T0330295

*Green Capitalism?*

HAGLEY PERSPECTIVES ON BUSINESS AND CULTURE

Roger Horowitz, Series Editor

A complete list of books in the series is available from the publisher.

# *Green Capitalism?*

Business and the Environment
in the Twentieth Century

*Edited by*

## Hartmut Berghoff *and* Adam Rome

**PENN**

UNIVERSITY OF PENNSYLVANIA PRESS

PHILADELPHIA

Published by
University of Pennsylvania Press
Philadelphia, Pennsylvania 19104-4112
www.upenn.edu/pennpress

Printed in the United States of America
on acid-free paper

10  9  8  7  6  5  4  3  2  1

*Library of Congress Cataloging-in-Publication Data*
Names: Berghoff, Hartmut, editor. | Rome, Adam, editor.
Title: Green capitalism? : business and the environment in the twentieth century / edited by
    Hartmut Berghoff and Adam Rome.
Other titles: Hagley perspectives on business and culture.
Description: 1st edition. | Philadelphia : University of Pennsylvania Press, [2017] | Series:
    Hagley perspectives on business and culture | Includes bibliographical references
    and index.
Identifiers: LCCN 2016052374 | ISBN 978-0-8122-4901-9 (hardcover : alk. paper)
Subjects: LCSH: Environmentalism—Economic aspects—History—20th century. |
    Capitalism—Environmental aspects—History—20th century. | Business
    enterprises—Environmental aspects—History—20th century. | Environmental policy—
    Economic aspects—History—20th century.
Classification: LCC HC79.E5 .G6885 2017 | DDC 338
LC record available online at https://lccn.loc.gov/2016052374

# Contents

*P r e f a c e*

Environmental historians and business historians have seldom looked to each other for inspiration. This collection hopes to change that. It grew out of a thought-provoking 2014 conference cosponsored by the Hagley Museum and Library and the German Historical Institute (GHI) in Washington, DC, held at the Hagley. In the conference call for proposals, the organizers explained that they sought to provide "historical perspectives on a question of obvious relevance today: Can capitalism be green—or at least greener?" Our title—*Green Capitalism?*—is admittedly drawn from contemporary discourse. But we are convinced that history can provide invaluable insights into the complex and changing relationship between business and the environment.

The conference was developed in dialogue with Hartmut Berghoff, at the time director of the GHI and now director of the Institute of Economic and Social History at the University Göttingen in Germany, and Adam Rome, then Unidel Helen Gouldner Chair for the Environment and Professor of History and English at the University of Delaware. Berghoff and Rome subsequently agreed to serve as editors for this volume. About half of the papers delivered at the conference are included in this collection after considerable revision. The volume also includes essays by Berghoff and Rome as well as several chapters that they recruited from other authors.

Part I asks readers to look at the "big picture" through three wide-ranging essays posing large questions and stretching over an extensive array of scholarship. In "The Ecology of Commerce," Adam Rome investigates a provocative question: is business becoming a participant in the environmental movement? Surveying literature among business and environmental writers, he shows how the interest in "greening" capitalism so it would be sustainable has overcome resistance in many quarters such that "the sustainable-business bookshelf [now] has hundreds of manifestos." Looking at similar issues from a different vantage point in "Shades of Green," Hartmut Berghoff seeks to correct business history's long neglect of environmental factors. He explores how in fact environmental concerns among firms have a long history and how those have become more prevalent and sophisticated since the 1970s. While granting the contradictions of "eco-capitalism," his essay charts a course toward an "eco-cultural" approach to business history. The final "big picture" essay, by Hugh Gorman, explores the emergence of systems of environmental governance, how "the rules that govern markets recognize the finiteness of earth systems," and the role played by business in their construction. His emphasis on the role of legal and political systems in green capitalism is a thread developed in many of the later essays; Gorman provides an overview of the literature and a review of the role of business that will allow readers to place those case studies into a larger frame.

Part II, "Conservation Before Environmentalism," pushes back the chronology to the late nineteenth and early twentieth centuries. Christine Meisner Rosen revisits the movements to regulate effluent from meat processing plants and to improve air quality in the urban North with the intent of tracing the leadership role played by business interests. William D. Bryan moves readers to the American South and looks at how local boosters combined promotion of economic development with conservation of natural resources in the hope that "permanent ways of using these resources would provide the basis of a new economy." Julie Cohn then examines the countryside and the surprising synergies between utility companies and conservation advocates over electrical power and the hope that hydroelectric development could lead to a reduction in pollution from coal-fired power plants.

"Failures and Dilemmas," the volume's third part, features essays on two complex and contradictory efforts by firms to venture into green capitalism. Both authors foreground the complicated task of establishing corporate intent within the shifting terrain of environmental governance. David Kinkela takes the case of a ubiquitous item—the plastic six-pack ring—to show how its emergence and subsequent refinement lay at a nexus of corporate strategy, scientific research, and environmental awareness. Developed to alleviate a waste issue of excessive packaging, these rings created a new environmental hazard, one that the firm then sought to alleviate—at the same time as it challenged new environmental rules developed to address the unintended problem it had created. Similar themes inform the essay by Leif Fredrickson about a very different product, Ford's Ecostar van. Here again corporate initiatives and research developed in tandem with changes to governance systems, in this case California's zero-emission vehicle (ZEV) mandate, with the objective to establish the company's authority in debates over environmental issues rather than to actually sell a "green" product. Both essays recall Gorman's stress on governance, as they draw attention to what Kinkela calls the "shifting legal terrain that shaped the marketplace" and thus influenced business initiatives.

The fourth and final part offers five cases of "Going Green." Moving away from the U.S. focus of the collection thus far, two essays discuss European countries and a third follows a comparative approach. Ann-Kristin Bergquist stresses the importance of Swedish environment policies to generate the will and technological innovation by the Boliden Company to correct the appalling pollution released by its Rönnskär copper smelting plant. Roman Köster explores how private firms moved quickly into the recycling of household waste in West Germany long before this practice became commonplace in other industrialized nations. Joseph Pratt brings in the curious case of a utility company promoting conservation through Consolidated Edison's "Save-a-Watt" campaign, provoked by the difficulties of meeting consumer demand while also complying with tougher environmental regulations. To explain the "skewed geography" of wind power, Geoffrey Jones stresses that considering "the external costs of conventional energy—such as climate change, air pollution, and water depletion"—in government policies was necessary to make wind power competitive with conventional energy sources. Governance, a theme throughout this section, is central to Brian Black's exploration of how hybrids and electric vehicles finally secured a corner of the U.S. auto market, a shift generated by the 1970s energy crisis and its impact on government policies and consumer attitudes.

This is the eleventh volume in the Hagley Perspectives on Business and Culture series that began in 1999 at Routledge, and now has a happy home at the University of Pennsylvania Press under the care of its remarkable history editor, Robert Lockhart. These collections aim to bring cutting-edge work to the attention of scholars; we hope you will find these essays stimulating and useful.

Roger Horowitz
Director, Center for the History of Business, Technology, and Society
Hagley Museum and Library
Editor, Hagley Perspectives on Business and Culture

# PART I

# The Big Picture

# Chapter 1

# The Ecology of Commerce: Environmental History and the Challenge of Building a Sustainable Economy

*Adam Rome*

"There is no polite way to say that business is destroying the world," Paul Hawken wrote in *The Ecology of Commerce* in 1993. "I don't mean to imply that business acts without principles. But sooner or later, we must recognize that despite the protestations of industry, it is completely lacking in ecological principles, and that what is good for business almost always is bad for nature."[1]

Hawken did not fit the stereotype of an environmental activist. He was an entrepreneur, not a grassroots organizer or a beltway lobbyist. In 1979, he co-founded Smith & Hawken, a mail-order garden-tool company. Drawing on that experience, he wrote a 1987 book about growing small businesses, which was a companion to a seventeen-part public-television series. He believed that business was indispensable: No other institution was as capable of meeting the world's needs. Yet he also was convinced that the industrial economy had to be reinvented. *The Ecology of Commerce* was his attempt to "save business"—to point the way toward a sustainable future, with "profitable, expandable companies" that do not wreck the planet. As he concluded, "Business is the problem and it must be part of the solution."[2]

*The Ecology of Commerce* became a best seller. The book changed Hawken's life—he soon became a guru of green capitalism. It also changed the lives of many readers. As the founding chairman of the U.S. Green Building Council wrote, Hawken's work gave many people "permission to be both a capitalist and an environmentalist."[3]

Does Hawken deserve a place in the teaching and writing of environmental history? Until recently, I never thought to lecture about *The Ecology of Commerce*, and my neglect probably is typical. Hawken also is missing from the scholarly literature about environmentalism. Yet I've become convinced that Hawken's work warrants our attention.[4]

The success of *The Ecology of Commerce* was the most visible sign of a new kind of environmental movement. By the early 1990s, some business leaders, management experts, and commentators were beginning to argue that capitalism needed to be greener. They saw business as the most dynamic force in society—but they admitted that business had caused serious environmental problems, and they took for granted that those problems would not just go away with greater wealth. What would be required to make business sustainable?

At first, the call to green capitalism was drowned out by the increasingly vociferous opposition to environmentalism in the 1980s and 1990s. The administration of Ronald Reagan tried to undo the environmental initiatives of the 1970s, and conservative intellectuals and pundits joined the attack. They argued that environmentalists grossly exaggerated the downsides of prosperity, that the free market ensured the wisest use of resources, that voluntary action to protect the environment was best, that private property owners were far better stewards of the land than government bureaucrats, and that environmental improvement required continued economic growth. As talk-show host Rush Limbaugh wrote in 1992, "The key to cleaning up our environment is unfettered free enterprise, our system of reward." When *The Ecology of Commerce* appeared, many conservatives saw the environmental movement as "anti-development, anti-progress, anti-technology, anti-business, anti-established institutions, and, above all, anti-capitalism."[5]

Despite the polarization of environmental politics, the effort to green business has engaged more and more people. Now the sustainable-business bookshelf has hundreds of manifestos. Some are the work of business-school professors. *Green to Gold*, for example, explains "How Smart Companies Use Environmental Strategy to Innovate, Create Value, and Build Competitive Advantage." A few business leaders have written about their efforts to lead a sustainability revolution. Some were keen from the first to do things differently, while others are recent converts to the cause. Because expertise in environmental management has become valuable, green consulting is a thriving business, and some of the new books are by successful consultants. Even environmental activists are getting into the game. Adam Werbach's *Strategy for Sustainability* offers insights from a Sierra Club president turned corporate adviser.[6]

Business schools are training green managers and entrepreneurs. Students at several top schools now can concentrate on business and sustainability. Yale University and the University of Michigan offer joint degrees that combine a master of business administration (MBA) with graduate training in environmental science or policy. Several business schools have green-capitalism institutes. The University of North Carolina has a Center for Sustainable Enterprise, and the Wharton School at the University of Pennsylvania has an Institute for Global Environmental Leadership. At the Haas School of Business at University of California-Berkeley, environmental historian Christine Meisner Rosen teaches MBA classes on corporate environmental management and strategy.[7]

Corporate practice also has changed. As Andrew Hoffman argued in *From Heresy to Dogma*, environmental management slowly became institutionalized in the decades after the inaugural Earth Day. At first, most companies responded defensively to calls for improved environmental performance. Their environmental departments had little prestige or authority—and some were part of public relations. By the early 1990s, however, the issue had become a "strategic" concern. Hoffman's evidence came mostly from the chemical and oil industries, but other evidence suggests that the trend is general. In the jargon of management, many companies have moved "beyond compliance" with environmental regulations. They have dramatically reduced how much energy they use and how much waste they produce per unit of output. Some have pressured their suppliers to do the same. Many companies also have redesigned products to lessen their environmental footprint. A few now take responsibility for the ultimate fate of some consumer goods.[8]

Here are a few examples drawn from the green-capitalism literature:

Among manufacturers, 3M was a pioneer in the pursuit of eco-efficiency. In 1975, as businesses were struggling to comply with the requirements of the Clean Air and Clean Water Acts, 3M launched the Pollution Prevention Pays program. The company's environmental manager did not want just to install scrubbers and filters: Pollution-abatement technologies were costly and might not work as well as expected. Could employees come up with cost-effective ways to reduce waste generation? They could. In 1990, after the first fifteen years of the program had helped cut emissions by 50 percent while saving millions of dollars, the company announced an expanded waste-prevention effort. That commitment affected product design, not just manufacturing operations. A few years later, for example, 3M's CEO vowed that the company would not develop new products that required use of a particularly polluting solvent. Keeping to that pledge sometimes slowed innovation, but executives were convinced that the loss in potential sales would be outweighed by lower pollution compliance and monitoring costs.[9]

Alcoa—the world's biggest aluminum company—has become a model of environmental planning. When the State of California denied the company a permit to expand a facility because of concern about water scarcity, Alcoa concluded that water use might become a huge constraint on future growth. Instead of expanding somewhere else, the company made reducing water demand a priority at all its facilities. Alcoa similarly realized that concern about climate change had strategic implications for the industry. It reengineered a key process to reduce emissions of a potent greenhouse gas, created a company-wide database to track all greenhouse-gas emissions, and redoubled efforts to lessen electricity consumption. At the same time, the company has supported efforts to raise automobile fuel-efficiency standards: One way to improve mileage is to lower vehicle weight, and aluminum is lighter than other structural materials. Because reusing scrap aluminum is twenty times more energy efficient than smelting bauxite and avoids the environmental costs of mining, Alcoa also has worked to improve can-recycling rates.[10]

Though not a household name, modular-carpet maker Interface has drawn attention for trying to make every aspect of its operations sustainable. Like 3M, Interface set a goal of dramatically reducing factory pollution and waste. But that was just the start. The company has made the use of its products more environmentally benign. The modular tile system allowed customers to replace pieces of carpet rather than entire rooms, and the company reinforced that efficiency by offering a line of nondirectional "entropy" designs that look attractive in any arrangement. To avoid the environmental hazards of using glue, Interface developed a no-glue method of installation. The company also pioneered in carpet recycling. A key part of that effort was offering carpet leases. Because Interface took back old carpet at the end of every lease, the company had to design products for reuse. Now Interface tiles are made for easy separation of the backing from the fabric cover, and the company uses recycled material to make new carpet.[11]

Working with environmental consultants, Wal-Mart launched an ambitious sustainability effort in 2006. In addition to making its stores and trucking fleet more eco-efficient, Wal-Mart began to use its tremendous purchasing power to improve the performance of suppliers. The company decided to stock more clothing made with organic cotton, and that decision encouraged farmers to switch to organic methods. To save energy in transportation, Wal-Mart pushed detergent manufacturers to sell their product in concentrated form. The company asked all computer makers to meet European standards that restrict toxic components in laptops and monitors. In 2009, Wal-Mart promised to devise a "sustainability index" for everything it sells. The index would help Wal-Mart's buyers to lessen the impact of the company's supply chain—and success in improving the sustainability of suppliers now is a metric in buyers' annual evaluations. Eventually the index will be made public. In the meantime, Wal-Mart is identifying "sustainability leaders" in many product categories.[12]

Of course, the corporate world still is far from sustainable. Many companies still resist efforts to enforce higher standards of environmental protection. Some companies have improved in a few ways while continuing in many other ways to degrade the environment. Almost every company remains committed to growth. As even the most ardent advocates of green capitalism acknowledge, that commitment is problematic.[13]

All of this begs for rigorous historical analysis. How much really has changed since 1970? Why have some companies and some industries done more than others? What have been the most formidable obstacles to reform?

Unfortunately, few environmental historians have shown any interest in those questions so far. No doubt some scholars in the field see the sustainable-capitalism movement as too recent—too present—to consider. Christine Rosen raised that issue in a provocative 2007 essay on the documentary *Who Killed the Electric Car?* "Do we have the temporal distance and perspective to study [sustainability initiatives] as historians?" she asked. "Or can we only report on them, like newspaper reporters and documentary makers?" For Rosen, those doubts were outweighed by her conviction that we urgently need to understand everything "that is paving the way, or standing in the way, or complicating the path toward environmental sustainability." But she recognized that other scholars might be put off by the difficulty of writing historically about developments that still are unfolding.[14]

I'm convinced, though, that the reluctance to explore the subject goes deeper. The effort to green business does not fit easily into the historiography of environmental history. Indeed, scholars in the field long have criticized business, with good reason.

In 1979, Donald Worster's *Dust Bowl* set an agenda for the field with a powerful critique of capitalism. Worster called capitalism "the decisive factor in this nation's use of nature"—and he meant that no other force had been as destructive. He acknowledged that capitalism was "constantly evolving." It took different forms in different places at different times. But he argued that capitalism had "a recognizable identity all the same: a core set of values and assumptions more permanent than these outer forms—an enduring ethos." In Worster's view, three ecological ideas were part of that cultural core. First, "Nature must be seen as capital." The environment only has value as a storehouse of commodities. Second, "Man has a right, even an obligation, to use this capital for constant self-advancement." That idea made capitalism "an intensely maximizing culture," always working to get more profit out of the world's resources. Third, "The social order should permit and encourage this continual increase of personal wealth." Those three ideas gave capitalist societies "a greater resource hunger than others, greater eagerness to take risks, and less capacity for restraint."[15]

Perhaps the best elaboration of Worster's argument is Theodore Steinberg's *Nature Incorporated*. Steinberg argued that the rise of industrial capitalism "involved a profound restructuring of the environment," at great cost. New England's pioneering industrialists had no regard for rivers as habitat or lifeblood. They saw flowing water as a productive input and a cheap repository for waste. Indeed, they transformed water into a commodity—the mill power. They also thought that society had a duty to use the productive power of water to the fullest. To let water go unused was irresponsible. Because the common law favored agricultural uses of water, the mill owners needed the help of the state, and legislators and judges eagerly acted to encourage industrial development: Officials rewrote water law to give manufacturing priority, and they allowed water pollution despite protests. The new factories produced great wealth, as the industrialists promised. But they also flooded fields, destroyed fisheries, and turned rivers into sewers.[16]

Many other scholars have demonstrated the environmental destructiveness of capitalism. We now know that turning beavers into "commodities of the hunt" nearly wiped them out in New England—and indeed in all of North America. In just a generation, the commercialization of the forests of the Great Lakes left a cutover wasteland. The drive to exploit gold and copper destroyed landscapes across the country. So did the creation of the fossil-fuel infrastructure. Even before the mechanization of fish harvesting, the expansion of commercial fishing in the Atlantic brought many species close to the breaking point. To meet the "insatiable appetite" of consumers for sugar, bananas, coffee, rubber, and beef, American companies destroyed many of the world's tropical forests. After World War II, the construction of millions of tract houses in new suburbs caused a host of environmental problems, from landslides to groundwater contamination. The list could go on and on.[17]

As Samuel Hays argued in 1987, business also has been the most vigorous opponent of environmental regulation. "In the mass media, in legislative, administrative, and judicial action, in educational materials distributed in public-relations campaigns, in scientific and technical circles, its resistance to environmental and ecological concerns abounded," Hays wrote in *Beauty, Health, and Permanence.* "Each segment of business, whether raw-materials production, manufacturing, commerce, transportation, or construction, had its own particular objection to environmental proposals and almost all business groups found common cause that produced a shared opposition. Only those firms with an economic stake in pollution-control technology remained apart from this massive onslaught against environmental policies and programs."[18]

The work of many scholars supports Hays's argument. To fight the Clean Air Act, the coal industry formed a powerful coalition of coal-dependent companies, from railroads to electric utilities. U.S. Steel fought antipollution regulations at the local level as well as in Washington. The chemical industry attacked the credibility of Rachel Carson's *Silent Spring.* Business groups also funded campaigns to cast doubt on the scientific evidence about the problems of acid rain, the ozone hole, and climate change. Developers rallied property owners to oppose land-use regulations. The ranching and logging industries opposed the creation of wilderness areas. Again, the list could go on.[19]

But a handful of studies suggest that the story is more complicated. Even before the rise of the modern regulatory state, businesses sometimes had bottom-line reasons to try to protect parts of nature, use natural resources more sustainably, or seek collective action to improve the environment. To ensure that logging did not harm tourism, the Board of Trade in Asheville, North Carolina, lobbied in the early 1900s for the creation of a state park in the Black Mountains. Because air pollution lowered property values and damaged dry goods, urban developers and merchants sometimes sought antismoke ordinances. Occasionally businesses tried to do better and failed. In the 1930s, Ford bought junk cars to salvage for scrap, but the company's "disassembly line" never made economic sense.[20]

If we turn our critical energies to analyzing the business response to environmental challenges, I'm confident that we will gain many fresh insights into a key dilemma of our time. The developments of the last twenty-five years are especially relevant. But we need to understand the efforts to green capitalism in historical context.

Hugh Gorman's study of the petroleum industry—*Redefining Efficiency*—is a model of what we might do. Gorman showed that oil engineers and executives in the early twentieth century readily acknowledged that every aspect of the industry caused environmental problems. Drilling produced briny wastes, blowouts spewed oil onto the land, refineries polluted the air and water, pipelines leaked, tankers emptied oily ballast into oceans and harbors, and slick port waters caught fire. Officials also understood that many industry practices wasted crude. Yet they resisted calls for corrective legislation. They argued that pollution and waste would diminish as the industry worked to make its operations more efficient. They were partly right. But Gorman made clear that the win-win ideal of eco-efficiency was inadequate to address all of the industry's problems. Though oil companies did better in many ways, air and water pollution still increased. Some environmental problems were not profitable to address. The reductions in waste generation per unit of output also were far outweighed by the tremendous growth in the scale of the industry. By the 1960s, therefore, the argument for self-regulation no longer was convincing. The pioneering environmental laws of the 1970s forced the industry to accept new management goals.[21]

To follow Gorman's lead, however, we need to do more to get inside the heads of entrepreneurs and executives. For business historians, that is second nature: the firm is their basic unit of analysis. But few works of environmental history focus on specific companies—and most of those books speak to the destructiveness of industrialization, not the response of business to concern about environmental degradation. When environmental historians write about specific industries, we rarely look at the subject from the perspective of insiders.[22]

Because environmental historians are not trained in management theory, we need help thinking about business decision making. The green-capitalism literature is surprisingly useful. To be sure, the sustainability manifestos address the future more than the past. They also are boosterish—they downplay the many barriers to reinventing the corporation. But they provide frameworks for analyzing key issues.

What might motivate businesses to become greener? Environmental historians have focused on government action and citizen activism as catalysts. But the management literature makes clear that pressure for reform can come from several other sources. Businesses can be challenged by other businesses. Insurance companies might demand action to reduce the risk of claims. Banks might refuse to lend money for projects that might not pay off if new regulations change the rules. Because environmental issues are becoming increasingly important in supply-chain management, companies might be forced to change to meet the requirements of their business customers. Of course, consumers might refuse to buy products that are not green enough. Stockholders might press for change as well, especially if they fear that failure to develop a more sustainable business model might make the company uncompetitive or devalue the company's assets. Even employees might put pressure on executives: most people want to be proud of their employer, and many companies now see sustainability as a recruitment issue.[23]

As the management literature acknowledges, some companies and some business sectors have more at stake than others. They face greater scrutiny, or they are especially vulnerable to changing ecological conditions, or they have more opportunity to gain competitive advantage from green innovations. Recruitment is particularly important in the high-tech sector, where talented employees often are a company's principal assets. The consumer-electronics industry is likely to face growing pressure as e-waste increasingly comes to symbolize the unsustainability of a throwaway society. To assure future supplies of essential natural resources, some businesses will need to organize conservation efforts. Companies with substantial "intangible value" need to be extra careful to avoid problems that might destroy "goodwill," while firms with great market power have more freedom to make decisions that might raise costs or pay off only in the long term.[24]

The management literature also offers useful ways to measure corporate change. Most companies have focused on eco-efficiency gains that directly benefit their balance sheets. That's the "low-hanging fruit." Some firms also have worked to reduce environmental risks. But the management literature points to many other possible sustainability efforts. Some are internal to the firm. Have companies changed what products or services they offer? Have they changed the kinds of skills they seek in employees? Other efforts involve rethinking relationships with business partners, customers, and environmentalists. Have businesses sought to lessen the environmental footprint of their supply chain, or worked with consumers to reclaim products that no longer are useful, or partnered with environmental organizations? Ultimately, the question is how deep the commitment goes. Are green initiatives "bolted on," or are they "embedded" in corporate culture? Are companies just "reducing unsustainability," or are they truly reimagining how they do business?[25]

Though writing about business will take environmental historians out of their comfort zones, the payoff will be great. The historiography of the field will become richer. Even more important, our work will contribute to public debate about the future of capitalism.

To radical critics of capitalism, the corporate environmental initiatives of the last generation are trivial. The critics are convinced that the dream of greening capitalism is a delusion, so they dismiss everything business does to become greener as greenwashing. It can't lead to a sustainable economy. Their argument essentially is definitional. They define capitalism as a system dedicated to endless accumulation of capital—and so, by definition, capitalism can't be sustainable, because the never-ending quest to turn nature into capital eventually will run up against the limits of a finite world.[26]

The green-business boosters see capitalism in much more flexible terms. They take for granted that the profit motive ultimately is compatible with many kinds of enterprise. Some even imagine that growth itself might not be essential in a capitalist system. The boosters disagree about how rocky the path forward will be, but they all assume that the pressure to green the economy will continue to intensify. Their hope is to encourage more business leaders to be proactive—to make the transition to sustainability smoother and faster. Because they want to show what is possible, they focus on companies they see as trendsetters.

For different reasons, then, neither the critics nor the boosters have offered a systematic assessment of the movement to green capitalism. I hope this volume will inspire many more environmental historians to take up that analytical challenge. To build an enduring economy, we need to understand the strengths and weaknesses of business efforts to address environmental problems, and that is impossible without a profound sense of history.

*Chapter 2*

# Shades of Green: A Business-History Perspective on Eco-Capitalism

*Hartmut Berghoff*

Green capitalism has become a popular concept in recent decades and has caught the imagination of different groups, from environmentalists to political and business elites. In 2009 President Obama promised "to invest $150 billion over the next ten years" in "alternative and renewable energy" and to "create millions of new green jobs."[1] In fact his administration's response to the recession of 2008–9, the American Recovery and Reinvestment Act, prioritized "energy efficiency and renewable energy."

Even a staunch Republican and cool-blooded business leader like Jack Welch, who publically called global warming a "mass neurosis" and "the attack on capitalism that socialism couldn't bring," emphatically advocated green capitalism.[2] Welch, the former CEO of General Electric (GE), one of the most admired and influential American managers, argued that there is no alternative to green products. "From a business standpoint, you've got a consumer now who thinks they've got to do it. . . . If I'm running a business, I want to be sure I'm green as can be. . . . Design products with a smaller carbon footprint; . . . make everybody feel you're in. . . . There's an enormous opportunity . . . whether you believe in global warming or not . . . get on this bandwagon, and go with it."[3] Green bonds that finance environmentally friendly investments have become a fast growing segment of financial markets. In 2012 \$3 billion of them were sold, in 2014 an astounding \$36.6 billion.[4]

Green capitalism offers a multitude of promises: saving the planet through a less noxious economy, a technological solution to ecological problems, and a new growth paradigm that combines ecological with economic benefits. People can have a quiet conscience without needing to revise their way of life. There seems to be no need for a zero-growth or even slow-growth policy. On the contrary, green products offer new growth and profit opportunities. At last, capitalism has found a sustainable growth model, and ecological modernization can follow a market-driven agenda.

Critics speak of a mixture of "slick marketing" and willful delusion as many so-called green products are by no means environmentally sound and cause severe, often hidden, ecological and social damages. Heather Rogers claims that "the market has a distinct inability to solve environmental crises because it can't adequately value nature."[5] In her recent book *This Changes Everything: Capitalism vs. the Climate*, Naomi Klein asserts that capitalism's internal dynamics prevent its greening. "Forget everything you think you know about global warming. The really inconvenient truth is that it's not about carbon—it's about capitalism." According to Klein, "A powerful message— spoken in the language of fires, floods, droughts, and extinctions—[is] telling us that we need an entirely new economic model."[6] Rejecting green capitalism, Klein states that the ecological crisis requires nothing less than a radically different economic and social system. Thomas Friedman takes the exact opposite position, propagating a "green revolution" to "renew" and "regenerate" American capitalism.[7] Paul Hawken and others suggest replacing "conventional" with "natural" capitalism via market-based productivity offensives as well as by "redesigning" products and processes "on biological lines" to eliminate waste.[8]

This ideologically charged debate underscores the relevance of the topic. Green capitalism touches upon a key question for the future. This essay looks at it from a business-history angle. The first section asks why business history has largely neglected studying the environmental footprint of corporations until now. The ecological implications of corporate action should be a central topic. An eco-cultural approach to business history is needed. Second, this essay demonstrates that green capitalism is not so new; environmental concerns and production methods have a long history. Third, it places capitalism in a comparative framework. Is it per se greener or dirtier than other economic systems? Fourth, it sketches the rise of the green-capitalism paradigm since the 1970s and looks at examples of how it has changed products and production methods. The fifth and final section briefly addresses the ambiguities and contradictions of eco-capitalism.

## Business and Environmental History: Contours of a Non-Relationship

Despite considerable thematic overlap business and environmental historians do not talk much to each other.[9] Environmental history devoted itself early on to investigating industrial pollution, its studies often treating corporations as external to nature, as polluters that disturb ecosystems.[10] They fail to analyze the logic and constraints of businesses. Many of these studies are implicitly or explicitly antibusiness and treat firms as the only culprit. Yet the complexity of environmental problems prohibits such simplistic blame games.

Increasingly, historians are recognizing that companies are not always entirely free in their action. Thus, the limits of firms' room for maneuver and the institutional and technological frameworks that determine their behavior come to the fore. Such perspectives, however, all too often focus on the regulatory actions of the state rather than the companies themselves.[11]

Economic theory, in turn, has long classified water and air as "free goods," with business history accordingly disregarding the environment and treating it at best as an external factor. The Chandlerian paradigm, which views firms from the perspective of organizational design, encouraged scholars to investigate shifts in the structure of companies as they grow from small enterprises run by their founders to large multidivisional and diversified giants run by salaried managers. Alfred Chandler's concept of a "market-cum-technology environment" refers to anything but the environment in the ecological sense of the term. Instead, it denotes external factors that create growth opportunities and trigger organizational responses. For Chandler, corporate growth correlates to a company's ability to secure a high-speed throughput of resources through the value chain and to operate near the lowest unit price. The institutional paradigm of business history has not addressed the ways that the stream of resources through enterprises affects the ecosystem and the ways that nature's transformation affects companies' operations and factor costs.[12]

Almost all aspects of Chandler's work have been criticized, giving rise to new directions in business history from the rehabilitation of the family firm to the discovery of corporate culture. Eco-cultural approaches have, so far, remained rare. Not one page of the 715-page *Oxford Handbook of Business History*, published in 2008, is devoted to the natural environment.[13] Despite the pioneering work of a handful of scholars, eco-cultural business history remains outside the mainstream.[14]

Business historians' disregard of ecological questions is all the more striking given the attention most corporations now dedicate to ecological issues. The cost of natural inputs and the intensity of regulation have increased dramatically, as have the risks of financial and reputational damage if business-related ecological scandals surface. The likelihood of public exposure and shaming has also heightened considerably. Shell's attempt to dump the oil platform Brent Spar in the Atlantic in 1995 and the subsequent campaign by Greenpeace or BP's Deepwater Horizon oil spill in the Gulf of Mexico in 2010 are obvious examples. Consumers increasingly demand green products. Organic produce sales have exploded in recent years. Retailers like Whole Foods flourish as customers pay higher prices for food they hope is healthier. Eco-labels and the idea of "environmental friendliness" have become important selling points for everything from detergents to tourism.

An eco-cultural approach to business history is essential not only because of the green wave of recent years. Industrial firms and the natural environment have always been inextricably interconnected. Nature has provided resources and places of disposal. Conflicts over natural resources have always influenced companies' cost structures, strategic orientations, and public images. Although firms have long been largely able to externalize the costs of using the environment, regulatory restrictions have now forced them to internalize these. If there is no cost for polluting a river, there is no need to treat or reduce sewage, but when real costs accrue businesses will take them into account. These costs are not recent phenomena. As Matthias Mutz's study of the paper mills in nineteenth-century Saxony has shown, there were virtually hundreds of court cases where neighbors, adjoining mills, or the authorities sued polluters. At the same time, procuring pulp for paper production had enormous consequences for local forestry and distant trade. Procurement of central inputs and, more generally, resource management are essential challenges for firms, not only for modern industrial corporations.[15] Businesses have to react to price signals; limited natural resources make these

inputs more expensive. Historically, dealing with the environment has always constituted a significant part of business development.

## Early Examples of Green Capitalism

Industrial capitalism has had green components right from its beginning. The
squalor of early industrial towns pervades common perceptions of industrialization. Friedrich Engels referred to Manchester as "hell upon earth": "my
description . . . is far from black enough to convey a true impression of the
filth, ruin, and uninhabitableness. . . . Everything which here arouses horror
and indignation is of recent origin, belongs to the *industrial epoch*."[16] The
boundless pollution associated with industrialism certainly could be found in
many urban centers of early industrialization, but much industrial development took place outside cities. Rural industrialization often relied on water-
power rather than steam power. In the Kingdom of Württemberg, a highly
specialized, export-oriented region in southwest Germany, not until 1895
did steam power overtake waterpower.[17] Industrial workers were often part-
time farmers and lived in villages and small towns. Due to the remoteness of
coal deposits and high transport costs in general, many industries in Württemberg and neighboring Baden were labor intensive rather than energy
intensive. For example, clock and musical and surgical instrument manufacturing were highly specialized industries there that served global markets. They relied on craftsmanship, quality orientation, and diligence rather
than on massive inputs of resources, energy, and machinery.[18] This is not to
say that industry outside urban agglomerations was generally clean. On the
contrary, pulp and dyeing mills, for example, often massively polluted rivers
they used as sustainable sources of water.

Another example of a partially green industry is forestry. Although industrialization manifoldly increased the demand for timber, the story of
wood usage in industrializing countries is not always one of ruthless depletion of natural resources. Even in the mid-seventeenth-century, forestry literature discussed the detrimental effects of overexploitation. Originally
forests were cut down for settlement or agricultural purposes or degraded
by littering, tanning, and intensive use for livestock fodder and as an energy
source. In early industrialization, then, the mining industry, especially, consumed whole forests for smelting ores. Wood was used for building material
and as an energy source, but reforestation would obviously take decades and

leave subsequent generations unsupplied. With forests disappearing without attempts to restore them, a Saxon mining administrator, Hans Carl von Carlowitz, first formulated the concept of *Nachhaltigkeit*—sustainability—in 1713, arguing for the cautious use of natural resources to safeguard their future availability.[19] Fears of an imminent wood shortage and interventions by the authorities played a decisive role in implementing sustainable forestry practices. Regulations in most Western countries tightened in the twentieth century in response to logging companies' increasing technological capacities and growing conservation concerns.

Alongside regulation, philanthropic and religious imperative, often mixed with marketing considerations, prompted early green practices in the food industry. Major problems of this sector were adulteration and contamination. The recipe for success became selling healthy food, with strong brands guaranteeing quality. Cadbury's involvement with the Quakers and the Temperance Society led it to provide tea, coffee, cocoa, and chocolate as alternatives to alcohol. Cocoa had been "heavily adulterated with starch substances like potato flour or sago to mask the excess cocoa butter." In 1866 Cadbury introduced a new cocoa press that "removed some of the cocoa butter from the beans, producing a less rich and more palatable cocoa essence." It was successfully marketed as " 'absolutely pure."[20] This production method became a model, influencing the passage of the Adulteration of Food Acts in 1872 and 1875. Excluding detrimental ingredients and promising healthy food helped Cadbury become a large, globally operating company.[21]

Overcoming the serious defects of the early food industry led to success for many other large firms and strong brands like Nestle, Kellogg's, Rowntree, Heinz, and Dr. Oetker.[22] Founder Henry Heinz advocated the safety and cleanliness of his company's production facilities and tried to cut waste to a minimum. "Although many food manufacturers opposed 1906's Pure Food and Drug Act, Heinz was a proponent of the measure. His advocacy for its passage helped increase sales, as customers felt they were able to trust the safety of Heinz's manufactured foods."[23]

There were also cooperatives and communes creating their own version of green capitalism, some of which enjoyed surprising and persistent success. The "life reform" movement that sprang up in Germany and Switzerland in the late nineteenth century propagated a back-to-nature lifestyle, emphasizing organic food, calisthenics, outdoor activities, alternative medicine, loose garments, as well as juices and vegetables. The still-existing "reform house" retail stores constituted one branch of this alternative economy. Around 1900 the first plants for such products sprang up, for example, the Eden Cooperative in Oranienburg north of Berlin. They produced juices and purees from berries grown on cooperative-owned land. Factories for organic salt and bread followed. This sector grew fast, forming the Neuform Cooperative in the 1920s, which by 1933 had about 1,200 member businesses. The vision of a green and healthy life, of an earthly paradise following on the self-reform of the individual was adaptable to ideologies from the left to the extreme right. Although this sector always remained tightly associated with alternative milieus, it survived all political ruptures of twentieth-century German history and continues to serve health-conscious customers, now with less ideological baggage.[24]

In many green businesses best-practice working conditions were part of their corporate culture. Cadbury, for example, provided canteens, sports grounds, and educational opportunities for its workers. In 1878–79 it moved its factory from the overcrowded and polluted inner city of Birmingham to an open area on the outskirts of town. It acquired land for a model village with low-cost housing for workers, each house with its own garden, later known as Bournville. The village in a way predated the Garden City idea, combining industry production and living with the benefits of semirural surroundings.[25]

Inner cities were far removed from this idea, but business owners did support initiatives to reduce air pollution in the decades before 1914, as the essay on the U.S. antismoke movement by Christine Rosen in this book (see chapter 4) demonstrates. Even if manufacturers typically reacted to complaints by heightening their chimneys and dispersing toxic fumes more widely, the resulting improvements for city dwellers were significant. Company housing projects inspired by the Garden City movement became a common sight in many industrial cities of the late nineteenth and early twentieth century, including Port Sunlight in northwest England (Lever), Siemensstadt in Berlin, Gartenstadt Welheim in Bottrop (the mine of Vereinigte Welheim), and Marktown in Indiana (Mark Manufacturing Company).

To sum up, there were islands of green capitalism during the industrialization period. They often had a compensatory or legitimizing function or a strong ideological component and did not heal the overall environmental damage of the "first, dark phase of industrialization."[26] Rivers tended to be discolored and foul smelling, cities filled with thick smoke, and growth relied on the extensive use of natural resources rather than on principles of sustainability.

## Capitalism in Comparative Perspective

If one considers capitalism an economic system particularly offensive to the environment, as Klein does, one should look at the environmental history of socialism, the primary political alternative for much of the twentieth century. The lack of constitutional checks and balances led to widespread disregard for environmental concerns in the Eastern bloc, as in most dictatorships.

German history makes it possible to compare both systems directly and evaluate the transformation of an entire economy from one system to the other. The German Democratic Republic (GDR), or East Germany, lacked money for modern filters and concern for citizens' health. Excessive use of brown coal and exhaust from technologically backward cars covered this state in a distinct vapor. The per capita energy use and emissions significantly surpassed those in the Federal Republic of Germany (FRG), or West Germany. GDR citizens inhaled about twice as much carbon dioxide and carbon oxide as West Germans in 1990, and, per capita, emitted 272.1 kilograms of sulfur dioxide, a toxic gas with a pungent, rotten smell, compared to 13.9 in the FRG.[27]

After unification, the discrepancies between East and West shrank dramatically. Emissions of sulfur dioxide leveled in 1997. Market mechanisms shut down the worst East German polluters because these formerly state-run combines could not compete in free markets. Between 1989 and 1997, the number of jobs in the East German chemical industry fell by 82 percent, while output was roughly halved. Productivity quadrupled and emissions dropped to less than 10 percent of their 1990 levels.[28] Where industrial production continued it was in thoroughly modernized factories. The energy mix drastically shifted toward oil, gas, and hard coal. In the Leuna-Buna-Bitterfeld Chemical Triangle, the center of the East German chemical industry, multinational corporations like Dow Chemical, Total, Bayer, Akzo Nobel, Linde, and Elf Aquitaine either modernized run-down plants or built new ones with the highest technological standards. Between 1990 and 1997, airborne emissions and hazardous waste in the regions of Bitterfeld and Wolfen fell by 98 percent, and the amount of sewage dropped by 91 percent.[29]

Does this mean that capitalism is greener than socialism? We should not jump to generalizations from this particular case. The legal and political frameworks are more important than the economic system. The lack of democratic accountability, the absence of the rule of law, as well as unfree media work against sustainability, irrespective of the economic system. Capitalism is not inherently green but might become greener for certain external reasons. The staggering reduction of pollution in East Germany in the 1990s was mainly due to the sudden application of strict West German environmental standards. It resulted from enforced regulation rather than voluntary action by firms. Corporations are unlikely to invest more money into environmental protection than they have to, especially if it weakens their competitiveness. Where regulation is absent or not enforced, where ecological atrocities will probably not be detected, capitalist enterprises have proven to be just as ruthless as combines in socialist dictatorships.

In the late 1960s, the Northeastern Pharmaceutical and Chemical Company (NEPACCO) produced toxic waste with a high concentration of dioxin. Instead of incinerating it, the best practice then, NEPACCO contracted the services of a company that had no experience in toxic waste disposal. This firm subcontracted the job to a small waste oil business. Whereas NEPACCO paid the first contractor \$3,000 per load, the subcontractor received \$125 and mixed the hazardous waste together with old crankcase oil. The resulting concoction was used to spray land to fight the local dust problem. Although birds dropped dead and other animals died or got ill, it was more than ten years before all 14,000 inhabitants of the small town of Times Beach, Missouri, were completely evacuated in 1983 because of the extreme dioxin contamination.[30] The Seveso disaster of 1976, an accident that higher and more expensive security standards could have prevented, in which Seveso's inhabitants were extremely highly exposed to dioxin, resulted from a similar derangement through a chain of incompetent and ruthless subcontractors. Barrels with the toxic chemicals disappeared and were later found in an abandoned slaughterhouse in a village.[31]

The profit motive, capitalism's main driving force, was clearly responsible for such ecological disasters. The same goes for systematic deforestation in Indonesia, the dumping of toxic waste in Third World countries, or illegal fishing in exclusion zones. These offenses typically go hand in hand with unenforced regulations and corruption and high chances of never being caught.[32]

## From the "1950s Syndrome" to the "Ecological Revolution"

According to Christian Pfister, the 1950s were the most important turning point in humanity's relationship to the environment. Rapid postwar economic reconstruction, the unprecedented rise in real wages, the sharp decline in energy prices, the explosive spread of motor vehicles and plastic products, as well as the widespread application of chemical fertilizers in agriculture put the world on a fatal path toward an accelerated loss of sustainability. The amount of greenhouse gas emission indeed climbed to unparalleled heights.[33] Even if Pfister's concept and periodization have been criticized, it is clear that the first postwar decades saw an escalating exploitation of non-renewable resources and a surge in ecological problems.[34] It is also clear that another turning point occurred in the 1960s and 1970s, as rising awareness of environmental problems prompted the search for more responsible use of natural resources.

Rachel Carson's book *Silent Spring* (1962), a warning against the dangers of pesticides like DDT, reached a mass audience and mobilized large numbers of people. The chemical industry reacted at first with fierce opposition. Its lobbyists claimed that a pesticide ban would endanger human health and make humanity "return to the Dark Ages, and the insects and diseases and vermin would once again inherit the earth."[35] *Silent Spring* became a rallying point for the emerging environmental movement. The creation of the Environmental Protection Agency (EPA), the introduction of Earth Day, and passage of the federal Clean Air Act, all in 1970, and the ban on the use of DDT in 1972 pointed to a fundamental reorientation. Environmentalism became an increasingly influential factor in society and politics.[36]

Another important impulse was the Club of Rome's study *Limits of Growth* published in 1972 and translated into thirty-seven languages. This alarmist tale of impending exhaustion of resources had an enormous effect, although it was not a shortage but rather the abundance and low cost of resources that generated the biggest ecological problem. As the book became a best seller, the two 1970s oil crises hit Western nations, spiking raw material prices. This forced industry to use them more economically, and states enacted a spate of regulations aimed at reducing emissions and resource consumption. Old fears of being starved for raw materials mixed with environmental concerns.

Industry initially fought the new rules and argued that they would hurt their competitiveness. Once the new regulations were in place, industry found ways to comply with them and indeed realized remarkable improvements in energy efficiency. The average fuel consumption of passenger cars in the United States improved from 13.5 miles per gallon in 1970 to 21.9 in 2000.[37] The steel industry, one of the most energy-intensive sectors, reduced

its energy consumption significantly. In Germany, the energy needed to produce crude steel fell by almost 40 percent between 1960 and 2012, which
corresponds to 393 kilograms of coal equivalents per ton. The emissions of
carbon dioxide sank by 44.4 percent, or 1,083 kilograms per ton.[38] These impressive reductions primarily resulted from legal requirements and innovations in process engineering.

In the last decades of the twentieth century, industry faced three types of
external pressure. First were the demands of environmentalist movements
and advocacy groups. In the 1970s and 1980s environmentalism became a
mass movement that profoundly influenced consumers. Later it made it into
mainstream politics and even into some governments. In Germany, the
Green Party, founded in 1980, became a coalition partner in several states
beginning in 1985. From 1998 to 2006, the Greens even formed part of the
federal government coalition as the junior partner of the Social Democrats.
After 1990 hardly any party platform could ignore environmental issues,
at least in Western democracies. Second was consumer demand. By 2000,
hardly any consumer durable could be sold without reference to its green
qualities. Saving the planet became part of consumers' mentality and most
people's rhetoric. For large corporations, being green became a crucial image builder. Third were regulation imperatives. The net of regulation became
denser, and in the course of the "compliance revolution" enforcement more
efficient.[39] Fines rose significantly, monitoring systems improved, and advocacy groups like Greenpeace, EcoWatch, Friends of the Earth, and Corporate Watch campaigned more aggressively and skillfully. They documented
offenses even in remote places and systematically damaged offenders' reputations. Shareholder activism has put environmental issues on the agenda of
annual meetings. All in all, the price and the risk of pollution have climbed,
so it might pay to become green.

Ecological atrocities in the Third World no longer remain hidden. In
2008 and 2009, Shell's failure to fix dilapidated pipelines along the Niger
Delta precipitated a gigantic oil spill. It destroyed thousands of hectares of
mangroves and the fishing grounds of the Bodo tribe. Shell had known about
these problems for years but failed to address them. Decades before, an incident like this would have generated no repercussions for the polluter nor
global attention. According to Nigerian government figures, there were more
than seven thousand spills between 1970 and 2000, two thousand of them
major. News and pictures travel fast in the Internet age, so it takes no time,
even in the remotest part of Africa, for someone to take cell-phone pictures

and disseminate them worldwide. Well-organized advocacy groups are actively monitoring corporations. Once unenforceable legal claims have become a real deterrent as fines have risen dramatically. Shell initially denied responsibility and offered the entire community $6,050 in compensation. As Bodo chiefs and elders, with the help of Amnesty International, Nigerian civil rights groups, and the renowned British law firm Leigh Day, were able to threaten the multinational with a trial at the High Court in London, Shell settled out of court for $83.5 million in 2015. The claim named 15,601 villagers, including 2,000 children.[40] Thus, the once invisible and powerless victims of corporate abuse have gained access to the courts. The costs of negligence and ecological crime have grown steeply. Spectacular cases like Shell's in Nigeria or BP's in the Gulf of Mexico powerfully deter practices that many companies used to get away with.[41]

The parameters in which businesses operate have profoundly changed. In short, rather than fighting environmentalism, many corporations now embrace it in their public relations and business models. The following example best illustrates the magnitude of change since the 1980s. Joschka Fischer, a former left-wing radical and leading figure in the German Green Party, was anathema to the corporate world, not only for his provocative demeanor in parliament but also for his antibusiness stance. His rise to Germany's foreign minister and vice-chancellor in 1998 was unforeseen. After the end of his political career Fischer became a lobbyist for large corporations like Siemens, once an important proponent of nuclear energy, BMW, a manufacturer of luxury cars, and the utility company RWE, which runs several nuclear power plants. Fischer was courted, as Siemens pointed out, for his "unique profile and network," his ecological competence and credibility.[42] Obviously both the corporate world and Fischer had changed considerably.

GE has a rich history of large-scale pollution. It disposed of toxic waste, as the U.S. Environmental Protection Agency put it in 2003, without "adequate protection of public health and the environment."[43] According to the Corporate Toxics Information Project, GE was the fourth largest corporate air polluter in the United States in 2000.[44] In 2005, GE of all companies rebranded itself as an ecological corporation and launched a program called "Ecomagination." In the words of CEO Jeff Immelt, it intended "to develop tomorrow's solutions such as solar energy, hybrid locomotives, fuel cells, lower-emission aircraft engines. . . . And we will use these technologies to improve our own energy efficiency and environmental performance."[45] By 2013 GE had invested $12 billion in research and development in Ecomagination products, generating more than $160 billion in revenues. GE claims to have proven that "green is green." "We have also made it a part of our competitive structure, reducing our greenhouse gas emissions 32% since our 2004 baseline and our freshwater use 45% since our 2006 baseline, while realizing $300 million in savings."[46]

The greening of corporate giants like GE and Siemens encompassed the acquisition of smaller companies that had pioneered green technologies like wind power. In 2002 GE bought the wind-power division of Enron, the only surviving U.S. manufacturer of large wind turbines at the time. In 2009 it acquired ScanWind and in 2011 Wind Tower Systems LLC. Siemens bought the Danish windmill manufacturer Bonus in 2004 and added several smaller firms later on. Wind energy became a huge success for Siemens, while investments in solar energy and water treatment failed. When Siemens took over Bonus in 2004, the firm had two plants in Denmark, 750 staff, and sales of €300 million. In 2010 the division had ten plants in four countries, among them Fort Madison, Iowa, 8,000 staff, and sales of €3.9 billion. The factories had moved from small-batch to automated mass production. Siemens followed GE from 2007 by focusing on four megatrends, among them climate change and the ecological modernization of large cities. Green products were defined as the future of the company. Just in time for the World Climate Summit in Copenhagen, which CEO Peter Löscher attended himself, he had created the full-bodied motto: "Siemens is marching at the forefront of the green revolution."[47]

What the self-laudatory narratives of greening firms conceal is their continued dependence on subsidies and political support, as the history of solar- and wind-energy companies demonstrates. Their success also depended on the price of conventional sources of energy. Solar energy especially, being expensive, was very vulnerable to boom and bust cycles. It received an enormous boost in the 1970s in the wake of the oil crises with a mixture of tax incentives, subsidies, and an obligation for utility companies to buy solar energy at above-market prices, that is, so-called feed-in tariffs.[48]

While the sector started with great hopes in the 1980s, falling oil prices dented its profitability. In the United States, the Reagan administration hurried to cut subsidies and tax credits while Japan and Germany rolled out new subvention programs. Germany, the pioneer in adopting a renewable energy policy, intensified its efforts following the Chernobyl disaster and the rise of the Green Party. Continued reliance on volatile political support makes it difficult for companies to plan for the long haul. Recently, Chinese government subventions to the point of dumping put many European and U.S. firms in crisis and made their existence depend on protective tariffs. The sector also suffered when governments cut subventions due to the recession following the financial crisis of 2007–8.

The history of the solar industry also reflects the problems large corporations have when turning small niches into big business. Massive investments by large oil manufacturers in solar energy in the 1980s did not work out and in most cases were abandoned. Siemens had been interested in solar energy since the 1950s but left the industry by 2012. Today it confines itself to supplying components like control systems and turbines. By contrast, GE builds entire solar-power systems.

Siemens also suffered from focusing on the wrong technological path. Rather than going for photovoltaics where silicon cells generate electricity it opted for high-temperature thermal energy. In this system, solar collectors (dishes) direct sunlight onto oil-carrying pipes. The heated oil generates steam, which is used by conventional turbines to generate electricity. In 2009 Siemens bought the Israeli corporation Solel Solar Systems and acquired shares in the Italian Archimede Solar Energy. Both firms specialized in solar thermal systems. Solel came with a huge order for a reference unit in Andalusia. One hundred seventy thousand dishes were to generate fifty megawatts, enough electricity for thirty thousand households. The dishes covered the space of fifty-eight soccer fields.[49] This project exemplifies all the risks of green innovations. Political decisions on access to the grid and feed-in tariffs, the bankruptcy of a project partner, and unresolved financing questions delayed the completion of the power plant, which only began operations in 2012. At this point, the market shifted and cheaper electricity generated by photovoltaic panels had undermined solar thermal energy's competitiveness. Generally, cuts in feed-in tariffs, the dumping of Chinese solar panels, and the subsequent price erosion plunged the sector into a deep crisis. In the case of Solel, losses exceeded sales. Siemens therefore sold its Archimede shares in 2012 and Solel in 2013. Siemens lost an estimated €1 billion through its investments in solar energy.[50]

Despite green capitalism's long history of failed projects, it came to be regarded as a megatrend for the future. Thus, in the 1990s large corporations began issuing sustainability reports alongside their business reports. Typically, these reports contain data on firms' emissions, products, and process innovations, pledges to cut waste, energy consumption, and greenhouse emissions, as well as pledges to enforce certain sustainability standards in the supply chain. Eco-audits supply data that are fed into prestigious indexes claiming to measure ecologically correct business behavior like the Dow Jones Sustainability Index, the KLD Global Climate 100 Index, and the Innovest Global 100 Most Sustainable Corporations in the World Index. Corporations use their rankings for self-promotion.

The *Siemens Sustainability Report 2012* has a cover picture with children playing in a park. CEO Löscher and Barbara Kux, the company's chief sustainability officer, admonished readers that "we must act today to ensure that future generations inherit a world worth living in." Sustainability is then defined as the company's overarching "strategic principle" with reference to von Carlowitz before impressive projects of ecological modernization spearheaded by Siemens are described.[51] GE claims to be "redefining what it means to be green," "inventing the next industrial era," and "finding solutions that benefit the planet, its people and the economy."[52] This kind of literature gives the impression that environmentalists have taken over the commanding heights of the economy and ousted old-style profit-seeking managers. Nowadays, CEOs seem to care only about saving the planet. But nothing could be farther from the truth.

Green capitalism in the twenty-first century is, first of all, as both GE and Siemens frankly admit, a business opportunity, a way to open up new markets and sources of growth and to deliver for investors.[53] When everybody wants to be green, no big corporation can be not green. Eco-capitalism is a marketing claim and a fashion, a reaction to changing markets, and an attempt to sell innovative and less damaging products. It also is the result of generational change. The present cohort of managers, having been influenced by environmentalism, take ecological concerns more seriously than their predecessors. Yet the greening of industry is more than greenwashing and is often accompanied by significant ecological benefits. How large they really are, how they compare to less advertised investments, and how much eco-capitalism matters in the face of relentlessly advancing global warming remains to be analyzed. The final section addresses the paradoxes and contradictions of green capitalism.

## The Paradoxes and Contradictions of Green Capitalism

Going green brings technological and financial risks for corporations but also opportunities and visions. The Desertec project, developed in the wake of the Chernobyl disaster, is a good example. In 2003, a transnational consortium decided to invest $507 billion to build an integrated, decarbonized power system based on renewable energies. The Sahara Desert was to generate most of the electricity, which a supergrid would transmit to satisfy much of Middle Eastern and North African and 15 percent of continental European demand by 2050.

Founded in 2009, the consortium Dii GmbH consisted of around fifty partners, including many multinationals like ABB, Siemens, Bosch, Deutsche Bank, Munich Re, E.ON, RWE, and ENEL. This megalomanic project was poorly conceived from the beginning. It would have created a fatal dependency on politically unstable North African countries and posed almost insurmountable cross-border coordination problems. Collaboration among several nations and fifty partners was an unrealistic endeavor. For the tumultuous Arab world, which was increasingly divided, Desertec looked like some kind of neocolonial takeover. Finally, the projected thirty-five-to-fifty-year time span was too long for publically traded corporations with significantly shorter investment horizons. Thus, by 2013 the largest engineering multinationals like Siemens, ABB, and Bosch had left the consortium.[54]

Desertec has been compared to another stillborn giant, the Atlantropa project of the 1920s.[55] It pursued a mammoth hydroelectric dam across the Strait of Gibraltar that would provide the entire Mediterranean region with electricity. This vision involved lowering the surface of the Mediterranean Sea up to 660 feet, building another dam across the Dardanelles, and opening up large new lands for settlement in an almost totally drained Adriatic Sea, which most likely would have devastated the regional ecosystem. The ecological risks of Desertec concerned local water supplies, which might have been depleted if used to clean dust off solar panels and cool turbines.

Historically, hydropower megaprojects and nuclear power plants started as "green projects" because they would supposedly replace fossil fuels and smoke-belching chimneys with a clean and inexhaustible source of energy. Both turned out to be "environmental risks of the highest order."[56] Huge artificial lakes like the Aswan Dam dried up valleys, became breeding grounds for epidemics, and caused massive evaporation. Huge sediment buildups caused biological damage and reduced biodiversity. For the Three Gorges Dam in China, thirteen cities, 140 towns, and 1,350 villages were flooded and 1.2 million people were relocated. Nuclear power has not only precipitated disastrous accidents like Chernobyl and Fukushima and created incalculable risks following terrorist attacks and airstrikes in wars but also produced the still unsolved problem of highly radioactive wastes that need to be stored in high-security deposits for a million years.

One possible tragedy of green capitalism might be that many successes are too small to noticeably impact the world climate, whereas large-scale technical projects either remain utopian or generate new ecological problems much worse than the original issues.

More evidence that a green label does not necessarily correspond to green contents comes from the production of so-called biofuels made out of biological materials, such as plants or waste. Their supporters claim that they can be burned with no or very little net emissions of carbon dioxide. The worldwide production of biofuels—principally ethanol and biodiesel—has grown rapidly since 2000. They emit 20 to 60 percent less carbon dioxide than fossil fuels, yet it is debatable whether biofuels are really green. Ethanol production in the United States relies on corn, which is less efficient than sugar and is often produced in refineries powered by coal. To compete with Brazilian producers, U.S. farmers need subsidies and tariffs.[57] As biofuels rely on economies of scale, crops are typically grown by large agribusinesses. They favor monocropping and intensive irrigation, as well as chemical fertilizers, herbicides, and pesticides. This possibly depletes local water deposits and poisons the groundwater. Nitrous oxide emissions result from fertilizer use and are much more harmful to the atmosphere than carbon dioxide. Biofuel production can also potentially contribute to deforestation, soil erosion, and loss of biodiversity. As biofuels are more profitable than food, they can raise food prices and starve the world's poorest.[58]

In Germany, high subventions have enormously spurred the cultivation of canola for biodiesel, resulting in small idealistic farmers—the pioneers of green agriculture—losing their land as agribusinesses outbid them upon lease renewal. Once agribusinesses have taken over, the formerly organically farmed acreage becomes flooded with fertilizers, falling victim to exhaustive monocultures.[59]

Indonesia, for example, is expanding oil palm plantations at the expense of rain forests and peatlands to benefit from the biofuel boom. This weakens an important carbon dioxide repository, while slashing and burning the forest releases a massive carbon dioxide load. According to one investigation one ton of palm oil generates ten times more carbon dioxide emissions than petroleum.[60] The overall ecological impact of biofuels is still controversially debated. The simplistic idea that biofuels equal green energy, which interested parties suggest, might be misleading.

Another ambiguity of green capitalism arises from the Jevons paradox, or "rebound effect." In 1865, the English economist William Stanley Jevons received wide recognition for his counterintuitive finding that increasing energy efficiency does not guarantee sustainability. "It is wholly a confusion of ideas to suppose that the economical use of fuel is equivalent to a diminished consumption. The very contrary is the truth." If some technological advance made it possible for blast furnaces to produce iron with less coal, he wrote, then profits would rise, new investment would be attracted, and the price of iron would fall, stimulating additional demand. Eventually, he concluded, "the greater number of furnaces will more than make up for the diminished consumption of each."[61] Even if this conclusion remains controversial, technological progress might well be a double-edged sword.

Environmental economists have detected a more recent rebound effect from greater fuel efficiency in cars since the 1970s, which increased automobile usage in the 1980s. The U.S. fuel-economy regulations of 1975—the first of their kind—did not result in a decline in U.S. motor-fuel consumption. Instead it rose significantly as car miles doubled (1980–2010), and horsepower, vehicle weight, and car ownership increased.[62] The story with air conditioners and refrigerators is similar. Today they are vastly more energy efficient than in the 1950s. These gains drove down the costs of both operation and manufacturing. As refrigerators got more efficient and cheaper, they became bigger. More people could afford them, prompting less thrifty usage. Stockpiling food until it spoiled became a common practice. Air conditioning once was a luxury, but by 2005, 84 percent of U.S. homes had it. Manufacturers worked hard to "green" air conditioning, achieving remarkable improvements (28 percent more energy efficiency between 1993 and 2005). Yet increased household consumption for air conditioning (37 percent) exceeded these efficiency gains, which, alongside price reductions, have transformed air conditioning from a luxury to a staple. The same factors hasten its dissemination all over the world, with China and India making the largest strides.[63]

Further examples are easily found. Today's jet engines are about 70 percent more efficient than those of the 1970s, but colossal growth in traffic has outstripped these gains. Passenger numbers increased between 1970 and 2010 by roughly 600 percent. Airfreight volume rose even faster.[64] Aviation is, in fact, one of the fastest-growing sources of greenhouse gas emissions. What is the net ecological effect when cars use only half as much gas as they used to while their number worldwide soars? Cleaning oil sands with less water can be flagged as green but still supports an activity with extremely high energy consumption and incalculable ecological risks.

## Conclusion

Green capitalism is neither a new nor an unambiguous concept. GE's slogan "green is green" could not been farther from the truth. Green comes in very different shades and is often undermined by unintended consequences. Going green confronts corporations with complicated technological and financial choices. One main problem is diverging time horizons. In this financialization era, capital markets put a lot of pressure on managers, and publicly listed companies live from one quarterly or yearly reporting period to another rather than planning for decades or beyond.

Going green makes sense for them if they perceive it as a business opportunity. Although there has been a remarkable change in boardroom mentalities, the main drivers of green capitalism have been outside forces, regulation, and market demand. Dramatically revised regulatory regimes and consumer attitudes gradually turned green capitalism into a commercial growth strategy. Green products and processes are indeed taken seriously, although greenwashing and marketing ploys are also involved. Corporations like GE prefer to talk about their green agenda rather than their abysmal cleanup record. It took massive pressure from the U.S. Department of Justice and the Environmental Protection Agency to force GE into a $250 million settlement in 1999 to clean the Housatonic River of pollution that the company's use of polychlorinated biphenyls (PCBs) caused.[65] Whereas GE widely touts its "Ecomagination," it is discreet about its past sins. Still, without industrial corporations seeking greater energy efficiency, the planet might be worse off.

The notion of capitalism that is entirely green, of a purely technological solution to the current ecological crisis, is highly unrealistic, not only because of the Jevons paradox. We might classify it together with past technological utopias that were to save the earth via hydropower or nuclear energy. In the early days of electricity, many people thought that this "white coal" would expunge air pollution. Instead of noisy, stinking factories covered in poisonous smoke, the industry of the future, the early twentieth-century forecast held, would be located in a "well-maintained park, in which only the birds' choirs interrupt the solemn tranquillity and where instead of former factory sewers a pristine creek meanders between gigantic trees."[66] In 1904, August Bebel, the leader of Social Democrats in Germany, sketched his vision of a green paradise based on inexhaustible solar and geothermal energy: "Mineral coal is hard to get and its supply decreases daily. Attention must be turned towards utilizing the heat of the sun and of the earth's crust. The hope is justified that both sources will be drawn upon without limit . . . all imaginable machinery may be put in perpetual operation on earth . . . numerous chemical problems will become solvable, among these the greatest of all—*the chemical production of food*." Hunger would be overcome once and for all. "The problem of removing dust, smoke, soot and odors could likewise be completely solved by modern chemistry and technology. . . . No longer will the face of earth be marred . . . by agriculture: it will become a garden in which, at will, grass or flowers, bush or woods, can be allowed to grow, and in which the human race will live in plenty, in a Golden Age."[67]

Today we know that that socialism as it materialized had a particularly devastating environmental record. The language of these failed visions, like Bebel's expectations, partly resembles the rhetoric of many proponents of green capitalism today. The history of green utopias teaches us to be skeptical. This does not mean that attempts at greening capitalism are futile. On the contrary, corporations must play a central role in limiting greenhouse emissions. Their initiatives—regardless of what motivates them—are an important step in the right direction. A critical eco-cultural business history can contribute greatly to our understanding of the logic these important actors of environmental history follow.

# Chapter 3

# The Role of Businesses in Constructing Systems of Environmental Governance

*Hugh S. Gorman*

How does environmental governance relate to the topic of "green capitalism"? Ultimately, "governance" is the entity whose "greenness" really matters. In general, the decisions of producers and consumers operating under a particular set of market rules is less important than the rules themselves and the choices embedded in those rules. Green capitalism, from this perspective, is a form of capitalism in which the rules that govern markets recognize the finiteness of earth systems and reward producers and consumers for operating within a set of socially constructed boundaries rooted in this finiteness.

The process by which systems of environmental governance are constructed is a messy one, often requiring action at different scales and jurisdictions and involving multiple social groups, each having its own vision of the future and level of influence. Efforts to construct new forms of environmental governance typically occur when a variety of people attempt to exploit the same set of resources for different purposes, giving rise to conflicts that can only be resolved by establishing clear rules about how those resources can be used.[1] Ideally, once those rules are well integrated into markets, producers and consumers develop practices that respect those particular boundaries.

However, even after a system of environmental governance is in place, innovation can alter uses of the environment and push a society into unexplored ethical and legal territory. For example, in the United States, the introduction of automobiles and the construction of paved roads connecting cities to national forests allowed masses of recreation-seeking tourists to interact with those forests in new ways, placing them at odds with those who valued the same forests as sources of timber or for their solitude and wilderness characteristics. Ultimately, political choices had to be made about how those forests—and access to those forests—were to be governed in the age of the automobile.[2]

What roles have business interests played in establishing past systems of environmental governance? It is an important question to ask if the goal is to develop systems of environmental governance that are considered "green." Producers and consumers operating in a market cannot, by themselves, alter the rules that govern their practices. Such changes, at their root, are political choices—and the role of business interests in embracing, resisting, or otherwise influencing those choices is important to understand. Indeed, the efforts of firms to alter the rules that govern their practices may be more important to examine than the greenness of their practices. After all, if we assume that competition generally results in firms having to adopt the most efficient practices available to them under a particular set of rules, then it may be misleading to judge them for adopting ungreen practices that are both allowed and available to their competitors. Whether those same actors embrace or resist forms of governance that would result in everybody adopting greener practices is just as important.

What follows is a review of the various roles that business interests have played in constructing past systems of environmental governance. The purpose is to provide insight into the challenge of constructing a greener form of capitalism, one that is capable of both sustaining uses of the environment that people value and rewarding innovation that makes it easier to do so. What role can producers and consumers be expected to play in this process? Can the power of business interests be harnessed to facilitate "green" changes? Or should the goal be to reduce the influence of businesses in the process of defining the rules that govern uses of the environment? This brief review of the topic suggests that an emerging approach is to facilitate transitions in environmental uses through forms of adaptive governance—that is, by employing transparent systems for reaching consensus on objectives, monitoring progress toward those objectives, and using what is learned to periodically adjust goals and strategies.

## A Brief Review of Broad Patterns

Here, I review the various roles that business interests have played in altering systems of environmental governance over the last couple of centuries. First, however, a brief look at the general concept of governance will be useful. The constitutional scholar Lawrence Lessig explains the notion of governance in terms of the factors that influence the practices people adopt. He emphasizes these four factors: laws, markets, norms, and what he refers to as "architecture."[3] Laws identify the boundaries of what we can do legally—that is, without any state-enforced consequences. For example, a law prohibiting smoking in public spaces does not mean that one cannot physically light a cigarette in a restaurant; it simply means that people who do so are potentially subject to some type of legal consequence, such as a fine. In practice, though, most behavior regarding smoking is regulated by social norms, not by the fear of legal action. The market is also a governing factor. It determines, for example, whether a person can afford to buy cigarettes in the first place or, if they can, whether they can afford to buy a car that permits them to travel (and smoke) in a private space. Finally, there is "architecture," which Lessig uses to refer to the physical constraints and capabilities that govern what one can do.

Lessig's focus is on the governance of cyberspace, not environmental governance. Writing on the topic in 1999, he noted that most people believed that net neutrality was built into the architecture of the Internet. But, as Lessig made clear, net neutrality was not built into the architecture of the Internet. Neither was it protected by law. Instead, at the time, social norms were the only factor discouraging companies from violating the principle of net neutrality. And as those norms eroded, Lessig pointed out, we would see rational, profit-seeking companies adopt practices that violated the principle of net neutrality. So, he argued, laws would be needed if people desired to keep the principle of neutrality intact.

When it comes to uses of the environment, these same four factors—laws, markets, architecture, and norms—also govern practices. Here, we can think of "architecture" as referring to the physical environment, both in terms of the natural environment (earth systems) and the built environment (technology), with the two becoming increasingly intertwined over time. In preindustrial societies, for example, the locations of mountains and rivers governed practices more than they do today, as did the rising and the setting of the sun and the distribution of resources on the landscape. However, a century of unrelenting technological innovation eliminated many constraints previously imposed on human practices, initially leaving markets and the search for profits as the primary governing force. Environmental regulations, from this perspective, can be seen as an effort to place boundaries on economic practices that had been previously governed by the architecture of nature. It is this general process of constructing policy-based systems of environmental governance, and the role of businesses in that process, that we examine here.

The categories that will be considered are: first, the role of businesses in the construction of systems of environmental governance that facilitated industrialization; second, cases in which business interests generally accepted societal efforts to place limits on their uses of the environment; third, efforts by businesses to address environmental concerns through self-regulation; fourth, cases in which business interests resisted societal efforts to place new boundaries on their uses of the environment; and, finally, efforts in which some business interests have pushed for greater limits on uses of the environment to achieve environmental objectives, with the intention of engaging in economic activity directed toward achieving those objectives. As one attempts to fit historical examples into these categories, it becomes clear that most cases do not fit cleanly into any one category. At the same time, this exercise does serve as a useful heuristic for examining the general range of roles that businesses have played in constructing past systems of environmental governance, providing some insight into how to facilitate, in a market society, interactions with the environment that are considered greener.

The first pattern, in which business interests helped to construct systems of governance that facilitated industrial uses of the environment, was the dominant one for most of the nineteenth century and a good portion of the twentieth century. We know about the details of such changes thanks to the many scholars who have explicitly examined the environmental history of cities, rivers, and their environs. For example, Marc Cioc's "eco-biography" of the Rhine River starts in 1815, just after the boundaries of Europe were redrawn by the Congress of Vienna and just before a period of rapid technological change.[4] Much of the story that Cioc tells involves the construction of a system of governance that facilitated greater use of the Rhine River as an industrial resource. That is, instead of placing limits on those with the power to alter the river in significant ways, a system of governance was constructed that facilitated changes in the service of industrial growth. One can tell—and many scholars have told—a similar story for most rivers that flowed through industrializing regions in the nineteenth and early twentieth century. For that matter, one does not have to confine oneself to rivers. For example, Brian Black's *Petrolia* tells the story of how efforts to extract petroleum from the earliest oil-producing region of Pennsylvania resulted in the entire landscape being integrated into the system of oil extraction.[5]

In some industrializing areas, where powerful groups with different economic interests clashed, rules affecting how one could (and could not) use environmental resources had to be negotiated. The creation of those rules often involved lawsuits and legislation, with the end result generally (but not always) favoring groups that desired to use waterways and other resources for industrial interests. For example, before they could use the river as a source of power, the operators of mills along the Merrimack River had to lobby for changes in Massachusetts law, which originally prohibited the building of dams that blocked fish and flooded fields.[6]

Even when efforts to change the law were unsuccessful and existing environmental uses continued to be privileged, companies often planted their operations just far enough away to avoid immediate conflict.[7] Firms could also locate operations in areas distant from urban cores, where few institutions capable of placing limits on industrial practices existed. In such cases, firms could operate with impunity. This lack of governance was certainly true in the oil-producing regions of Pennsylvania in the 1860s and true some fifty years later when the U.S. Steel Corporation located a massive industrial complex in a relatively remote part of Indiana where nobody had the power to interfere with the company's practices (establishing, in the process, Gary, Indiana, in honor of U.S. Steel's founding chairman, E. H. Gary).[8] Firms that conducted operations far from nineteenth-century industrial cores, such as the sugar industry in Hawaii or the guano industry in Peru, also tended to alter landscapes at will.[9]

A second category involves cases in which business interests accepted limits on uses of the environment being advocated by others. Although efforts in this category sometimes addressed environmental concerns, those concerns were not necessarily the motivating factor behind the change in governance. For example, business interests generally embraced efforts by Progressive Era reformers to set aside large tracts of forested land for resource conservation. Although such efforts addressed environmental concerns—such as deforestation, the loss of habitat and wilderness, and soil erosion—we know from classics such as Sam Hays's *Conservation and the Gospel of Efficiency* that the conservation movement had more to do with using resources efficiently than achieving environmental objectives.[10] After all, when efficient use and environmental objectives clashed, the former generally trumped the latter.[11]

Another example that illustrates the conservationist mind-set and its gradual embrace by business leaders can be found in the U.S. petroleum industry. In the nineteenth century, oil fields were messy, dangerous, and largely ungoverned places—resulting in far more drilling than necessary and huge quantities of oil being lost to fire and spills or trapped underground due to the flaring of viscosity-reducing natural gas. Leaky wells also allowed water and oil to move between formations, contaminating aquifers and, when water entered an oil formation, limiting the ability of the oil to flow freely. In addition, producers often lifted large quantities of briny water along with their oil, which they separated and discharged in streams. Downstream users affected by this contamination often sued. Gradually, over the course of about a half century, leaders in the U.S. petroleum industry came to accept rules that called for the cementing of wells, the use of blowout protectors, the return of brine to underground formations, limits on releases of natural gas, limits on the number of wells drilled in certain areas, and even the practice of managing an oil formation as an integrated unit. Small companies, which could no longer rush into a newly discovered oil field and inexpensively extract large quantities of petroleum at the expense of others, opposed any change in governance. Over time, however, conservationists were able to convince industry leaders to support the new rules by showing that the change increased the net wealth that could be extracted from a particular oil field. The new set of rules also addressed a variety of environmental concerns, such as reduced cases of stream pollution, and resulted in fewer costs associated with lawsuits.[12]

Another example of an effort to place limits on uses of the environment that did not meet with resistance from business interests was the urban campaign to prevent outbreaks of waterborne diseases such as typhoid and cholera. When civic leaders attempted to govern practices associated with the securing and disposal of water, business interests generally supported them. They gave their support, in part, because they valued clean sources of water for industrial uses and because the initial focus was on the safe removal of pathogen-filled municipal sewage, not the treatment of industrial wastes. In addition, the consequences of inaction—thousands of people dying due to outbreaks of disease—could lead to a city gaining a reputation for being especially unhealthy, making it difficult to attract new workers. Finally, the main actions involved the construction of municipal sewers and, later, municipal wastewater treatment plants, both of which represented a significant amount of economic activity.[13] Similarly, the City Beautiful movement, which placed parks and other urban spaces off limits to development, also received the support of many business leaders. Among other things, they hoped that access to green space would contribute to a more harmonious social order.[14] Likewise, the establishment of rules that required urban residents to dispose of their garbage in a systematic manner caused no reason for alarm.[15]

Systems of governance that mandated the use of sewers, established parks, and required people to dispose of their garbage in a systematic fashion not only placed limits on uses of the environment but also demanded some level of public investment without a direct economic return. However, business leaders generally supported these efforts, partly because these actions did not require significant change in their own practices and partly because the new rules meshed with the type of urban, industrial society they hoped to see flourish. In any event, these efforts resulted in new forms of environmental governance that were generally embraced by business interests.

A third category involves efforts by industrial interests to address environmental concerns by governing their own practices, mainly through the voluntary adoption of practices more restrictive than legally necessary. By the 1920s, trade groups and engineering societies routinely governed industrial practices through the use of standards that affected everything from wire sizes and connector designs to processes for producing and testing materials. Over the course of the twentieth century, when faced with environmental concerns linked to industrial practices, industry leaders have often argued that the same system of governance could be used to address environmental concerns.

The initial impulse toward standardization came from nineteenth-century engineers seeking to create product specifications that could be referenced over and over again, eliminating the need to prepare new specifications each time.[16] In general, these engineers desired to make the world a more efficient, safer, and predictable place by creating and controlling a body of such standards through their nascent professional societies. However, from works in the history of business and technology, such as Edwin Layton's *Revolt of the Engineers*, Bruce Sinclair's *Centennial History of the American Society of Mechanical Engineers*, Steven Usselman's *Regulating Railroad Innovation*, and Amy Slayton's *Reinforced Concrete and the Modernization of American Building*, we know that process of setting industrial standards proved to be more controversial than these early engineers expected. After all, if a group of engineers agreed to embrace a particular standard, it also meant that their employers, their employer's competitors, and all consumers, large and small, would be governed by that standard as well. And that did not always go over so well.[17]

We also know how the story of industrial standardization unfolded over the course of the twentieth century. A process for creating standards by "voluntary consensus" emerged, involving the members of hundreds of professional societies and industry trade groups. Today, much of the coordination associated with establishing a new standard by voluntary consensus is provided by the International Organization for Standardization (ISO), the members of which are national-level standardization bodies, one for each country. In their book on ISO, Craig Murphy and JoAnne Yates explicitly describe the standard-setting process over which the organization presides, along with the resulting standards, as a form of global governance.[18] And it is a form of governance in which business interests hold significant power.

The overlap between standardization and environmental governance has occurred whenever technical experts involved in the creation of industrial standards have turned their attention to environmental practices. For example, in the 1930s, when faced with potential federal regulations aimed at limiting oily discharges into water bodies, the American Petroleum Institute (API) turned to the committee system that it normally employed for standardizing things such as pipe sizes and processes for measuring the quality of crude oil. A new committee was formed and charged with setting expectations for refiners in terms of what pollution-prevention practices they should adopt. The main goal was to fend off regulations by demonstrating that the industry could govern itself.[19]

The practices recommended by the API were framed as voluntary. Furthermore, no attempt was made to identify specific environmental objectives. The hope was that as engineers designed new refineries and integrated the recommended types of pollution control into their designs, concerns associated with the discharge of pollution-causing wastes would gradually disappear. In short, they assumed that economic incentives associated with saving material and avoiding lawsuits would drive the adoption of new practices—and up to a point, they were right. Over the course of several decades, significant progress was made in reducing the quantity of wastes released by refineries for each barrel of oil processed. Those improvements, however, were overwhelmed by dramatic increases in the number of refineries and the scale at which they operated. Hence, by the 1960s, economic incentives associated with reducing releases of pollution-causing wastes had been exhausted—yet pollution concerns remained. Furthermore, public expectations associated with environmental quality were rising.[20] Eventually, state officials and others waiting for the long-promised improvements in water quality concluded that self-regulation would not, acting alone, achieve the desired goal. In the absence of government-enforced regulations, refiners (and the operators of other industrial plants) had no reason to take the level of action necessary to significantly improve air and water quality.[21]

A more sophisticated twist on the desire to promote sound environmental practices through self-regulation involves the use of eco-labeling and green certification programs. Here, the goal is to set up a system for consumers to reward firms that manage their operations in an environmentally friendly way. An example might be a lumber company that sells wood harvested from sustainably managed forests or a food distributor that only does business with farms that do not use pesticides. These firms, in essence, hope to fill a market niche occupied by consumers who are willing to pay extra for products produced in a way that meshes with their values.[22]

By the 1980s, a tangle of green certification programs, eco-labels, and voluntary industrial initiatives led the leaders of the ISO to direct their attention toward the business of environmental governance. Initially, they had hoped that the organization could coordinate the creation of environmental standards that would be broadly accepted by companies throughout the world. The end result, however, was another certification program, one spelled out in the ISO 14000 series of standards. Essentially, this series of standards establishes a procedure for certifying that companies employ a continual improvement process for setting and meeting internally defined environmental goals. In most cases, these internal goals involve complying with existing environmental laws as efficiently as possible. In practice, therefore, the decision of firms to become ISO 14000 certified matters less than the strength of the laws with which they are expected to comply.[23]

We see the same technocratic impulse—and faith in self-regulation—at work today in the promotion of "Green Chemistry" and "Green Engineering."

In general, these concepts refer to a set of principles that, if followed, would result in practices and products that place less stress on earth systems. For example, Green Engineering principle 2 is: "It is better to prevent waste than to treat or clean up waste after it is formed."[24] And Green Chemistry principle 4 is: "Chemical products should be designed to effect their desired function while minimizing their toxicity."[25] Over time, proponents argue, industrial practices will come to be less and less environmentally disruptive as engineers incorporate these principles into their designs. The major proponents of these principles tend to frame the process of making something "greener" as a purely technical matter. That is, they see it as an engineering problem, not a political choice associated with placing boundaries on uses of the environment so as to encourage innovations and practices that respect those boundaries. Some proponents even suggest that environmental regulations are undesirable in that they constrain the ability of technical experts to find creative solutions.[26]

Governing environmental practices through self-regulation has generally failed due to the problem of free riders. Firms that voluntarily adopt environmentally friendly practices (and, for that matter, the consumers who pay extra for green products) put themselves at a disadvantage in the market relative to nonadopters. In the case of a conventional industrial standard, such as one that specifies the size of a standard-sized cargo container, the opposite is true. Adopters of conventional standards are not placed at an economic disadvantage relative to nonadopters. In fact, if the standard is successful, adopters are likely to enjoy an economic advantage over nonadopters. Therefore, although it may take intense negotiations to reach consensus on a standard size for cargo containers, it is perfectly reasonable to describe the use of that standard as voluntary. After all, there is no problem with allowing a shipping line to use a nonstandard container. That company (and its customers) will not necessarily benefit economically from the decision to use a nonstandard design. If anything, over time, they would be likely to bear extra costs for ignoring the standard. The same is not true when a firm chooses to ignore an environmental standard.

In the case of voluntary environmental standards, nonadopters have the economic advantage. For example, if expectations associated with controlling emissions of sulfur dioxide were voluntary, an energy company could choose not to install sulfur-control equipment on its coal-fired power-generating stations. This nonadopter would save the cost of purchasing, installing, operating, and maintaining that equipment. As a result, either its customers would benefit by having to pay slightly less or its shareholders would benefit by receiving slightly larger profits. And given that the people who bear the brunt of sulfur dioxide emissions often live hundreds, if not thousands of miles away, consumer choices would not push a resistant utility to voluntarily alter its practices. On the other hand, firms that voluntarily adopt the limit on sulfur emissions would experience higher costs, placing themselves at a disadvantage relative to nonadopters. Hence, if all environmental standards were voluntary, producers and consumers that ignored them would be rewarded.

The potential ability of the insurance industry, which has been called a "technology of governance," to influence the environmental practices of its customers must also be considered in this category of self-regulation.[27] But free riders also complicate the story here. Consider a hypothetical example: the use of insurance to regulate the design and operation of nuclear power plants. It is a hypothetical example because all countries with nuclear power plants have state-enforced regulations that govern the design and/or operation of those facilities. In the United States, there is also legislation (the Price-Anderson Act) that complicates the issue by relieving the operators of nuclear power plants of most liability associated with accidents and placing that responsibility on the federal government.[28] But consider what would happen if nuclear power plants were completely ungoverned by the state. Utilities that purchase liability insurance would be governed by the firms that insure them, with insurance companies requiring the adoption of safe practices as a condition of being insured. But what about companies that might choose to save costs by operating their facilities without insurance and, perhaps, by adopting riskier and less expensive practices than their competitors? Who would govern them?

In general, the insurance industry is not able to serve as a "technology of governance" without laws that empower it in that role. Unless legislation requires all firms to obtain insurance, some firms—the uninsured ones— would fall outside of this system of governance. Also, laws must be in place that hold firms liable for the environmental consequences of their practices; otherwise, why would firms purchase insurance to protect against the costs of those consequences? A good example of this intertwining of insurance, standardization, laws, corporate practices, and environmental consequences can be found in the governance of the maritime industries.[29] In that industry, private classification societies inspect and rate ships according to a set of industry standards, providing insurers with the information they need to assess risks. And given that international treaties and national laws now hold ship owners (and, hence, the companies that insure them) liable for the consequences of events such as oil spills, the risk of such events are taken into account when a ship is inspected and the cost of insurance is calculated.

A fourth category involves societal efforts to place boundaries on uses of the environment that met with resistance from business interests. In most cases, this resistance has come from industries in which companies would be expected to change their practices in significant ways. We see this resistance, for example, in the early twentieth century, when urban reformers sought to place limits on the amount of soot that coal-fired boilers could legally release, and a few decades later, when officials in Los Angeles sought to address concerns associated with photochemical smog. In the case of photochemical smog, obtaining cleaner air meant that car manufacturers, oil refiners, and the operators of power plants would have to significantly reduce emissions of compounds that were practically invisible, and resistance was substantial.[30]

In the United States, as elsewhere, a wide range of other efforts to impose limits on uses of the environment have also triggered resistance, such as efforts to slow the loss of biodiversity by limiting the development of important habitats, efforts to reduce acid precipitation by placing limits on emissions of sulfur dioxide and nitrogen oxides, and efforts to eliminate the use of industrial and agricultural chemicals that are toxic, persistent, and capable of bioaccumulating in fish and wildlife. Resistance to placing limits on carbon emissions so as to reduce anthropogenic climate change also, of course, falls into this category.

Potential forms of resistance vary, but some general tactics that have been employed by firms in the past are:

- Participating in fact-finding hearings and promising action but failing to change practices in any substantial way unless forced to do so by courts or legislation.[31]
- Controlling the production of and access to data necessary for decision making, including the results of internally funded research.[32]
- Restricting access to industrial sites.[33]
- Framing an issue in terms of utilitarian conservation and self-regulation and arguing that the problem will disappear as technology improves in a competitive free market.[34]

- Opposing regulatory action by framing the issue as an economic "taking" that results in private wealth being used to fund a public good.[35]
- Funding lobbying efforts to defeat legislation or challenging a rule in court.[36]
- Arguing that a scientific consensus does not exist and introducing uncertainty into decision-making.[37]

Does the manifestation of such resistance suggest that the rules governing a market are not "green?" At some level, of course, yes. However, even when the rules are already relatively green, we would still expect businesses to resist changes that would affect the value of their investments. After all, at the beginning of a policy cycle, when issues are not particularly clear and the level of consensus on policy solutions is low, firms and investors can be expected to be wary of regulatory action that would affect the value of their assets and potentially undermine their entire business model. For that matter, good decision making requires some level of resistance and debate; "greenness" is not a well-defined direction, and there are always choices to be made.

Perhaps it is more important to examine how the forms of resistance available to various actors have changed over time. For example, a half century ago, firms in the United States could generally prevent officials from accessing and inspecting their facilities. Today, such a strategy is no longer a viable option. That change, in itself, represents a shift in environmental governance that many would consider a step in the direction of greenness. Other changes that improve the decision-making process would also represent a step in that direction.

This brings us to the last category, which is the case in which firms actively support placing limits on uses of the environment for the purpose of engaging in economic activity in support of an environmental objective. Today, one can point to companies in the photovoltaic and wind turbine industries as having business interests that would benefit from stronger environmental regulations, such as carbon caps or some other policy instrument that would integrate ecologically justified limits on carbon emissions into the economic system. Although such companies can be viewed as supporting a policy change for economic reasons, their interests are also strongly tied to environmental objectives. After all, their business models revolve around an intention to produce products and services that make reaching those objectives possible.

Entrepreneurs who would have benefited from the integration of environmental limits into markets can, of course, be found in the past. In general, though, early entrepreneurs tended to believe that all innovations worth pursuing would eventually be economically justified by market forces alone. For example, Frederick Cottrell, who invented the electrostatic precipitator in the early twentieth century, hoped that all companies would use this piece of equipment to capture the material escaping from their smokestacks, not only to avoid pollution-related lawsuits but also to capture valuable material that may be going up the stack. However, even Cottrell, a philanthropist who donated all of his profits to a research foundation, saw no need to lobby for stricter limits on the emission of contaminants into the atmosphere.[38]

The insurance industry, which would benefit from stronger limits being placed on some uses of the environment, should be discussed in this category as well. As mentioned earlier, insurance companies tend to be good at getting customers to adopt safer practices. But they hold no sway over the practices of noncustomers, even when those practices have a direct influence on the insurance business. In the early twentieth century, for example, a fire insurance company could not prevent a noncustomer from storing gasoline in an open container or using shoddy wiring techniques, even if that customer were surrounded by homes insured by the company. The company, however, could lobby for a law to prevent such practices—and, indeed, insurance companies routinely supported such ordinances.[39] Today, insurance companies might be expected to support efforts to reduce emissions of carbon. Climate change not only introduces a level of uncertainty in the ability of insurance firms to set prices but it also increases the possibility of extreme events—floods, storms, droughts, and so on—that could reduce profits in the future or even overwhelm the capacity of the industry to meet its obligations. That said, the response of the insurance industry to issues related to climate change generally has not been proactive.[40]

To what extent is the willingness of forward-looking companies to push for policies that place limits on uses of the environment so as to achieve environmental objectives a fundamental characteristic of something we would call "green capitalism"? Certainly, if most businesses engaged in an environmental "race to the top," and if most consumers rewarded businesses for doing so, then markets would encourage practices to become greener. However, it is difficult to imagine that companies would advocate for a change in environmental governance if the change would result in significant financial losses. For example, it is highly unlikely that the fossil fuel industry, which has trillions of dollars' worth of assets invested in oil and coal reserves, would back a policy change that would cause the value of those reserves to plummet.[41] Neither, for that matter, might individuals who have their retirement funds in pensions and mutual fund-based accounts that are heavily invested in oil and coal.

In many ways, the challenge is for societies to facilitate the transition from one set of rules to another. For reasons already mentioned, we can expect resistance whenever new forms of environmental governance are first proposed and choices are being debated. However, after changes come to be embedded in an effective and well-designed set of policies, businesses that successfully adjust their practices and plans are likely to embrace the new policies as legitimate. For example, in the 1980s, after refiners in the United States and elsewhere had invested tens and hundreds of millions of dollars in chemical processes capable of raising the octane level of gasoline without the use of tetraethyl lead, investors in those companies certainly did not want to reverse the recently imposed limits on the use of lead.[42]

The degree to which policy transitions are managed is a societal choice. In Sweden, for example, companies have tended to work more closely with the government to manage the transition from one set of practices (such as chlorine-based processes for pulping wood and making paper) to a greener set of practices (nonchlorine processes).[43] Even in the United States, some transitions in environmental governance have been managed. For example, the use of tradable "lead" credits, which gave the air quality experts at the U.S. Environmental Protection Agency (EPA) their first experience in developing allowance trading programs, was specifically designed for the purpose of managing the transition from a system of governance that allowed for the use of leaded gasoline to one that did not.[44] Indeed, the mark of "green capitalism" may be the extent to which institutional systems for facilitating transitions in environmental governance, such as identifying and integrating ecologically justified boundaries into the rules governing markets, are in place.[45]

At one level, the transition to a greener economy, one that recognizes the finiteness of earth systems and rewards producers and consumers for operating within a set of socially constructed boundaries rooted in this finiteness, has been under way for about fifty years. In the past, this effort has largely been unmanaged, with significant policy action not being taken until a focusing event—a particularly intense incident of urban smog, bald eagles disappearing, a Bhopal-scale industrial accident, a large tanker spill, a blowout in a fragile environment, levees collapsing, unusually devastating floods, or a sustained public protest—places the spotlight on an issue, at least for a while, until public attention gradually drifts away, only to snapped back by another focusing event.[46] However, depending too much on focusing events is not necessarily a good strategy. For one thing, some environmental concerns, such as mercury- and PCB-contaminated fish in the Great Lakes or the dead zone in the northern Gulf of Mexico, are not likely to capture the public's attention on the scale necessary to deal with the problem. Indeed, environmental concerns as complex as these, in which causes and effects are separated by great distances and actions have to be coordinated at many different scales and jurisdictions, will take multiple generations to address. Maintaining the requisite political will may be impossible without some institutional structure in place.

Consequently, many social theorists are calling for adaptive forms of governance to be used in addressing the most complex environmental concerns. By adaptive forms of environmental governance, I mean processes in which a broad range of actors first reach consensus on a set of environmental objectives, develop general strategies for achieving those objectives, monitor progress in the desired direction, and periodically review that progress and make adjustments to their strategies and goals based on what has been learned since the last review. It is also important to note that decision making can be a nested process, occurring at many different geographic scales and jurisdictions at the same time.

An example of such a process is the strategy of "adaptive management" being used to reduce the size of the dead zone in the northern Gulf of Mexico. The dead zone is an area of little to no oxygen that forms each summer due to the decomposition of large quantities of algae, the growth of which is fueled by a springtime rush of nutrients delivered by the Mississippi River. To address this concern, a task force empowered by the Harmful Algal Bloom and Hypoxia Research and Control Act of 1998 first had to engage a wide range of scientists, resource managers, and governmental officials and reach consensus on a set of goals and strategies. In this case, the main goal is to reduce the size of the dead zone to 1,900 square miles, down from a peak of about 8,500 square miles. The main strategy involves reducing the quantity of nutrients being delivered to the Gulf of Mexico by the Mississippi River, which involves altering the practices of farmers and municipalities throughout the entire Mississippi River basin. To accomplish this objective, the task force gave each subbasin of the Mississippi River targets to achieve in terms of reducing nutrients. Within each subbasin, targets also have been propagating down to local watersheds. Periodically, participants in these decision-making processes (at all geographic scales) have been reviewing progress toward their targets and adjusting their strategies based on what has been learned in the process of implementation. Scientists have been monitoring the size of the dead zone for about two decades, with the size of the 2014 oxygen-deprived area measuring 5,052 square miles, a little over half way toward the long-term goal.

In short, adaptive forms of environmental governance can be viewed as a continual improvement process on a grand scale, coordinating the actions of many actors in multiple jurisdictions over several generations in the face of many unknowns, with the question of who gets to define "improvement" being a significant one. Another example of an adaptive process is the one being used to achieve ecosystem objectives in the Great Lakes, such as reducing levels of mercury in fish tissue so as to eliminate the need for consumption advisories.[47] Progress toward this specific objective is being determined by monitoring the concentrations of mercury in fish tissue.

Scholars in the Netherlands have also been promoting an adaptive approach to facilitating transitions. In this case, the focus is on the governance of sociotechnical systems, which are often part of the architecture that shapes a society's interactions with the environment. This process is being referred to as "transition management" and is conceived as a way to facilitate complex changes likely to require several generations to complete, such as the transition to a smart grid that facilitates the decentralized use of renewables.[48] Efforts to address concerns associated with climate change would also benefit by a more adaptive approach.[49] In this case, an indicator such as the concentration of greenhouse gases in the atmosphere or the rise in the average annual global temperature could be monitored, with more specific objectives and strategies set at the regional level. (In many ways, the Kyoto Protocol embraced this approach by setting carbon caps and giving nations significant flexibility on how to reduce their emissions of carbon dioxide—but the approach failed due to issues of design and cooperation.)

What is the role of businesses in such processes of adaptively managed change? In many ways, the potential roles are no different than in unmanaged, less-structured transitions. The power of large companies and industry trade groups to shape strategies and to resist rapid changes in governance certainly remains strong. But that power is countered by the establishment and monitoring of long-term objectives and the continual review of progress toward those objectives. Focusing events will still occur and trigger change; indeed, some focusing events will be tied to long-term monitoring. For example, today, a steady rise in the size of the dead zone would focus attention on that concern and the need for stronger action. However, in the absence of systematic monitoring and review, few people beyond those directly affected by the phenomenon would even notice until the degradation of the aquatic ecosystem triggered serious concerns in coastal economies. In general, then, adaptive forms of governance keep the focus on environmental concerns that are too complex to be solved through the event-driven policy cycle that emerged in the twentieth century.

Even more important, perhaps, is the role of adaptive governance in facilitating transitions in business models. Among other things, the cycle of establishing objectives and monitoring progress toward those objectives can help participants, including industry leaders, explore options and learn about the ways in which practices might have to change. Policies that place socially defined limits on certain uses of the environment will still be needed, but—in the ideal—the transition to greener policies will be better managed. And, if transitions are better managed, businesses might be empowered to compete on their ability to produce goods and services that make it easier to achieve the environmental objectives motivating the transition.

# PART II

# Conservation Before Environmentalism

# Business Leadership in the Movement to Regulate Industrial Air Pollution in Late Nineteenth- and Early Twentieth-Century America

*Christine Meisner Rosen*

Grassroots movements to regulate industrial air pollution took place in many industrial cities from the end of the Civil War and into early twentieth-century America. They proceeded in two phases. In the first phase, which peaked during the 1870s, the proponents of regulation focused on forcing the owners of slaughterhouses, packing plants, rendering plants, and livestock yards to abate their disgusting stenches. In the second phase, which started in the 1880s and 1890s and continued into the twentieth century, popular concern turned to a new kind of air-pollution problem: the coal smoke pouring out of downtown chimneys and factory smokestacks.[1]

The movements were popular ones in both periods. They usually involved a variety of interest groups, including business organizations, working in collaboration with each other. They were partially successful, with activists achieving important victories in many cities without, however, eliminating the air-pollution problems they hoped to solve. Those who fought against the stench problem in the 1860s and 1870s sought to protect the people from property damage as well as the discomfort and disease that came from living near the pools of putrefying blood and the piles of decaying animal matter and manure around urban slaughterhouses, rendering establishments, and livestock yards. The antismoke movement's goal was to eliminate the dark pall of thick, black, greasy coal smoke that covered urban skies and made its ways into homes and offices as a result of the burning of vast quantities of soft bituminous coal for power and heat. The smoke choked the people living and doing business in many U.S. cities, putting a film of soot on buildings, clothing, personal belongings, and commercial goods, as well as people's lungs.

This chapter addresses an important but currently still poorly understood aspect of how these movements were mobilized and carried forward: the leadership role that businessmen played in them. For the most part, the task of writing the history of the movements to regulate air pollution in this period has fallen to historians who have been predisposed to play up the leadership of other groups of reformers and downplay the leadership of businessmen and their organizations. With a few notable exceptions, the history of slaughterhouse-stench regulation, for example, has been written by public health and legal historians for whom this kind of regulation is a small part of the larger drama of nineteenth-century sanitary reformers' long and heroic struggle to protect public health in the nation's terribly unsanitary cities. Though these historians sometimes note, where relevant, the help that some business reformers provided the sanitarians who led the health-reform movement, they frame their narratives of these anti-stench movements as battles between the forces of good, the sanitarians, and the forces of evil, which include (especially for public health historians) public apathy and ignorance of "sanitary science," as well as the butchers and owners of packinghouses, rendering-houses, and other nuisance industries who viewed such regulation as a threat to their livelihoods and were determined to fight it to the bitter end, and their allies, the corrupt politicians who treated sanitation as lucrative extensions of their patronage machines.[2]

The urban and environmental historians who have taken up the history of the fight against smoke have done something very similar. They, too, have cast the grassroots struggle for smoke regulation as battles of good versus evil, with the villain role played by the entrenched business interests that sought to thwart regulation to protect their profits at the expense of a broader public interest. For Robert Dale Grinder, the first historian to study nineteenth-century smoke regulation in any depth, and, more recently, Harold Platt, Angela Gugliotta, and David Stradling, the heroes of the war against smoke are the groups of mostly upper-class women who did battle with the business interests who opposed regulation. These historians credit public health reformers, civic improvement groups, and mechanical and boiler engineers with playing a valuable supporting role, helping the women prepare ordinances and mobilize public support for regulation and, in the case of engineering societies, developing smoke-abatement technologies. They also acknowledge, at least in passing, that business-led reform organizations also took part in these movements. However, they characterize the leadership role played by men (the engineers as well as business leaders) as conservative and limiting compared to the women's—and sometimes even hostile to the goal of smoke abatement. They argue that the men sought to enact regulations that were less strict (and so more easily complied with) than what the women reformers demanded. They are also critical of the male leaders because they were more interested than the women in providing technical assistance to the owners of smoke boilers and furnaces to help them come into compliance with the requirements of smoke regulation and so were less prosecutorial in their approach to enforcement. Platt and Stradling are particularly hard on the business leaders who got involved in these movements, rarely identifying business-led organizations as such, except when criticizing their impact.[3]

The purpose of this chapter is to outline a different, much more complex narrative, one that goes against the grain of the conventional approach to framing business's role in the antismoke movement. In this story, business interests actively opposed regulation, often successfully bringing it to a standstill. Paradoxically, however, they also played crucially important, positive leadership roles in the movements. In fact, in some instances they were the primary or even the only leaders of these movements. In many other cases, they were the allies of the women, newspaper editors, and health reformers who initiated many of the antismoke crusades, providing help that was absolutely essential to their success.

What follows are a series of brief case studies of business leadership in the grassroots movements to regulate stench and smoke pollution in New York City, Chicago, and some other cities that illustrate business's leadership role. These case studies are based on research I have conducted for the book I am writing on the history of the American response to industrial pollution between 1840 and 1920.

My analysis is intended to stimulate discussion and debate. I am not attempting to be comprehensive. Nor am I trying to completely debunk work of the historians responsible for the mainstream view. Quite the contrary, I agree that business opposition was the bane of these movements. Rather, my purpose is to offer a few suggestive examples to point out the need for further analysis of business's positive roles in these movements. My goal is to bring their leadership role forward to the light, so that we can examine it in all its paradoxical contradiction to all we know about how business interests thwarted regulation. Much of what I will write about here is actually in the articles and books by the other historians who have studied these movements. The problem is that it is typically there in repressed and unacknowledged form, outside the authors' interpretive frames. I will argue that only by broadening these frames can we fully understand the creative, remarkably collaborative nature of the movements to regulate air pollution that took place in late nineteenth- and early twentieth-century American cities.

## My Cases

My first case concerns the New York Metropolitan Board of Health. Lauded by public health historians as the "first effective municipal health department in a major [U.S.] city," the Metropolitan Board is important in the history of pollution regulation because its leaders used their unprecedented regulatory powers to impose tough zoning regulation and innovative technology-based pollution-abatement regulation on the hundreds of butchers, packinghouses, fat renderers, soap manufacturers, bone boilers, and other animal waste processing businesses in New York City, as well as to pressure the city's manufactured-gas companies into installing technologies to abate their stench nuisances. The movement to establish this powerful new health board began in the late 1850s. It was spearheaded by public health reformers concerned about the role stenches and miasmas played in the city's skyrocketing death toll from epidemic disease. The physicians who led the movement agitated unsuccessfully for years for the establishment of a government health agency with enough power to deal with New York City's mounting sanitary problems and death rates. They finally turned their losing battle around in the late 1850s by reaching out beyond the boundaries of the medical profession and joining forces with influential business and professional reformers who were fighting the corruption and machine politics of Tammany Hall. This alliance led to the formation, in 1859, of the short-lived New York Sanitary Association, the first public health organization in

U.S. history in which laypeople constituted the majority of members and officeholders. After this group faded away, its leaders formed a new group, the Citizens' Association of New York, in 1863.[4]

The public health reformers' decision to work with the city's business leaders proved to be an incredibly politically astute move. Some of the most talented, politically and legally savvy members of the city's business and professional elite used their connections to those in power in state government to lobby for the legislation that led to the formation of the Metropolitan Board. They helped the public health reformers prepare increasingly well-crafted bills to advance their cause, as well as sophisticated legal arguments to support endowing the new board with strong regulatory powers. Perhaps most important, they supported the undertaking of an elaborate sanitary investigation of the city by a committee of the Citizens' Association physicians. Modeled on sanitary surveys being conducted in England to document the city's many public health problems, this ambitious project not only produced the detailed information the reform leaders used in testimony before the state legislature to advance their cause, it also provided the fodder for a well-orchestrated publicity campaign to publicize the Citizens' Association's findings and whip up public support for the legislation whose passage in 1866 by the state legislature created the Metropolitan Board.[5]

In a sign of how intimately involved the business community was in this struggle, the state legislature appointed Jackson Schultz, a major figure in the city's leather industry, as the first president of the Metropolitan Board. He led the board's effort to impose tough new regulations on the slaughtering and animal waste processing industries. The regulations forced these trades to move uptown above Fortieth Street, as well as to install stench-abating technologies in their establishments, like running water and asphalt floors and rendering tanks equipped with seals and condensers and other mechanisms for abating stenches.[6]

The business community's role in the regulatory process was hardly a lovefest. Many butchers, fat melters, soap makers, and the like fought bitterly to avoid having to comply with the Metropolitan Board's stench regulations. Angry tradesmen sued to stop the board from enforcing its regulations, embroiling the Metropolitan Board in litigation that dragged on for years. The regulations reduced stench pollution in New York City but did not come close to eliminating it. Even the most advanced model sanitary abattoirs built in the city in response to the Metropolitan Board's efforts were less than perfectly stench proof and many lacked facilities for on-site waste processing, a feature particularly prized by sanitary reformers.[7]

Nonetheless, it is interesting that business reformers did so much, at their own expense, to help public health reformers get the state to create the Metropolitan Board and further its efforts to reduce the stench nuisance. A leather merchant, a member of the animal waste processing trades, led the Metropolitan Board's regulatory initiatives during its crucially important first year. Some in the meat and related industries did more than comply with the board's regulation. They established sanitary abattoirs with facilities for stench abatement that, while less than perfect, went far beyond the board's regulatory requirements.[8]

A similarly complex picture emerges in the history of air-pollution regulation in Chicago, where business reformers also had a powerful impact. Even more than the New York Citizens' Association, which seems to have been active for only a few years, the Citizens' Association of Chicago epitomized the business-led, environmental reform groups that are the focus of this chapter. The Chicago Citizens' Association was an organization of businessmen who were dedicated to reforming political and environmental conditions in the city. During the late 1870s and 1880s, its members studied and proposed regulatory solutions and lobbied for legislation to deal with a broad range of air, noise, and water pollution problems, in addition to a wide range of the city's many other physical, social, and political ills.[9]

They were particularly impactful in the realm of air pollution. Their first target was the infamous stench emitted by the city's enormous meatpacking and slaughterhouse waste processing industries. Although the city's Board of Health promulgated several technology-based pollution regulations similar to those instituted by the New York Metropolitan Board in the late 1860s and early 1870s, it was never able to enforce them due to a variety of political and legal problems. Conditions deteriorated until 1875, when the city's former sanitary superintendent John Rauch called on citizens to help the desperately underfunded board out. In response, the Chicago Citizens' Association began conducting investigations to document the extent of the regulatory violations being committed by the packers and animal waste processors and strenuously agitating for enforcement of the city's sanitary regulations. Its leaders worked closely with public health officials and reform-minded city council members and newspaper reporters and editors for three years, conducting joint investigations of problems, publicizing findings, lobbying for

the appointment of a strong leader for a newly constituted Health Department (to replace the toothless Board of Health), and for the passage of legislation to give the Health Department real power to enforce its sanitary
regulations, testifying in court cases, and even paying the salaries of some
staff people working on the issue for the city's Health Department. Their
help was crucial to the passage of the city's "stink ordinance," a law that required any company engaged in slaughtering, meatpacking, and animal
waste processing within a mile of the city limits to obtain a city license that
required them to obey all the sanitary laws of Chicago and the State of
Illinois and subjected them to a penalty of $100 or imprisonment for viola-
tions. Association members helped the department enforce the law and, as
witnesses for the prosecution, played a key role in the court battles that finally forced the city's packers and animal waste processors to come into
compliance with the ordinance.[10]

Though this victory did not eliminate the industry's pollution emissions,
it did lead to significant reductions in the stenches coming from the rendering
tanks at the city's packinghouses and glue and fertilizer factories. This improvement was palpable enough for the leaders of the Citizens' Association
to realize that the rendering tanks were not the only source of the stenches
emanating from the packinghouse districts, inspiring them to study and begin making recommendations to solve the water pollution problems caused
by the discharge of vast quantities of sanitary and industrial waste into the
Chicago River. The association's work on this problem eventually helped
lead to the construction of Chicago Ship and Sanitary Canal, the enormous, multimillion-dollar public works project that reversed the flow of the
Chicago River, allowing the city's industrial and sanitary effluents to flow
westward to the Mississippi River.[11]

The Citizens' Association leaders also turned their attention to the city's
worsening problem with coal smoke. In 1881, they succeeded in persuading
the city council to pass a smoke ordinance that required the owners of commercial buildings to install smoke-abating equipment on their coal-burning
furnaces and steam boilers to reduce their emissions of heavy black smoke
to specified levels. The 1881 smoke ordinance authorized the Department of
Health to impose fines of $10 to $50 on violators. Though it was not the first
municipal smoke ordinance in U.S. history, this law appears to have been the
first to have been actually enforced by city officials. Litigation led to a state
supreme court ruling that allowed the city to continue to prosecute violators.

Following the precedent set in the battle against the packinghouse-stench nuisance, the Citizens' Association members helped the Department of Health identify violators and testified against them in court.[12]

After a few years of apparently quite remarkable improvements in air quality, enforcement of the 1881 smoke ordinance declined, due to a lack of inspectors to monitor compliance and the refusal of local juries to convict violators. In 1892, however, a new business-led reform organization, the Smoke Prevention Society (SPS), stepped into the gap, going even further than the Citizens' Association had to help the city enforce its smoke laws in preparation for the 1893 World's Columbian Exposition. The SPS leaders not only began a new campaign to call public attention to the city's filthy skies, but also hired a staff of engineers to inspect smoking boiler plants and advise their owners about how best to control the smoke. When a hard-core group of property and tug boat owners continued to balk at coming into compliance with the 1881 smoke regulations, they took the even more radical step of hiring their own attorney to prosecute violators. Prosecution did much to clean up the skies in 1891 and 1892, but some of those charged with violations decided to fight the SPS in court. Once again, local juries refused to convict and the SPS withered away.[13]

Chicago's early, entirely business-led antismoke movements were the exception, rather than the rule, in the late nineteenth- and early twentieth-century smoke wars. In some instances, women reformers supported business-initiated regulatory initiatives by staging events that publicized the harm done by smoke and the need for reform. In St. Louis, for example, the most important impetus for smoke regulation occurred in 1891, when the leaders in the city's business community and government, including the mayor, convened a large meeting of "prominent citizens, representing fifteen city clubs and commercial bodies" to discuss the smoke problem and find a solution to it. This group appointed the committee of engineers who developed the smoke ordinances passed in 1893, the first enacted in St. Louis, which required businesses to abate their emission of "dense black or thick gray smoke," while creating the city's first smoke regulation agency (the St. Louis Smoke Commission). The members of the Wednesday Club, an elite women's club, helped get the ordinances enacted by helping the men mobilize public support and lobby city council members. After the ordinances were enacted, the businessmen who began the movement helped officials in the newly created Smoke Abatement Department enforce their provisions by deploying members to serve as observers who reported on violators. According to historians Joel Tarr and Carl Zimring, the "ordinances appear to have been relatively successful in reducing some of the worst smoke nuisances"—until 1897, when the state supreme court invalidated them.[14]

In other instances, the women initiated antismoke crusades. Typically, however, they quickly realized they could not succeed on their own and moved to enlist male business leaders in their cause. Like the public health reformers who persuaded the New York state legislature to create the New York Metropolitan Board of Health, they reached out to business-led reform organizations and professional organizations, as well as individual business leaders for help for strategic reasons, well aware that they needed their political clout—and their technical expertise—to achieve their goals. And time and time again, in city after city, the men and their organizations rallied to the antismoke cause, constructively engaging with the women—not always instantly, but in sufficient numbers and passion to make a difference.

For example, in Cincinnati, in 1904, after years of desultory, unproductive discussion and complaint within the business community, fed-up leaders of the city's Woman's Club and local health reformers began a crusade to force the city to enforce its almost twenty-five-year-old, but long dead letter, smoke ordinance. They soon realized that they needed to bring powerful business leaders into the fold if they were to be effective, and so two years later, in 1906, they formed the gender-neutral Smoke Abatement League. The organization counted the presidents of Procter and Gamble, Stearns and Foster, and other important manufacturing firms as members and financial backers, as well Charles P. Taft, the editor of the *Cincinnati Times-Star*, as well as industrial companies such as the American Smelting and Refining Company and Cincinnati Milling Company. The Smoke Abatement League played an important role in strengthening smoke regulation in Cincinnati into the 1930s. Early on it hired a superintendent to investigate smoke problems and make citizens' arrests of offenders, while using its powerful members' political clout to persuade the city council to enforce the antismoke law. After the city acceded to its demands and hired a smoke inspector in 1907, the league deployed members to watch towers to identify and document violations.[15]

I do not mean to imply that these coalitions eliminated business opposition to smoke regulation in America's smoky cities—or that the smoke ordinances the reformers achieved were well-crafted pieces of regulation that eliminated urban smoke pollution problems. Quite the contrary, business opposition remained intense and often strong enough to ensure that ordinances were full of loopholes and exceptions and that enforcement would be weak. Worse, their opposition led to litigation and adverse court decisions that sometimes completely hamstrung enforcement.[16]

My point is that business opposition was not the whole story of Progressive Era smoke regulation. Business leaders played key leadership roles in the struggle for air pollution regulation, as well as in the fight against it. As a result of their involvement, smoke regulation grew stronger over time and became better enforced in most cities—even though coal smoke remained a problem until after World War II, when cities switched from coal to natural gas and electricity for power and heat for residential as well as commercial and industrial activity.

Nothing illustrates the willingness of the leaders of the antismoke movement, women and businessmen alike, to engage in very long-term struggles against immense odds better than the battle to regulate smoke in Pittsburgh, one of the United States' most infamously smoky cities. To briefly summarize: in 1891, an upper-class women's organization, the Ladies' Health Protective Association, began to campaign for the institution of an enforceable smoke ordinance. They quickly reached out to the Engineering Society of Western Pennsylvania, an organization whose members included all of the city's leading industrialists. Their proposal divided the members of the society, eliciting particularly strong opposition from the city's iron manufacturers. With limited business support, they were able to persuade the city council to enact a smoke ordinance in 1892 that was weak, difficult to enforce, and excluded the manufacturing districts. This resulted in little, if any improvement, and so the women and their allies began lobbying for a stronger law. In 1895 the city council obliged them by passing a new smoke ordinance that was slightly stronger than the 1892 law in some ways, though still much too weak to clear the air in any significant way. Their movement continued, with the men and women uniting to form the gender-neutral municipal improvement organization the Civic Club. As the movement gained steam, and the smoke nuisance worsened, Andrew Carnegie became a convert to the antismoke cause. A speech he gave in 1899 inspired the Pittsburgh Chamber of Commerce to join the movement. In 1902 the courts overturned the 1895 law. Working closely together, the Chamber of Commerce and the Civic Club lobbied strenuously for enactment of a rigorous new smoke ordinance with real enforcement teeth and that covered mills and factories as well as commercial buildings. Their campaign kicked into high gear in 1906, when the newly established and reformist *Pittsburgh Sun* and other city newspapers entered the fray. With the help of front-page reports and editorials on the cost of smoke and the need for strong regulation, finally the antismoke coalition forced the city council to enact a strong and enforceable smoke ordinance.[17]

There was no rest for the weary, however. The new ordinance immediately sparked an intense backlash from members of Pittsburgh's business community who were not in the antismoke fold. The resulting litigation led to a state court decision that declared the 1906 ordinance an illegal abuse of the city's police power, forcing the city to revert to the much weaker 1892 ordinance. Undeterred, the men and women in the antismoke camp regrouped and waged a new campaign to persuade the state legislature to pass a bill that officially authorized Pittsburgh to regulate smoke. This law was passed in 1911. The city then passed a new ordinance that provided for professional inspectors and other much-needed enforcement mechanisms. This ordinance was much stronger and more enforceable than the 1892 ordinance and did a great deal to help clean up the smoke emanating from commercial buildings. But it was weaker than the 1906 regulation, because despite significant support from the business community, the antismoke forces were not able to replicate that earlier hard-won success. Caving in to pressure from angry manufacturers, the city council exempted most of Pittsburgh's factories from its strictures, setting the stage for many more years of struggle to extend and further strengthen smoke regulation.[18]

## The Challenge of Constructing a New Interpretive Frame

At first glance, it would appear to be a relatively easy and straightforward thing to articulate a new interpretive frame for the history of air pollution regulation in late nineteenth-and early twentieth-century America that addresses the concerns outlined here: simply add reform-minded businessmen and their professional and civic organizations to the roster of people and groups that spearheaded the movements to regulate smoke and packing- and rendering-house stench. Complicate the story a little by showing how these early environmental movements divided the business community and by probing the creative way in which the desire to control some kinds of industrial air pollution led some businessmen to develop productive political collaborations and partnerships with reform-minded members of their city's medical communities and, later, upper-middle-class women reformers.

When we take this more complex narrative as our frame, we can begin to interrogate these early antipollution movements in new ways. Historians have looked quite closely at some of the women who led the urban smoke crusades. What about the business leaders who worked so hard to empower government authorities to regulate industrial stench and smoke? Who were they? What distinguished them from the far more numerous members of their communities who actively opposed regulation or who refused to take sides in the battles to clear the air? What motivated the activist business-men to take on such a controversial problem? Were most driven primarily by their own economic interests? By their wives? Or were they primarily moti-vated by a more altruistic and economically self-sacrificing desire to solve serious urban problems? How hard was it for them to take on their fellow businessmen in these battles?

It is beyond the scope of this chapter to offer definitive answers to these questions. What I will say, however, is that they will not lend themselves to simple answers. It will not be possible, for example, to drop the businessmen who supported smoke regulation into clear-cut, one-off categories based on whether they were merchants or manufacturers, big businessmen or small shopkeepers, big polluters or small ones, and the like. While the owners of coal-powered factories appear to have been, in general, more likely to oppose smoke regulation than merchants, the men who joined the smoke regulation movement and participated in the business-led organizations that advocated for smoke reform came from many backgrounds, including manufacturing. The leaders of Chicago's Smoke Prevention Society, for example, included Bryan L. Lathrop, a real-estate developer and investment banker, James W. Scott, the publisher of the *Chicago Herald*, and two well-known leaders of the city's industrial community, William J. Chalmers, the president of Fraser and Chalmers, a large, multinational manufacturer of mining machinery, and Samuel W. Allerton, the owner of the Allerton Packing Company and various stockyards in Chicago and the rest of the United States.[19] The engi-neering societies whose members studied the smoke abatement problem in-cluded factory owners as well as professional engineers among their members.[20] Andrew Carnegie, the biggest steelmaker of them all, helped galvanize Pittsburgh's smoke reform movement in 1899 with the speech to the city's Chamber of Commerce in which he blasted the smoke nuisance and called for change.[21]

Nor will it be an easy matter to fully explain the motives of the business-men who led and co-led the movement to regulate urban smoke. Economists like to think that businessmen will support regulation only when they be-lieve it will benefit them personally in a financial sense. Lance Davis and

Douglass North, for example, argue that business interests will support regulation that changes the institutional structure of the market (as pollution regulations do) when there is "the possibility of profits that cannot be captured within the existing arrangemental structure." The problem for historians seeking to use economic reasoning to attribute motive is that business participation in anti-air-pollution movements was often in poor alignment with the most obvious costs and benefits of regulation.[22]

Take, for example the issue of merchant and professional support for smoke reform. The costs of smoke bore especially heavily on businessmen in the merchant and professional classes. Smoke not only got into downtown stores, dirtying the products on public display, it made its way into warehouses, where it damaged inventories in goods. In 1892, J. V. Farwell, one of Chicago's leading dry goods merchants, for example, estimated that it cost him $17,000 a year to replace goods damaged by smoke. A decade later, Marshall Field and Company reportedly lost $150,000 to smoke damage. The smoke also swept into downtown offices, choking the bankers, lawyers, accountants, clerks, and other men and women at work, covering their clothing and office supplies with soot, forcing them to work extra hard to keep their premises and clothing clean and tidy. To keep the dirty, black smoke out, these people had to keep their windows closed during the long, hot days of summer. The smoke also led to respiratory and other illnesses. These conditions were not only an inconvenience; they also reduced productivity, lowering profits. The desire to save these costs undoubtedly served as a powerful incentive for merchants and professional men to join the antismoke crusades. The difficulty is that many did not do this. Many were not supporters of, much less active participants in, these movements, despite the many factors that would have made it economically advantageous for them to do so. Why did some merchants and professional men step up and get involved in the movement to regulate smoke when so many others did not?[23]

On the other side of the coin, some factory owners, downtown real-estate developers and operators, and other big smoke emitters got involved in smoke regulation movements, even taking leadership roles in them, despite the high cost of smoke abatement. Smoke pollution epitomized what economists call an "externality" or "social cost" problem. Businesses that polluted "externalized" a cost of production by shifting the cost of dealing with stench and smoke to the people living in their local communities who suffered from the discomfort and lower property values resulting from packing- and rendering-house stenches and the property damage, extra cleaning costs, and health problems resulting from the smoke problem. By externalizing these costs, factory and commercial building owners were able to charge less for their products and services, thus expanding their markets, and, depending on the supply and demand for their goods, services, and real estate, enjoying higher rates of return. This was a big incentive for them to oppose smoke regulation.[24]

American antismoke activists argued that factory owners and other businessmen stood to save a great deal of money from the improved efficiency of combustion associated with smoke abatement.[25] While this claim seems to have captured the imagination of the antismoke forces, including many in the business community, however, it is not at all clear that the economic benefits of more efficient combustion actually outweighed the costs of smoke abatement on a consistent basis prior to the development, testing, and dissemination of information about reliable and effective abatement technologies in the late 1910s and 1920s, and later by the Mellon Institute and other research organizations. Effective smoke abatement required the monitoring and continual fine-tuning, maintenance, and repair of smoke abatement equipment. Before reliable mechanical stokers became generally available, it also depended on the more careful firing of furnaces and boilers and/or the use of more expensive coal. These needs added to the cost of labor. Furthermore, it was well known in engineering circles and, due to publicity surrounding the problem, among the general public as well that smoke abatement equipment that worked well in one factory often failed miserably in another. The equipment was expensive to purchase and install. The risk that it would not work properly, or that it would break down long before it paid for itself through fuel savings, no matter how well the engineering staff maintained it, in combination with the externality savings associated with not abating pollution should have made it economically irrational for manufacturers and commercial building owners to embrace the idea that it would be good to enact regulations that would have required them to choose an abatement technology and install it. Nevertheless, some manufacturers and real-estate operators played important roles in early urban smoke crusades. Why?[26]

To answer these questions, historians must look beyond the logic of economic theory and probe more deeply the personal economic situations, social relationships, and life experiences of the individuals whose activism they want to explain, as well as the kinds of business they owned or managed, their professional backgrounds, and the availability of abatement technologies suitable for use on their properties. The factors behind the business community's leadership and coleadership of movements to regulate slaughterhouse stenches were as varied as the individuals involved and the cities and the times in which these movements took place. Thus, for example, while the businessmen of the Chicago Citizens' Association were driven into their fight to force the city's rendering plants and packinghouses to comply with Chicago's sanitary ordinance by outrage at their disgusting odors and fear that these smells represented a serious threat to public health,[27] the businessmen who helped New York City's public health reformers found the New York Citizens' Association and lobby for the establishment of the Metropolitan Board of Health were reacting (at least in part) to the Civil War draft riots. They believed that sanitary problems were contributing to social unrest in the city and hoped that by improving living conditions, they could make the city a less volatile as well as healthier place for the populace to live.[28] In contrast, the businessmen who most determinedly helped public health reformers in New Orleans win passage of that city's slaughterhouse regulation were the capitalists who were competing with one another to obtain the franchise to build the abattoir that that regulation was going to force all of the city's butchers to work in. They sought to profit from a monopoly on the city's meat trade, while taking advantage of the money-making efficiencies of large-scale assembly-line production, proximity to a large integrated livestock yard, and on-site facilities for utilizing slaughterhouse wastes.[29]

The reasons businessmen got involved in smoke regulation were equally varied. Take, for example, the men who founded Chicago's Smoke Prevention Society. All but one (Bryan Lathrop, the president) were directors of the World's Columbian Exposition. These men had not only created a joint stock company to raise the funding to pay the cost of the exposition, they had also invested their own money in the stock. With value of the stock as well as their reputations and egos on the line, they were desperate to ensure that a black pall of smoke not ruin the fairground's beautiful "White City." This was not, however, the only reason they took leadership on the smoke problem. They were civic leaders, not just business leaders. Like many Chicago businessmen, they were members of groups like the Citizens' Association, the University Club, and the Union League that encouraged members to raise their sights beyond the everyday grind of making a profit in business by reading great books, supporting symphonies and art, and engaging in political reform and city beautification. At least two of SPS leaders had been actively involved in smoke abatement for years before the formation of the society. Bryan Lathrop, the SPS president, was a zealot for the smoke reform cause who had served on the Citizens' Association's Smoke Committee during the 1880s and would continue to take a leading role in smoke reform for years after the SPS disappeared from the scene. These men believed that cleaning the air would not only help ensure a successful exposition, but also enhance the image of Chicago as a good place to do business and thus provide long-term economic benefits in the form of new opportunities for the city's entire business community.[30]

Similarly, while it is undoubtedly the case that some of the businessmen who supported Pittsburgh's women-led antismoke crusade were strongly encouraged to do so by their activist wives, they were also inspired by Andrew Carnegie. In his pivotal 1899 peroration in favor of smoke regulation, Carnegie declared that he had come to believe that Pittsburgh's ability to continue to advance to the ranks of a great city depended as much on eliminating the smoke nuisance as on the continuing construction of "magnificent parks and coming boulevards, the zoo, the golf links, the conservatory, halls and hotels, picture galleries, libraries and orchestra" and other things "not material." Calling for a savior to step forward, for someone like George Westinghouse, the founder of Westinghouse Electric Company, or Dr. John Brashear, a well-known astronomer, "to work the miracle of our salvation from this nuisance," Carnegie laid out a path to redemption that captured the imagination of his listeners. With the supplies of natural gas that had cleared the city's air for several years in the late 1880s and early 1890s exhausted, Carnegie argued that the solution to the smoke nuisance was manufactured gas "produced from our coal at the mines and supplied to homes in Pittsburgh in place of natural gas for all purposes." He envisioned the establishment of a commission of "Pittsburgh's able, well known citizens" who, after consulting the experts, would "purchase a vast field of coal on the river" and construct a model plant and the pipelines that would bring the invisible gas from the coalfield to Pittsburgh and distribute it throughout the city. The speech was so inspiring that members of Pittsburgh's Chamber of Commerce immediately established a special smoke committee. It joined forces with antismoke activists in the Civic Club to lobby for the passage of a new, more comprehensive and enforceable smoke ordinance. This collaboration led to the passage of the city's ambitious 1906 smoke ordinance and, after the courts overturned that law, years of mostly business-led agitation for stronger smoke regulations.[31]

As a smoke reformer, Carnegie embodies the ambiguities and contradictions of business involvement in the smoke regulation movement that this chapter seeks to highlight. Carnegie was, of course, the owner of many of the iron foundries, blast furnaces, steel mills, and coke ovens that were blackening the skies around Pittsburgh. As Angela Gugliotta points out in her dissertation on the history of smoke and smoke regulation in Pittsburgh, Carnegie began experimenting with manufactured gas in his mills in 1891. Although he made a large investment in a manufactured-gas-powered mill in Bellefonte, Pennsylvania, in 1892, however, he does not appear to have converted any of his existing plants from smoky bituminous coal to the fuel. The cost was too high. Nonetheless, he was not faking his conversion to the smoke abatement cause. While expressing confidence in his 1899 speech that inventive Pittsburghers would eventually be able to find a way to make the price of manufactured gas competitive with cheap coal, he urged his listeners to persuade the city fathers to subsidize the new manufactured gas plant with public funds until the costs came down enough for the plant to sell its power profitably without the subsidy. A notorious penny-pincher, Carnegie simply was not prepared to convert his own operations to manufactured gas without subsidies, at least not until the price came down, and was not interested in other, more piecemeal forms of smoke abatement. And yet some manufacturers in Chicago, men who lacked Carnegie's financial resources, were willing to invest in costly smoke abatement at their own factories and did so with great determination and enthusiasm, even when not required by city officials to do so, despite the cost and the technical difficulties.[32]

To explain the role of business reformers in late nineteenth- and early twentieth-century movements to regulate air pollution as fully as possible, historians will have to find a way to fit these paradoxes into an interpretive narrative that coherently addresses the sometimes-ironic nature of their leadership. To further complicate things, it will also be necessary to relate some horror stories that call into question the very idea that businessmen could serve as authentic leaders of the antismoke movement.

The most vivid example of such a debacle is the episode in Chicago's history of smoke reform that Stradling and Platt both present as the truly iconic moment in the war against smoke: the women-led movement to force that city's railroads to substitute electricity for soft coal as their source of fuel within the city limits by electrifying their terminals and tracks. Platt treats their ultimately unsuccessful movement as the defining moment in the history of smoke reform in Chicago. For Stradling it is the defining episode in the whole history of smoke reform in the United States. It is an appalling story of betrayal as well as regulatory failure. I will briefly recapitulate it here, because it illustrates the compelling nature of the mainstream frame that demonizes business's leadership role in smoke reform, as well as the challenges that historians face trying to responsibly evaluate and frame the role business leaders played as leaders of these antipollution movements.

The episode began in 1908 when a group of South Side women declared war on the filthy smoke pollution of the Illinois Central Railroad (IC) with attention-getting parades, petitions, and threats that they would stop cleaning their homes and washing their children if the city did not use its power to solve the problem.[33] In *Shock Cities*, Platt calls the South Siders' movement the "revolt of the housewives." Like female smoke reformers elsewhere, the South Side women quickly reached out to Chicago's male business community for help. They formed the Anti-Smoke League and quickly enlisted endorsements from what Platt calls a "diverse coalition of women's clubs, neighborhood improvement associations, and professional groups [i.e., business organizations]."[34] The women and their antismoke business allies also developed a good working relationship with Mayor Fred Busse, a former coal dealer, and his chief smoke inspector, Paul Bird, and his inspectors, who had been installed in city government as a result of the previous business-led movements to regulate the smoke nuisance. Bird ordered a crackdown on smoke ordinance violators. As the movement gained steam, the city council met to consider legislation to force the Illinois Central to abate its smoke. The IC responded by agreeing to burn cleaner burning, but very expensive, hard coal.

This victory in hand, the city council began debating a proposal to force all the railroads to abate their smoke. The high cost of hard coal, coupled with the success of railroad electrification in New York City led the council to replace the hard coal mandate with a more open-ended ordinance that would also allow the railroads to eliminate their smoke through the electrification of their trains and their passenger and freight terminals. The huge up-front costs of electrification made this alternative to hard coal extremely expensive and even more controversial than the original plan, but it appealed to reformers who saw it as a way to modernize the city's train system, while solving its smoke problem much more completely than a switch to burning hard coal ever could.[35]

In 1909, the Chicago Association of Commerce, a business-led reform group that supported the smoke regulation movement, stepped into the fray.

The Association of Commerce offered to undertake a study of the smoke problem to help the supporters of smoke reform make the positive case for electrification with documentary evidence of its benefits and technical feasibility. Such studies, like the sanitary survey undertaken by the New York Citizens' Association and the reports the Chicago Citizens' Association made on the terrible condition of the Chicago River in the 1880s, were often undertaken by reform organizations to document the need for regulation and other government initiatives. The Association of Commerce's report, completed in 1910, concluded that electrification was both practical and economically feasible and recommended that it begin immediately.[36]

So far, the story aligns well with the new interpretive frame outlined above. An antismoke coalition that included both women and business leaders successfully pushed a city council to enact an unprecedentedly strong smoke ordinance. But—and this is a big "but"—before the Association of Commerce made this report public, its leaders double-crossed the women and their antismoke allies. They decided to run the report by a number of railroad officials.

Chicago was a major railroad hub, filled with the tracks and terminal facilities of all the nation's many railroad companies. Taken aback at the cost of having to electrify their systems and seeing little or no economic or managerial advantage in doing so for their companies, simply to reduce smoke, and concerned that the U.S. Senate was beginning to look into the feasibility of electrifying the railroads entering Washington, D.C., the leaders of the industry persuaded the leaders of the Association of Commerce to quash the report and begin a second, more "scientific" study, one that the railroads would generously fund. While keeping the original report secret, the association's leaders and their railroad company allies persuaded the city council to postpone its vote on the regulation to force the railroads to abate their smoke until the study was completed so they could make their decision on the basis of a new committee's well-researched evidence of the costs and benefits of electrification.

The new committee studied the issue for four years—two more than originally planned. The women leaders of the Anti-Smoke League and their allies continued to press for electrification, but as the years dragged on and the city council waited for the association's report, their movement lost momentum, while the railroads, through their intermediary the Association of Commerce, gained control over how the smoke problem and its possible solution would be defined. For them it was a question of economics, not public health or civic beauty. The new report was finally published in 1915. Weighing in at an impressive 1,177 pages and loaded with charts, graphs, and tables that gave it a distinguished air of scientific objectivity, it concluded that electrification was neither economically necessary nor economically feasible. Taking note of the committee's well-researched conclusions, the Chicago City Council refused to enact an ordinance to regulate the industry's smoke.[37]

You can see why Platt and Stradling like this story. The Association of Commerce's betrayal of the women (and other) smoke reformers fits their framing of the history of smoke regulation perfectly. Women were good reformers; businessmen reformers were untrustworthy, self-dealing, and bad.

This framing makes sense in the context of this particular episode. The problem is that both historians projected its significance backward, allowing it to shape their interpretation of the earlier stages of Chicago's antismoke movement, when reform-minded business leaders were the instigators of efforts to strengthen smoke regulation policy and enforcement. Platt characterized the Smoke Prevention Society as a "city beautiful" organization, not a business organization, obscuring the fact that it was not only led but also entirely composed of businessmen. Stradling relegated the work of the SPS to a mention in a footnote and did not discuss the Citizens' Association's role in the passage and enforcement of the 1881 smoke ordinance. He also said nothing about the role the business community played in the establishment of the city's highly regarded Smoke Inspection Department, instead characterizing this improvement in regulatory capability as a power play by trained engineers to "shift power away from non-expert anti-smoke activists" to themselves.[38]

Was the Chicago Association of Commerce's betrayal of the smoke regulation cause emblematic of a historic turning point in the history of American smoke regulation? Did it mark the point at which reform-minded business leaders stopped working with the women and other more authentic antismoke leaders and became the enemies of regulation? It is certainly the case that the railroads' mobilization of ostensibly "objective" scientific expertise, under the Association of Commerce's reformist auspices, to "prove" that railroad electrification was not in Chicago's interest had parallels in other developments in the response to industrial pollution in the early 1900s. A transition in the field of industrial hygiene began in the 1910s and 1920s when corporations began hiring their own physicians to study occupational disease among their workers.[39] Mining corporations also began hiring their own physicians and plant scientists around this time in order to conduct research into the impact of smelter smoke on human health and plant life. Though these doctors and scientists were in theory potential allies of anti-pollution reformers, they were under pressure to produce research and recommendations that supported their employers' economic interests.[40] I plan to argue in my book that environmental reformers began to lose momentum when corporations began to funnel their resources into research on the toxicological effects of industrial pollution, using their wealth to challenge and preempt the investigative research that reform groups had previously used to mobilize support for regulation. A new kind of business leadership came to the fore—one with the capability to counter the political influence and technical expertise of business reformers and their allies in the public health and women's reform movements.

Alas, however, as illuminating as it might be of some aspects of the history of the American response to industrial pollution in this period, this dramatic turning point narrative also constitutes a misleading frame for the very complicated story of the grassroots politics of smoke regulation in the early twentieth century. Business support for and leadership of the antismoke movement did not disappear during the 1910s. Nor did the professional research that justified regulation and provided guidance to smoke reformers seeking to strengthen regulation and improve abatement.

In Pittsburgh, for example, in 1911, Andrew and Richard B. Mellon, scions of one of Pittsburgh's premier industrial and banking families, founded a research institute at the University of Pittsburgh and commissioned it to study the city's smoke problems—at the very time that the Chicago Association of Commerce was preparing its thousand-plus-page report proving that it would be a big economic mistake to electrify the city's railroads. The Mellon Institute's widely publicized smoke investigations documented the scale of the smoke problem in Pittsburgh and its high economic, social, and public health costs, as well as its harmful impacts on local vegetation, providing scientific credibility for the argument that Frank Uekoetter argues was one of the distinguishing characteristics of the American antismoke movement compared to German smoke reform: its reliance on the argument that smoke abatement made economic sense.

Publication of the first of the Mellon Institute's reports on the smoke problem inspired the Pittsburgh Chamber of Commerce to convene a meeting in 1913 of the city's commercial and women's organizations that led to the formation of a new antismoke organization, the gender-neutral (but male-dominated) Smoke and Dust Abatement League. The league lobbied for passage of a stronger smoke ordinance. It succeeded in securing passage of such a law less than one year later. This victory in hand, its members pressed city officials to enforce the tough new regulations stringently. They also initiated campaigns to educate the public to the harm caused by smoke and the many economic and public health benefits of smoke abatement, as well as the availability of various kinds of equipment for reducing smoke emissions. These efforts were so successful that the number of Pittsburgh's "smoky days," as defined by the U.S. Weather Bureau, declined by 50 percent between 1912 and 1917. Of course, the 50 percent reduction of smoke was a far cry from complete elimination, but this was still a significant improvement. The reductions not only took place in the central business district, but also in industrial parts of the city that were not covered by the smoke ordinance. In fact, so many of the city's factories voluntarily reduced their smoke emissions (to save fuel costs) that it became obvious that the opponents' claim that it was economically and technically impossible for industry was wrong, and the city council expanded the smoke ordinance to cover the manufacturing district.[41]

The movement to regulate smoke also continued in St. Louis, Cincinnati, and other cities. One of most successful movements in the 1920s and 1930s took place in St. Louis, where the gender-neutral Citizens' Smoke Abatement League (founded in 1923) experimented with smoke abatement technologies and smokeless fuels, worked with the city's Division of Smoke Regulation to help ordinary citizens as well as businesses reduce their emissions, raised hundreds of thousands of dollars to educate the public about how to abate smoke, and lobbied for more power for smoke inspectors, tough controls on the types of coals that could be sold in the city, and other changes to improve smoke regulation. When the league's energy began lag in the late 1930s, the *St. Louis Post-Dispatch* began a new antismoke campaign that led to the formation of a new antismoke committee composed entirely of local business leaders in 1939. It succeeded in getting enacted a new smoke ordinance that required all coal users, manufacturers, commercial businesses, railroads, and residents alike to use mechanical stokers and smokeless fuels. These achievements became a model for smoke reformers around the country after World War II.[42]

As Stradling and the other historians who have tracked the movement into the twentieth century point out, women generally began taking less active roles in urban smoke regulation movements in the 1900s, while business leaders and professional engineers took more and more leadership roles. As the generation of women who got active in smoke reform in the 1890s grew older, they began to retire from leadership, giving way to a younger generation of men who not only had the technical expertise to help polluters come into compliance with the strictures of smoke regulation but, as Adam Rome has pointed out, also felt a need to emotionally distance themselves from the femininity of women activists. Stradling characterizes the growing importance of men in the movement in declensionist terms, as the "surrender" of the women and other laypeople who represented the more "radical" wing of the movement to the more conservative experts and engineers and their corporate employers who put economic considerations ahead of the more humanitarian and environmentalist concerns of public health as aesthetic issues. Grinder interprets it as the victory of male efficiency and engineering prowess over an insurgency composed of indignant middle- and upper-class ladies. Focusing on the successes of the movement in Pittsburgh, Gugliotta argues that the decline of female leadership ironically went hand in hand with another important shift: the "ascendancy of women's values" in the administration of smoke regulation and the management of fuel use in industry.[43]

The point I want to make here is that business leadership of these movements was nothing new in the early twentieth century. Business's involvement in grassroots movements to force industry to regulate its air emissions goes back to the movement to regulate slaughterhouse stenches in the late 1860s and 1870s and the early battles over smoke in Chicago. These movements were, for the most part, collaborations between business and non-business activists. The activists, whether businessmen, public health reformers, or women, worked together because they realized they needed each other and could help each other achieve their goals.

## Conclusion

As the people who have attended recent meetings of the Business History Conference know, American business historians are struggling to figure out how to raise the visibility of our field in the post-Chandlerian era in a way that connects American business history with mainstream American history. I believe we can use the complex and controversial history of business's positive as well as its negative role in the history of pollution regulation (and other kinds of environmental reform) to engage the interest of historians who study culture, politics, and political economy, as well as the environment in the study of the history of business. It may also offer us something even more important—a way to engage the interests of nonhistorians who are looking for historical perspective on the struggles taking place today over climate change and the other increasingly serious environmental problems facing the peoples of the globe as a consequence of industrialization. We can provide them with valuable historical insight into the growing role that the so-called green business movement is playing in the development of regulatory and technological solutions to these problems.

Again, the question is how to most insightfully frame and interpret this history in its complex entirety. The challenge is to find a balance that gives the positive leadership role played by reform-minded businessmen much more attention and credit than historians have yet provided, without creating a new frame that hides the negative role that business opposition played in preventing smoke reformers from achieving their goals—and that some business-led reformist groups played when they pressured the more radical smoke reformers to make politically expedient but arguably unnecessary compromises and otherwise undermined and even betrayed their more activist, often female allies. Too much cynicism distorts the reality of businesses' involvement in the antismoke movement. Too little cynicism is just as distorting.

Finding the right balance will not be an easy task. Characterizing the role business leaders played within the grassroots movement that agitated for the regulation of industrial air pollution problems is difficult not only because their involvement was complex and often contradictory and because the movement's successes, though real, were at best mixed, but also because the whole subject is so highly politically and emotionally charged today.

The bitter fights that have raged between business interests and environmentalists over pollution regulation since the 1960s not only influence public perception of business's role in today's battles over industrial pollution regulation, climate change, green chemicals policy making, natural resource conservation, and all the other environmental issues confronting society in the twenty-first century; they also affect how people, historians included, tend to view past battles. They breed an anger and distrust that can make it difficult to tell the story of business leadership a century and more ago in an even-handed way. They also breed incredulity on the part of audiences. This raises the stakes in the historical enterprise of narrating the business history of pollution regulation. The controversial nature of this subject must not, however, stop us. The whole history of the movement to regulate air pollution in late nineteenth- and early twentieth-century U.S. cities needs to be told.

*Chapter 5*

# "Constructive and Not Destructive Development": Permanent Uses of Resources in the American South

*William D. Bryan*

On September 1, 1913, Woodrow Wilson sent a telegram from the Oval Office to open the nation's first exposition devoted to the conservation of natural resources. The National Conservation Exposition was different from the hundreds of other fairs and exhibitions held throughout the United States in the late nineteenth and early twentieth centuries. While most promoted economic development by showcasing the transformation of natural resources into commodities through grand displays of machinery and manufactured products, the Conservation Exposition was intended to teach "by concrete example . . . the best methods of conserving these resources."[1] To this end, the event featured over one hundred thousand square feet of exhibits devoted to conservation. Noteworthy displays included a sixteen-thousand-square-foot bas-relief map of the South's natural resources, an exhibit sponsored by the East Tennessee Audubon Society that showcased the state's "desirable and undesirable" birds, a Forest Service model showing the effects of deforestation on streams, and even a five-acre model farm intended to demonstrate the "most approved methods of scientific agriculture."[2]

At the time conservation was prominent on the American public agenda. Yet the exposition was organized and held in Knoxville, Tennessee—in the heart of a region little known for protecting its natural resources. Its organizers were not trained in resource management. They were businessmen who saw this as an opportunity to promote the South. By 1913 the Southern economy lagged far behind the rest of the nation, and organizers hoped that the exposition would attract new enterprises to the area and help pull the South out of its economic torpor. For every exhibit promoting conservation there were others sponsored by railroad, mining, and manufacturing companies encouraging new development by displaying products made from Southern resources, including furniture, mattresses, machinery, textiles, asphalt, lumber, bricks, and a variety of regional crops. After viewing these displays a manufacturer from Pennsylvania even remarked, "If there is anything that typifies the spirit of the new South better than this great exposition could, I have failed to see it or to hear of it."[3]

The National Conservation Exposition therefore served a dual purpose: it promoted the conservation of natural resources and Southern economic development. Organizers saw little tension between these two goals, and they intertwined conservation and development in their vision for the South's future. Rather than worrying that conservation would hinder the South's desperate search for economic development, the fair's organizers believed that it would help build a new economy that would better serve the long-term interests of the region. As one organizer explained, the exposition would "advance the highest development and best use of all natural resources," while another claimed that it would "go beyond the promotion of mere development." Instead, it was "directed toward making the development permanent, and toward turning the natural resources of the country into perpetual sources of wealth."[4]

As these comments suggest, "permanence" was the watchword of the exposition, and it shows how changing ideas about the best uses of the South's natural bounty were helping to redefine the region's development strategies. William Goodman—the director-general of the exposition—explained this when he told Atlanta's Chamber of Commerce that "there has been some talk of building a greater nation on a greater south, but neither can become permanently greater with the present waste going on in our forests and on our farms." Because "present methods of development are not what they should be," Goodman worried that Southerners were "creating problems which posterity will find difficult of solution." He implored the region's leaders to reevaluate their needs and distinguish between "development" and "waste" in order to solve these problems.[5] Goodman was echoed by Atlanta banker

Robert Lowry, who went one step further when he urged fellow Southerners to practice "constructive and not destructive development"—a path marked by the stewardship and wise use of natural resources.[6] In this light the exposition's commercial and conservation displays did not work at cross-purposes. They simply encouraged Southerners to use permanence as a blueprint for new patterns of economic growth that would not deplete the region's valuable resources.

Goodman, Lowry, and other officials were vague about how to implement this vision, but their interest in permanence suggests that by 1913 boosters were rethinking strategies for economic development as they struggled to come to terms with the South's environmental limits. Since the end of the Civil War natural resources had been one of the region's most valuable assets. Southern leaders always wanted to make the most of them, and their ideas about permanence were shaped by nearly five decades of debate about the best uses of these resources. As businesspeople and public officials confronted drastic declines in resources in the late nineteenth century, they hoped that permanent ways of using these resources would provide the basis of a new economy that addressed their most pressing problems without requiring difficult decisions about where to rein in resource use. Permanence was at heart a conservative strategy: it offered economic stability and the possibility of lasting growth, posed no challenge to the racial hierarchy, and promised to keep lining the pockets of Southern elites in perpetuity. Rather than selling off land, timber, water, and minerals without considering how they would be used, then, business and municipal officials argued that the region could only prosper by attracting industries that would be better stewards of these once-abundant resources. In short, they advocated making conservation a part of the fabric of the region's economy.

This vision fueled efforts to make the region's economy greener. In the first decades of the twentieth century permanence was beginning to shape everything from the decisions that municipal officials made about what industries were best suited for the South to the strategies used by corporations to maintain a steady supply of raw materials. As Southern officials worked to ensure that their natural resources would be available indefinitely, they transformed the region's economy and environment in important ways.

Yet the South's experience with permanence is mostly a lesson in the challenges of greening capitalism. Despite success protecting certain resources, by the mid-twentieth century the region served as a cautionary tale about the environmental consequences of unchecked development—a point underscored by authors like Erskine Caldwell and Stuart Chase. Although conservation measures sometimes did not work as planned, the South's twentieth-century environmental problems more often stemmed from boosters' use of permanence as a benchmark for Southern development. Because permanence only required finding efficient ways of using the South's natural resources, businesses were able to secure long-term stocks of raw materials without addressing the most exploitative uses of the Southern landscape. Permanent uses of natural resources often intensified resource use or created environmental problems like soil erosion, pollution, and flooding that could not be fixed by using resources more efficiently. In short, efforts to sustain business as usual through permanence never mandated that firms fundamentally rethink the way that they used Southern natural resources— often with dire consequences for the natural environment.

In this, permanence shares a great deal with sustainable development. Although sustainability was popularized in the 1970s and 1980s, it has roots in attempts to find solutions to localized instances of resource depletion reaching back to the eighteenth century.[7] For three hundred years people have tried to cope with environmental limits while maintaining economic growth and the use of valuable resources. Although advocates of sustainable development now speak the language of ecology, sustainability is just the newest iteration of strategies for using natural resources to "meet the needs of the present without compromising the ability of future generations to meet their own needs."[8] Sustainable development and permanence are both predicated on finding developmental solutions to environmental problems— solutions that do not require radical changes in corporate behavior. One proponent even recently summed up sustainability as "a lifestyle designed for permanence."[9] Because of these commonalities, understanding why Southern corporate leaders embraced permanent uses of resources can help to explain the popularity of sustainability with business leaders today. It can also suggest how sustainable development fails to address the issues that are at the heart of many environmental problems.

Southerners had long worked to make the region more self-sufficient, but the idea that permanent uses of resources should dictate strategies for economic development was a product of the post–Civil War era. For decades prior to the Civil War agricultural reformers argued that Southern planters needed to adopt scientific methods of cultivation to avoid soil depletion, make the region more independent, and keep from having to migrate west for fertile land. Reformers like Edmund Ruffin urged planters to stop using their land until it was exhausted, concluding that planters who were adept at getting "the greatest *immediate* production and profit" from their soil should instead work for "the greatest *continued* products and profits."[10] Although reformers often framed their solutions in the language of permanence, antebellum discussions about new economic paths were muted by the profitability of plantation agriculture and by fears that any attempt at reform might threaten slavery.

The end of the Civil War provided a unique moment when Southerners had to reimagine the fundamental structure of their economy as well as their systems of labor, political beliefs, and social organization. There were many visions for the future, but it was clear that a "New South" would have to replace the region's antebellum plantation society. This was an unprecedented challenge. As the region's land and resources took on new significance after the destruction of war, people throughout the nation were optimistic that the South's "matchless resources" would make successful development possible.[11]

In the decades following Appomattox, growing classes of urban professionals and businesspeople worked to put these resources to profitable uses. These groups sought to remake the region in the image of the North through industrialization, urbanization, and the diversification of agriculture. This "New South Creed," as historian Paul Gaston explains, began as a strategy for the future but was quickly fashioned into a "myth" that papered over the region's continued underdevelopment.[12] The manufacturing revolution that boosters like Atlanta's Henry Grady had predicted did not materialize, and industrial growth in the late nineteenth century was characterized by extractive industries that exploited cheap labor and abundant resources.[13]

By the twentieth century, visible declines in resources and the burgeoning national conservation movement fueled efforts to find more efficient ways of using Southern resources that were being extracted at breakneck speed. Community officials throughout the region were in the same boat as one newspaper correspondent from Greenville, Alabama, who predicted in 1898 that "in a few years at most the various mills contiguous to Greenville will have consumed all the timber in their territory and will have to seek other fields." Like this correspondent, the same public officials and businesspeople who had promoted economic development often realized that it was "time to be looking out for something to take the place of these industries."[14] As a postwar generation of leaders confronted this task, they were attracted

to permanent uses of resources that promised to free the South from its colonial relationship with the North, avoid antebellum patterns of constantly
declining land productivity, stave off declines in resources, and make the region prosperous once again.

The fate of the New South was being worked out in the midst of the
American conservation movement, and conservationists outside the region
also played a key role in shaping Southern ideas about permanence. The belief that there could be permanent ways of using natural resources had a long
history, ranging from Malthusian reactions to global population growth to
nineteenth-century programs of sustained-yield forestry in Germany. These
early efforts to conserve resources were always bound up with maintaining
the power of the nation-state and typically focused on resources with military or political importance.[15] As the United States faced the possibility of
resource depletion in the second half of the nineteenth century, federal
officials similarly promoted conservation as a way to expand the nation's
global reach and realize American imperial aims. These geopolitical goals
were necessary to ensure the "safety and continuance of the Nation" for generations to come.[16] Theodore Burton—the chairman of the 1908 Conference
of Governors—explained that conservation was a way to maintain the "material resources on which the permanent prosperity of our country and the
equal opportunity of all our People must depend."[17] As they justified extending American influence abroad by securing long-term supplies of resources,
officials like Burton hitched conservation to the permanence and prosperity
of the nation in ways that Southerners could not help but notice.

Gifford Pinchot did more than anyone else to popularize the idea that
conserving resources could lead to permanence. Pinchot's study of forestry
in Europe convinced him that sustained-yield management would spawn
"permanent forest industries, supported and guaranteed by a fixed and annual supply of trees."[18] As the nation's leading conservationist and chief of
the U.S. Forest Service, Pinchot formulated the concept of "wise use" as a
strategy for efficiently using all of the nation's resources. Pinchot famously
explained, "Conservation means the wise use of the earth and its resources
for the lasting good of men. Conservation is the foresighted utilization, preservation, and/or renewal of forests, waters, lands, and minerals, for the
greatest good of the greatest number for the longest time."[19] This philosophy
guided his work to conserve the nation's forests and became the mantra for
all federal efforts to manage timber, minerals, and other natural resources.
"Wise use" also demonstrated that conservation affected "both the present

and the future," and codified the idea that certain resources could be used in a permanent and renewable manner.[20] Theodore Roosevelt more directly translated the ideas of Pinchot into the language of permanence for the Southern Conservation Congress in 1910. Roosevelt encouraged the businessmen gathered in Atlanta "to profit by the mistakes that have been made elsewhere and to see that this marvelous development, this extraordinary growth of the new South, takes place in such fashion that it shall represent not a mere exploitation of territory, not a mere feverish growth in wealth and luxuriousness on a honeycomb foundation of morality and good judgment, but that it represents a solid and abiding and enduring prosperity and growth which shall not only be great but permanent."[21] By urging the South's leaders to see their resources as a guarantee of long-term growth and their responsibility to maintain for future generations, conservationists like Pinchot and Roosevelt drew on long-standing fears that population growth and industrialization were outstripping the global capacity for survival. They believed that the South was one of the last remaining places where these problems could be headed off before they had run their course, and they pressed Southern leaders to find ways of using resources that would not exploit them to depletion.

Many of the South's leaders were attracted to the ideals of wise use and conservation, but they adapted these principles for the South—a region characterized by private ownership of land and resources. Because they were also struggling with a sluggish economy, conservation had to "come not from a lessening of activity, but from a quickening of those forces in the best possible way," as Georgia's governor Hoke Smith explained.[22] Like Smith, boosters of permanence believed that the best uses of their resources should be determined by private interests, not federal bureaucrats. In 1909 William Finley—a Mississippian and the president of the Southern Railway—acknowledged that "the South is interested in the application of Conservation to the wise use of its soils, its minerals, its timber, and its streams" and laid out a typical vision for conservation in the region. While in some cases conservation "may involve a measure of present self-denial" in other cases Finley claimed that it "may mean the use of resources so as to obtain the maximum present profit."[23] To this end, he promoted private conservation measures instead of federal or state initiatives. Finley urged farmers to diversify, rotate their crops, and use fertilizer to improve their soils; he urged the owners of private forestland to selectively cut their timber; he urged private utility companies to build dams to generate hydroelectricity and prevent flooding; he urged landowners to maintain forest cover to decrease soil erosion. Finley even claimed that factories were private avenues for conserving resources because they could utilize wasted raw materials that had not yet been used for production. For Finley and other Southern boosters, the only role that the state should play was to reform the tax system to provide financial incentives for conservation.[24]

Despite his focus on private methods of conservation, Finley's vision was less unique than he made it seem. Gifford Pinchot had long acknowledged that the development of resources was an important part of the conservationist agenda. Throughout his career he sought to balance private and public uses of the nation's resources and was criticized for working with corporations to promote conservation.[25] In this context, Southern boosters like Finley simply magnified the developmental imperatives that were already at the heart of the conservation movement. As conservation became a priority, they sought to conserve resources not by funding state conservation agencies or enacting restrictive legislation but by attracting enterprises that would use the region's resources more efficiently—whether by using idle resources for the first time or better managing resources that had already been tapped.

By the first decade of the twentieth century municipal officials and businessmen were using permanence as a yardstick to weigh which enterprises were best for the South. The math was simple: an industry was permanent if it managed resources rather than exploiting them to depletion. The best explanation of this strategy came from Robert Lowry—a prominent business leader in Atlanta. In 1913 Lowry wrote, "The development of these resources [of the South] should be of a permanent and not a temporary nature." As the president of a bank that depended on Southern economic growth, Lowry acknowledged that he was not opposed to "industrial development" and did not believe that resources should be preserved from use. He simply hoped to find ways of using the South's natural resources that would leave them in "better shape" for later generations. Lowry wrote, "I favor all forms of development, but I also favor a conservative use of natural resources, which results in constructive and not destructive development. All the natural resources of this wonderful section, in which our thriving city of Atlanta is located, can be turned into permanent productive sources of wealth for this and all future generations." Simply put, permanence could be achieved by finding enterprises that promoted "constructive and not destructive development."[26] Lowry's description does not fit with standard caricatures of

Southern boosters as development-crazed industrialists with little interest in the health of the region's natural resources. Yet Lowry was not an idealistic nature lover. He was a businessman. He was enthusiastic about permanence only because it provided long-term profits and required little sacrifice.

Faith in the gospel of permanence was not just talk, and it shaped the paths that business and municipal elites believed were ideal. Instead of mandating that businesses change their exploitative ways, Southern boosters worked to attract industries that would be better stewards of their natural resources. The best example was the enthusiasm for waste industries. As resources became scarce, officials latched onto nearly any enterprise that could use discarded by-products from existing industrial processes, resources that had been idle, or raw materials that never had much commercial value—a trend that Richard Edmonds called the "utilization of Southern wastes."[27] These enterprises attempted to wring as much money as possible out of the earth and assured the South's leaders that perpetual growth was possible— even in a region up against its environmental limits. This appealed to businesspeople and public officials who did not want to make difficult decisions about which resources to use and which to conserve. Local boosters, corporate officials, and even some state governments put money into efforts to discover new ways of using resources that had gone to waste, supported research on private industrial and demonstration farms, and sometimes even provided direct incentives like tax exemptions and subsidies to enterprises that promised to transform wasted resources into lasting economic growth.

These efforts often paid off. Waste industries gained a foothold in the South as the region industrialized in the mid-twentieth century. For instance, timber-producing areas experimented with products like Masonite, which was made by applying steam and pressure to wasted sawdust.[28] Phosphate mining in South Carolina and Florida provided raw materials for making cheap commercial fertilizers and used a resource that had gone unnoticed. Cottonseed oil manufacturing gave farmers a market for their seed and fueled the growth of a new industry in the Cotton Belt that was producing more than one billion pounds of oil annually by 1940.[29] Chemist Charles H. Herty developed a method for extracting turpentine from pine trees that did not kill the tree—keeping an industry threatened with resource exhaustion afloat. Even the production of Portland cement was praised for lessening the strain on other resources, and in 1909 a Georgia public official predicted that making this product from his state's slate and lime would "largely relieve the pressure upon our iron-ore beds."[30]

Hope for permanence through new technology also gave momentum to the chemurgy movement in the 1920s and 1930s. Chemurgists sought to use applied chemical research to discover new industrial uses for agricultural goods in order to stimulate economic growth and make agriculture and manufacturing more interdependent. It is no coincidence that many of the nation's outspoken advocates of chemurgy were Southerners who had promoted permanent uses of regional resources. For instance, in 1937 a manufacturer from Florida described chemurgy in terms that could have been lifted directly from earlier statements about permanence when he claimed that chemurgists wanted to develop "raw materials . . . that can be perpetually produced at a profit from the soil without impairment of the soil." He concluded that "this is the only source of perpetual cumulative wealth."[31]

The best example of how waste industries and permanent uses of natural resources reshaped Southern economic development is pulp and paper manufacturing. In the 1890s entrepreneurs developed a method for manufacturing low-grade paper used for packaging—known as kraft paper—out of yellow pine, which opened up the region's piney woods to paper manufacturers for the first time. It would take several more decades for chemists to determine how to manufacture higher-quality paper from resinous pine, but in the 1910s and 1920s a number of paper manufacturers opened their doors in the South. By 1930 the region's kraft mills even led the nation in the production of low-grade paper products.[32]

As paper manufacturing expanded, boosters declared that it was the ideal industry for the South. Because paper mills needed wood chips to fuel their operations, they provided markets for pieces of wood that never had much commercial use because of their small size or poor quality. Building a paper mill also required a massive outlay of capital, and corporations could not afford to pursue the cut-and-get-out strategies used by other forest industries. Reforestation was not optional for these firms. They relied on fast-growing slash pine that quickly replenished stocks of raw materials. Paper companies even ensured that they would receive a steady stream of pulpwood by employing the region's first corporate foresters.[33] All of these qualities added up to permanence for Southern boosters, who lauded the industry for using forest resources that other industries had wasted in more long-term ways. For instance, in 1923 an official from North Carolina's Department of Conservation and Development praised the pulp and paper industry both for its "omnivorous appetite" in utilizing "formerly neglected woods" and because it promoted "more permanent means of reforestation."

He concluded that these factors made pulp and paper ideal for the South because it had a "permanent nature."[34] Unlike naval stores operators and loggers, pulp and paper manufacturers seemed to be moving into the South to stay.

Southern boosters faced an uphill battle before pulp and paper could become permanently profitable, however. As William Boyd notes, by the twentieth century, lumber and naval stores operators had already cut through a huge swath of the region's forests. Tax codes throughout the region penalized timber owners for keeping standing timber, and the structure of industry financing mandated that loggers get as much money as possible out of their trees to keep operating. Compounding these problems were a lack of experienced foresters in the South, a regional penchant for fire that made it risky to keep timber standing, and an abundance of privately held land that was not easily subjected to industrial forestry.[35]

Despite these problems, boosters worked to bring pulp and paper enterprises to the South. States and municipalities became more active in providing incentives to industry in the twentieth century, and a few began exempting enterprises that manufactured paper from taxation or providing them with bounties and other subsidies to lure them into the region. Although this can be explained by the South's general mania for industrial development, evidence also suggests that conservation played a role. For instance, in 1922 the Mississippi General Assembly passed a law that exempted "all factories for making paper or paper products out of wood pulp, cotton stalks or other material" from having to pay taxes for five years in the hopes of encouraging pulp and paper manufacturing. When the meaning of the law was challenged just a few years later by a corporation that did not process wood pulp but still hoped to take advantage of the tax break, the state's supreme court ruled that "it was the manifest purpose of the legislature to encourage the conservation of such raw materials as were going to waste, such as wood from which wood pulp is manufactured and cotton stalks from which a form of paper may be produced."[36] From the 1930s onward municipal and state enticements were commonly provided to pulp and paper manufacturers as part of a far-reaching campaign to "sell the South" to industry. These efforts were wildly successful, and by 1950 the region was producing more than half of the nation's wood pulp.[37]

As paper manufacturers moved into the South, they implemented policies that would keep their mills continuously supplied with pulpwood. Although the largest corporations were typically managed by outsiders with little interest in the health of Southern forests, their need for steady access to raw materials prompted officials to manage certain resources in long-term ways. Perhaps the best example was Louisiana's Great Southern Lumber Company, which added a pulp mill to its operations in the second decade of the twentieth century as a way to head off a potential timber famine. The firm had been located in Bogalusa—thirty miles north of Lake Pontchartrain— ever since 1908, when it constructed the largest sawmill in the world there. Although the company owned more than four hundred thousand acres of yellow pine in Louisiana and Missouri by 1914, officials still worried that their days of cutting timber were numbered.[38] These fears came to a head when the Great Southern failed to find a new source of timber in South America and plans to resettle its cutover lands in the South did not work as well as expected. After touring pulp and paper facilities in Sweden, the firm's president—A. C. Goodyear—lauded the "wonderful system" that "assured" that country of a "perpetual undiminished forest." He proposed paper man- ufacturing as a solution to the company's declining stocks of timber, and in 1916 Great Southern officials financed the construction of a pulp mill in Bo- galusa that ran on the waste generated by their sawmill.[39] When the pulp mill began operating in 1919, the company converted the five hundred cords of "slabs, edgings, branches and trees too small for saw logs" that it had burned each day into raw material for its operations.[40] Company officials even me- morialized the "death" of the mill's refuse burner by inscribing its steel sur- face with a note explaining that "the complete utilization of the sawmill refuse in the manufacture of paper has my fire forever extinguished."[41]

Providing for more efficient uses of waste was only one aspect of perma- nence. The new pulp and paper mill also pushed Great Southern officials to develop a program of reforestation that would maintain a steady supply of pulpwood by hiring corporate foresters, establishing nurseries, developing methods for fire control, and replanting pines on cutover lands. Company lobbyists even pressed the General Assembly of Louisiana to make parish tax codes more favorable to reforestation, and foresters educated local farmers about how "the poor rugged and waste acres can be profitably used in grow- ing fast loblolly pine trees for pulp."[42] Although this entailed enormous costs, the firm's president explained that pulp production and reforestation were "not the product of impractical idealism" but "the healthy offspring of busi- ness necessity." Goodyear admitted that this strategy might be considered an "adopted child," but he argued that it was "adopted because it pays" and would provide the company with a means of operating indefinitely.[43]

Obtaining a perpetual supply of raw materials also gave company officials a unique way to ensure the stability and availability of labor. Municipal
and corporate officials incorporated permanence into their paternalistic
management of Bogalusa and championed the city as an example for other
Southern communities that depended on resource extraction for their daily
bread. No one was more enthusiastic about the civic possibilities of pulp and
paper than William Sullivan—the company's general manager and Bogalusa's
mayor. While Sullivan acknowledged that "no sawmill town has ever been
considered permanent," he claimed that Bogalusa was bucking this trend.
Sullivan's vision for Bogalusa was intended for "our children and our
children's children," and he outlined a broad program that involved the
construction of an expensive new high school, pay raises for teachers, an
ambitious program of residential construction, and "building regulations
that give no possible chance for congestion if the present population of
15,000 grows to 100,000." Coming just two years after attempts to unionize
workers at his lumber company ended in violence, Sullivan likely hoped to
bring stability to an unsettled city and promote a positive image that would
attract new residents and workers. These ambitious plans depended upon
the success of the Great Southern's papermaking experiment. As Sullivan
explained, "the minute it became clear that we could put our finger down on a
point in the calendar and say: 'Here's where the lumber gives out,' why, that
minute we began to work on plans to make Bogalusa permanent," and he
concluded, "It's on paper that we're depending to make Bogalusa permanent." Sullivan understood that there were "profits . . . in paper," but he was
attracted to permanence for more than just profit.[44] Social and civic visions
for the New South were always intertwined with decisions about how to use
natural resources, and Sullivan's vision for a permanent Bogalusa suggests
just how much issues like civic growth and labor availability could depend
upon the wise use of Southern natural resources.

The Great Southern Lumber Company was one of only a few firms that
drastically modified their business strategies to promote permanence in the
1920s, but their reforms became more popular in the next few decades. Indeed, Great Southern officials did more than perhaps any other group to
publicly link permanent uses of resources with the pulp and paper industry, and people throughout the nation took notice. After visiting the town,
the president of a northern paper company claimed that "while Bogalusa, the
lumber town, would come to an end soon, Bogalusa, the paper city, is
built for all time."[45] In January of 1921 Richard Edmonds—editor of the

*Manufacturers' Record* and one of the most influential of all Southern boosters—even commissioned a series of articles on the company's efforts in Bogalusa. In his editorial comments Edmonds noted that although the "destruction of . . . forests" was one of the most pressing problems facing Southerners, the company's work "gives assurance of the feasibility of reforestation and also of the profitable operation on a large commercial scale of paper mills using the waste products of pine sawmills and other pine timber." The subtitle of the articles proclaimed what Edmonds saw as the main lesson provided by Bogalusa, that the "perpetual timber supply through reforestation" was the "basis for [the] industrial permanency of Bogalusa."[46] The Great Southern might not have touched off a complete revolution in private forest management, but the company firmly established the connection between waste industries and permanent uses of natural resources—at least until it folded in 1938—and suggested that other firms could profit by securing permanent supplies of raw materials.

As the pulp industry expanded into the South's forests and clashed with other stakeholders, industry officials also found that framing their operations as permanent helped to justify access to the South's forests and make it seem like they were good corporate neighbors. For instance, in 1926 Robert W. Griffith—the president of the Champion Fibre Company in Canton, North Carolina—defended his company's role in western North Carolina for an audience of Asheville residents. Like other boosters, Griffith predicted that waste industries, especially pulp and paper, were the future of the Southern economy. Griffith's firm was one of the pioneers of industrial forestry, and he claimed that Champion's efforts to reforest its one hundred thousand acres of forestland were "evidence of the company's faith in the practice of sound conservation of forest resources." He ultimately suggested that the company's role in providing a pulp market for waste products and eliminating waste on their own land through reforestation proved that Champion expected to run "a permanent industry in this location . . . with the purpose of obtaining a continuous supply of raw material."[47]

At the time Griffith was a key player in a fierce conflict between industrialists and a coalition of businesspeople, tourist promoters, preservationists, and federal officials over whether the federal government should create a national park in the southern Appalachians. Given that much of the land in the proposed park was controlled by Champion, it should not be surprising that Griffith argued that the park would remove the region's valuable resources from use and "inevitably handicap its future development." He invoked the permanence of his company's operations to convince the public that Champion would be just as good a steward of these resources as federal foresters. Griffith also sought to distance his company from logging companies that were prevalent in the southern Appalachians, and he contrasted Champion's "efficient" operations with lumbermen who had no plans for "conducting a permanent industry."[48] Framing the benefits of the pulp and paper industry in this way worked to solidify its claim to the region's forests over other industries, justify investment in the industry, and smooth over relations between manufacturers and locals. In short, it helped to justify corporate control of the South's natural resources.

The pulp and paper industry therefore provides a window on the different ways that permanence shaped Southern economic development in the decades after the Civil War. For these firms permanence was always an aspirational goal—one that was contested by stakeholders with different visions of how to achieve it and who should benefit from it. In a context in which enterprises were constantly vying with one another for access to resources, "permanence" sometimes seemed like little more than a buzzword used by corporations to distinguish themselves. Yet the experiences of the Great Southern Lumber Company and Champion Fibre Company suggest that corporate officials were keen to improve aspects of their environmental performance and modified their business strategies to prolong their supply of raw materials.

Permanence did not just shape the fate of the Southern pulp and paper industry; it was an important consideration in all New South development efforts. As the region moved into the twentieth century, Southern leaders were less inclined to embrace economic growth without considering the cost. Boosters and corporate officials never saw a conflict between jobs and permanent uses of resources, and they adapted their business strategies to deal with a declining resource base. Long-term uses of resources may not have always won out as Southerners remade the region's economy, but permanence led boosters to look for more efficient means of using resources, to work to replace what they had already used up, and to attempt to lure more permanent industries into the region. Taking the environmental vision of New South boosters seriously shows that while they may not have been "green," to adapt Char Miller's phrase, they were "green*ing*."[49]

By World War II the region was narrowing the economic gap that had long separated it from the rest of the United States. But these accomplishments never went as far as boosters hoped, and they never improved the lives of most

Southerners. Despite progress by companies in greening parts of their operations and municipal efforts to attract more permanent industries to the region, too much of the South's growth was unsustainable. Given that corporate leaders and public officials often embraced permanence, how then do we explain the gullies, the exhausted fields, the dammed rivers, and the air and water pollution that have pockmarked the Southern landscape for much of the twentieth century?

For one, conservation did not always work on its own terms. People, and even corporations, sometimes continued to waste resources. Conservation may have transformed the acres owned by large firms, but it was less popular among private landowners and small companies without the money and manpower to throw at maintaining stocks of raw materials. The region's emphasis on private avenues for conservation also meant that clashing visions for what permanence was and how to achieve it were difficult to resolve because they pitted private interests against each other.

The bigger issue was that attempts to secure permanent uses of resources were myopic. Southern businesses may have tried to use resources more efficiently or reduce their production of wastes—and many succeeded—but these efforts never went far enough to avoid environmental problems. The very definition of permanence meant that business leaders could ensure the long-term availability of resources without ever having to radically rethink their operations. Municipal officials who hoped to attract more permanent industries to their community also never had to reconsider their obsession with industrial development. Above all, this was because permanence never challenged the logic of capitalist development. It was just a way to cope with environmental limits and maintain growth. Attracting new enterprises to the region, using resources that had been idle, and eliminating waste in industrial processes all quickened the pace of development. Permanence allowed business leaders to modify their strategies in order to deal with resource depletion without cutting production. In this way, it never challenged the most exploitative uses of the South's natural resources and reinforced what Donald Worster calls the "maximizing creed" that is a key characteristic of capitalism's relationship with the environment.[50] By defining conservation as the permanent use of corporate resources, then, leaders of the New South found a goal that they could work toward without reining in development or addressing other pressing environmental issues.

Efforts to achieve permanence sometimes even made environmental problems worse by intensifying the use of certain natural resources or creating problems that could not be addressed simply by using resources more efficiently. Manufacturing paper from wood pulp promoted forestry but also created water and air pollution; using slash pine for reforestation led to industrial forests that simplified complex ecosystems; commercial fertilizers temporarily boosted soil fertility at the expense of the long-term health of soils; the manufacture of Portland cement eased pressure on forest resources but resulted in significant air pollution; scenic tourism preserved certain landscape features but paved the way for sprawl and pollution. These issues were only defined as problems by people concerned about quality of life or ecological ethics. They did not figure into the developmental calculus of public officials and businesspeople, who saw permanence as a way to maintain stocks of profitable raw materials for industrial uses. Even as environmentalists tried to widen the frame and call attention to these other aspects of environmental quality in the 1960s and 1970s, Southern corporate officials clung to their conception of environmental quality as simply replenishing corporate resources for continuous production.

If the history of the American South is a study in irony, as C. Vann Woodward contends, the role that permanent uses of resources played in hastening environmental degradation provides yet another twist.[51] Whereas Woodward uses irony to call attention to the distinctive aspects of the regional experience, the ironic implications of the Southern search for permanence seem all too familiar in an era in which sustainability is heralded as the key to solving global environmental woes. Although our current struggle for sustainable uses of resources is almost a century removed from the South's struggle for permanence, the lessons from this experience should provide optimism that businesses can and will make central aspects of their operations greener. Yet the experience of the post–Civil War South also suggests that unless we conceive of environmental quality in the broadest possible terms, and unless we are open to fundamentally rethinking the relationship between business and the environment, we will have little success in heading off environmental problems.

# Utilities as Conservationists? The Paradox of Electrification During the Progressive Era in North America

*Julie Cohn*

In 1902, Professor John Perry, protégé of Lord Kelvin, lamented the "ruthless waste of the world's fuel," that is, coal.[1] He proposed more efficient transformation of coal energy directly into electricity, full use of water powers for industrial plants, and, perhaps, development of techniques to harness the sun's power. Perry described the world as conservationists saw it at the turn of the last century. Industrialists wasted finite natural resources. Electrification promised greater energy efficiency. It was time for mankind to turn to renewables. And scientists held the key to resolving these matters.

At that moment in America, the relatively young electric power industry had already transformed lighting, transportation, and manufacturing practices. While only a small percentage of citizens used electricity, the industry was growing rapidly. This meant, in turn, that the consumption of coal and the damming of rivers proceeded apace. The utility companies occupied an equivocal position within the conservation movements. On the one hand, expanding power systems threatened resource overuse, and on the other they offered a panacea for long-term clean and efficient energy production. Even more provocatively, power companies sought and adopted energy-saving innovations and at the very same time encouraged increased consumption.

Early twentieth-century conservation initiatives indisputably focused on electrification. Conservation leaders advocated full development of river basins for irrigation, flood control, and power production. They believed that not a drop of water should be wasted before it reached the ocean. Further, they argued that hydroelectric power generation could displace, if not fully replace, coal-fired power plants. This had multiple benefits, including reduced reliance on resources potentially in short supply, "free" energy from falling water, and less smoke pollution. Some deemed electricity the ideal alternative to other forms of energy used in manufacturing, both for its increased efficiency and its flexibility. These utilitarian conservationists focused on the wise use of natural resources so that they would be available to future generations, unlike later environmentalists who addressed the possibility of reducing overall consumption to protect natural ecological systems.[2]

While electrification was the "green" alternative for some, it represented the worst aspects of overreaching capitalist enterprise to others. Preservationists, nature lovers, and local populations argued that hydroelectric dams marred the scenic beauty of remote mountain areas, destroyed fisheries, and flooded upstream landscapes. In some areas residents protested that power lines threatened human health, safety, and aesthetic preferences.[3] Urban activists complained that coal-fired generating stations caused noise and smoke pollution. Antimonopolists objected to increasing consolidation in the private sector portion of the industry. Further, increased reliance on electricity for light and power led to increased resource use. The power industry operated at the nexus of conservation and consumption.

America's power companies had a vested interest in the resource management side of conservation. They offered a product that had peculiar characteristics rendering it useful only at the instant of demand. They faced long-term amortization of their capital investments. They had to attract a widely diverse market over many years both to achieve operating economies and to repay investors. While power companies had direct control over their own generators, they often depended upon the vagaries of nature and fluctuating resource markets for their primary energy supplies. Power company concern for steady and predictable access to energy resources aligned neatly with conservation ideas about resource management.

This chapter investigates a central paradox in the electrification and modernization of North America. Through both stated intentions and operating practices, the power industry joined the ranks of conservationists who sought efficient resource use, as well as cleaner air and water. Yet the very techniques adopted by power companies to achieve these laudable goals entailed a growing customer base that used electricity more often and in greater amounts for a wider variety of applications. In other words, the power companies promoted consumption as part of the process of conservation.

## The Electric Power Industry in North America

Diversity characterized electrification in North America in general and in the United States in particular. In the late 1800s, licensees of various lighting and power systems brought electricity to cities and towns.[4] Both public and private concerns entered the market, often in direct competition. By 1902, there were 2,805 commercial companies and 815 municipal companies providing 2.5 billion kilowatt-hours (kWh) of electricity to American consumers.[5] Figure 6.1 illustrates the dynamic relationship between commercial and municipal companies: as the numbers of the latter increased, the total share of generation by the former also increased. Figure 6.1 also indicates the dramatic growth of electrification. While initially sold as an expensive and prestigious commodity, by the early 1900s, power companies pushed to provide electricity as a service. As one engineer mused, "Every step upward in the overall efficiency means a chance for a more economical supply and a larger market . . . it should be possible to make electrical supply a necessity and not, as it now is in many instances, rather a luxury."[6]

Regional variation characterized the primary energy resources used for electric power. Along the Eastern Seaboard, power companies preferred anthracite coal. On the Gulf Coast, after the Spindletop gusher of 1901, power companies used crude oil. In the Rocky Mountains, and along the West Coast, falling water provided the primary energy source for electrification. As Figure 6.2 illustrates, fossil fuels powered the majority of electric plants through the early twentieth century.

In addition to many participants, and much geographic variation, the power industry in the United States operated under a very loose regulatory system. In the absence of state or federal government regulation in the late 1800s, private companies negotiated franchise agreements with municipalities, with which they were occasionally in direct competition. Shortly after the turn of the century, state governments began to establish regulatory authority over the regions in which power companies operated and the prices they charged. Private companies generally acceded to these regulations in return for monopoly control over markets and rates that assured cost recovery

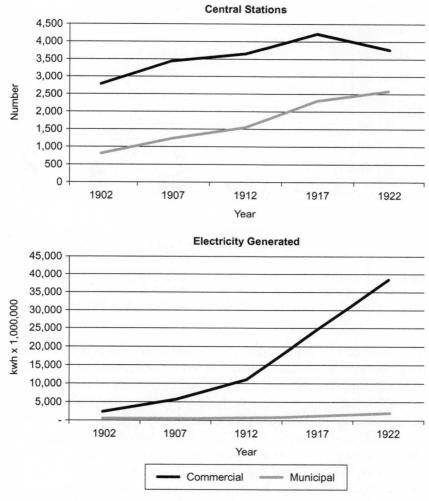

**Figure 6.1.** Comparison of commercial and municipal power stations, both in terms of number of stations and electricity generated, 1902–22. *Sources:* Data from *Central Electric Light and Power Stations and Street and Electric Railways, with Summary of the Electrical Industries, 1912* (Washington, D.C.: Government Printing Office, 1915); *Census of Electrical Industries, 1917* (Washington, D.C.: Government Printing Office, 1920); *Census of Electrical Industries, 1932* (Washington, D.C.: Government Printing Office, 1934).

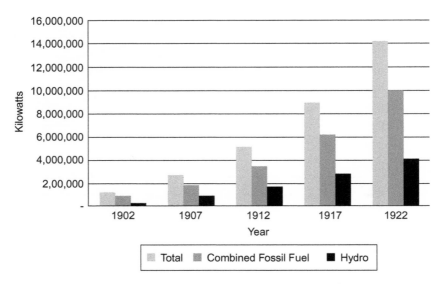

***Figure 6.2.*** Comparison of installed generating capacity by type of prime mover and thus type of primary energy resource used, 1902–22. *Source:* Data from *Historical Statistics of the United States, 1789–1945* (Washington, D.C.: Government Printing Office, 1949).

with profit. As part of the bargain, the private companies promised equitable power sales at affordable prices. By 1914, commissions in forty-three states regulated rates and entry for electric utilities.[7] Yet there was and is great variability. Nebraska, for example, forbade private power companies, and Texas waited until 1975 to institute electric utility regulation.

In the United States, the central government joined the regulatory process late in the game. The federal government controlled access to resources on government-owned land, regulated use of navigable waterways, and authorized treaties for international power sales, but otherwise exerted almost no authority over electrification until 1920. Interstate sales of electric power took place outside of any regulatory oversight until the Supreme Court articulated the federal responsibility for this activity in 1927.[8] During the 1930s, President Franklin Roosevelt instituted policies and Congress passed several laws that brought the federal government more thoroughly into the power sector.[9] Federal agencies financed infrastructure, built hydroelectric dams, and transmitted electricity. The Securities Exchange Commission regulated the financial organization of privately owned power companies and the Federal Power Commission controlled access to hydroelectric dam sites. A key feature of these relationships is the lack of any central planning or oversight. Electrification took place, for the most part, on an ad hoc basis as individuals and companies chose to enter markets and expand.

## Economics of Electrification

For both investor-owned private power companies and government-owned public power companies, the economics of electrification were challenging. Power companies faced long financial horizons and very short-term operating realities. The initial costs of building generating stations, hydroelectric plants, power lines, and distribution networks were quite high. To lure and keep customers, companies promised reliable electricity and developed attractive rates targeting each portion of the market. But the generally affordable rates meant slow repayment of capital. And the availability of primary energy resources—both coal and falling water—proved to be variable. The economic stability of power companies depended upon a reliable, steadily paying customer base and predictable access to primary energy resources over the long term.

Keeping a power plant operating at its ideal capacity was tricky. Electricity is useful only if it is available at the instant of demand. For a typical urban power station serving private homes in the late 1800s, peak demand occurred at night, for lighting, and in the winter, for heat. On a bright, sunny, temperate day, demand was almost zero. The power company operating this imaginary plant would have to slow or stop the generators during the day and power them up again at night, causing wear and tear on the equipment and undermining the ability to operate at ideal capacity. The graph in Figure 6.3 depicts this type of daily and seasonal fluctuation. While the data represents utility operations in 1919, the principal held true for all the preceding years as well. Power companies sought to diversify their demand (also called load) to include residential customers, businesses, industry, retail stores, and electric transit as a way to spread out the load over the course of the days, weeks, and year. Through advertising, sales of appliances, carefully constructed rate schedules, and extension of transmission and distribution lines, power companies expanded their markets and improved their operating economies.[10]

At the heart of economic operations was an irony: consumption and conservation advanced hand in hand. Manufacturers designed larger and more efficient generators and the per-unit cost of power production fell steadily from the late 1800s to the 1960s. The improved economy was achieved, however, only when a plant operated at its ideal capacity. As they installed larger

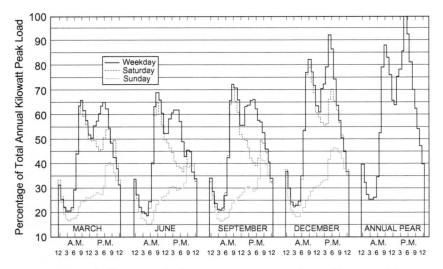

*Figure 6.3.* Graph illustrating the fluctuation in customer demand by time of day and by season of the year—aggregated from utilities operating along the Eastern Seaboard. *Source:* Reprinted from W. S. Murray et al., "A Superpower System for the Region Between Boston and Washington," United States Geological Survey Professional Paper 123 (Washington, D.C.: Government Printing Office, 1921), 41, fig. 8, "Typical seasonal loads of electric utilities in superpower zone in 1919."

plants, power companies sought a greater number and more varied consumers. For these power companies, more consumption spread evenly across time equaled improved energy efficiency, which led to lower cost of unit of power produced and greater profits. Energy efficient operations also offered the possibility of reducing rates, to increase consumption, and thus realize even greater profits. More efficient generating technologies, economies of scale, and careful operating techniques, combined with rising demand led to a steady and measurable decline in the primary energy needed to produce one kilowatt of electricity. With affordable rates, strong marketing and advertising programs, new technologies, and a willing public, power companies in turn achieved a huge expansion of electrical systems through the early 1900s.

## Conservation Initiatives and Power System Experts

The term "conservation" has a mixed history in North American usage. The word itself originated from the Latin *conservare*, meaning "to keep, guard, observe."[11] In the nineteenth century, physicists formulated the law of conservation of energy, stating that the total amount of energy in a closed system, while it may move or change form, remains constant.[12] Inventors, engineers, and others working on electrification studied the laws of physics and adopted terminology from that scientific field to describe phenomena in power systems. In the later nineteenth century, the notion of conservation was applied to various initiatives that arose to protect scenic beauty and manage natural resources. By the early twentieth century, political leaders appropriated the word to define elements of Progressive Era activism that sought greater central control and increased scientific authority over management of North American resources, including energy resources. Over the course of the mid-twentieth century the meaning of conservation expanded to include protection of natural resources against destruction by pollution and overuse. By the end of the twentieth century, the word "conservation" was often conflated with "environmentalism."

In the early 1900s, President Theodore Roosevelt and his chief forester, Gifford Pinchot, appropriated the term "conservation" to describe their particular initiatives to manage and develop the nation's resources. When Roosevelt addressed a meeting of foresters in 1903, he invoked "wise use" and linked careful management of forests to mineral extraction, transportation, manufacturing, commerce, agriculture, and water supply.[13] In his 1907 letter appointing the Inland Waterways Commission, Roosevelt called upon this entity to plan for "all the uses to which streams may be put," and to "co-ordinate the points of view of all users of water."[14] Roosevelt termed this a policy to "consider" and "conserve" natural resources because industrial development had largely depleted many resources already. In November of that year, the president called for the country's governors to meet in 1908 to discuss the "conservation of our natural resources."[15]

On May 13–15, 1908, the governors met with the president, Pinchot, representatives of numerous federal agencies, and individuals from a wide array of interests groups, including the electric power industry. They discussed the status of the nation's natural resources and the opportunities for managing those resources for the country's long-term benefit. Henry St. Clair Putnam represented the American Institute of Electrical Engineers (AIEE) at the Governors' Conference, and said of electric power, "New economies are possible of accomplishment and the resulting effect upon the conservation and utilization of our power resources is of the greatest importance."[16] He lamented the pending disaster if the rate of coal exhaustion could not be slowed and lauded the possibility of garnering more energy from rivers. Putnam closed with a plea for "wise governmental guidance" to assure development of the nation's resources with the "highest practicable degree of economy which scientific knowledge and engineering skill can attain."[17]

The status of coal reserves framed debates about electrification. During the first decades of electrification, utilities strongly preferred anthracite (hard) coal over bituminous (soft) coal for its flammability and minimal smoke production. In the early 1900s, there were multiple forecasts of anthracite coal shortages, causing some alarm among the generating companies. Representatives of the power industry measured the failure to exploit waterpower sites in terms of coal used. Yet, the "reckless and destructive" practices of the prior fifty years had lessened "the availability of our water powers."[18] Experts reported in 1907 that anthracite would last only fifty more years, and repeated the warning in 1908.[19] Pinchot told a special conservation meeting of the AIEE that only 50 percent of the available coal was extracted properly, and of the quantity mined, 90 percent was wasted.[20] Utility engineers lamented the coming depletion of coal reserves and acknowledged that shifting to waterpower offered only a partial solution. Many advocated building power plants at waterpower sites and using long-distance transmission lines to bring energy to industry.[21] In 1912, the predicted shortage, called the "anthracite scare," was deemed "fictitious," yet in 1918 experts continued to worry about the alternatives should coal "fail."[22]

The power companies addressed coal conservation in several different ways. In the face of reduced anthracite reserves, electricity producers attempted to use lower grades of coal, refuse coal, gas, and other combustibles, including vegetation. Smokeless electricity production became a secondary goal of the power industry, especially for plants located in urban areas.[23] Engineers debated whether more energy was lost as trains brought coal from mines to urban generating stations or across long electric transmission lines. A power company in Hauto, Pennsylvania, realized the industry's "dream of conservation" with a plant located at the mouth of a coal mine and a transmission system carrying the electricity to more distant users.[24] The electrical industry encouraged factory owners to switch from coal-fired steam plants to electricity because, they argued, electricity increased the "efficiency" of energy production from coal.[25] Often factory owners then purchased in-house power plants. As power companies installed larger and more efficient generators, they promoted their central station service to factory owners as cheaper and more reliable than in-house power plants. By 1914, the Association of Edison Illuminating Companies reported that a large plant used only 3.3 pounds of coal per kilowatt-hour of electricity produced, while small isolated plants used three times that much. Large central stations saved the country 1,750,000 tons of coal per year.[26]

In addition to saving coal, conservationists and power system engineers sought to reduce waste, which had multiple meanings. The overuse of natural resources, without consideration for maximizing utility and assuring stores for future generations, represented one kind of waste. As an engineer reflected in 1900, "we have been frightfully wasteful also of our forests, our oil, our natural gas, our resources of the soil."[27] Failing to use a resource to the full represented another kind of waste: "water under high heads is so valuable that throwing it away unused comes in the category of sinful waste."[28] Both power company executives and conservationists touted the benefits of waterpower over coal power and advocated the full use of rivers through strategic planning. In the 1910s, engineers estimated that one horsepower of hydroelectricity could displace the burning of twelve tons of coal. The U.S. secretary of agriculture estimated in 1916 that anywhere from 30 million to 200 million horsepower of water sat unused in the United States.[29]

Utilities claimed waterpower development as a number one conservation goal, for their own long-term economic interests and for the wellbeing of the country. The AIEE told the National Waterways Commission in 1911 that every cubic foot of water unused represented a "definite monetary loss to the nation."[30] Some argued that hydroelectric power had the potential "to change the fate of nations," in much the same way that a wealth of coal and minerals had in the prior century.[31] The secretary of the interior agreed that "the water power that is developed is perpetual and continuous, and its use is the most living and vital example of conservation."[32] Many engineers concurred that once waterpower was made profitably productive, then "definite saving is made in the apparently exhaustible fuel assets of the nation."[33]

Reflecting the diversity of the industry, not all who worked for the power companies agreed that waterpower was a conservation panacea. "Many of the best engineers . . . have arrived at the conclusion that, on the whole, any new installation of steam power can be employed with much greater chances of profit than almost any water power in any part of the United

States, except where coal is very high in cost."[34] Waterpower sites were located at a long distance from markets, use was often restricted by federal and state actions, the construction cost of hydroelectric dams was high, and long-distance transmission was both difficult and costly. Utilities faced many challenges to gain access to these seemingly ideal and inexhaustible sources of energy.

Control of waterpower sites occupied the attention of politicians, government officials, power company managers, and the public in the early twentieth century. Conservationists favored full river development following planning by engineers and scientists at the federal government level. Some state leaders advocated for local levels of control. Even a few municipalities joined the wrangle over regulatory authority. Within this negotiation, private utilities lobbied against government ownership of facilities, but over time favored a role for the federal government that might include some degree of planning or even regulation.[35] Power company executives also feared a regime of federal oversight that excessively favored wilderness protection, although they found common cause with forest preservation. Regarding Niagara Falls, for example, one engineer argued against preservation "just" for aesthetic reasons, and later suggested that full development would cause the falls to be "more beautiful than ever" when finished.[36] As another engineer put it, "saving Niagara from the aesthetic standpoint, is a sorry joke."[37] Yet, power system engineers shared a concern that deforestation resulted in changes in rainfall patterns and water flow, thus wreaking havoc on the reliability of hydroelectric power. Care should be taken, they said, "to preserve the forests, the great storehouses of rain and flywheels of river flow."[38]

Over time discussion of waterpower development and resource management converged on the idea that interconnection achieved conservation goals. As early as 1908, engineers observed that in regions like the Pacific Northwest, with roughly one-fourth of the United States' potential waterpower, "great combinations" would provide "general and conclusive value . . . in electrical generation and transmission," and that an interconnected network could "do in efficiency and reliability what no one plant can reasonably hope to accomplish."[39] Even if aggregation of hydroelectric plants gave the appearance of an emerging power trust, interconnection tended "distinctly toward conservation of our natural resources."[40] In praising the interconnection of seven systems in the South in 1914, one journalist noted that it was the means by which each plant "could be utilized to its greatest advantage and the waste of water . . . could be averted."[41]

## Controlling Resources Through Interconnections

American power companies began to interconnect almost as soon as they built long-distance transmission lines. Westinghouse Electric Company first demonstrated the efficacy of long-distance transmission of alternating current at the 1893 Columbian Exposition in Chicago. By 1899, *Electrical World*, the most widely distributed publication on electrification, reported on links between autonomous power companies in California, and soon thereafter in Utah.[42] Within a few years, engineers lauded interconnection as the wave of the future, as the editor of *Electrical World* noted, "Probably the most important present tendency in power transmission is the union of several plants in feeding a great network."[43] Over the course of the twentieth century, interconnections between discrete companies became a defining characteristic of the North American power system.

Interconnection extended the advantages of long-distance power transmission. Long-distance transmission lines allowed a power company to carry electricity from a hydroelectric plant located at a remote mountain waterfall to a demand center, such as a mine, a manufacturer, a large agricultural concern, or a dense urban area. Likewise, a power company with an urban generating station used long-distance transmission lines to carry electricity beyond the city center. An interconnection exists when two or more autonomous entities build a link across which they share electric power. Through these links, power companies moved electricity even farther than transmission lines allowed. Interconnections also enabled power companies to shift load between different generating stations depending upon which offered the next most economical source of electricity. With an interconnection, access to diverse resources and markets extended farther.

Just as important, companies shared power across interconnections during planned maintenance outages and in emergencies. Fairly early in the process of electrification, company managers realized that reliability mattered to their clients. As one noted in 1897, "with the growth of systems, the service which was in its early days rather fitful and liable to shutdowns at any time has become more reliable, and the feeling has grown up that the shutting down of a line is something almost criminal."[44] Another offered that "continuity of service has been one of the prime requisites of commercial success" and with growth it "has become imperative."[45] Strategies for assuring access to backup power in case of an outage included installing extra generating capacity, called "spinning reserve," installing storage batteries that could be charged during times of low demand and used to respond to high demand and outages, and linking with another system. When companies interconnected, they could reduce their individual investment in spinning reserve and storage batteries by relying on the neighbor for backup power.

Interconnections grew slowly, but steadily, in North America. Only a handful of companies operated long-distance, interconnected power lines in 1908. By 1918, there were a few clear networks. At the start of World War II, the skeleton of what is now called "the grid" appeared. In 1967, the Eastern and Western Interconnected Power Systems finally completed links across the Rocky Mountains, establishing a network of power lines that reached from the East Coast to the West Coast and from Canada to the Mexican Baja. As power companies built links in different regions, they pursued different operating objectives.

One of the oldest interconnected systems, in Southern California, offers a perfect example of the resource management power companies achieved. In 1899, the San Gabriel Electric Company relied primarily on a hydroelectric plant on the San Gabriel River to provide power to customers.[46] The company built a link with the Los Angeles Railroad Company to share power. The railroad operated a power plant reliant on fossil fuels. When the river ran low, the company bought power from the railroad and when the river ran high, San Gabriel sold excess power to the railroad. San Gabriel "gives or takes a 500-volt direct current from the Los Angeles Railroad Company ... the very quintessence of novelty, originality and boldness of design."[47] San Gabriel competed for customers with the Southern California Electric Company, which transmitted power from the headwaters of the Santa Ana River to Los Angeles on an eighty-three-mile transmission line, deemed the world's longest in 1899.[48] Southern California also employed a temporary interconnection, with the Redlands Electric Light and Power Company. In this instance, the interconnection assured continuous electrical service during construction of a new powerhouse.

In a similar vein, companies in other regions managed the variability of hydroelectric power through interconnections. Companies in Colorado and Utah that relied on hydroelectric plants interconnected with each other. In this way, when one river ran low, the companies could draw power from others that were running high.[49] In 1910, the Holtwood Dam on the Susquehanna River in Pennsylvania promised large quantities of electricity for the city of Baltimore in Maryland. The Susquehanna is a long and wide river with great variability in flows. Thus to insure a steady supply of electricity, investors linked the hydroelectric plant to a network of coal-fired plants also serving the region and shifted electricity production between generating stations depending upon river flow.[50]

Companies that operated coal-fired power plants also found interconnections beneficial for managing energy resources. By linking multiple power stations, companies gained significant advantages. First, the units of coal used to produce each kilowatt-hour of electricity varied from generator to generator, and thus from station to station. Additionally, each power station served a slightly different market with different demands. By sharing the load across multiple interconnected stations, the companies together realized greater diversity in the total market and perhaps a more balanced demand schedule across time. Interconnected companies planned out operating schedules that allowed them to take advantage of the most efficient generators for the base load and use the more expensive generators when loads increased.

## Electrification in Terms of Conservation

As the power companies introduced technical and operating innovations like interconnections, they increasingly described their work in conservation terms. The word itself crept into the technical literature between the 1890s and the early 1900s. Figure 6.4 indicates the increasing frequency with which "conservation" and its variants appeared in engineering and science publications. In the late 1800s, "conservation" in technical publications specifically referred to capturing a greater percentage of energy from burning fuel, building reservoirs to save water for future use, minimizing the evaporation of moisture from irrigated soil, and purifying dirty rivers. By 1908, the term was often used to address saving forests from overcutting, finding economies within the process of resource use, protecting labor, eliminating urban smoke, and increasing the use of resources through careful development. For technical professionals, the term "conservation" encompassed the major ideas of efficient resource use, long-term resource management, and reducing pollution.[51]

When writers first used "conservation" in articles about electrification, it specifically meant reserving a resource for future use. One engineer suggested that "conservation of rainfall" would be key to making long-distance

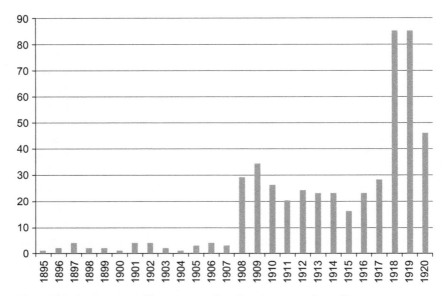

***Figure 6.4.*** Appearance of "conservation" and variants in technical literature, 1895–1920. *Source:* Data acquired from Compendex, s.v. "conserv," accessed October 1, 2012, http://www.engineeringvillage.com/.

transmission cost effective in southern Vermont.[52] Another, in reference to debates over the use of Niagara Falls, suggested that waiting to build more power plants until coal became "too expensive" would have the result of "conserving a tremendous block of power until such time as it may be utilized to greater public benefit."[53] By 1908, the power industry journals contained many submissions that addressed resource depletion, efficiency of generating plants, economy of the industry, and the relative merits of long-distance transmission in overcoming the challenges of accessing distant energy resources.

Power experts often used the terminology of conservation when talking about the work of operating power systems. Before 1900, journal articles routinely reported on reduced operating costs, avoided "first cost" (in other words, lower capital investment), load factor, losses on the transmission line, and profitability. Those concerns did not disappear, but increasingly, after 1900, success was also weighed in terms of coal saved, pollution reduced, waste averted, and water used. For example, one engineer reported to the AIEE that, among other benefits, a large system "solves the smoke problem by wiping out small coal plants."[54] Another told his colleagues, "The transmission of electrical energy generated by water-power which would otherwise be wasted is the most important work engineers of the present day have accomplished."[55] When the dispatcher of the "World's Largest Transmission System" operated all plants in parallel, it resulted in use of each plant to the fullest degree and "economy of water and fuel."[56]

World War I highlighted the advantages of interconnection as a conservation strategy. The United States experienced its first serious energy crises during the war. Power companies collaborated with the central government to generate needed electricity for the war industries and explicitly used "electrical interconnections to conserve fuel."[57] As Figure 6.4 illustrates, the appearance of "conservation" in the technical literature spiked in 1918 and 1919. Even after the war, engineers often talked about the benefits of interconnection in conservation terms. For example, a contributer to *Power* magazine offered that "large savings in coal, labor and transportation . . . would be possible from electrical interconnection on a give-and-take basis."[58] And journal articles continued in the same vein, reporting, for example, that in Vermont "the interchange of energy now attained between both industrial and public utility plants is making it possible to handle rapidly increasing loads more effectively, conserve water, avoid the importation of coal or oil on any appreciable scale, utilize labor to better advantage and, last but not least, to keep down the investment burden."[59] Likewise, an interconnection opportunity in Philadelphia "indicates that 62,000 tons of coal could be saved by holding in reserve inefficient stations," and a project in Massachusetts resulted in an annual savings of 10,000 tons of coal per year.[60]

The notion of electrification as a conservation tool held a place in public discourse throughout the mid-twentieth century. After World War I, every significant proposal for large-scale interconnection, from the "superpower" idea for the Eastern Seaboard to the north-south transmission line to link northwestern Canada to Los Angeles, described conservation benefits.[61] Congress enshrined the link between interconnection and conservation in the 1935 amendment to the Federal Power Act. The act designated a role for the Federal Power Commission in voluntary interconnections "for the purpose of assuring an abundant supply of electric energy throughout the United States with the greatest possible economy and with regard to the proper utilization and conservation of natural resources."[62] In 1964, the United States released its first comprehensive National Power Survey and proposed that a national grid promised both equity of service and conservation of resources for the American public.[63] By the 1960s, however, activists seeking to protect the country's natural resources no longer looked to power companies as allies and electrification as the solution to conservation problems.

## Conclusion

The legacy of America's diverse and unorganized power industry includes a huge and aging electrical grid, giant dams blocking every major river, hundreds of thousands of tons of coal consumed daily at power plants across the country, and a nuclear industry of indeterminate merit in the public eye. Late twentieth-century and early twenty-first-century activists have often targeted power companies as the perpetrators of environmental wrongdoing. There is no denying that the process of electrification wrought irreversible and often deeply damaging changes on the landscape. In the early 1900s, however, power companies may have been the "green" industry of their day.

Early twentieth-century conservationists and power system experts alike viewed electrification as a benefit for public health and welfare and for resource management. Electric power offered more efficient and cleaner use of the energy locked up in coal. At the same time, expanding reliance on hydroelectric power hinted at the possibility of reducing reliance on coal. Technological advancement in the design of generators and the employment of interconnections offered sophisticated tools for achieving improved energy efficiency and careful resource management. With these tools, power companies achieved real savings in the per unit consumption of coal for each kilowatt-hour of electricity produced.

Between 1900 and 1920, power system experts embraced conservation ideas as their own on several levels. Early in the century, engineers repeatedly lamented the profligate waste of finite resources like coal as well as the unused potential of renewable resources like falling water. They participated in the public discourse on conservation through technical journal publications, through appearances at high-profile conferences, through discussions at their own technical and industry-specific meetings, and through the lobbying of government leaders. Even more potently, engineers and power company managers used the terminology of conservation when describing their technical innovations, operating practices, and system achievements. Electrification proceeded with the advance of conservation movements during this period.

Through water used, waste averted, and coal saved, the power industry established its conservation credentials in the early twentieth century. At the very same time, however, the technologies and economics of electrification led to increased consumption of power and accelerated use of natural resources. So, this green industry embodied a paradox. The energy efficiencies of electrification that were so attractive to conservationists and power moguls relied entirely on an operating paradigm that called for bigger generating stations, more dams, longer transmission lines, and ever more consumption. From the investor-owned utility to the municipal generating plant, power companies made choices that conserved natural resources. Yet across this diverse industry, increased consumption was paramount, not only to the bottom line, but also to the very energy conservation strategies at play. This episode in energy history indicates that an industry's "greenness" may be intentional and measurable at a certain time, yet not so green over the long run. For power companies, the technologies and practices that led to better stewardship of natural resources depended upon a willing customer base eager to use more and more electricity.

Assessing the role of businesses in both protecting and damaging the environment is complicated by this central paradox. The term "conservation" is malleable and relative to the social context in which it has been used, and thus a company's actions may be deemed conservationist in a particular time and place. But two factors mitigate the effects of "green" choices. First, individually and across an industry, companies tend to seek market growth, so that overall consumption increases even as the per unit resource cost decreases. In the case of electrification, customers were complicit in finding more uses for "clean" energy, underscoring the importance of the consumer side of the equation. And second, in some industries, like the electric power industry, the technologies and practices that enable conservation depend on increased consumption. Though highly capitalized, not every power company in North America was, or is, profit seeking. Yet the paradox holds. The history of electrification adds details to the early project of conservation and underscores the multiple ramifications of industrial practices across the complex environmental history of America.

# PART III

# Failures and Dilemmas

# Chapter 7

# Plastic Six-Pack Rings: The Business and Politics of an Environmental Problem

*David Kinkela*

In 1959, Ougljesa Jules Poupitch, a research engineer for Illinois Tool Works (ITW), received his first patent for his design of the plastic six-pack ring. Over the next six years, Poupitch would continue to refine his design, receiving two more patents for his innovative work. It was his first design, however, that established the formula and rationale for his invention. "It is an object of this invention," he wrote "to provide such a device which is in itself, inexpensive, simple and economical to assemble with beverage cans." To emphasize the significance of his design, Poupitch described the industry standard beverage package. "Beverage cans," he wrote, "heretofore have been held together in package units by means of paper or paste board containers; or by means of metallic clips."[1]

For Poupitch, paper packaging was not only costly but also extremely inefficient. "Paper or pasteboard containers which have been sufficiently strong to be accepted commercially are unduly expensive, and require rather complicated packaging machinery. Such paper containers substantially completely 'encase' a plurality of cans, thus insulating the cans, and requiring that they be removed from the paper container for efficient refrigeration."

His plastic six-pack ring design solved these issues. Not only did his flexible plastic rings assemble beverage cans in a convenient, take-home package, but they were less costly and more "environmentally friendly." Indeed, his plastic rings offered the possibility to solve problems of waste. Poupitch's design would enable soda and beer to cool faster without the bulky cardboard packaging, thus lowering energy costs. And its slim plastic design greatly reduced the waste generated from packaging, meaning that less material would enter the waste stream. For its time, Poupitch's invention seemed like a perfect solution.[2]

Over time, however, the plastic six-pack ring emerged as an environmental problem. Six-pack rings littered American waterways, entrapping birds, fish, and other animals in its unforgiving yokes. Unlike paper substitutes, plastics did not decompose. Estimates indicate that the first generation of six-pack rings have a life span of 450 years.[3] The once-promising packaging solution proved to be an environmental pollutant.

Because of its environmental hazard, by the late 1970s, a number of state governments prohibited the use of plastic six-pack rings. By 1986, the federal government began hearings to decide the fate of the plastic six-pack ring. Through it all, however, the Hi-Cone division of Illinois Tool Works (hereafter, ITW Hi-Cone) developed new photodegradable plastic technologies to mitigate the dangers of entrapment, entanglement, and permanence. With photodegradable plastics, ITW Hi-Cone sought to address environmental concerns, while challenging new environmental legislation that threatened the company's profit margin. ITW Hi-Cone's innovation in plastic packaging and subsequent commitment to recycling programs advanced an environmental ethos within the company that has been recognized by such environmental groups as the Ocean Conservancy.[4]

This chapter examines the history of the six-pack ring, a ubiquitous piece of plastic designed to reduce shipping costs for producers and to simplify the purchase of soda and beer for consumers. Because of its cost, weight, and relative "invisibility" compared to the product being sold, the plastic six-pack ring has become an almost forgotten product, despite being the standard packing device for canned and bottled beverages. The Vitra Design Museum in Weil am Rhein, Germany, for example, celebrates the six-pack ring as one of the "hidden heroes" of modern design.[5]

Yet, the story of the six-pack ring reveals a complex history at the core of this volume: green capitalism. Indeed, the history of the plastic six-pack ring offers an intriguing case study to explore the contested meaning of waste, environmental regulation, and the corporate response to local and global environmental problems. For example, ITW Hi-Cone's response to state and federal regulation of plastic six-pack rings suggests that government regulation created the context for capitalism to go green. ITW Hi-Cone, however, began developing its innovative photodegradable plastics prior to state and federal regulation, indicating that the company sought to mitigate its environmental impact within the parameters of the free market. In other words, while actively challenging state and federal regulation of the plastic industry, ITW Hi-Cone responded to environmental problems through innovative problem solving and market solutions.

This chapter analyzes the driving forces in creating more environmental-friendly forms of capitalism—state regulation or market innovation. More significantly, it addresses a key question: can capitalism actually be green? By examining the very tensions embedded within the construct of green capitalism, the story of the plastic six-pack rings underscores changing notions of environmental problems over time, while calling attention to what Berghoff and Rome have called "the shifting legal terrain that shaped the marketplace" for plastic products in the United States. It is a story that explores the impact of plastic waste in our world and how corporations and governments attempted to remedy the waste problem at a critical moment in its very formation. In the end, however, it is a story that also reveals that neither regulation nor market innovation can fully grapple with the environmental impact and permanence of plastic waste.

## Making Bottles and Cans

As a matter of design, the plastic six-pack ring had little to no use after consumers took their beer or soda home, and thus entered into the waste system as a matter of design. Indeed, aside from packaging and moving beer and soda, the six-pack ring offers no value in and of itself. Its history, therefore, is intrinsically connected to the emergence of other disposable products, namely aluminum cans and plastic bottles.[6] This shared history reveals a complex story that undergirds the quest to provide soft drinks and beer to the marketplace as cheaply and efficiently as possible.

Unlike our own time where disposability and recyclability of plastic bottles and aluminum beverage cans are the norm, the culture of reuse was embedded in the early formation of the beverage industry. The cost of producing glass bottles, all of which were handblown until the beginning of the twentieth century, discouraged beverage producers from simply giving away bottles as the cost of doing business. According to historian Finn Arne

Jørgensen, "Beverage producers organized deposit programs . . . to buy the bottles back from the consumers." So by the early twentieth century, bottlers in concert with retail stores developed a comprehensive system to ship, sell, buy, clean, and refill bottles. On average, bottles were reused twenty-three times by the start of World War II.[7]

In 1935, however, the American Can Company began manufacturing a specially coated, disposable can for beer producers. Krueger Brewing Company in Newark, New Jersey, began test-marketing the canned beer in Richmond, Virginia, and quickly saw an increase of sales of 550 percent. Despite costing more than bottled beer, the cans did not require a deposit, which encouraged disposability over reuse. By the end of the year nearly two hundred million cans had been produced and sold. Canned beer also got a boost during World War II, as GIs enjoyed the cold taste home delivered in the relatively lightweight, unbreakable, and disposable package.[8]

Amid these modest discoveries within the beverage industry, most single-serving containers, whether glass or tin (and later aluminum), were shipped in wooden crates or boxes of twenty-four or twelve and sold individually. In 1923, however, Coca-Cola introduced and experimented with the six-pack, a convenient take-home size that we know today. Pabst brewery introduced the six-pack of cans in 1940. Nevertheless, brewers remained reluctant to sell their products in take-home carriers. By 1949, *American Brewer* estimated that only about sixty U.S. breweries used "take-home" or "carry-home" packaging (both six-packs and twelve-packs)—out of an estimated four hundred or so breweries existing at the time.[9]

For those selling for the take-home market, most six-packs (or three- or four-packs) were shipped and marketed in cardboard or paper packaging. Of those, glass remained "the dominant beverage container material in the world" up until the 1970s.[10] The production and shipping costs associated with the sales of beer and soda would lead manufacturers to look for more cost-effective means to sell and transport their product.[11]

## Making Plastic Rings

Plastics emerged after World War II as a transformative product. According to the industry's trade journal, *Modern Plastics*, the postwar period offered plastic manufacturers unlimited potential to transform the marketplace. "There is no end to the uses of plastics," the industry proclaimed in 1948, "not as replacements, not as substitutes, not as alternates, but decidedly as materials which offer characteristics and availability unattainable with metals, wood, leather, fabrics, and the like."[12]

The moldable possibilities of plastic produced much enthusiasm within the industry and across the business community. Not an animal, plant, or mineral, plastic was a "fourth" material that could be molded into seemingly anything with an endless array of color options. Visually, this idea of a new building material was perhaps best expressed in the map "Synthetica: A New Continent of Plastics," in the October 1940 edition of *Fortune*. On the new continent of Synthetica, the map's caption explained, "the countries march right out of the natural world . . . into the illimitable world of the molecule." *Fortune*'s map of the imaginary new continent is suggestive of the new chemical terrain in which anything may be possible. According to historian Jeffrey Meikle, "The map of Synthetica firmly rooted plastic in the extractive materials culture of the past," but not surprisingly ignored any mention of how the disposal of plastics may have been different from resources derived from natural sources.[13]

Nevertheless, the growth of the plastics industry in the years following the Second World War was pronounced. By 1962, the industry produced nearly 7.4 billion pounds of plastic, up from 6.3 billion pounds the year prior. The increase was attributed to the innovative uses of polyvinyl chloride (PVC)—pipes, floor coverings, foam, and surface coating—and polyethylene (PE)—wire coating, injection molding, and plastic bottles (these bottles are not the familiar water bottles of today, which are made from polyethylene terephthalate, but largely storage bottles one might find at a large wholesaler).[14] Today, the industry produces around two hundred billion pounds of plastic a year, approximately 30 percent of which is for packaging.[15]

More important, however, was the way in which the plastic industry evolved during the postwar period. Throughout the postwar period, the volumes of *Modern Plastics* call attention to the shift from providing permanent or durable plastics to disposal—or, in other words, from plastics in consumer goods, like irons, insulation, and refrigerators to disposable food and beverage containers. In 1964, *Modern Plastics* reported on the development of "thin-wall containers," claiming that the "industry [wa]s on the threshold of a market expansion that could dwarf most earlier success."[16]

It was in this context that the six-pack ring was born. Developed by the Conex Division of Illinois Tool Works in 1959, the "Hi-Cone" carrier was made from two pieces of extruded polyethylene, which allowed for the "full visibility of the lithographed cans for maximum display impact." According to *Modern Plastics*, "The Hi-Cone multiple pack stack rapidly for story display, cool up to twice as fast as paperboard carriers when refrigerated, and are not affected by water, chemicals, or detergents." And once the last can was removed, *Modern Plastics* proclaimed, "the carrier is discarded, taking only a small amount of space in the wastebasket."[17]

From a marketing, waste, and transportation perspective, the six-pack ring seemed like a perfect packaging solution. It was light, thus reducing the cost of transportation. At a cost of one cent per pack, it was nearly 35 percent cheaper than cardboard packing. And it enabled consumers to inspect the can for possible damage, while allowing for the label to become the means to attract consumers. In one case, "sales of six-packs in Hi-Cone carriers ran 123% higher than sales in conventional paperboard containers. In another area . . . test store sales of a brand packaged in Hi-Cone carriers increased 23%, while other retail outlets registered a 21% sales decline of the same brand in conventional carriers."[18] By the end of the decade, the plastic six-pack ring became the predominant packaging system for canned beverages.

Not surprisingly, throughout the late 1970s, sales of ITW Hi-Cone plastic products soared. Revenues jumped from $29.1 million in 1970 to $63.8 million in 1979. Product innovation as well as a growing domestic and international market contributed to ITW profits. By the early 1980s, the company proclaimed, "The Hi-Cone carrier was a vital contributor to the growth and profitability of ITW."[19] To add to its product array, in 1977 Hi-Cone introduced a twelve-pack carrier, which, according to ITW, offered "considerable savings over standard paperboard carriers."[20]

## Making Pollution

Disposable plastics, as well as aluminum cans and bottles, became pollution. Indeed, postwar consumerism had a profound environmental impact both near and far, leading to such initiatives as the Highway Beautification Act and the "Keep America Beautiful" campaign, the latter of which was funded by beverage giants Anheuser-Busch, PepsiCo, and Coca-Cola—all ITW Hi-Cone customers. These initiatives focused primarily on the escalating pollution problem at the local level, while serving to mitigate any culpability on the part of the beverage industry in creating a "throw-away culture."

Waste, in other words, had become an individual and a community problem, not a production, packaging, chemical, or corporate issue. Bartow

Elmore's recent work on the environmental history of the Coca-Cola Company, for example, analyzes the concept of "natural capital," while exploring the shift from reusable bottles to single-use aluminum cans and plastic bottles, claiming that recycling programs created to alleviate waste and the public relations problem for the soft-drink giant were "built from the ground up, largely by city governments and largely with taxpayer dollars."[21]

Yet the problem and impacts of plastic waste proved to be more complex. Wind carried lightweight plastic bags far and wide. Water transported floating plastic into and through river systems and into the world's oceans and seas. And soils were incapable of breaking down the chemical structure of man-made plastics. Indeed, unlike animal, mineral, or vegetable, the "fourth" great building block of the twentieth century had serious long-term consequences that were foreseen but not completely understood.

For scholars, scientists, and social critics, pollution represented a uniquely, if not depressing, symbol of American postwar prosperity. In his influential 1961 book *The Beer Can by the Highway: Essays on What's American About America*, scholar and social critic John A. Kouwenhoven, for example, expressed his dismay at "the sodden banks of garbage between which rivers of industrial waste flow into the sea, [and] at the beer cans strewn along the shoulders of our highways." Artist John McHale lamented about the fleeting nature of the disposable society in his 1967 essay "The Plastic Parthenon," "in which astronomical numbers of artifacts are mass produced, circulated, and consumed." Futurist Alvin Toffler also extolled the dangers of a rapidly changing world in his 1970 book *Future Shock*. While concerned about how the speed of technological change affected the world, Toffler also commented that "the flight against pollution, aesthetic blight, crowding, noise and dirt well clearly absorb tremendous energies." And in his 1971 book *Design for the Real World*, industrial designer and social critic Victor Papanek condemned designers for their shortsighted and profit-making motives. "Over and over I want to stress in pollution," Papanek wrote, "the designer is more heavily implicated than most people." Papanek, however, had a soft spot for biodegradable plastics.[22]

Similarly, environmentalists forcefully condemned the narrow vision of industrial designers, capitalists, and consumers. In his 1971 best seller *The Closing Circle*, Barry Commoner wrote, "Huge numbers of chaotically varied plastic objects have been produced. Apart from the aesthetic consequences, there are serious ecological ones. As the ecosphere is increasingly cluttered with plastic objects nearly infinite in their shape and size, they will—through the workings of nature and the laws of probability—find their way into increasingly narrow nooks and crannies in the natural world."[23]

By the early 1970s, stories of birds, dead fish, and entangled seals and turtles called attention to the scale of the plastic waste problem. A 1973 *New York Times* article on bird watching indicated that "discarded plastic rings that are used to bind together six-pack beverage cans often become fatal or near fatal nooses for waterfowl, including Canada geese. Some fish have been trapped in this manner also." In 1974, *Field and Stream* reported on "plastic, six-pack beverage carriers in which ducks, geese, and small animals sometimes get caught." To emphasize the scope and unattractive nature of plastic pollution, the article also indicated, "A wild flower beside a trail does not look so pretty when it grows up through a plastic beverage carrier."[24]

Throughout the 1970s, the scale of the plastic pollution problem also increased. Plastic pollution was no longer a local or national problem, but one global in scope. And the oceans, once considered immune to the wastefulness of modern society despite the long history as being a dumping ground for human waste, became part of a growing debate over the meaning of waste, disposability, and plastics in the environment.

In 1972, for example, *Science* published the findings of two Woods Hole marine biologists found high concentrations of plastic particle waste in the Sargasso Sea. Their study indicated that "the source of the particles may have been the dumping of waste from cities or by cargo and passenger ships. However, no metropolitan dumping occurs in the areas sampled," although some samples were collected "within major shipping lanes from Europe to Central America and the Panama Canal." By 1973, the journal *Ocean Management* asked, "Pollution of the oceans: an international problem?" Another report noted "plastic materials accumulating in Narragansett Bay." And in 1975, the *Marine Pollution Bulletin* published a report titled, "Plastic Cups Found in Fish."[25]

Initially, the international community responded to ocean plastic waste by attempting to regulate ocean dumping. In 1972, Intergovernmental Conference on the Convention on the Dumping of Wastes at Sea drafted the Convention on the Prevention of Marine Pollution by Dumping of Wastes and Other Matter, called the "London Convention," which created an international framework "to prevent marine pollution caused by dumping" and required signatories to "harmonize their policies in this regard."[26] This agreement did not take into account pollution streams from land-based sources. A year later, working under the auspices of the International Marine Organization, delegates drafted the International Convention for the Prevention of Pollution from Ships, which was designed to reduce ocean pollution, including oil, noxious liquid substance, exhaust, and waste disposal. For example, Annex V of the agreement called MARPOL—short for "Marine Pollution"—prohibited oceangoing vessels from dumping all waste into the sea, including plastic waste, and made provisions for creating port reception waste facilities. Amended in 1978, Annex V prevented the dumping of "all plastics, domestic wastes, cooking oil, incinerator ashes, operational wastes and fishing gear."[27]

MARPOL, however, did not (and does not) regulate the waste present throughout the oceans, nor did it address how to prohibit the floating plastic that originated from land-based sources. Despite its international scope and regulatory approach to reduce plastics entering into the ocean world, the inability to address land-based plastic waste streams or recommend possible remediation efforts for the plastic debris already present limited MARPOL's effectiveness in promoting ocean health.

Throughout the 1970s and 1980s, biologists, ecologists, oceanographers, and chemists, continued to study and work on the escalating problem. In 1984, National Marine Fisheries Service organized a series of international workshops to examine "the source and quantification of marine debris; the impact of debris on marine resources; and the fate of marine debris in the world's oceans. Because of the broad public interest in the topic, particularly as regards the entanglement issue, a fourth, general session was held to focus on identification of management needs." Aside from general proposals to raise public awareness and to study the issue more thoroughly, the 580-page report also proposed that disposal of plastics should be regulated that results "in high negative impact on resources" and scientists should "investigate use of biodegradable materials in gear construction and the recycling of net materials."[28]

Other studies continued to reveal the scope of the problem. In 1986, the Northwest and Alaska Fisheries Center reported on a national beach cleanup effort in eleven coastal states. The coordinated effort identified an array of plastic debris washing up on beaches throughout the United States—six-pack holders, plastic containers, straps, fishing line, plastic nets, and bags. Spearheaded by local community groups, the consolidation of information gathered by the Northwest and Alaska Fisheries Center exposed the ecological connections between land and water through the disposal and migration of plastic waste. To emphasize the plight of marine animals and the environ-mental activism of beach cleanups, the report stated, "Going after marine debris as 'litter' does not have the same impact and gain the same public sup-port as focusing on the issue of entanglement and ingestion by fish and wildlife."[29] Protecting nature, it seems, made more of an impact than pick-ing up "litter."

## Making New Plastics/Creating New Laws

The negative publicity resulting from stories of entrapped marine animals in the yokes of plastic six-pack rings encouraged Hi-Cone and other plastic manufacturers to develop a second-generation of disposable plastics. As early as 1975, Hi-Cone chemists developed photodegradable six-ring carri-ers, which broke down into smaller and smaller pieces with exposure to the sun. Marketed under the "E/CO" trademark, whose acronym stood for the copolymer "ethylene carbon monoxide," Hi-Cone recognized the economic value of being "environmentally" friendly.[30] Indeed, the new Hi-Cone six-pack ring not only made a future where entangled marine animals might be a thing of the past, but it increased the company's position within the bever-age packaging industry.

Somewhat surprisingly, given ITW's corporate culture of innovation, the E/CO ring received scant attention within the company. Throughout the 1970s and 1980s, ITW's annual reports did not identify the photodegradable six-pack rings as a major technological achievement. In fact, it was not acknowledged at all. Instead, ITW highlighted how the company "reduced costs of production permitting lower costs to the users," created carriers "which offers the advantage of using less material," made "a series of changes to further minimize material used," or improved design "to reduce material used and to meet the changing packaging requirements of both cans and plas-tic bottles."[31] For ITW, pollution was about volume, not a product's lifecycle. According to one ITW executive, "the less material, the less solid waste."[32]

Volume was a critical factor in ITW Hi-Cone's calculus of waste. From the first patent application to the decades that followed, ITW understood its plastic six-pack rings took only a small fraction of the landfill space required for other packing options. It was a point of emphasis that ITW Hi-Cone made consistently to underscore its commitment to environmental steward-ship. It was also sound logic if all waste was the same. But plastics, like other industrial and chemical compounds, were (and are) inorganic compounds, producing new categories of waste that challenged older notions of trash and disposability. The proliferation of industrial chemicals in the postwar world made waste a question not only of volume but also of toxicity, risks, and time.[33]

Moreover, Hi-Cone's innovations were not entirely altruistic or market driven. Government action also was a prod. Led by the State of Vermont, which prohibited the use of disposable, nondegradable six-pack rings in 1977, pressure from a number of state governments escalated. Concern about local environmental impacts of six-pack rings propelled landlocked and coastal states to assess and regulate plastic six-pack rings. By 1987, eleven states had banned nondegradable six-pack rings.[34]

Nationally, the debate about plastic ocean waste intensified as well. In 1987, President Ronald Reagan, through the White House Domestic Policy Council, convened an Interagency Task Force on Persistent Marine Debris. Charged to "assess the problem and the need for research, identify potential reduction measures, and consider alternative actions to address the problem of plastic marine pollution," the task force brought together representatives from seven departments and four federal agencies to review existing data and make recommendations a year later. The task force made five recommendations—increase federal leadership, coordinate efforts with state and private industry, vigorously implement all laws related to marine debris, conduct additional research on the sources of marine debris, and promote beach cleanup and monitoring. It did not call for additional federal regulation.[35] Given the administration's pro-business philosophy, this was not surprising.

Even as the Interagency Task Force launched its fact-finding work, Senator Frank Lautenberg of New Jersey introduced legislation limiting plastic waste, which was titled the Marine Plastic Pollution Research and Control Act. Lautenberg remarked, "The evidence continues to grow about the entanglement of marine animals in plastic debris and the ingestion of plastics by marine organisms." The bill, he claimed, "would specifically prohibit disposal of plastic products. Such prohibition would apply to our waters, including the exclusive economic zone 200 miles from our coasts. It would also apply to disposal in areas, such as beaches and landfills, where such material could be washed or blown into the water." It also required the Environmental Protection Agency to conduct a six-month study to determine "the feasibility of using alternative products for . . . making . . . degradable plastics [which were] determined to cause significant harm to marine life, wildlife, birds, or their habitat."[36] Finally, the bill would ratify Annex V of MARPOL, ensuring U.S. compliance with the international accord.

Despite these state, national, and international measures, public and political scrutiny continued to focus on the plastic six-pack ring. In December 1987, Senator Quentin Burdick of North Dakota introduced a bill (S. 1986, the Plastic Pollution Control Act of 1987) that would require that all "plastic ring carrier devices be degradable."[37] The bill was predicated on two discoveries: first was the growing body of scientific literature indicating the hazards plastic six-pack rings posed to marine wildlife; and second was the emergence of new plastic chemical formulas that potentially could photodegrade or biodegrade after disposal. Operating from two distinct scientific disciplines, chemists and biologists sought to both recognize and rectify an ecological problem that had local, national, and international implications. However, despite a shared purpose, debates over the federal regulation of plastic six-pack rings underscore profound differences in how to protect of marine ecosystems based on the science at hand.

The subcommittee hearing on the hazards of plastic six-pack rings was one arena where these differences were most pronounced. Held on July 26, 1988, the Subcommittee on Fisheries and Wildlife Conservation and the Environment of the Committee on Merchant Marine and Fisheries and the Subcommittee on Transportation, Tourism, and Hazardous Materials of the Committee on Energy and Commerce invited representatives from the plastics industry, environmental organizations, and federal environmental regulatory agencies to debate the merit or limits of the law. According to Rep. Gerry Studds (D-Mass.), chairman of the Subcommittee on Fisheries and Wildlife Conservation and the Environment, "The six-pack ring epitomizes the plastic pollution problem: a highly successful product that is functional and durable, and yet ugly and deadly when improperly discarded."[38] Barbara Mandula, a staff scientist for the Environmental Protection Agency (EPA) commented separately that "thousands of birds and other animals die accidentally each year when they encounter such plastic debris as strapping bands, six-pack rings and fishing line and nets."[39] Led by Lautenberg and Burdick, the federal government sought to "ban the disposal of plastic products in our waters and on beaches and landfills."[40]

Members of the scientific and environmental community testified on behalf of the bill. Al Manville, a senior staff wildlife biologist from Defenders of Wildlife, claimed that the law would "send a message not only to the plastics' industry, but to product users and the general public that Congress does consider degradability a viable option."[41] Manville appeared on behalf of the Entanglement Network, an affiliation of environmental organizations that sought to publicize the science of plastic marine pollution. In submitting his testimony, Manville's written statement recognized the challenges of understanding the scope of the plastic debris problem from a scientific perspective. He wrote, "Although scientifically documented evidence of entanglement is often anecdotal—most deaths going unobserved by man— there are rough estimates of annual mortality worldwide, including at least 100,000 marine mammals and 1 million seabirds that are believed to die in plastic debris, including six-pack yokes as well as nets and net fragments. Death is by drowning, from exhaustion, by starvation, by strangulation, from infection, or by predators."[42]

For its part, ITW and the plastics industry expressed its commitment to reduce waste but rejected the premise of the proposed law. Mike Hudson, the vice president of public affairs of Illinois Tool Works, claimed, "One of the reasons the customers have adopted our product is because of its light weight and relative lack of material. So we think already the carrier in and of it- self is making a major contribution right now to reducing the amount of solid waste that stems from packaging, particularly of beverage cans." In fact, Hudson told the subcommittee, ITW "did not jump at this idea of degradable plastic quickly." According to Hudson, the company "did a lot of investigation and looked at a variety of different kinds of systems during the 1970s." ITW "tested and produced" the E/CO product and "knew it would work through the commercial environment prior to the passage of the first state law which was the State of Vermont, in 1976."[43]

From ITW's perspective, the Plastic Pollution Control Act of 1987 "could be interpreted to say that you can only make degradable carriers." Given ITW's expansion into international markets, the company expressed con- cern that they would not be able "to supply them with non-degradable carriers. . . . We would lose that export market." Despite ITW's innovative manufacturing process that made photodegradable plastic six-pack rings possible, the company sought to limit regulation because it was concerned about market competition. "The product," Hudson reported to the subcom- mittee, "has enjoyed a great deal of success . . . [but] it is not without its competition." Since the E/CO carriers cost more than 6 to 8 percent more than the Hi-Cone plastic six-pack carrier, ITW believed that its customers would reject paying more for six-pack rings if given the choice. Mandat- ing photodegradable rings nationally, ITW argued, would put them at a competitive disadvantage for other packing options, including paperboard or shrink-wrap.[44]

Competition, both domestic and global, shaped ITW Hi-Cone's thinking about federal regulation. Indeed, ITW's response to federal regulation was not surprising. Beginning with its 1976 Annual Report, ITW introduced a new feature into its annual reports, titled "The Business Environment." In it, ITW executives called attention to "uncontrolled government growth" and the "tremendous costs associated with the need to comply with the regulations generated by the never-ending array of new agencies and programs." Calling for the "proper balance between the public and productive sectors" to be "restored and then maintained," ITW leadership challenged the cost and imposition of the regulatory state. Subsequent reports (in 1977 and 1978) drew on the Federalist Papers and Adam Smith's *Wealth of Nations*.[45] By 1983, however, these overtly political statements dissipated from ITW's annual reports. Nevertheless, the company's scorn for federal regulation underscored its response to the Plastic Pollution Control Act of 1987.

On October 28, 1988, President Reagan signed the Plastic Pollution Control Act of 1987, which required all plastic six-pack rings produced in the United States beginning in 1990 to be photodegradable. Despite its protests and fears that the legislation would impact its profit margin, ITW Hi-Cone did not lose its market share. Instead, the company continued to innovate, developing carriers and application machines for plastics bottles, which were first utilized by Coca-Cola by the mid-1980s.[46] What's more, beginning in 1992, ITW Hi-Cone sold only photodegradable rings to foreign buyers.

## Questioning Degradable Plastics

Despite state, national, and international regulation, plastics and plastic six-pack rings continued to flow into the oceans. And the search for technological solutions to offset this growing environmental problem grew more complex, politically, scientifically, and environmentally. Degradable six-pack rings were clearly superior to earlier generations of plastic carriers, but they were not without their problems. Concern mounted over whether they degraded at all. And if they did degrade, what happened to the degraded pieces of plastic?

Shortly after passage of the Plastic Pollution Control Act of 1987, environmentalists challenged the notion of degradable plastics. While Hi-Cone produced photodegradable plastics, other plastic manufacturers began marketing "biodegradable plastics," which incorporated sugar or cornstarch to promote decomposition. In 1987, Jeanne Wirka from the Environmental Action Foundation, called degradable plastics "a hoax." Richard Denison, a senior scientist from the Environmental Defense Fund argued that "degradable is a warm and fuzzy word, like organic and natural. . . . The concern is that if people think you can toss plastic away and it magically disappears, they will just toss it away." And following the release of the scientific report on the degradability of plastics in 1991 by Cornell University professor William J. Jewell, Nancy Wolf of the Environmental Action Coalition called degradable plastics "a marking ploy whose time has run out."[47]

While degradable plastic rings certainly reduced the potential for entanglement, other problems existed. First, photodegradable six-ring carriers break apart in one to six months, making them dangerous for wildlife and marine animals unfortunate enough to come into contact with them before they degrade. And second, as plastic breaks into smaller and smaller pieces, some tiny enough to be ingested by even small marine animals, the ecological impact of plastics in the ocean is not only pronounced but unknown. In 1989, Daryl Ditz, a chemical engineer at the Cornell Waste Management Institute, reported, "As the molecules become smaller, they become more mobile. They may migrate or become volatile."[48] Since then, scientists have discovered that these smaller pieces of plastic also have become magnets to other pollutants, like DDT and other persistent organic pollutants, which further exacerbates the problem.[49] The ecological impacts of plastics have only begun to be understood.

## Conclusion

In 2012, celebrating the company's one hundred years of innovation, ITW published a retrospective history. In it, ITW acknowledged how the Hi-Cone carrier "revolutionized the beverage industry, noting, "More recent innovations have made the carriers photodegradable, recyclable, and non-toxic."[50] Not surprisingly, the Plastic Pollution Control Act of 1987, or any other regulatory action, was not mentioned as part of the company's history. The packaging revolution came from within the company.

Regardless, ITW Hi-Cone continues to promote itself as a green company. A recent Hi-Cone publication on sustainable development identified the six-pack ring as "highly sustainable packaging." "Because the Hi-Cone ring carrier is so light in weight," the company claimed, "there are lower overall environmental burdens for production and there are less pounds of post consumer packaging waste to manage at its end of life." Essentially, ITW Hi-Cone simply reasserts the same calculus it used during the 1980s, "Less material going into landfills is better for everyone."[51]

Not only has ITW Hi-Cone secured its dominance in the beverage packing industry, but it has also promoted a vision of good corporate citizen. In 1999, ITW Hi-Cone developed the "Ring Leader Recycling Program," a program that encouraged community groups to collect ring carriers for "open loop recycling" by the company. According to a company publication, "more than 12,000 schools, business and groups around the world have participated in the free Ring Leader Recycling Program and helped to save the environment."[52]

ITW Hi-Cone's transformation from a reluctant producer of photodegradable six-pack rings to corporate citizen recognized for its recycling initiatives is rather remarkable. This change has not been without its causes. And as I have shown in this chapter, technological innovations, market demands, state regulation, and changing conceptions of waste have all contributed to the changing fortunes of the Hi-Cone six-pack ring. However, this is all part of a larger story.

Packaging generates an enormous amount of waste. According to a 2015 report *Waste and Opportunity*, sponsored by the National Resources Defense Council, "Less than 14 percent of plastic packaging—the fastest-growing form of packaging—is recycled."[53] Like the six-pack ring, most packaging is simply designed to facilitate the movement of goods from the producer to consumer. Once that is done, packaging becomes waste. In our own time, industrial designers in the spirit of ITW's Ougljesa Jules Poupitch have made impressive strides to reduce packaging waste, while using more sustainable materials to facilitate the flow of goods around the world. Packaging can become environmentally sound.

With the advent of plastic packaging, however, the long-term consequences of this waste stream are more pronounced. Plastic waste remains a serious, global environmental problem, which will impact the natural world well into the future. Within the context of the plastic pollution problem, the story of Hi-Cone beverage rings could be read as a success story. Photodegradable six-pack rings are superior to their predecessors. But the story is not a success. Even though photodegradable plastics break down into smaller pieces, they do not degrade. Plastics attract pollutants like PCBs and DDT, creating new forms of toxic waste that were largely unknown decades earlier. Birds, fish, and other organisms also ingest smaller pieces of plastics that have long-term ecological impact that scientists are only beginning to uncover.[54]

So despite the corporate and legislative actions that made plastic six-pack rings more environmentally friendly, chemistry and industrial design affirm another story. Green capitalism may not be compatible with industries or products that are based on disposability, fossil fuels, or industrial chemistry. The ecological impacts of plastics—both known and unknown—suggest that no matter how innovative or rule-bound the production of products like plastic six-pack rings have become, they are inherently in conflict with the ambitions of green capitalism.

# The Rise and Fall of an Ecostar: Green Technology Innovation and Marketing as Regulatory Obstruction

*Leif Fredrickson*

For several days in May 1994, dozens of electric vehicles zipped across the northeastern United States in the Tour de Sol, a "real world" race with drivers obeying laws and navigating traffic. The rules emphasized endurance, efficiency, and reliability because the overarching goal of the race was to "bring practical electric vehicles into everyday use." In 1989, its first year, only six cars entered the Tour. But by 1994, fifty vehicles queued at the starting line, and the race had attracted its first entrant by a major automobile company— Ford's Ecostar. The Ecostar was an impressive electric vehicle on paper. Its sodium-sulfur battery yielded a top speed of seventy miles per hour and a one-hundred-mile range. And the race proved it was a real-world electric vehicle: the Ecostar won the Tour de Sol. It was a triumph for Ford. The company's marketing agency went into high gear publicizing the win. Oddly enough, however, Ford hoped the win would *curb* what it saw as excessive enthusiasm about electric vehicles.[1]

Ford's Ecostar strategy was the result of asymmetries of information between businesses, consumers, and regulators. In many contexts, businesses had informational advantages that they could use to influence, or manipulate, consumers and regulators. Influence was built on credibility. But the perception, among regulators, consumers, or the public in general, that they were being manipulated, not just influenced, could undermine the credibility of business. That made it hard for businesses to influence consumers and regulatory policy. Businesses might then seek to rebuild credibility in order to regain influence. In this essay, I show how the Ford Motor Company tried to do just that in an elaborate strategy that involved developing, testing, and marketing the Ecostar electric vehicle.

The regulatory policy Ford tried to influence was California's 1990 zero-emission vehicle (ZEV) mandate. This mandate required the major automobile companies to sell a quota of ZEVs in the state, beginning in 1998. The automobile companies vigorously objected to what they saw as an unreasonable policy, and they used various strategies to combat it. In particular, they tried to get the chief regulator, the California Air Resources Board (CARB), to revise or eliminate the ZEV policy. But for years, CARB held fast.

Ford tried another strategy. In the context of public and regulator distrust, Ford sought to improve, test, and market an electric vehicle, the Ecostar, that would demonstrate that the company was genuinely pursuing electric vehicle (EV) technology and that it was, in fact, the leader in that technology. With the help of a green marketing pioneer, the J. Walter Thompson Company (JWT), Ford publicized its EV. But Ford did not hire JWT to sell the Ecostar. It hired the company to sell the idea that the Ecostar was the most advanced electric vehicle in order for Ford to appear as a credible and authoritative expert on environmental technology. With public trust, Ford hoped it could undermine CARB's ZEV mandate and shape public policy more broadly.

## The Zero-Emission Vehicle Mandate

In 1990, California's Air Resources Board promulgated a "zero-emission vehicle" mandate. It required that by 1998, 2 percent of the vehicles sold by major automobile companies in the state could emit nothing. The mandate pushed the quota to 5 percent for 2001 and 10 percent for 2003. As a part of a larger "low-emission vehicle" (LEV) program created by the state, the ZEV policy initially garnered little attention. But it soon became known as one of the most aggressive and controversial environmental regulations in the history of the United States.[2]

The LEV program was the outcome of California's long, and often failed, attempt to improve its air quality. California cities like Los Angeles had long struggled with air pollution as a result of their geography, climate, and heavy automobile use. The state had been a leader in trying to deal with air pollution since the 1940s. But while state and national regulations on air pollution had improved some of the worst conditions, air pollution continued to be a serious problem. Automobiles had become cleaner, but as population and affluence increased, people bought more cars and drove them more miles. Air pollution districts in Southern California in particular were not able to meet national air quality standards, which meant that the state risked losing federal funds. In 1988, the legislature passed the California Clean Air Act and that, along with a bill to study alternative fuels, gave CARB the authority and impetus to create regulations for a Low Emission Vehicle Program. The program relied on the idea of affecting *average* tailpipe emissions by requiring car companies to sell vehicles that fell into different emissions categories: transitional-low emissions, low emissions, ultra-low emissions and, the most stringent category, zero emissions.[3]

The ZEV program was an extraordinarily assertive law, combining a strong technology-forcing mandate with a strict production schedule. Technically, the ZEV policy was a performance-based approach that set an environmental standard that businesses had to attain, without specifying what technology should be used to attain the standard (as opposed to a technology-based standard that required the adoption of some particular existing technology). In theory, car companies could develop any kind of technology they wanted to meet the zero-emissions standard. In reality, there was only one technology that was close to being widely marketable and could also meet these standards: battery electric vehicles (BEVs). The ZEV policy thus forced automobile companies toward innovation (as performance-based standards were intended to do), but forced them in a very specific direction (as technology-based standards did).

CARB's ZEV policy was developed in the context of notable improvements in electric-vehicle technology. Electric vehicles emerged with steam- and gasoline-powered vehicles in the nineteenth century, but their development and use dried up after the 1920s. In the 1970s, electric-vehicle research crept back in slowly, as companies responded to air pollution standards and the oil crisis. Independent inventors also began developing electric vehicles.[4] More immediately for CARB, research in the late 1980s funded by Southern California Edison showed that BEVs were a promising technology for reducing air pollution.[5]

Despite a lot of knowledge about batteries and electric vehicles, CARB was still at an inevitable information disadvantage regarding how much technological innovation and change automobile companies could bear. This was a position regulators increasingly found themselves in in the postwar era. Tort law, statutes, and regulations had long struggled to balance the benefits created by businesses against the social costs and risks that resulted from the capitalist pursuit of profit. In the 1960s and 1970s, that balance shifted more toward protecting consumers, workers, and the environment from the externalities of business. Some environmental statutes, like the 1972 Clean Water Act, contained provisions that focused on the benefits of regulations to the nearly complete exclusion of cost. Others, like the 1970 Clean Air Act, the original technology-forcing policy, put businesses on a brisk march of technological change.[6]

The power of environmental regulations, however, depended on knowledge of the regulated industry. Regulators had to set standards that were neither too weak, and hence pointless, nor unreasonably strong, thus liable to undermine the regulators' authority. Industries, however, could outmatch regulators in expert capacity. Moreover, businesses had knowledge of many practices, technologies, and forecasts that were not available to regulators. That meant that industries could manipulate regulators or outmaneuver them in the court of public opinion in order to eliminate or weaken regulations.

But manipulation was a double-edged sword because it resulted in regulators (and a public) that did not trust the proclamations of businesses about regulations. Some of the most infamous stories of this type featured the automotive and oil industries, who claimed that the adoption of the catalytic converters fuel-efficiency standards were impossible goals that would sink the industry. By the 1990s the narrative of industries who claimed disingenuously that they could not accommodate new regulations and technologies was as familiar as was the story's ending: in a matter of years, commercially viable technologies belied the impossibility of these accommodations.[7]

The ZEV mandate was a direct outcome of this dynamic. Automobile companies may have been experts on ZEV technology and its marketability, but they were not reliable experts. "The key balancing act," one CARB official stated, was to "push hard enough to [accelerate] investments, but not so hard that they [CARB] lost their credibility." CARB thus sought a ZEV goal that it could defend on scientific grounds, but one that would also force the auto companies to develop ZEVs at a faster pace. The ZEV mandate included a review process by which CARB could adjust its mandate if it believed it had gotten it wrong. But the car companies would have to prove the goal was not attainable.[8]

Although CARB did not trust the auto companies, it relied on clues from these companies, in addition to its own assessments, to infer what technological goals were possible. Here, another informational problem contributed to the mandate. As in other industries, automobile manufacturers guarded their technological research (and marketing analyses), sometimes hiding their technological progress and sometimes overstating it. At a Los Angeles auto show in January 1990, General Motors (GM) chairman Roger Smith introduced the Impact, a totally electric vehicle, by saying that "issues like global climate warming and energy conservation demand fundamental change from all industries in all nations." Smith did not emphasize that the Impact was only a prototype at the time, and GM subsequently put a team together to see if the vehicle could realistically become part of GM's lineup.[9] The car, in other words, was not nearly as ready for production as GM implied. But GM wanted to present itself as a technological leader, to hype its brand to the American public and scare its rivals. And it wanted to present itself as a company pursuing environmentally friendly cars. What the showing was not intended as was an attempt to influence policy, and in that sense the gambit backfired. After unveiling the Impact, Smith reportedly asked a CARB spokesman, "You guys aren't actually going to make us build that car, are you?"[10] At the time, CARB was already considering a ZEV mandate, but it read the confidence with which GM unveiled its EV as a sign that the mandate was indeed reasonable. CARB understood that EVs were not yet a commercially viable product, but the Impact and their other research indicated to them that by 1998 they could be.[11]

Automotive companies were not opposed to producing EVs, so long as they were profitable, and indeed they had been researching and developing EV technology to varying degrees.[12] General Motors was well ahead of the other major auto companies with the Impact. Chrysler was the farthest behind, with Ford in the middle. Ford had a long history of innovating in electric and alternative fuel vehicles, however. Henry Ford's mass production of the Model T dramatically reduced the price of gasoline-powered automobiles, helping to put the final nail in the coffin of the first round of electric vehicles in the early 1900s. But in the 1960s Ford started investigating electric vehicles again and made significant progress with a novel sodium-sulfur (NAS) battery. Ford continued developing electric vehicles and began to dabble in hybrids in the 1970s. These experiments were promising enough that research continued. At the same time, Ford's marketing research suggested that light-duty vehicles for fleets held the most promise, and it oriented its electric vehicle program toward producing this type of vehicle. In the 1980s, Ford developed an Aerostar van with an NAS battery that could achieve a one-hundred-mile range.[13]

Although the automobiles companies did not oppose EVs per se, the ZEV mandate alarmed the auto companies, who saw it as unrealistic and a threat to their profits. California had a huge automobile market, and the state was extremely culturally influential, but the implications went even further. According to the 1990 Clean Air Act, California was the only state allowed to adopt air quality standards more stringent than the federal law, but other states could adopt California's standards rather than the federal standards. During its initial passage, the ZEV mandate caught the automobile companies in a moment of distraction as they focused their attention on the major components of the Clean Air Act in 1990 and other California pollution regulations.[14] After the ZEV mandate passed, however, the auto companies shifted into high gear, researching the possibilities of EV production and strategizing about how to soften or rollback the ZEV mandate.

The auto companies took different strategies for researching and creating EVs. General Motors continued to focus its research on the Impact, later renamed the EV1, a two-door, sporty, and somewhat futuristic looking electric car designed for commuters. The Impact ran on conventional lead acid batteries, but it was an entirely new vehicle, built from the ground up. Chrysler, the runt of the Big Three, did the smallest amount of research of the group, focusing largely on retrofitting one of its vans, now dubbed the TEVan, with a conventional lead-acid battery. Ford reinvigorated its EV research, falling in between the ground-up approach of GM and the retrofitting of Chrysler. Ford used an Escort van body with an NAS battery to build its Ecostar, an EV designed to be used in fleets by companies or agencies that drove in cities (that is, not commuters or individual owners). With the help of the Department of Energy, the Big Three also formed the United States Advanced Battery Consortium (USABC), an endeavor that resulted in the sharing of some ideas but which was also hobbled by questions of proprietary information and funding.[15]

While the auto companies did start pouring more funding into research, and ultimately into producing some EVs, they also pursued strategies for countering the mandate. Specific reactions and strategies varied, however. Their responses differed by company and by the groups they tried to influence to undermine the ZEV mandate. The companies all engaged directly with CARB, fighting expertise with expertise. The problem was, however, that CARB, an agency that prided itself on independence, did not trust the auto companies.[16] So long as the evidence for the viability of the ZEV mandate remained equivocal, CARB gave the impression that it would not budge. The auto companies thus looked for other ways to influence the debate.

Outside of CARB, the auto companies banded together to fight the ZEV policy in the courts, the bureaucracies, and the legislature. As northeastern states adopted the ZEV mandate, the auto companies sued in court, sometimes with success. The auto companies also helped spearhead the Electric Transportation Coalition (ETC), an organization promoting the interests of industries who stood to benefit from electric transport, including utilities, automobile companies, and battery and metals manufacturers. The ETC contained dozens of powerful corporations from across the United States. The coalition pressed both for greater flexibility in the ZEV mandate and for more government subsidies for research on EVs.[17]

Although the Big Three all opposed the mandate, joining in lawsuits and the ETC, they also diverged in important ways in their strategies of opposition. GM believed that it would be able to negotiate with CARB to change the mandate in later years, and it believed there would be breakthroughs in batteries. Thus GM took a relatively accommodating position. Chrysler and Ford initially worried that strong opposition would hurt their public image.[18] But Ford's opposition increased. By 1994, it saw Chrysler and GM as taking a "promotional" approach to electric vehicles in contrast to its aggressive opposition to the ZEV mandate. Internally, Ford acknowledged that the public perceived Chrysler and GM as more "environmentally proactive" than Ford. Internal memos show that Ford did take an increasingly hard-line stance against electric vehicles.[19] As one Ford representative wrote at a strategizing meeting at the Electric Transportation Coalition in 1994, "Our task is to show beyond question of a doubt that EV's proponents are the ones who can't be trusted."[20]

## ZEV Green Technology and Marketing

Ford turned to the public to try to undermine, in a more subtle fashion than stated in closed-door meetings, the credibility of EV proponents. To do that, Ford hired the advertising giant J. Walter Thompson (JWT). But here Ford and its marketing agency confronted another trust problem: consumers, and the public more broadly, had grown wary of green marketing, even as that approach to marketing expanded in the 1990s.

In the decades after environmentalism emerged in the postwar era, businesses used green marketing to sell their products, enhance their public image, and influence policy. In many ways, green marketing was highly successful. Burgeoning in the 1970s, it flourished by the 1990s as consumers and businesses embraced it as never before. But problems haunted the idea of buying green, in particular whether consumers and environmental activists could trust the environmental claims of businesses about themselves or their products. As green marketers like JWT discovered in the 1980s and early 1990s, consumers were often confused by or distrustful of green marketing. It was not clear to consumers what labels like "biodegradable" or "natural" meant, or if they meant anything at all.[21] How could green consumers, a dispersed interest group with little capacity to investigate particular green-marketing claims, know if products or companies were actually "green"? Environmentalists and regulators concerned about manipulation, and businesses who had a genuinely green product to sell, sought to overcome this problem in two ways in the 1990s. One was third-party certification, in which a nongovernmental organization (NGO) would vet the claims of businesses, using ratings or explicitly defined labels. Another was government regulation. In the early 1990s, the Federal Trade Commission developed and held hearings regarding the standardization of green-marketing terms. In 1991, it cited three corporations for misleading consumers with green advertising. Although far from foolproof, these regulations did curb some of the most brazen attempts at greenwashing.[22]

But what if a business did not want to sell a product so much as an idea? What if it wanted to sell the idea that certain government regulations were unreasonable? Third-party certifications and regulations were not as amenable to ensuring trust in these cases.

Nevertheless, auto companies sought to court public opinion in their favor. The Big Three auto companies all used some form of marketing to prop up their green images during the ZEV controversy, but they also used marketing in other ways. GM's green marketing of the Impact in 1990 resulted in the unintended consequence of supporting the ZEV mandate. In the aftermath, GM attempted to reel in its bold rhetoric about the Impact and the promise of EVs. This strategy also reflected dissension within GM about whether the Impact would be viable commercially in 1998.

Ford took a different strategy. It feared it would be forced to build subpar EVs with lead-acid batteries because an NAS-battery-powered EV would not be commercially viable by 1998. Instead of downplaying its technology, Ford hoped that by aggressively pursuing, testing, and demonstrating that it had the best EV technology, it could regain public influence as a trustworthy expert. Ford developed a marketing strategy that it hoped would at once boost its green image, position it as the leader in green technology, and at the very same time draw upon that stature to roll back the rising tide of ZEV mandates.[23] Put another way, Ford faced two forms of distrust: The first was that it was an interested party and therefore unreliable. This was CARB's unyielding position. The second was that Ford, and perhaps other auto companies, had not established their expertise because they were simply not far enough along in their research to speak authoritatively. The public, at least in Ford's estimation, believed Ford was untrustworthy for both reasons, so the company wanted to show that it was both "green" and a technological expert in order to sway the public to its position. What Ford really highlighted with regard to its "greenness," however, was that the technologies it was pursuing would be good for the environment. It shrank away from presenting the company as one driven by environmental values rather than profits for fear it would come off as disingenuous.[24] The strategy that ultimately emerged, therefore, was one that emphasized Ford's green technology expertise and the positive environmental consequences of that technology.

An incipient form of this strategy was evident in 1992 when Ford made a presentation to show to civic groups, the media, and others "involved with AFVs [alternative fuel vehicles] and the environment." The presentation included a video titled "Driving Toward a Cleaner, Greener Environment: How Ford Motor Company Is Pioneering the Search for Alternative Fuels" and a speech with slides titled "Change Is in the Air," both of which told of Ford's efforts in alternative fuels, including its electric vehicle, the Ecostar.[25] After the first draft of the script, a reviewer for Ford's public affairs department asked that the writing do more to emphasize that while these technologies were promising, there was considerable uncertainty about which would work out, to what extent consumers would accept them, and, overall, that there was still much work to be done. But the reviewer also wanted more emphasis placed on showing that Ford was a "committed participant" in environmental technology. And he noted that the presentation should make Ford's "technical competence" a theme. A revision of the presentation asked, "Is Ford still on the cutting edge of fuel technology as it was when Mr. Ford switched from oats to oil?" The answer, of course, was "yes."[26] The presentation went on to detail Ford's research into alternative fuel vehicles and noted that concern about pollution was prompting greater interest in AFVs. Government regulations, including both incentives and sales requirements, also pushed for AFVs, the script stated. Ford was committed to remaining a leader in AFVs, touting that it would soon have the Ecostar on the road, but, Ford noted, just because car companies could build AFVs that did not mean consumers would buy them, and ultimately Ford owed its allegiance to those consumers.[27]

Ford's nascent move toward establishing environmental technology expertise took a big step forward, in 1993, when it hired J. Walter Thompson to take on the marketing of the Ecostar. J. Walter Thompson developed several marketing tools for Ford, but what it was selling was an idea, not a car. Although Ford planned to lease a number of Ecostars to company fleets that year, it did not intend to sell the Ecostar to individual consumers.[28] The brochure for the Ecostar developed by JWT was thus aimed not at sales but at image. JWT wanted the brochure to "leave the impression that Ford is the leader in electric vehicles." The brochure was directed at "target audiences," reflecting a common understanding in marketing about how beliefs were spread: specific social groups were receptive to certain types of messages and likely to spread them. JWT wanted to target "tree huggers" and "technoids." "Tree huggers," JWT noted, were "into all that reduce, reuse, recycle stuff. They view the big three as bad guys." The "technoid," on the other hand, was interested in the newest technology. The "key response" JWT hoped to get from "tree huggers" was recognition that Ford was the leader in EV technology, whereas the key response from "technoids" was that the Ecostar was an "advanced sophisticated" technology. Overall, JWT wanted to convey the impression that the Ecostar was a "technological masterpiece," not a golf cart.

JWT and Ford engaged in more elaborate forms of green marketing as well. The first of these was the Eco Expo in Los Angeles, which was designed to show off green products, a phenomenon that was very much the outcome of the new era of green consumerism. The fair's president, Marc Merson, wrote to JWT urging them to join the fair. "As we discussed," Merson wrote to JWT's Vince Doyle, "Ford has taken [the] leading role in urging the relaxation of existing Zero Emission regulation in California." While that may be a reasonable case, Merson wrote, Ford needed to communicate that it was committed to solving the problem of clean air, not just dragging its feet. At the Eco Expo, therefore, JWT sought to demonstrate that Ford was "actively pursuing environmental improvements in our products and our processes." In addition to handing out the aforementioned brochures, Ford would display parts of the Ecostar and allow some riders to test-drive the car.[29]

JWT and Ford's most ambitious attempt to establish the environmental tech expertise of Ford came the following month, May 1994, with the Ecostar's entry into the Tour de Sol race. For JWT, the situation was this: the public perceived auto companies as opposing "anything that makes them work hard" like fuel economy, safety, and quality. To the public, opposition to the ZEV mandate was just the latest example of auto company obstructionism. Moreover, Ford had been the most vocal in its opposition to the mandate. Even though all manufacturers opposed the mandate, Ford had received the most negative publicity. "But people are generally unaware that Ford has the 'best' EV out there today," JWT wrote, "and is dedicating a huge amount of energy to make it work." Ford needed to be positioned at the head of the pack, to be seen as the "consumers' champion for viable transportations solutions of the future." JWT wanted to make it clear that the Ecostar was the "best" thing anyone has come up with, but that it was not yet good enough for customers, and that the ZEV mandate was "arbitrary and unrealistic," ignoring "constraints of the real world." So how could Ford do that? Enter the Tour de Sol and win, demonstrating that its efforts were sincere, but also emphasizing that the solution may be a "few years" away. Key public responses to such a win, JWT hoped, would be:

- "Ford has the best electric vehicle, I mean they won, right? They must know more than anyone else about EVs. Perhaps I should listen to their side."
- "I think Ford has the best EV out there today, I feel they are making an honest attempt to meet the mandate, I believe that there is more to the limits of EVs than the government or environmental fanatics are telling us."[30]

Ford sent its Ecostar to the race with a video production team, an educational team to explain the vehicle to the public, and a treatment that made it glow "as though its crew had waxed it overnight."[31] The Ecostar won, but would that victory translate into the public authority that Ford sought? While Ford and JWT had met some of their goals, the ZEV mandate was still popular and still favored by CARB.[32]

CARB's research up to late 1995 suggested that the ZEV mandate was technologically and commercially feasible, and the Ecostar and the sodium-sulfur battery were important components of this belief. According to CARB's Battery Technology Advisory Panel (BTAP), the key technological issue for ZEVs was the amount of work batteries could do for a given amount of weight, or the "specific energy" as measured in watt-hours per kilogram. Standard nickel-cadmium and lead-acid batteries (like those used in the EV1), could not and would not be able to provide the specific energy required—about 80–100 watt-hours per kilogram, which was about the amount that would a yield a one-hundred-mile range in an urban/suburban setting. Several other types of batteries, however, did promise a specific energy in this range, and researchers were actively developing four of these: lithium-ion, nickel-metal hydride, sodium-sulfur, and zebra. Nickel-metal hydride and lithium-ion were both promising but had considerable inherent cost issues. The sodium-sulfur and the zebra batteries, on the other hand, were mainly expensive because they were not in mass production, so they had the potential to be much cheaper. Their main downside was that they had to be kept at a high temperature to work properly. They had to have heaters, which added cost, and had the potential to deteriorate, or "freeze up," if allowed to cool too much. Of all these advanced-technology batteries, the sodium-sulfur battery provided the longest range and was the one that had the most real-world testing. Thus, while CARB pushed for the development of all these kinds of batteries, the promise of sulfur-sodium certainly played into its optimism about fulfilling the mandate. In addition, CARB believed that there was good consumer demand for these vehicles, noting that people who had previewed the GM Impact and the Ford Ecostar had "very, very positive things to say about their readiness . . . to purchase EVs." Manufacturers, they noted, were less enthusiastic, believing that when it came down to buying a new car, many consumers would be comparing EVs to traditional vehicles and that the higher price of EVs would be decisive.[33]

But there was another problem with NAS batteries that the Ford Ecostar illustrated. Twice in 1994, once before the Tour de Sol race and once after, the batteries overheated, catching fire. One of these fires included an Ecostar leased to CARB itself. Although Ford believed the problem was not inherent to the batteries, after the second fire it decided to discontinue the NAS batteries. It switched over to conventional lead-acid batteries (used in a Ford Ranger body). In 1995, Ford's supplier of NAS batteries stopped making them, leaving only one other NAS battery manufacturer in the world (which stopped making them in 1998). In 1996, the major manufacturer of NAS batteries stopped producing them, and the U.S. Advanced Battery Consortium stopped researching NAS batteries. This closed off one of CARB's major hopes for a viable battery.[34]

In the meantime, CARB came to believe the technology was indeed further off and had started softening its stance on the ZEV mandate. In 1996, CARB did away with the mandated ZEVs for the years 1998 and 2001, but kept the same quota for 2003 (10 percent). In the following years, CARB further amended the mandate allowing "partial zero emissions vehicles" (PZEVs) to form a large part of the quota. Lawsuits followed these amendments, followed by more amendments in the first decade of the twenty-first century. Ford and JWT's strategy was largely a failure. They never gained the public's trust that Ford was the expert to be looked to on environmental regulation. But in an indirect way the campaign contributed to the demise of the initial ZEV mandate by highlighting the problems with the sodium-sulfur battery.

## Conclusion

What can the Ecostar story tell us about green capitalism? The most salient theme is the protean, and troubling, dynamic of informational asymmetry between business, consumers, and regulators. Because capitalism is about producing profit, first and foremost, making capitalism green means (and has meant) constraining that profit seeking through regulation, public censure, and consumer choice. But those means of constraining capitalism, if they are to work, rely on good information and trust between these groups, and these have clearly been inadequate in many cases.

As the detailed history of the Ecostar presented here is just one case, there is a limited amount that can be extrapolated from it to a broader argument about green capitalism. But there are a few interpretations that it can suggest that could be examined in other case studies and syntheses.

One interpretation is that the technology-forcing aspect of the ZEV mandate was misguided. Some analysts have argued that the air pollution standards that the ZEV mandate was supposed to contribute to could have, and indeed were, achieved primarily through making conventional internal combustion engines more efficient.[35] The electric vehicle focus was thus unnecessary, and it put an unnecessary burden on car companies. Instead of putting resources into developing and marketing the Ecostar, for example, Ford could have focused more on producing fuel-efficient vehicles. In this interpretation, the Ecostar was a waste, rather than a move toward green capitalism.

Another interpretation is that the ZEV mandate was a failure because the auto companies were able to successfully weaken it and avoid producing ZEVs on the original schedule. Although Ford did not successfully position itself as trusted expert, the Ecostar campaign was helpful to the broader strategy of delay and doubt that the auto companies sowed. The Ecostar, in other words, compounded the informational problem surrounding regulation. In this way, Ford's strategy was a common, if elaborate, example of how businesses monkey-wrenched the move to greener technology and, perhaps, greener capitalism.

A final interpretation, and the one I think fits best with the Ecostar story, is that the ZEV mandate was successful in flushing out knowledge about electric vehicles that was either unknown or hidden from the view of regulators and the public. Although, in the short run, efficient internal combustion engines allowed California to reach air quality goals, in the long run, even efficient gas-using vehicles would produce pollution. Just as before, as population and use increased, so would pollution. In addition, as concern about automobile technology shifted more toward the production of greenhouse gases, the expansion of electric vehicles has become more important. Since the ZEV mandate forced automobile companies to invest in electric vehicle research, it helped make electric vehicles a viable, mass-consumer option for automobile consumers in the twenty-first century.[36] For the Ecostar specifically, the ZEV pushed Ford to demonstrate that its electric vehicle was technically viable as a way (in Ford's strategy) of demonstrating its broader authority about regulatory reasonableness. But, in fact, the Ecostar was not fully technically viable, and the ZEV mandate helped to bring that to light. Subsequently, Ford and other companies sought to fix problems with the NAS battery or moved on to other types of batteries. At the same time, CARB recalibrated its LEV program, including the ZEV mandate, based on better information about what technologies were desirable and possible. In this interpretation, the troubling issue of asymmetric information in the achievement of green capitalism was partly overcome by aggressive regulation.

What the Ecostar story tells us for sure is that capitalists will go to extraordinary ends to maintain their informational advantage. Unpacking the potential of green capitalism will mean unpacking the dynamics of this strategy as it has played out among businesses, regulators, consumers, and the public.

# PART IV

# Going Green

# Dilemmas of Going Green: Environmental Strategies in the Swedish Mining Company Boliden, 1960–2000

*Ann-Kristin Bergquist*

As in many other Western countries, the environmental awakening started in Sweden in the late 1960s. Sweden was actually the first country in the world to establish an Environmental Protection Agency in 1967. After a process initiated already in 1963, a new act, the Swedish Environmental Protection Act, was implemented in 1969, radically changing the conditions for how key industries, such as the pulp and paper, iron and steel, and other highly polluting industries could operate. In Sweden, the Boliden Company (hereafter Boliden) constitutes an exceptional case in terms of pollution and complexity. Even though the company had made substantial efforts to handle air pollution issues before 1969, it was discovered in the early 1970s that the Rönnskär plant, a nonferrous metal smelter owned by Boliden, emitted arsenic and other heavy metals to an extent that potentially threatened the entire Baltic Sea. However, from the late 1960s to the late 1990s, emissions of arsenic and other heavy metals came to be reduced by 99 percent and emissions of sulfur dioxide by more than 90 percent. Today the Rönnskär plant is one of world's most efficient copper smelter facilities and is a world leader in the recycling of copper and precious metals from electronic scrap. This chapter seeks to explain the driving and intermingling forces behind this transition and how it actually was accomplished.

Indeed, the environmental awakening in the 1960s and the enforcement of new regulations added a new institutional dimension to the business environment as well as a new managerial challenge. Much research in business history has paid attention to the time before the 1960s, while the highly complex recent business environment has been neglected.[1] This chapter seeks to add perspectives and open up the "green box" of technological and organizational development that any polluting industry critically needs to address. The complexity and remarkably broad scope of pollutants discharged from the Rönnskär plant presented a great challenge to the company, including especially gaining access to vital environmental knowledge, technology, financing for investments, and also addressing ethical and reputational concerns. While the Rönnskär smelter had been equipped with the latest state-of-the-art environmental technology when it was built in the late 1920s,[2] the 1960s saw a growing awareness of both the scope and the complex effects of emissions from the Swedish industry. In this chapter, I argue that even though companies might want to do "good" and define themselves as taking social responsibility seriously, they may still encounter several difficult dilemmas.

Environmental history has been criticized for concentrating on the negative sides of business without delving deeper into ongoing processes inside firms. Some business historians have responded to this and called for a more balanced approach to historical studies of the environmental relations of businesses.[3] Analyzing why industrial history has evolved as it has, or how one can conceptualize the history of corporate change related to the environment, embraces a complex analysis of the social dynamics of environmental behavior.[4] In this context, it is impossible to ignore the strong influence of the regulatory framework that took shape in the 1960s and 1970s. Divergent strategies among firms in addressing pollution problems developed in response to a set of complex factors wherein a country's institutional history holds important explanatory value, such as the evolution of a country's legal history, industrial structures, state-industry relations, markets, and business attitudes.[5]

In any institutional or historical context, however, the process of greening polluting industries embraces a comprehensive and in-depth technological dimension that can generate severe bottlenecks if pollution problems must be addressed quickly. It is easy to underestimate the implications of technology and the time dimensions involved to change technological paths, especially in capital-intensive industries. Nathan Rosenberg's conceptual understanding of technological development implies that it is a risky and uncertain activity with outcomes that cannot be fully assessed in advance.[6] Rather, technology development requires a lot of information, which makes the process very costly, but also path dependent.[7] Placed in a context of the greening of industry, there were certainly no ready technologies waiting "on the shelf" when the environmental debate broke out in the 1960s and strict regulations came to be enforced. It is reasonable to expect serious difficulties when firms try to become greener due to technological path dependencies and technological lock-ins. At the same time, positive economic outcomes of developing cleaner technologies could also come about, as suggested in the "Porter hypothesis" put forward in the seminal work of Michael E. Porter and Claas van der Linde.[8] The hypothesis holds that environmental regulation affects the information firms have available, which can make them realize new opportunities for improved productivity and efficiency.[9] The interplay between industry behavior and regulation still depends on timing and context. It can take decades for a company to achieve both an improved environment and productivity and efficiency when "going green." In this chapter, I will show how trade-offs between the environment and the economic and technological realities polluting companies face are often present. The chapter maps key events in Boliden's greening history after the 1960s and how the company interacted with shifts in national and transitional environmental politics, market situations, and, not least, organizational learning.

## Boliden: A Brief History

The mining sector has been and still is responsible for a tremendous and global impact on the environment. Despite irreversibly changing the landscape by leaving huge craters in the earth's crust that can never be repaired, mining and smelting of nonferrous metals also cause a release of sulfur and heavy metals into the air and water systems. Pollution from mining and metal smelting is, of course, not a phenomenon that began with industrialization and the takeoff of modern economic growth. There are even elevated levels of lead in Swedish mosses and sediment that date back to Bronze Age, which, amazingly, have been traced to metal smelting activities in the Roman Empire in the Mediterranean area.[10] Industrialization, however, generated a strong demand for metals, which marked the earth's surface with thousands of open pits, mainly in the United States, Russia, Germany, and Australia.[11] Pollution problems became extremely severe in North America in the early twentieth century, especially in Montana due to the activity of the Anaconda Company.[12] Northern Sweden has been no exception. Rather, intensive extraction of copper and iron ore was a central part of the social and economic development in that part of the country during the twentieth century.

The inevitable release of mercury, cadmium, lead, nickel, and other heavy metals, which are a natural composition of nonferrous ores during the process of enrichment and smelting forms the backdrop to the severe environmental problems Boliden faced. Even though the noxious effects of arsenic and sulfur were well known when the company started up in the 1920s, still other substances, such as mercury, lead, and cadmium, were not yet even acknowledged as "polluting." In this particular industry, it is certainly easy to "do bad" from an environmental point of view, and much more complicated to "do good."

Boliden was founded in the 1920s when one of the world's largest gold deposits was discovered in the northern part of Sweden, outside the town Skellefteå. Right from the start, environmental issues concerning the composition of the ore made it to the very core of the company's boardroom. As it turned out, the ore contained not only a sensationally high concentration of gold but also an unusually complex composition of arsenic and sulfur. In fact, never before had ore with such a high concentration of arsenic been treated on an industrial scale.[13] Despite substantial efforts to find a "safe" method, including transfer of technological knowledge from the United States and building the highest smokestack in Europe, adverse effects related to both the internal and external environment emerged in only a few years. The peak of sulfur dioxide ($SO_2$) emissions occurred in 1943 when they reached a level of 130,000 tons.[14] This contrasts with 2013 emission levels of about 3,000 tons.[15]

Production at Boliden involved treating a very complex ore with technological processes developed in-house, a trend that continued when it came to environmental technology as well. Boliden today still specializes in treating very complex materials such as electronic scrap, including cell phones and computers. Along with copper, which is the company's most important product, other substances central to the business are gold, silver, lead, and zinc, as well as sulfur products.[16]

Boliden has undergone several phases of development during the last eighty years, including shifts in terms of management and corporate ownership. These shifts have played a role in the formation of new strategies, including environmental management and challenges related to pollution control. When Boliden started, the business involved only mining and smelting and was based in the northern part of Sweden. During the 1950s, however, the company diversified, and in the mid-1980s, Boliden was one of the largest industry groups in Sweden with foreign offices on several continents. In 1963 Boliden had 4,000 employees while twenty-five years later, the company, now dealing with mining and metals, chemicals, construction, wholesale, and finance, had 15,000 employees.[17]

Very much in line with international trends, the company de-diversified and concentrated on its core activities, that is, mining and metals operations, beginning in the mid-1980s. The big shift occurred when the Trelleborg Group acquired all of Boliden's shares in 1986, making it a subsidiary. Aside from streamlining the business, this also increased its international engagement in mining and smelting. In the mid-1980s, the Trelleborg Group, which had previously focused on rubber and plastics, started to act as a broad industrial conglomerate aiming to expand into the mining and metals industry. Between 1987 and 1992, the group acquired production facilities in the Netherlands, the United Kingdom, and Belgium. Expansion was also taking place in Spain and in North America.[18] In 1997 the Trelleborg Group formed the Canadian Boliden Ltd. and transformed Boliden's mining and smelting activities into a Canadian company.[19] Already in 1999, however, Boliden was restructured, Boliden's shares were listed on the Stockholm Stock Exchange, and in 2001 the company moved back to Sweden. Among the acquisitions was the Spanish company, Apirsa SL, in 1987. In 1998, the dam at Apirsa's mine in Los Frailes burst, allowing 4.5 million cubic meters of tailings to flow into the nearby Rio Agrio. This was an environmental disaster, though it lies outside the scope of this chapter.[20]

The strongest driving and formative factors behind the greening of Boliden and the Rönnskär smelter, as will be discussed below, were after the 1960s environmental regulations. Yet there were strong external factors that affected the company's ability and willingness to undertake expensive environmental investments. Fluctuating metal prices, which are very characteristic of the metals market, is one central external factor affecting profits, along with the overall current economic situation. Market changes, as well as access to technology and scientific knowledge, shaped the company's approach to environmental issues.

## The Challenge

The greening process, and the scope of the challenge it presented, can be illustrated by the data of emission reductions from the Rönnskär smelter throughout the period discussed in the chapter (Tables 9.1 and 9.2).

Behind the emission figures shown in Tables 9.1 and 9.2 and beyond technology and investments lie hidden factors that include a lengthy and complicated process of clarifying the relationship between pollutants and their impact on the environment. When the Swedish regulatory system was designed, there was a close interaction between the polluting firms and the authorities in advancing knowledge. The environment around the Rönnskär smelter came to be the country's most "researched" polluted area,[21] which, of course, had to do with the remarkable scope of pollutants in this specific case. Without going into detail about the legal procedures, we can describe the big picture as a development that went through different stages related to the licensing process in accordance with the Environmental Protection Act (EPAct). The company handed in its first application in 1973, and the Swedish government made its first decision in 1975. The next license hearing started in 1980, and the license was then renewed in 1981, 1986, and 1998, with all decisions entailing strict requirements for emission reductions, improved waste management, and further investigations into the impact of the polluting substances on the environment.

When the environmental issue broke in the 1960s, not much attention had been directed toward environmental concerns within Boliden since the 1920s and 1930s. On only a few occasions in the 1940s and the 1950s had Swedish authorities made inquiries about the smelter's water emissions, and the reason behind this was essentially that protection against water pollution was included in the Water Act in 1941. Regulation in the area of water pollution developed earlier in Sweden than air pollution and was, in practice, unregulated in Sweden until 1969.[22] Due to the country's low population density, significant hydropower resources, and lack of major coal deposits, urban smoke never became a truly critical issue like it was in big cities such as London or Pittsburgh. Rather, it was water pollution and odor emanating from pulp and paper industries and sugar mills that spurred the first public pollution debate.[23] Despite efforts to control water emissions, the Water Act

Table 9.1  Emissions of heavy metals to air from the Rönnskär smelter (tons)

| Year | Arsenic | Lead | Cadmium | Copper | Mercury | Zinc |
|---|---|---|---|---|---|---|
| 1965–69 (mv) | 154.0 | 684.0 | 13.4 | 190.0 | 3.5 | 488.0 |
| 1975–79 (mv) | 68.0 | 230.0 | 5.4 | 192.0 | 1.0 | 266.0 |
| 1985 | 40.0 | 101.0 | 2.7 | 41.0 | 0.6 | 145.0 |
| 1990 | 4.7 | 52.0 | 1.3 | 18.0 | 0.25 | 33.0 |
| 1995 | 0.8 | 9.0 | 0.2 | 5.0 | 0.07 | 11.0 |
| 2000 | 0.17 | 4.0 | 0.06 | 2.0 | 0.15 | 6.0 |
| 2005 | 0.23 | 3.4 | 0.07 | 1.4 | 0.13 | 5.1 |

Sources: Västerbotten County Administrative Board's Archive (VCABA), Dossie för miljövård 2482-24-107, vol. 03-06, "Miljörapport Rönnskärsverken 2005"; for the years 1969–85, data have been provided by Boliden.

Table 9.2  Emissions of heavy metals to water from the Rönnskär smelter (tons)

| Year | Arsenic | Lead | Cadmium | Copper | Mercury | Zinc |
|---|---|---|---|---|---|---|
| 1965–69 (mv) | 2,078.0 | 214.0 | 7.2 | 165.0 | 5.2 | 93.0 |
| 1975–79 (mv) | 744.0 | 14.0 | 1.5 | 15.0 | 0.5 | 62.0 |
| 1985 | 0.4 | 3.1 | 0.4 | 7.2 | 31.0 | 7.6 |
| 1990 | 8.0 | 1.4 | 0.07 | 2.3 | 0.03 | 5.4 |
| 1995 | 0.6 | 1.3 | 0.02 | 0.6 | 0.02 | 1.8 |
| 2000 | 0.5 | 0.5 | 0.04 | 0.5 | 0.04 | 2.5 |
| 2005 | 1.2 | 0.5 | 0.06 | 0.5 | 0.01 | 2.4 |

Sources: Västerbotten County Administrative Board's Archive (VCABA), Dossie för miljövård 2482-24-107, vol. 03-06, "Miljörapport Rönnskärsverken 2005"; for the years 1969–85, data have been provided by Boliden.

did not lead to any direct actions to control pollution in the Rönnskär case before the 1960s. While air and water emissions containing substances from almost the entire periodic table continued to be discharged, both the authorities and the company remained surprisingly unaware of the situation. This, however, took a sudden turn in the 1960s when Sweden experienced a period of rapidly growing knowledge on industrial pollution and the environment, coupled with mobilization in the regulatory arena.[24]

Needless to say, it was not only in Sweden that environmental issues ended up on government agendas. In different parts of Europe, political mobilization concerning air pollution occurred, partly because of the severe sulfur dioxide episode in London in 1952. The first European international convention concerning air pollution was held in Milan in 1957, where Sweden was among twenty-one participating states.[25] In 1963 the National Air Pollution Control Board was established in Sweden to address air pollution, mainly through research on air quality. Sweden never experienced a particular air pollution episode like that of London in 1952. Rather, the mercury debate in the early 1960s has been emphasized as a possible trigger there.[26] In the early 1960s Swedish scientists and ornithologists found injured and dead birds resulting, it turned out, from the use of mercury in agriculture. A scientific debate ensued, followed by a political and a public debate, which coincided with the release of Rachel Carson's book *Silent Spring* in Swedish.[27] In Sweden, the mobilization of environmental interests in the 1960s never really grew out of environmental pressure groups. Instead it was channeled through a level-headed policy process involving participation of state agencies and industry experts and, not least, representatives of the scientific community. When the EPAct was implemented in 1969, the process of environmental policy making had been going on since 1963.[28] The regulatory framework to control pollution was formed in a collaborative context that involved industry typically by having industrial representatives on different committees. Scholars have argued that the act was a typical expression of the tradition of consensus-seeking solutions in Swedish politics often vaguely but commonly referred to as the "Swedish Model."[29]

Boliden made its first effort to survey water emissions (lead, copper, arsenic, sulfur dioxide, and sulfuric acid) at the Rönnskär smelter after a visit from the state water inspection agency in 1963.[30] The results showed that there was no real reason to worry, or so they thought. At the beginning of 1966 the company nevertheless decided, on its own initiative, to analyze samples of the seawater around the smelter, motivated primarily by its application to the Water Court to discharge waste into the sea.[31] A "working group" focusing on water emissions was also formed and the first "environmental manager" (*miljöchef*) was appointed. There were different factors propelling the increased urgency of the environmental issue in 1966. One of the company managers, Folke Nilsson, was involved as an industrial expert for the committee working on the EPAct.[32] At the same time the Institute for Water and Air Protection, a joint collaboration between the Swedish government and the industrial sector, had been formed and convened the first conference on industrial pollution and legal issues in 1966.[33] The company was well informed about the work on the EPAct, and concerns about the extent and effects of the company's emissions seriously increased. Then, in 1968, the mercury issue hit.

Aside from the mercury issue having received priority in Sweden in the early 1960s, an international debate on the so-called methylmercury issue arose. It was discovered that methylmercury could be absorbed by fish and accumulate in the biological food chain. Interest in Sweden was directed particularly against the chlor-alkali industry due to its big size in the country, but virtually all industries came under surveillance.[34] The Swedish Environmental Protection Agency (EPA) therefore contacted Boliden in 1968 concerning the new findings.[35] There was an "urgent need," the agency wrote, to discuss possible mercury levels in the ores used by Boliden, including any potential risks of the spread of mercury from processing and refining them.[36]

The concern about mercury affected the whole Boliden Company. An organization to coordinate research and possible measures to reduce the emissions was established and chaired by the CEO of Boliden, Åke Palm. The primary goals were to coordinate the issue within the company and to organize in-house research.[37] Pressure soon came from two directions. Not only the EPA, but also the company's customers for sulfur products, such as the pulp industry, were concerned about mercury in the products.[38] Overall, the debate on air pollution intensified, and in addition to mercury, emissions of acidic substances, especially sulfur dioxide, ended up on the political agenda. Due to the fact that Swedish soil (as in the other Scandinavian countries) is poor in lime, the country experienced an acute acidification problem in the late 1960s, not least since large amounts of sulfur dioxide originating in the United Kingdom and Eastern Europe hit Sweden as "acid rain."[39] Boliden was in trouble on both counts. Its emissions of mercury were high, and in terms of $SO_2$, it appeared that the smelter was the biggest point source of $SO_2$ in the country.

## Dilemmas of the Spring Cleaning During the 1970s

In 1972, a new working group was formed: the "Anti-Pollution Group" connected to the research and development department at the Rönnskär smelter. The group included, in addition to some technicians, the environmental manager Bengt Rudling and the Rönnskär CEO Folke Nilsson. The CEO's presence in the group signaled the strategic importance of handling the issue. A new sulfur plant was opened in 1971 with a selenium filter that allowed gaseous mercury to be captured from sulfuric gases, a method that had been developed in-house. In 1971, CEO Folke Nilsson stated during an internal meeting: "In the event that a conflict would occur with scarce resources, on-going operations must be prioritized. Secondly, environmental issues must come first, and only then expansion and long-term research projects."[40]

In addition to the company preparing an application for a license to operate according to the EPAct, another factor was the public debate, which was in full swing. As the Swedish environmental historian Erland Mårald has emphasized, there was an ongoing normative formation concerning "right" and "wrong" in the issue of the environment, and strongly value-laden words were common in the debate during the period.[41] The company did not argue at this stage, however, that the demand for far-reaching emission reductions was not justified. The management had declared that it was committed to undertaking any measures that were required by law. What concerned the management was rather the fear that stakeholders would expect things to happen too quickly. As the Rönnskär manager expressed it: "We need time to work on any adjustments that may be necessary. From the authorities, as well as the EPA, the County Administrative Board and at the municipal level, we have noticed a good understanding of this realistic requirement. I hope that the same realism and understanding will come from all others working for a better environment in our society. Just as Rome could not be built in a day, the work for a better environment will take time."[42]

In 1971, the company started to prepare an application for a license (the smelter then consisted of fifteen different production units) with the intent to obtain a permit for future operations, including production expansion, to present to the Licensing Board for Environmental Protection (LBEP).[43] Production expansion was considered necessary to adjust to the fast-growing competition on the international market. It was a tedious process, with intensive assessment work that involved several research and consulting institutions outside the company.[44] The first sampling results were worrying. In a meeting with the Swedish EPA in 1972, the company explained that all the investments undertaken up to that point had not had the expected results. More emission sources had also been discovered, while higher levels of emissions had been detected due to improvements in the measuring technique. It turned out that the entire heavy metal pollution problem in Sweden seemed be concentrated in the Rönnskär smelter at the time.[45] Measurements undertaken by the agency also showed that the arsenic concentration in the Baltic Sea was four times higher than normal and ten times higher than the natural levels in the northern part of the Baltic Sea.[46] The EPA regarded these levels as a big "exclamation mark" since they were directly attributable to one single point source. Another issue concerned $SO_2$. With annual emissions of 40,000 tons of $SO_2$, the agency concluded that the smelter was the biggest point source in the country. The question now was what to do.[47]

Closure of the business was in fact discussed between the company and the EPA. It is difficult to determine if the company discussed this in order to exert pressure on the authorities with warning shots.[48] However, though the emissions were exceptionally high, detailed knowledge of the effects from all the pollutants was still poor. For instance, it was mentioned during a meeting between the EPA and the company that knowledge about the ability of fish to absorb heavy metals and the impact of this absorption on lower organisms was scarce.[49] When the company handed in its license application to the LBEP in 1973, knowledge about the environmental effects of heavy metals was still not yet clarified. This made it impossible for authorities to determine what emission level standards should be required in the Rönnskär case. Further studies would be required, not only on arsenic and mercury, but also on cadmium. Another critical point was the connection between acidification and the leeching of heavy metals bound in soil.

When the LBEP reviewed the license application, it concluded that the overall picture was so alarming that the business could not be judged as admissible from an environmental point of view. But then, on the other hand, there was a big trade-off. More than two thousand people were directly employed at the smelter, and there were more indirect jobs in the mining sector and other companies that resulted from its activity. Thus, Boliden had strong support and loyalty in the region despite the national media buzz about it. The smelter was also of national strategic importance for Swedish "self-sufficiency" concerning strategic metals such as copper.[50] In such cases of severe trade-offs, according to the EPAct, decisions were to be transferred to the government. Thus, the LBEP handed the case over to the Swedish government in 1974, which announced its decision in 1975. The company was now given a short-term license—a "trial period" of four years—which involved forty-nine points of measures (including emissions cuts, further research about effects in the recipients, but also on health effects on workers and people living nearby the smelter, and so on).[51] In fact, between 1970 and 2000 over a hundred studies would be conducted at the company's expense, including studies on the impact of the emissions of sulfur dioxide and heavy metals on humans, birds, foxes, plants, and fish, as well as on metals in mosses and in bottom sediments. Thus, the area around the Rönnskär smelter became the country's most "researched" region.[52]

At the time of the government's decision, however, the company's situation had changed substantially. In 1975 the economic recession in the wake of the first oil crisis generated liquidity problems. The public debate turned increasingly radical, partly fueled by the book *The Limits to Growth* published by the Club of Rome in 1972.[53] The environmental issue was linked to an overall critique of the capitalist system. Boliden was seen as the archetypal "environmental villain."[54] In its 1978 annual report, the company devoted many pages to discussing this sensitive issue and tried to communicate its progress in environmental work.[55] It was obvious that the company also found itself unfairly accused in the media. In its view, the whole industrial sector had come to bear the environmental debt that really should have been shared by all who ultimately enjoyed the fruits of industrial production. Industrial companies closest to the natural resources in the production chain, and thus far away from consumers, according to Boliden, had been criticized the most severely. The annual report stated: "An industry often seems to be far away from the everyday and human needs in society. In fact it is the opposite. It is the community, the people themselves, who have created industries for themselves to meet their growing needs. Without the people, no industry. Without industry, no welfare society."[56]

Whereas the company had embarked on a positive, even sympathetic, attitude to undertaking environmental commitments in the late 1960s, this now changed. The oil crises and decreasing metal prices on the world market reduced profits. Productivity increases and production expansion were therefore needed. At the same time, all the environmental investments that were tied to the four-year temporary license crowded out scope for productive investments. The situation appeared paradoxical: to offset the costs of environmental investments, production expansion was necessary, but the liquidity was too low to finance both, at least temporarily. Also many uncertainties still remained, not least concerning environmental effects, with investigations still under way. A new strategic approach to managing necessary investments was therefore needed for the 1980s.

## Economic Dilemmas and Proactive Strategies in the 1980s

New strategies and organizational changes followed the challenge of the 1970s. As mentioned, the government's decision in 1975, which coincided with the deep worldwide economic recession, forced the company to make serious trade-offs in investment decisions due to liquidity problems.[57] The combination of a negative earnings trend and substantial environmental investments put a serious financial strain on the entire Boliden Company.[58] Entering the 1980s, the company had developed a new, fairly far-sighted strategy to avoid a similar situation in the future. In short, the basic strategy was to avoid short-term requirements from authorities by elaborating a "framework program," which included a set of environmental investments that the company committed itself to undertake in the new license application. The framework approach was developed as an integral part of the company's total investment plans stretching over a ten-year period and was presented to the authorities before the license hearing in 1986. According to the company, this approach was justified because consideration must be given to the dynamics of technology development and a constantly changing economic situation. Experiences from the years 1973–80 had not shown that technological development processes created new possible approaches in the least, reflecting a need for greater flexibility in the selection of technological measures.[59]

So far, not much has been said about the technological development that followed the greening process. Based on the stepwise decisions of the Swedish government in 1975, and the LBEP licenses of 1981 and 1986, deeper emissions cuts were required. According to the licensing stipulations of the LBEP in 1986, the company was allowed to emit 10,000 tons of $SO_2$ annually until 1989, then 8,000 tons annually until 1991, and then finally in 1994 5,000 tons applied as a strict "limit value," which meant that if emissions exceeded the limit value, the company would be forced to shut down.[60] It is no exaggeration to say that the company's survival depended on how it handled the environmental issue. To handle it effectively and to survive, of course, technology and financing for investments were needed.

A level of emissions at any given point in time is restricted according to prevailing technological knowledge. For the environmental authorities, as well as for the company, there was a great challenge to determine "technologically achievable" emissions levels. In practice, the task was to identify best available technologies (BAT) for benchmarking. Swedish environmental authorities developed a practice that generally avoided method-based standards. Instead, emissions level standards were prescribed that gave the company the flexibility to choose measures to reach the targets. In order to identify BAT, the company was ordered by the LBEP to do "study trips" to several countries together with representatives from the Swedish EPA. Thus, in 1974, the company traveled to visit smelters in the United States and Canada, in 1983 to the United Kingdom and the Federal Republic of Germany, and in 1986 to Belgium, Japan, the United States and Canada.[61] Yet, according to the company's reports from these trips, not much technology could be directly transferred for several reasons. The smelters in North America had generally low standards, especially in Canada. One of the visited smelters, Noranda Horne Smelter, lacked sulfur treatment facilities and released 470,000 tons of $SO_2$ per year in 1980.[62] In Germany, England, and Belgium, the standards were higher, but the smelters did not process the same complex materials as Boliden did. Japan's smelters, however, it could be concluded, were world leading in terms of low emissions and environmental technology. The travel report of 1985 suggests that Japanese smelters held a significantly higher environmental standard in relation to other countries, primarily with respect to emissions of $SO_2$.[63]

Due to the difficult task of finding transferrable solutions, a substantial part of the needed environmental technologies had to be developed in-house. Thus, between 1975 and 1979, engineers at the Rönnskär smelter developed an integrated water purification works that separated heavy metals such as mercury, copper, lead, zinc, cadmium, and arsenic from the process water and recycled the metals back into the metallurgical process.[64] It was development work that required a lot of the company's technicians and engineers. As one of the engineers explained, "sometimes our books in chemistry did not match with reality. In 99 cases out of 100, the experiments failed."[65] Due to this water purification works, Boliden became a world leader in technology for mercury and arsenic purification and water treatment for heavy metals.[66] Also in areas related to the processing of "secondary material" (such as electronic scrap) Boliden invented successful technology. Already by the 1980s, the Rönnskär smelter had developed into one of the world's most advanced smelters in terms of smelting complex materials (for example, mineral concentrates, ashes from the steel and brass industry, and scrap). It was also at the beginning of the 1980s that Boliden, under CEO John Dahlfors, made the strategic decision to invest in the capacity to process more complex materials, such as scrap from the electronics industry, including computers.[67] Combustion tests of copper scrap were initiated in the "lead Kaldo furnace" in the 1980s, a metallurgical process originally developed by Boliden to treat lead-containing intermediates from the copper process. The result was viewed as successful, and the treatment of copper-containing scrap such as PVC could be smelted with good results. The technology received great interest on the market as an environmentally friendly method for treating secondary materials, and at the end of the 1980s the company had already sold three plants.[68] These examples, which are some of the underlying factors behind the emissions reductions presented in Tables 9.1 and 9.2, show that some factors are difficult to detect without a thorough study of the technology. The time and space to experiment are conditions of technological development, and they are not always compatible with the requirements of rapid environmental protection. This was undoubtedly one of the more difficult problems for the company to communicate to its critics.

## Stricter Requirements and New Strategies After the Mid-1980s

After several changes in ownership in the early 1980s, the Boliden Group was taken over by the Trelleborg Group in 1986. The change in ownership, which involved replacing most of the executives, including the board of directors and environmental managers, coincided with intensified competition on the international market for nonferrous metals. Moreover, the changes in ownership also coincided with the big license hearing in 1986. Even though the company had managed to cut its emissions considerably since the early 1970s, the situation was still critical. Investigations had shown that there was a strong mercury load in the area around the plant. According to the EPA, the soil and water also showed serious acidification, causing "dissolution" of accumulated historical emissions.[69] The acidity was also crucial to the uptake of arsenic and many metals. Heavy metals, such as mercury, also had impacts on the land as well as on the lake systems.[70] To obtain the license in 1986, therefore, the company had to achieve far-reaching emissions cuts, especially of $SO_2$. From the level of 10,000 tons of $SO_2$ in 1986, the new license bound the company to reduce this to a level of 5,000 tons in 1994 with Japanese standards as the benchmark.[71] This requirement was unrealistic in the company's view. The Trelleborg Group, with its tough manager Kjell Nilsson, openly confronted the EPA and appealed to the government. Nilsson argued strongly that the new environmental standards forced the management to consider closing the smelter, which threatened Boliden's whole mining business in Sweden. In this case, again, the Rönnskär smelter and Boliden had become the center of a media storm. Trelleborg CEO Rune Andersson and Boliden CEO Kjell Nilsson wrote directly to Swedish Prime Minister Ingvar Carlsson, in short, outlining a very tough situation for the nonferrous mining business in Sweden, comparing the situation to those in competing countries.[72] Taking the offense in this way turned out to be successful. In 1987, the Swedish government announced a "package" of subsidies for Boliden to finance fifteen minor mining projects to support the development and growth of the region and strengthen the company's competitiveness.[73] The result was, in brief, that the company withdrew its appeal against the license, and the environmental requirements were applied at the Rönnskär smelter. In exchange, the company received subsidies for other parts of its business to offset the environmental costs at the smelter.[74]

The new owners appointed a new environmental manager, Per G. Broman, a metallurgist with experience in the mining sector, whose task was now to figure out how the environmental requirements could be achieved while enhancing the firm's competitiveness. In short, his solution involved structural changes in the production lines and ruthless rationalization. Streamlining all the activities was seen as the recipe for staying in business. In other words, the "structural plan" aimed not only to comply with the limit values for $SO_2$ but also to achieve cost savings and increased productivity. In addition to improving the efficiency of the copper and lead production, the company also phased out arsenic production in 1991, downsized service units, and changed the direction of technological development. Between 1986 and 1989, 838 jobs at the Rönnskär smelter disappeared. The rationalization continued in the following years, so that by 1995 there were 1,208 fewer employees than in 1986.[75]

The management perceived that the most critical issue was to reduce the $SO_2$ emissions. In contrast to the 1970s, developing new technology and calling upon engineering and technological competence were no longer viewed as the sole solution. To achieve the emissions targets, the new environmental manager considered it necessary to break down the license conditions to local responsibilities, covering everyone who handled an emissions source. Responsibilities came to follow department structures and an "environmental auditing" routine developed in-house was also introduced. When $SO_2$ emissions fell by 25 percent during the first quarter of 1988, the increased involvement in environmental issues on the part of both the management and operators was considered the main reason. Already in 1990, the company had achieved the lowered limit for $SO_2$ emissions that would not apply until 1994. The management even arranged courses in "basic chemistry" to raise awareness within the organization. However, though the company had accomplished rather impressive results since the mid-1980s, new challenges were just around the corner. Already at the beginning of the 1990s, the authorities were signaling that stricter environmental standards were in the works for the entire Swedish industrial sector.

## The 1990s: Sustainable Production and "Green" Copper

In the late 1980s and early 1990s, new targets were set for Swedish environmental policy. Increasing cooperation between the Baltic Sea countries, European Union, and international conventions came to influence national goals and industrial rules more heavily. More laws and increasingly stringent requirements were added to the previous environmental restrictions stemming from the EPAct. According to the Swedish government, a more holistic approach was needed that would cover the environmental impact not only of production but also of the product, from "cradle to grave." Life-cycle analysis—evaluating the total environmental impact of material and energy flows for the production, use, and disposal of a product—arose as part of this development.

A basic thrust for the internationalization of environmental policy was increased acknowledgment of the transnational nature of environmental problems and the need for more effective cooperation. One example was the pollution of the Baltic Sea, which was indeed affected by emissions from the Rönnskär smelter. Countries had been cooperating since the establishment of the Baltic Marine Environment Protection Commission, sometimes also referred to as the Helsinki Commission (HELCOM) in 1974, but the organization had been unable to deal successfully with problems in national implementations.[76] In 1990, the Swedish and Polish prime ministers invited the governments of Finland, the Soviet Union, Czechoslovakia, East Germany, West Germany, Denmark, and Norway, as well as the European Commission, to a conference on the Baltic Sea environment in the Swedish town of Ronneby.[77] The conference resulted in the Baltic Sea Declaration, which, among other things, announced that a working group would be established to develop a specific action plan to restore ecological balance to the Baltic area. Participating countries would develop concrete national action plans. The Swedish EPA identified a handful of industries that had a significant environmental impact, such as the steel industry, pulp mills, and, of course, the Rönnskär smelter. Stricter conditions were needed in the Boliden case, primarily to reduce mercury and cadmium emissions into the Gulf of Bothnia. When HELCOM presented a list of the worst sources of pollution around the Baltic Sea in 1992, the Rönnskär smelter topped the list.[78] A bill in 1991 also aimed to crackdown more severely; not least, this bill suggested that the EPAct should be used to renew the licenses for the most polluting industries.[79] Both the action plan for the Baltic Sea as well as the environmental bill attracted Boliden's attention.[80] The company expressed disappointment that the EPA, which, despite very good insight into the technological and economic realities in the Rönnskär case, put forward several proposals that clearly violated the EPAct's stipulations concerning "fairness."[81] License renewal would take place in 1996. Boliden's competitive situation in the 1990s was affected by an international trend toward larger production units. To stay in business Boliden had no choice, it concluded, but to follow the trend. Even if acceptable profitability was achieved in the 1990s, the management ascertained that competition in the international market would become considerably more fierce in the following years. The company therefore decided to make one of the biggest investments in its history and double the production levels of copper. In the planning of the project, a much broader survey of environmental factors was made than before. The Brundtland Commission Report of 1987 and the Rio Conference in 1992 had an overall focus on global environmental problems. The Rio Conference made it clear that climate issues, natural conservation, protection of endangered species, and long-term sustainable development were new issues at the focus of the conventions adopted. The restrictive elements of the environment relevant to the metals market, according to Boliden's analysis, were resource conservation and risk management. Since the recovered metal could not be considered resource consuming, recycled metals had potential for the future. From the company's analysis, environmental classification of copper was to be expected. There was a possibility that recycling, which had previously been driven by economic incentives, could now be used more strategically with a strong connection to the concept of sustainable development. The management even discussed the notion of "green copper" as a form containing a high proportion of recycled metal. It also chose technological processes that favored recycling.[82] A broader view than just the goal of managing license requirements formed the basis of investment choices. Overall, in the 1990s, the company had an opportunity to brand its business in a more environmentally friendly direction.

Much had changed since the 1970s. The impact of emissions on the environment was fairly well investigated, greatly reducing previous uncertainties. Moreover, environmental work had gradually been institutionalized and "routine management" had been developed, both within the company and among state organizations. In the 1990s, compared to 1973, both the companies and the environmental agencies were equipped with completely different skills, experiences, and support. Information costs for accessing knowledge from natural sciences and technological fields had also been greatly reduced. At the same time, $SO_2$ emissions into the air and metal emissions into both air and water were still significant. The Rönnskär smelter was still, in fact, the largest point source of several of hazardous substance emissions in Sweden.

After the smelter's license was renewed in 1998, it was extensively renovated and rebuilt. The production capacity increased from 100,000 tons of copper to 240,000 tons at a cost of two billion Swedish crowns ($279 million). Around 30 percent of the total project cost was related to environmental investments. The project's investments included a new flash furnace as a smelting unit. Flash smelting is characterized by very high utilization of the internal energy in the smelted material. With high enrichment of oxygen in the blast air, the materials can today be smelted without adding any external energy. Flash technology was thus very advantageous from an energy perspective. The energy issue, however, was not a big environmental concern before the 1990s. But energy had received increased attention in the business since the oil crises in the 1970s drove up energy costs. Work to reduce emissions and improve waste management was taken up alongside energy conservation. From 1983 to 2001, energy consumption was reduced by 16 percent, while overall metal production increased by 61 percent. Energy consumption per unit decreased during the same period by 42 percent.[83]

It is also worth noticing that the Rönnskär smelter today is connected to the municipal district heating system, providing households with surplus heat from the smelter. Moreover, the Rönnskär smelter has the capacity to process 75,000 tons of electronic waste per year, scrap that is converted to 14,500 tons of copper per year, plus 32 tons of silver and 2 tons of gold. Also minor amounts of palladium, platinum, and rhodium are recovered. Of the raw material 20 percent comes from Scandinavia, 70 percent from other European countries and the remaining 10 percent from the rest of the world.[84] In 2012, the company made a deal with the multinational giant Apple, which had contacted the Rönnskär smelter in searching for a company that could handle its electronic waste in an environmentally reversible manner.[85]

## It Is Complicated to Do Good and Very Easy to Do Bad

Boliden's greening process has reflected ongoing changes in society since the 1960s, both in market and environmental regulations. Yet it has not been beyond reproach in its history. Even though the company complied with the laws, things can still go very wrong. In the early 1980s, the company concluded that it could not process all metallic residues and searched for various options for disposing of the material. One alternative was having another company reprocess the material. A deal was set with the Chilean company PROMEL. Boliden's environmental director at the time, Rolf Svedberg, visited the Chilean company twice in 1984 to ascertain that PROMEL had the capacity to reprocess the material. The Swedish EPA was also informed about the deal. Between 1984 and 1985, Boliden delivered a total of about 20,000 tons of metallic residues from the Rönnskär smelter to the Chilean company. The sludge was a residual material from Rönnskär's arsenic works and included arsenic, lead, iron, gold, and silver. Once the material was delivered, contacts between Boliden and PROMEL ceased.[86] A complicated problem had been easily solved in the short term.

Then, in the early 1990s, PROMEL went bankrupt, and the sludge was left lying open in a location on the outskirts of the city of Arica. Meanwhile, the Chilean authorities had begun to take an interest in the land, and construction work on residential areas began in early 1990 on the site. People unaware of the material's toxicity moved into the area and injuries caused by lead poisoning and other diseases thus ensued. It all came to light in the Swedish media in 1998. On September 16, 2013, the company Arica Victims KB filed a writ of summons against Boliden.[87] The lawsuit is ongoing, and the trial is scheduled for the spring of 2017, with Boliden claiming it has no responsibility for what happened in Arica. The scandal has been the subject of intense debate in the Swedish media and has also been discussed in the Swedish parliament.[88] Boliden's export of toxic waste in the 1980s raises truly concerning questions about responsibility, about companies doing both good and bad, and about changes over time in normative opinions about what good and bad behavior is. In Andrew J. Hoffman's words, "there is no such thing as a 'green company.' The best one can do is to describe the progression of how companies are going green."[89]

## Conclusion

Boliden managed to cut emissions from its smelter up to 99 percent between 1960 and 2000, while production more than doubled. In terms of sheer numbers, this is impressive and reflects corporate behavioral adjustments to an evolving competitive market and a society that was shifting its concern about the natural environment and human well-being and continues to do so. This change was largely knowledge driven. During the formative period of the 1960s, there was a major knowledge deficit concerning both the scope and effects of emissions from Swedish industry. One striking example is the question of mercury, which put the environmental issue on the political agenda in Sweden in the early 1960s. At this stage, tons of mercury were released from the Rönnskär smelter without any concern, as the hazards of mercury were not known before it was determined to be the cause of Minamata disease in Japan in 1959. Mercury was, in fact, used worldwide in agriculture to control seed-borne diseases. Both the scope and effects of emissions of mercury, arsenic, and cadmium, as well as sulfur dioxide, were not clarified when the state began issuing licenses according to the EPAct in 1969. Once the Boliden license hearings began, however, the state totally changed the parameters because it could threaten to refuse to grant licenses, which it did to Boliden in the early 1970s. Thus, the rules of the game for Swedish nonferrous mining and smelting businesses had changed substantially; the legal threat put the company under maximum pressure to redefine long-term investment strategies and related research and development. It is not an overstatement to say that the future of Boliden relied on solving the environmental issues, which depended fundamentally on acquiring new knowledge and developing technological innovations.

The dilemmas that the company experienced have been many, mostly since there were severe short-term trade-offs between profitability and environmental investments, including research and development, in the 1970s. For Boliden, the trade-offs seem to have changed from the mid-1980s, when the work to reduce emissions was more strategically coordinated with the restructuring and rationalization of production, which raised productivity substantially. From the 1980s, it is even possible to talk about a win-win situation between environmental improvements and productivity growth, a dynamic effect confirming the Porter hypothesis. Though environmental regulations in the 1970s and the 1980s complicated business considerably, they eventually also generated opportunities, though not without causing the company to struggle. Besides enhanced productivity, Boliden's strategic decision in the early 1980s to specialize in metals recycling could also be linked to sustainable production in the 1990s. This was at least changing on the market level, leading the company's brand in a more environmentally friendly direction. Swedish citizens goodwill toward the company, however, is not high, both because it has a poor reputation because of its polluting history and because of the current "poison scandal" in Chile caused by

Boliden's export of hazardous waste in the 1980s. Yet despite the very critical debate in the national media, the company has always had strong regional support, and local resistance against its pollution has never really been organized or manifested. This support can possibly be traced back to Boliden's history of taking social responsibility in the local community. Also, when the smelter was built in the late 1920s, the company undertook voluntary action to avoid air pollution damages based on accessible environmental knowledge at the time. However, national and later transnational regulations, constituted the most important and driving forces in its environmental development from the late 1960s to the first decade of the twenty-first century.

The environmental "revolution" of the 1960s generated some great complexities at the firm level that largely remained hidden. In the Swedish context, business and environmental authorities interacted a great deal in advancing green knowledge, essentially on the effects of pollution in the ambient environment. When the attention to environmental issues increased in 1960s, it seemed that both Boliden and the Swedish EPA were taken by surprise concerning the scope of emissions. Furthermore, there were also great uncertainties related to the effects of metal pollution and sulfur. It goes without saying that the situation was messy at the start, and the solution to many of the problems involved chemistry, biology, engineering, measuring, experimentation, and construction. It was difficult to communicate these difficulties in the vitriolic national debate of the 1970s.

The greatest challenges for the company had to do with funding major environmental investments in technology. This was an essential characteristic throughout the 1970s and the 1980s, and, as noted above, it is easy to underestimate the time needed to develop and implement new technology. The company, in many cases, especially in the 1970s, was forced to develop a specific technology in-house because existing technology could not be directly transferred from abroad. In this context, the design of the regulatory framework was decisive, as it provided scope for innovation and long-term coordination between investments to benefit the environment and production. In the Swedish context, corporate environmentalism took off in a very collaborative regulatory framework, with knowledge flowing openly between the environmental authorities and the regulated industry. Boliden was no exception in this case. These characteristics changed over time, however, and already in the 1980s, the company grew more proactive, shaping its environmental strategies more independently of the Swedish EPA. This was a response to the dilemma that occurred in the wake of the oil crisis and the economic recession in the mid-1970s when the company ran into liquidity problems. The strategy was to develop long-term investment plans where coordination could be achieved by means of productive investment. Cleaner technologies and more efficient use of raw materials became an integrated part of the overall modernization of the company from the early 1970s and onward, and particularly after the mid-1980s.

Finally, this chapter has touched upon the "black box" of ongoing processes inside a multinational company that generates pollution. Appearing to be only profit seeking, dirty, and polluting from the outside, the company included managers, engineers, technicians, and ordinary workers struggling inside industrial gates in order to learn and accomplish the changes that society demanded. Some individuals made mistakes and bad decisions, and the "poison scandal" in Chile will be a big part of the company's image despite its tremendous improvements since the 1960s, including a considerable decrease in energy consumption. It is obvious that the company has caused damage to the natural environment and inevitably still does so by the nature of its work. Mining and smelting are simply not green activities and never will be, though these processes pollute much less than they did five decades ago. An important task for historians focusing on business and the environment is to really incorporate actual environmental impact outcomes and compare successes and failures. Just as environmental historians need to delve deeply into multifaceted processes inside firms to understand their subject fully, business historians with an interest in the environment also need to carefully consider the actual impact of business on the environment and the institutions that set the long-term rules to fully understand theirs.

# Private Companies and the Recycling of Household Waste in West Germany, 1965–1990

*Roman Köster*

Germany is—together with the Scandinavian countries and some U.S. states—a forerunner in the "modern" recycling of household waste—the systematic collection and industrial processing of different parts of garbage.[1] Already in the late 1960s, the first attempts at implementing systematic collection of waste paper and glass were made. In the 1970s, a sustainable infrastructure for recycling household waste was created, and in the 1980s it was improved and extended so that glass, paper, some metals, and potentially dangerous chemicals could be separated out and collected on a regular basis. These efforts finally led to the "green dot" system being introduced in 1990, one of the first systematic attempts to institutionalize the recycling of household plastics.[2]

Private firms played a decisive role in this development. In the late 1960s, they were among the first to regularly collect waste glass and paper from households. They invented new collection systems and built up large-scale infrastructures for collecting, processing, and selling secondary raw materials, including sorting plants, processing facilities, and so on. The institutionalization of a modern recycling infrastructure in West Germany would not have taken place without private waste management companies providing these logistics and expertise. These, therefore, became key players in environmental protection not out of idealism but to earn money. This demonstrates that the history of modern environmentalism has a business aspect that—in business history just as environmental history—is too often ignored.[3]

This chapter aims to outline the reasons the private sector played such an important role in the recycling of household waste beginning in the early 1970s. This seems to be astonishing not least because big cities were the "sovereign territory" of public sanitation departments until the early 1990s. I aim to explain how recycling actually became a "green" business and how the private sector evolved over the course of this development. I start by describing the ascent of private waste management companies in West Germany since the 1960s. Then I explain the reasons modern recycling (mainly of waste paper and glass) became institutionalized and outline the role private firms played in this development.

## Private Waste Management and the Salvage Business in Germany up to the Late 1950s

The origins of private waste management in Germany go back to the nineteenth century, when there were two main fields of activity: the removal of garbage from cities, and trade in reusable items and raw materials. The nineteenth century saw many changes that impacted garbage removal: Germany was rapidly urbanized, leading not only to massive social problems but also to declining hygienic conditions.[4] Traditionally, solid waste had been collected together with feces in cesspools and then used as fertilizer in agriculture, but this method simply could not manage the new scale of waste produced; moreover, other, more effective artificial fertilizers were introduced in the second half of the nineteenth century.[5] Furthermore, beginning in the 1860s, canalization systems were built, leading to feces being disposed of in rivers and other places. Solid waste alone, however, was only suitable as a fertilizer together with feces. Without them, it was merely a nuisance.[6]

This situation made it necessary for municipalities to organize the regular collection of solid waste from households. In the beginning, mostly local peasants were hired by the towns to carry the waste out of inner cities—usually the same people who had formerly discharged the cesspools.[7] They typically utilized extremely simple methods—one or a few horse-drawn vehicles with no equipment for avoiding the spread of dirt and dust in the streets. Thus, it is not surprising that they rapidly provoked plentiful complaints from public authorities and citizens that their service was unhygienic and not very reliable. Such criticisms must be seen in the context of the emergence of the concept of *Munizipalsozialismus* (municipal socialism), which suggested that the public authorities were better suited than private contractors to performing public services. In the last quarter of the nineteenth century, almost all German cities municipalized their waste collection and created sanitation departments.[8]

Only a few cities resisted this trend: the city of Berlin took over waste collection as late as 1927, and it was not until 1950 that the city of Munich municipalized waste collection,[9] but these were exceptions. Municipalization, however, did not immediately push private firms out of business. Municipal waste collection usually handled densely populated city centers with the most severe hygienic problems, whereas the garbage in outer districts was very often still collected by local peasants or other private contractors.[10] It was just a question of time, however, before public waste collection was extended to the whole surrounding area of cities, occurring in most towns by the 1930s, with the process being completed in the 1950s.

As for the second area of activity, trade in discarded materials and secondhand goods,[11] markets were well established by the nineteenth century. As Georg Stöger, Laurence Fontaine, and others have shown, regular markets for secondhand goods (clothes, kitchenware, and so on) had emerged as early as the seventeenth century.[12] They reduced scarcity and offered lower prices but also opened up more consumption options. The trade in used clothes in the eighteenth century, for instance, made it possible even for relatively poor people to wear a greater variety of clothes, and the collection and trade of rags was important in the fabrication of paper. Scrap was among the most valuable materials that could be separated, recycled, and traded from trash, alongside bones, organic waste, and so on.

While the markets for secondhand goods were on the retreat during the second half of the nineteenth century in many industrialized countries, the trade in secondary raw materials was extended and professionalized. The scrap trade, for instance, took advantage of new methods of steel production (especially the dominant Siemens-Martin method, up through the 1950s), but also the trade in rags and bones became more professional and took part in the globalization of Germany's economy before World War I.[13]

The First and the Second World Wars, however, precipitated massive state intervention in these markets. Especially when the National Socialists introduced the "Vierjahresplan" (Four-Year Plan) in 1936, which aimed to diminish Germany's dependence on imports, the state started to monopolize secondary raw materials trade and pushed most private firms out of the market.[14] During the war, salvage collections became ever more frequent as raw materials grew more and more scarce. Even when these collections remained more or less voluntary, they were very unpopular.

After this, the 1950s were a difficult time for private waste management as the infrastructures for recycling and waste removal by private firms had been destroyed. Most cities had municipal waste collection, and smaller municipalities very often did not need a collection at all. One waste management expert stated in 1947 that the United States was the only place where private firms seemed to be able to gain traction in waste management, in contrast to the rest of the world: "While the stance that only purely municipal sanitation departments fulfill the requirements is acknowledged all over the world, this point of view is somehow contested in America where often private firms manage to succeed."[15] Private firms in Germany, however, continued to engage in industrial recycling, the scrap trade, and the collection of wastepaper from industrial plants. The recycling of household waste, on the other hand, did not actually recover from the wartime constraints in Germany. What would later become a billion-dollar industry, beginning in the 1960s, was then just a dim reflection of a formerly prospering business.

## The "Comeback" of Private Waste Management Beginning in the 1960s

In the early 1960s, garbage was increasingly regarded as an unwanted side effect of growing wealth as the amount of waste, especially in the cities, experienced a steep rise. This resulted not only from increasing consumption but also from the introduction of self-service in retailing (which increased packaging waste) and the replacement of coal ovens by closed heating systems that prevented people from being able to burn organic waste and paper at home. The cities were faced with massive disposal problems because of the lack of space and the pollution of groundwater, which gradually became a hotly debated issue in the early 1960s as well.[16]

In addition, the blessings of consumer society were extended to the countryside. Motorization and the extension of traffic infrastructure made it possible to live in the countryside and work in the city. The same development made supermarkets accessible to rural townsfolk, and coal ovens were slowly replaced by oil and gas heating systems in these areas, as well. This "catch-up" process mainly occurred during the 1960s and 1970s, accelerating in the latter decade.[17] As a result, the causes of growing waste in the cities applied to smaller towns and rural areas as well, generating a need for regular waste collection. In most cases, however, public authorities were unable to establish a regular waste collection service because procuring a vehicle for a small number of people simply cost too much money. Cooperation between small municipalities normally collapsed because of administrative difficulties and regional jealousies. Therefore, it was easier to hire a private contractor who could cover a bigger area and thereby seize the economies of scale.[18] This development brought about a new field of business for private companies.

The problem of industrial waste was put on the agenda in the 1960s as well. An important factor in this regard was the water protection law (*Wasserhaushaltsgesetz*), which went into effect in 1960 and made firms rather uncertain about how to dispose of their waste.[19] Moreover, a growing sensibility to the potential dangers of chemical residues and other problematic kinds of waste opened up a new market for private firms. By 1970 already, private firms were responsible for the disposal of 70 percent of industrial waste in Germany.[20] They offered solutions to this problem, even though—at least in the 1960s—this did not mean that industrial waste was disposed of in a manner matching even low environmental standards. This fact was revealed in numerous toxic waste scandals in the early 1970s.[21]

The waste management firms that became important in the 1960s—Remondis, Trienekens, Altvater, and many others—were mostly founded in the 1950s. They normally started from scratch with one truck or merely a few. Sometimes, they emerged when a farmer needed someone to extract his sludge, or they formed to collect the household waste of a few small towns. A growing number of industrial companies needed someone to carry away chemical residues and other kinds of problematic waste.[22] Many firms were also involved in the scrap trade. So it is no exaggeration to say that private waste management was actually a "grassroots business," sometimes operated as a secondary employment. It was therefore essential to the survival of this business that firms become more professional, not least to cope with the stricter environmental regulations.

A clear indicator of this professionalization was the foundation of the VPS (Verband privater Städtereinigungsunternehmen [Organization of

Private Waste Management Companies]) in 1961. In the beginning this organization had merely forty-one members, all of them very small companies. It demonstrates the dynamic development of private waste management, however, that this association had grown to three hundred members by 1970, and to five hundred by 1980.[23] The VPS rapidly became a powerful lobby group for private waste management. It acted not only as a pressure group for the branch but also as an organization to spread knowledge about new technologies. Numerous scientific presentations were given at its annual conventions, which also constituted a meeting point for firms from all over Germany. Journals informed the firms about new developments.[24]

In the late 1960s, private firms started to break into the field of regular waste collection in bigger cities. Mannheim's public authorities, for instance, received numerous letters from the Altvater company, a subsidiary of the garbage-can producer Sulo since 1963, explaining that it had taken over the service in some medium-sized cities in southern Germany and asking Mannheim to follow suit.[25] The public authorities in Mannheim doubted that a company like Altvater would be able to provide regular service in a major city with about 300,000 inhabitants, and probably these letters were actually intended as a provocation. But to a certain degree they marked the beginning of a new era: from that point on, public sanitation departments had to take private firms seriously.

A turning point in the history of German waste management was the Abfallbeseitigungsgesetz (Waste Removal Act) of 1972, which had a profound effect on private firms. The most important clause in the act established the municipalities' responsibility for the collection and disposal of their solid waste. The VPS vehemently protested the first version of the law, interpreting this clause to mean that public authorities could throw private contractors out of the business without any reason. After some negotiations, however, a passage was included that permitted public authorities to hire private contractors to fulfill the task. Nevertheless, the new law enabled cities and counties to quit existing contracts, and this actually happened in a few cases until a court verdict from 1977 put a stop to this.[26]

Even today numerous VPS publications maintain that the purpose of the waste removal law was to damage private waste management companies.[27] Such a "conspiracy theory" seems to be unfounded, though. As Heinrich von Lersner, the first director of the Federal Environmental Agency (Umweltbundesamt [UBA]) established in 1974, stated, even the original version of the law without the added clause made it possible for municipalities to hire private contractors.[28] However, in some cases the law could be interpreted in different ways. In particular, the distinction between residues that have to be declared to be rubbish (*Abfall*) and those that are economic goods (*Wirtschaftsgut*) remained highly contested.[29] But von Lersner was certainly right that the law was not written in bad faith; at that point in time, the people in charge simply did not care much about private waste management companies and saw them as of minor importance and by no means as "dangerous" competitors to public sanitation departments.[30]

Private waste management actually had no reason to complain about the waste removal law because it actually did the branch a big favor. It was no longer possible for municipalities to avoid regular waste collection, which some rural towns had still managed to get away with before. As these smaller municipalities were unable to provide the service themselves in most cases, they were forced to contract private firms to complete the task. During the 1970s, private business in waste management grew increasingly important. In the early 1970s, 25 percent of household waste was collected by private firms, in 1975 this number had grown to 35 percent, and by the decade's end approximately half of all household waste was collected by them.[31] At that point in time, regular waste collection took place in almost all of West Germany.

But it was not private firms' dominance in rural areas alone that prompted their success. In most cases, they proved to be more cost effective than public sanitation departments, despite having to pay a sales tax that sanitation departments were exempt from.[32] The first reason private firms could provide cheaper service was that they had lower labor costs. During the 1960s, when the West German economy achieved full employment, the labor market was very tight and public sanitation departments had to pay high wages to attract workers for a very hard and unpleasant job.[33] Ten years later, however, West Germany experienced a resurgence in unemployment, allowing private firms to hire workers for lower wages. They also successfully recruited workers who wanted to stay in their home village or small town.

They also lowered costs by means of rationalization. During the 1950s and 1960s, cities made every effort to raise waste collection standards and to mitigate the problems caused by the severe labor shortage. While money was not a problem, the growing amount of waste and the very tight labor market were what mattered most for German cities, making technological efficiency more important than cost effectiveness. Vehicles and bins were expensive and the collective wage agreements for garbagemen relatively high. Private firms, in contrast, focused on rationalization, mainly striving for cost effi-ciency. Consequently, they took advantage of the introduction of lighter plas-tic containers and new sizes of garbage cans that made it possible to make processes more efficient[34]—something public sanitation departments always had problems with.[35]

A good example of such a rationalization measure was the introduction of the MGB 240, a plastic garbage can with two wheels for easier handling. This garbage can was developed by the Edelhoff Company from Iserlohn in close cooperation with the Sulo Company from Herford in the early 1970s. While most garbage can innovations came from public sanitation depart-ments in the 1960s, this changed in the following decade. The MGB 240 provided twice as much space as the traditional standard garbage can and was light and just as stable. Moreover, it became possible to demand assis-tance from customers. The people had to bring the garbage can to the side-walk whereas formerly the garbagemen had had to carry them up from the cellar, causing considerable time loss and making the work much harder. With the new cans, some firms even refused to empty them when they were not placed in the correct position.[36]

All in all, even when waste collection remained a "closed shop" in bigger cities, private waste management became a serious competitor to public san-itation departments during the 1960s and 1970s due to technological inno-vations, the rationalization of labor, and consistent uses of economies of scale. The relationship between private waste management companies and public sanitation departments became strained, not least because public de-partments accused private firms of exploiting their employees and of dishon-est advertising.[37] Thus, it is all the more astonishing that the two came together to cooperate in the field of recycling household waste.

## The Institutionalization of Household Waste Recycling

As has already been mentioned, "recycling" had been a common practice for centuries. Markets for secondhand goods, rags, paper, glass, and especially scrap had long existed. But while the scrap trade survived the Second World War because of the high value and easy processing of steel, copper, and such, the recycling of household waste (paper, glass, and such) came almost to a complete halt in the 1960s. There are several reasons for this,[38] but the main factors were growing wealth during the 1950s and 1960s and full employ-ment, eliminating an economic need for recycling.[39] Moreover, the Nazis had destroyed the traditional salvage business, which had been dominated by Jewish traders.[40] The introduction of self-service in retailing created a huge amount of packaging that could not be reused (at least not without serious social consequences). As city structures changed when German towns were rebuilt after the war, they were less amenable to recycling than the old ones.[41] Finally, the growing productivity gap between production and repair services made reusing things uneconomical. Rising hygienic standards for housework during the 1950s and 1960s were also hostile to traditional practices of reusing and recycling things.[42]

The end of traditional household waste recycling during the 1950s and 1960s did not mean that there was no recycling at all. Already in the mid-1960s, West Germany, in the case of wastepaper, had one of the highest recycling rates in the world (almost 30 percent). This paper came from industrial operations, department stores, and other businesses, where a large amount of mono-fraction paper could be picked up, while almost no paper from private households was collected.[43] This, however, changed in the late 1960s. In 1967, the German packaging industry started an advertising campaign called "Ex und hopp," promoting the easy disposal of plastic bottles and aluminum cans. At the same time, German beverage traders announced that they planned to abandon the traditional deposit systems for beer bottles that had existed since the nineteenth century, and in 1969, the German Federal Mail announced its abandonment of its traditional practice of taking back old telephone books in exchange for new ones.[44]

On the one hand, these measures caused new troubles for municipal sanitation departments because they were already struggling with scarce disposal space, unreliable incineration plants, and a constantly growing stream of waste. On the other hand, these symbolic acts generated retaliatory action on the part of the government, which became aware that it could play a role in business interests (an attitude that was not very common during the economically liberal 1960s).[45] Lobbying groups from the brewing industry also protested, finally impeding the abandonment of the deposit system.[46] Charity organizations started to collect old telephone books, and ordinary people initiated local recycling initiatives. The late 1960s therefore marked the relaunch of household waste recycling, even though it was rather erratic at first.

Right from the start of these renewed recycling efforts, three major players provided recycling services: people's initiatives, charity organizations, and private firms. While people's initiatives very often started local recycling activities, almost none of them could be sustained. Charity organizations, by contrast, benefited from volunteers, who collected valuable materials for free, remaining a major factor in recycling household waste until the early 1980s. Private companies, however, provided the most professional service and had decisive advantages over the "amateurs" in the business.[47]

From the early 1970s, public authorities in big cities like Frankfurt, Berlin, Freiburg, and Mannheim contracted private companies to collect waste paper and glass inside their territory.[48] Why did municipalities do this and why did they not perform this job themselves? Mainly, it was money: municipalities had financial constraints once the high growth rates of the 1950s and 1960s became history. Hiring private firms had the advantage of taking some pressure off the city's budget (and reducing the waste stream) and, moreover, proved to be much more flexible. Contracts could be cancelled quite easily while it was very difficult to release employees from public service against the opposition of trade unions.[49]

In 1973–74 there was something approaching a "recycling euphoria" in West Germany. The oil crisis created an incentive for people to look for new opportunities to save raw materials and energy. At the same time, the price of wastepaper experienced a steep rise, bringing environmental protection motives together with the profit motive of private firms. The big problem, however, was that the price of wastepaper did not remain high from the mid-1970s (Figure 10.1). On the contrary, the markets for secondary raw materials, especially wastepaper, proved to be very volatile, due to a number of variables, including the supply and demand of paper (especially wastepaper), the price of groundwood pulp, currency rates (in the West German case especially the dollar-mark rate),[50] and the capacity of processing facilities.[51] In the 1970s and 1980s these interacted in such a way that even experienced experts were perplexed. Moreover, people who recycled out of idealism were especially disappointed by this development because recycling services ended when the prices hit bottom. Even charity organizations stopped collecting wastepaper because the costs of storage turned out to be too high.[52]

The volatile price of wastepaper disrupted the market in the second half of the 1970s so that collection from households almost stopped completely. The situation was better for waste glass though, where prices developed more evenly and the amount of cullet used in glass production steadily rose. So while wastepaper recycling failed in the short term, in the second half of the

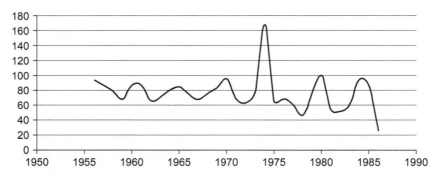

***Figure 10.1.*** Prices for wastepaper (1980 = 100). *Source:* Wolfgang Schneider, "Sekundärrohstoff Altpapier: Markt- und Marktentwicklung in der Bundesrepublik Deutschland" (Ph.D. diss, Technische Universität Dortmund, 1988), 63.

1970s, collection points and processing facilities for the separate collection of waste glass were slowly installed.[53]

## A Green Business? Private Waste Management and the Institutionalization of Household Waste Recycling

In 1978, the government of the state of North Rhine–Westphalia surveyed the existing recycling service in the state. The disillusioning answer was that none existed because the prices of secondary raw materials were simply too low. At that time, even charity organizations stopped collecting wastepaper on account of storage costs.[54] At the same time, society grew more environmentally conscious[55] (evidenced, for example, in the foundation of the Green Party in 1980) and the waste stream continued to grow (creating enormous disposal problems)—a factor at least equally important to municipalities. Thus, it was decided that something had to be done about recycling. At that point, municipalities had not merely begun to allow private waste management firms to collect secondary raw materials inside city territory but had also started to guarantee prices for glass and especially wastepaper.[56] This was a remarkable development because it made recycling the earliest example of the privatization of public services—and because of the history of conflicts between public and private waste management operations. By guaranteeing prices sanitation departments opened up their field of activity to private contractors and also created an almost "foolproof" business for them. Unsurprisingly, many practitioners in the field strongly disliked this policy,[57] but without it there simply would have been no recycling service.

However, there were other reasons private firms were able to compete successfully in this market. First of all, they took advantage of a decade's worth of experience in collecting waste from big areas. The requirements for collecting and disposing of waste in the countryside were quite similar to the requirements for large-scale recycling. The MGB 240, in particular, was a decisive precondition for the installation of so-called "carry systems," which proved to be more effective than "bring systems." Furthermore, private firms were not confined to the municipal area and could thus build up a large-scale recycling infrastructure and gain much higher market power—in relation to paper companies, for instance—than municipalities. A good example of this is the Rhenus Company from Essen in the Ruhr district. This firm started to build an infrastructure for the collection, sorting, and processing of waste glass from bigger cities. Rhenus was actually a logistics company and used this expertise to become a major player in the recycling business. That Rhenus was a subsidiary of VEBA, formerly one of the big energy suppliers in Germany (before becoming part of the Eon Company in 2000), demonstrates that "big business" was already involved in recycling.[58]

In 1985, the rate of return of wastepaper from private households was 33 percent, while in 1972 the return rate was merely 11 percent.[59] More successful (but also easier) was the recycling of waste glass (see Table 10.1); during the 1970s a comprehensive infrastructure of bottle banks (containers with different slots for white and colored glass) was installed.[60] The city of Frankfurt already had 300 bottle banks in 1980,[61] and the city of Dortmund had 531 bottle banks in 1985.[62] The providers of these facilities took advantage of the fact that glassworks were processing more and more shards in the smelting process. While the share of waste glass in the production of container glass was merely 6 percent in 1974, it was already 23 percent in 1983.[63] This also had to do with adequate prices, which made such an infrastructure worthwhile.[64] Furthermore, once these markets were developed, public authorities were able to cut subsidies because established infrastructures were much more profitable than emerging ones.[65]

But how "green" was the recycling service provided by private companies actually? First of all, it seems to be clear that private firms were anything but idealistic. They were striving for profits and stopped the service when the business was no longer profitable. What made recycling actually "greener," however, was the professionalization that went along with private firms'

Table 10.1  Collection of waste glass in West Germany

| Year | Glass |
|------|-------|
| 1974 | 150,000 tons |
| 1975 | 200,000 tons |
| 1976 | 260,000 tons |
| 1977 | 310,000 tons |
| 1978 | 370,000 tons |
| 1979 | 410,000 tons |

Sources: Umweltbundesamt, *Fünf Jahre Abfallwirtschafts programm* (Berlin: BDI, 1980), 19; Memorandum BDI: Developments of German Waste Management Policy and the Waste Management Program (July 1978), Federal Archive Koblenz, B 106, Nr. 69723.

growing market shares and new tasks in the waste management business. Private firms could no longer afford to dispose of toxic waste illegally or violate environmental standards as they often had in the early 1970s when controls were lax and there was little infrastructure to fulfill the requirements of new laws, not least because of the legal consequences of doing so.[66] Had they done so, they simply would have endangered the business model of private waste management.

In the late 1970s, many firms actually started to use lowered costs and environmental protection as sales points. A VPS flyer from 1977 announced: "The world we live in is perpetually in danger. Our earth needs help. . . . We all have to think about natural preconditions, about legal frameworks, about technological, scientific, and financial issues of environmental problems— and we have to act!"[67] In the early 1980s, the Rethmann Company, one of the biggest firms in the business, began using a tree as a logo, and the "Entsorga" trade fair for private waste management began advertising with the well-known recycling symbol.[68]

The involvement of private firms in recycling enabled them to subsume their activities under the label of "environmental protection," something that Finn Arne Jørgensen observed in the case of vending machines for glass and plastic bottles too.[69] But these were not just words: the Trienekens Company, for instance, built a sorting plant for solid waste in the Rhineland in 1985 and declared it the largest European facility of this type.[70] There are substantial reasons to doubt this statement, and it appears likely that this plant was a bit of a camouflage, but it demonstrates that private firms had realized that "environmental protection" was a promising field of business. Indeed, this business model did not prevent private companies from being prone to corruption as in the case of the infamous incineration plant in Cologne in 2002, where a massively overcapacitated plant was erected due to the bribery of the decision-makers by the company that finally built the plant. Even though these cases were related to garbage disposal (not recycling), they nevertheless show once again that most firms regarded environmental protection as a field of business, and nothing else.

All in all, the 1980s saw a continuously growing importance of private waste management companies. At the end of the decade they collected approximately half of all household waste, 80–90 percent of industrial waste, and they were highly involved in the recycling business. While in the late 1970s the West German Ministry of the Interior still had thought of private companies as a negligible factor, at the end of the 1980s private firms had become the model for public sanitation departments seeking to restructure their service.[71] This was not least due to the daily "competition" between public and private waste management operations inside cities' territory. This "paradigm shift" also became obvious when the "green dot" system of plastics recycling was introduced in 1990–91, with public authorities merely playing a minor role. The system was funded with an extra tax that firms had to pay for using the green dot symbol and was run exclusively by private companies that collected and processed plastic packaging.[72]

## Conclusion

Private waste management companies offered a solution to growing disposal problems of firms and municipalities beginning in the late 1950s, when and where no regular waste collection existed and new laws created new standards that public authorities very often could not fulfill. By providing their service in the countryside and for industrial firms, private companies gained experience in the efficient collection of waste in large areas. This proved to be very helpful when more and more small towns and firms hired them, and when recycling became a new major business in the late 1960s. Furthermore, during the 1970s and 1980s private waste management firms became the technology leaders, replacing public sanitation departments in this respect. These findings, however, demonstrate that waste management was first of all a business. In most cases, private firms were neither idealistic nor had much concern about the environment. New laws and necessary professionalization made private firms actually "greener," though, and from the mid-1980s "environmental protection" became a label they seized upon to market their business.

A combination of new laws and directives, on the one hand, and the economic approach toward recycling by private firms, on the other, spawned the modern recycling infrastructure in Germany. Private firms utilized their expertise in collecting and disposing of waste in large areas, while incentives such as state controls forced private firms to professionalize and actually become "greener." While contracts and price guarantees by the municipalities ensured a sustainable recycling service, it was private firms' profit motive that precipitated the emergence of an efficient recycling infrastructure. This, however, calls the distinction (very often found in environmental economics) between markets (as efficient) and the state/government (as inefficient) into question. In the West German case it was the state that "created" a market where private firms could successfully compete and actually contribute to environmental protection.

# Chapter 11

# Kill-a-Watt: The Greening of Consolidated Edison in the 1970s

*Joseph A. Pratt*

In May 1971 Charles Luce—the CEO of Consolidated Edison of New York—stunned the utility industry with the announcement of a new program called "Save-a-Watt." This initiative marked a sharp break with the industry's tradition of aggressively promoting the consumption of electricity. Instead, Con Edison turned to a comprehensive approach for educating its customers about both the need to save electricity and practical ways to do so. This pathbreaking program sought to address conditions unique to Con Edison, which led the nation in both the highest electric rates and the highest concentration of sulfur dioxide, a dangerous air pollutant. Facing long delays in siting new power plants, the company had pressing problems in supplying the growing demand for electricity in the New York City area. As it found itself blocked from other options, Charles Luce and Con Edison choose the available option, conservation, to help reduce demand.

This was an unprecedented choice for a public utility executive, but Luce was not an ordinary head of a public utility. He was an unusual choice to lead Con Edison, where he served as chairman from 1967 to 1982 and CEO from 1967 to 1981. A Kennedy Democrat who came to the company from a position as undersecretary of the interior under Stewart Udall, Luce was an outsider to the company and a relative stranger to the New York City area. As a former head of the government-owned Bonneville Power Administration, he was viewed with suspicion within the public utility industry. He was a lawyer, not an engineer, and he also was a member of various environmental groups. He brought to his job a pragmatic approach that included the willingness to engage the many critics of Con Edison and to look beyond traditions for solutions to problems. His selection to run the company was an announcement of the need for change, and he delivered far-reaching changes that pulled Con Edison through the difficult transition from the model of utility management inherited from the post–World War II boom to a new greener order that began to emerge in the 1970s.[1]

## Con Edison in the Old Order

As the primary supplier of electricity, natural gas, and steam to the greater New York Metropolitan Area, Con Edison was one of the largest and most visible of the urban utilities. It flourished in the post–World War II economic boom by building new plants to supply the power needed to meet its growing region's surging demand for electricity. Rate regulation by the Public Service Commission (PSC) of New York State provided this "natural monopoly" a predictable return on capital investment, giving the company a strong financial incentive to invest in large new power plants. The traditional rate structure granted the largest users of electricity preferential, low rates, and promotional advertising also encouraged the growth of demand. The company's engineers relished the opportunities to push the envelope on fossil-fuel technology while also remaining a leader in the development of emerging technologies such as nuclear power.[2]

An engineer's company, Con Edison had thrived as a leader in the development and use of new technology and in the construction of large traditional fossil-fueled plants. By the mid-1960s, its fuel mix for electric power generation was about 40 percent coal, 40 percent oil, and 20 percent natural gas—with a small but growing percentage of nuclear power. At this time, system planners at Con Edison, who projected future demand with a straightforward extrapolation of past growth, assumed that the trends of about 5 percent annual growth in electricity demand would continue. The overriding imperative for Con Edison was to keep the lights on, and this meant meeting future load by building new power plants in anticipation of future demand. A historical record of proposing, siting, and building new plants in two to three years gave reason for optimism, and the engineers at Con Edison looked forward to the challenge of building a new generation of giant power plants with cutting-edge technology.[3]

A second big challenge for the company as it moved into the 1960s was air pollution. As one of the largest users of fossil fuels in a densely populated city, Con Edison was a natural target for environmental regulators and the general public in the quest for cleaner air. City government had taken the lead in air pollution control in New York City from the late nineteenth century forward. Con Edison's giant gasworks, which produced gas from coal for heating, cooking, and industrial uses, were an early focus of government officials. But the steady growth of coal- and oil-burning power plants after the turn of the century gradually placed these plants in the bull's-eye for pollution controls. The smog that thickened with the passing decades contained dangerous levels of particulate matter and a nasty mix of sulfur dioxide, nitrous oxides, mercury, heavy metals, and even arsenic. Few yet recognized just how dirty and harmful to human health were the emissions from the largely unregulated burning of coal; the generation of power with oil and natural gas produced somewhat similar, yet less visible, emissions.

At the local level, New York City's Bureau of Smoke Control—renamed the Department of Air Pollution Control in 1952—regulated pollution in New York City. Con Edison monitored the level of particulate matter and other air emissions from its fossil-fuel-burning plants and cooperated with local authorities in addressing problems that arose. The company's management understood that it was both good business and good public relations to help fight air pollution. The old order's focus on economic growth gave Con Edison considerable flexibility in managing environmental issues; in general, the company limited its emissions to politically acceptable levels when this could be done economically. The resulting efforts by the company, other industries, and city government did not, however, prevent the steady deterioration of air quality.[4]

Con Edison reached the mid-1960s confident in its ability to continue to succeed within the rules of the old order by building new plants and doing enough about air pollution to dampen public concerns. Its plans for the new power plants it needed to meet its projections of future loads stressed a combination of traditional fossil-fuel-burning power plants and two promising new cleaner technologies: nuclear power and pumped storage. Con Edison became an early leader in nuclear power, the as-yet-unproven power source being widely touted as the clean and inexpensive fuel of the future. Its top management treated nuclear power as just another type of power plant and assumed that these plants could be sited and constructed under the rules and the general timetables of the old order. After building Indian Point 1, a relatively small experimental nuclear plant forty miles up the Hudson River near the town of Buchanan, in 1962 Con Edison announced plans to build Ravenswood A, a large one-thousand-megawatt nuclear plant in Queens. Soon after, it put forward ambitious plans to construct a cluster of nuclear plants at Indian Point. This embrace of nuclear power reflected the nation's nuclear enthusiasm in the 1950s and 1960s; the company assumed that nuclear power would gradually reduce its need to construct more base-load fossil-fueled plants while also helping to reduce air pollution.[5]

Con Edison chose pumped storage for its future peaking power. During off-peak periods at night, base-load nuclear and fossil-fuel-fired plants would pump water from the Hudson River through a two-mile-long tunnel up to a large reservoir behind Storm King Mountain, near West Point. When demand peaked, this water could be released back down the mountain into the river through traditional turbines, generating as much as two thousand megawatts (MW) of peaking power. This simple, efficient design pleased the company's engineers; it promised great benefits to the company in closing the growing gap between base-load capacity and the additional power needed to meet peak demand. In 1962 the company proposed to build a large pumped storage plant on Storm King Mountain near the town of Cornwall fifty miles up the Hudson north of New York City. Assuming traditional construction costs and timetables, the project was economically attractive in comparison to available options. As a bonus, this "man-made hydropower" produced very little air pollution compared to fossil-fuel-burning plants, and other environmental impacts would be minimized by the facility's location far outside of New York City in a sparsely populated region.[6]

At roughly the same time Con Edison announced its intent to build a new generation of nuclear plants and the pumped storage facility, it also announced plans to build the largest fossil-fuel-burning plant in the world, a one-thousand-megawatt behemoth, at its Ravenswood site. Nicknamed "Big Allis" after its manufacturer, Allis-Chalmers, Ravenswood 3 would be triple the size of the company's largest operating plant. It was a strong statement that the company sought to retain leadership in the coal- and oil-fired plants that had been the hallmark of the old order in the utility industry.[7]

## Cracks in the Old Order

This plan for future growth in capacity and the reduction of harmful emissions seemed logical and forward looking to company leaders in the mid-1960s. Yet cracks in the old order became apparent soon after. The most troubling of these were the growing delays encountered by Con Edison in seeking to site and build new power plants. Unfortunately, historically based assumptions of the relatively short time needed to move new plants from the planning stage to operations proved far off the mark. Instead, long delays became the norm for large projects of all sorts in the dawning of a new day of environmental concerns. These delays undermined the best-laid plans of the company, exposing the thin margin of error planners had allowed for completing the plants on a tight timetable.[8]

When Charles Luce joined the company in 1967, he surveyed conditions and concluded, "to say the least, Con Edison was not well managed." He found a company that "seemed to have turned inward, and to be defensive and almost paranoid, a wagon train drawn in a circle to fight off Indians." Customer relations and public relations left much to be desired. Company officials at times seemed impatient and condescending when dealing with the public, especially when outsiders raised questions about technical issues. High electric rates and problems with customer service added to the company's poor public image, which reached a low mark in 1966 when *Fortune*, a business publication, published a highly critical article, "Con Edison: The Company You Love to Hate."[9] Of even more concern to Luce was the lack of preventative maintenance and even everyday housekeeping at headquarters and in the power plants. As shown by a scandal uncovered early in Luce's tenure, contractors had developed cozy relationships with officials in order to fleece the company in rigged bidding schemes. From Luce's perspective as an outsider, it seemed that a once proud company that had built a great utility system in New York City had slipped badly.[10]

Although the new CEO had many concerns about the past management of Con Edison, he had no serious qualms about the company's projections that the demand for electricity would continue to rise at historical rates. At this time, Luce remained a self-described "power pusher" intent on expanding the use of electricity to open the way for building larger plants and capturing economies of scale. He shared this attitude with most other utility executives. He did not initially question the strategy of expanding generating capacity with nuclear for base load and pumped storage for peaking power. Luce forcefully agreed that the company's capacity would have to double by 1980 to meet projected demand: "The one thing not subject to change is the growing demand for electric energy. Therefore, if any proposed project is removed from the schedule, another must be proposed to replace it with the same completion date."[11]

Luce did voice concerns about the uncertainties from growing delays in the permitting of new power plants. He was, of course, especially concerned about completing the planned nuclear and pumped storage plants. When Con Edison announced its intention to build Ravenswood A in 1962, it chose a site in the middle of New York City. According to company spokesmen, the plant's design would be the "ultimate in safety." If the plant was considered safe enough to build and operate, it was safe enough to be placed "well within the city limits," where transportation costs for its electricity would be the lowest possible.

The intensity of public opposition stunned the company's top officials, who responded with patronizing remarks to serious reservations voiced by those who lived near the site in Queens. The experts at Con Edison remained unconvinced by critics who argued that it was reckless or at least premature to place a largely untested technology in the middle of a densely populated city. By the time Luce arrived, Con Edison had given up its losing battle to convince both its customers and regulators of the wisdom of constructing Ravenswood A, but not before the initial controversy had created public doubts about nuclear power and about Con Edison's leadership. These doubts greeted Luce as he settled into his new job and began to develop his own plans for the construction of nuclear power plants both inside and outside the city.[12]

Much the same happened to another pillar of Con Edison's plans for the future in the 1960s, its Storm King project. The company expressed pride in its proposed pumped storage plant by placing a drawing of the facility on the cover of its annual report for 1963. Those who lived in New York City and needed electricity to run air conditioners in the summers probably glanced at the drawing with interest and perhaps even a measure of enthusiasm. Those who fished this beautiful stretch of the Hudson River or had homes in the region reacted with anger that fed the growth of opposition to the Storm

King project. In what historians have called the birth of modern environmentalism in New York, those who would be directly affected by the project
organized to protest as strongly a possible. Their efforts even included a letter in 1968 from the Scenic Hudson Preservation Committee to one Charles
Luce. His name and address no doubt was pulled off a mailing list from another environmental group. The letter, which had been mailed to a previous
residence and forwarded to his office at Con Edison, made an emotional plea:
"We are fighting to establish firmly that the country's natural beauty belongs to all of the people and must not be ruined for any narrow economic
purpose.... Will you please join in the fight by sending your generous contribution to us?"[13] Luce, of course, had already joined in the fight on the other
side, but Scenic Hudson built an effective grassroots coalition to press its efforts to block the pumped storage plant on Storm King Mountain. In this
sense, the use of "Not in my backyard" (NIMBY) to characterize opposition
to environmentally destructive projects had its birth in New York State as
NIMHH—Not in my Hudson Highlands.[14]

The resulting controversy demanded much of Luce's attention in the first
thirteen years of his fifteen-year career at Con Edison. Government reviews
of the Storm King project began in 1963, when the company applied for a
construction permit from the Federal Power Commission (FPC), which regulated all hydropower sites in the nation. The commission granted the permit in April 1965. But in December a court of appeals handed down the
landmark *Scenic Hudson* decision. In addition to ruling that environmental
groups had standing, the court sent the case back to the FPC for study of the
impact of the project on natural beauty and recreational uses of the Hudson.
Three years later the FPC again recommended approval of the now modified
project, but New York City entered the legal battle on the grounds that the
project might pose a threat to the city's aqueduct. The battleground shifted
dramatically in 1970 with the creation of the federal Environmental Protection
Agency (EPA) and the beginning of the enforcement of the Environmental Impact Statement (EIS) requirement mandated by the National Environmental
Policy Act of 1969. The EIS shifted more of the burden of proof on companies
to justify permits for major construction projects. Con Edison now faced a
new requirement to prepare and submit to the FPC a detailed study of potential environmental impacts of its pumped storage plant, including analysis of other options that might be used to accomplish the goals of the proposed
project. The law also called for public input into the EIS process while opening
it to legal challenges.

The evolution of Con Edison's efforts to gain permits for the project illustrates the fundamental change in the old order brought by the new wave of environmental regulations. The original application to the FPC stressed the economic benefits of the project; its discussion of potential environmental impacts simply asserted that "there will be no palpable effect on the natural regimen of the river or upon navigation." *Scenic Hudson* forced Con Edison and the FPC to consider impacts on natural beauty and recreational uses. The EIS requirement in 1970 opened all sorts of issues to greatly increased regulatory and public scrutiny. Charles Luce believed in the project, but as the delay, controversy, and cost all increased, he accepted the reality that the project would be completed—if at all—much later than initially projected. He prudently moved on to one of the few options available to him to replace the much needed peaking capacity promised by Storm King by installing 2,500 MW of new capacity from gas turbines on land and barges around the system.[15]

As its nuclear and pumped storage plants faced long delays, the company also encountered unexpected technical problems with the third pillar of its plans for the future, Big Allis. The giant fossil-fueled plant at Ravenswood 3 proved to be a technological leap too far. The plant began operations in 1965, just in time to sustain serious damage in the major blackout of November of that year. This first of its size plant proved difficult to repair, since both the parts and experience needed were not yet readily available. Because it provided about 15 percent of the company's total capacity, problems with Big Allis reverberated throughout the system. Its shakedown period and return to dependable service proved long and difficult. Customer complaints grew. Indeed, even the chairman of the Power Authority of the State of New York called Big Allis "a lemon" after its frequent breakdowns contributed to a series of "brownouts" caused by insufficient capacity to meet the load. These problems and the fallout from the major blackout in 1965 fueled outrage in a public already angry about Con Edison's high electric rates.[16]

The coming of new government powers and processes to enforce stricter standards of safety and environmental protection had obvious benefits to the society, but they also held high costs for Con Edison. In the old order, the company's nuclear plants and Storm King would have been granted construction permits quickly and would have been in operation in three or four years. In the evolving regulatory system of the late 1960s and 1970s, however, environmental groups delayed to death the pumped storage plant while slowing to a walk the construction of the Indian Point 2 nuclear plant.

In retrospect, confusion and uncertainty were inevitable in the transition to a more demanding and open process for siting and building power plants. New regulatory and legal frameworks with broader public input and stricter environmental standards took time to establish. The greatly strengthened environmental laws of the late 1960s provided new legal weapons with which environmental activists could oppose what they considered unnecessary or destructive projects. In addition, new government powers at the national, state, and local levels had to be sorted out in a federal system. It was no easy task to create legal and institutional frameworks that gave regulators greater power over a range of decisions about power plant siting, fuel use, and pollution control that traditionally had been left primarily in the hands of the utilities. These changes cracked open the traditional approach of the old order and introduced new realities, especially on the design and location of new power plants and the time needed to site and construct them.[17]

The dangers were real for Con Edison. The company had hundreds of millions of dollars on the table, and construction costs escalated as delays mounted in an inflationary era. Continued stalemate threatened Con Edison's ability to perform the basic requirement of all utilities, meeting the load. The construction of gas turbines was a quick fix for additional peaking power, but Con Edison had no such quick fix to expand its base-load capacity. The company's fuels of the future remained in regulatory limbo. The clock kept ticking, and Con Edison's options kept shrinking.

## Muddling Toward a Greener New Order: 1967–1973

Meanwhile, Con Edison faced what amounted to a war on coal, the dominant fuel of its past and present. In the years just before the energy crises of the 1970s, local and federal regulators moved aggressively to reduce the health impacts of air pollution by limiting the sulfur content of the fuels used in the New York City region. Lower sulfur content had long-term implications for fuel use and, ultimately, for the siting of plants. In practice, lower and lower sulfur content standards meant a forced march from coal to oil in power plants, since sulfur could be more easily removed and emissions more effectively managed with oil than with coal. Con Edison strongly objected to the impact of rising oil prices on its already high electric rates. It also pointed out the long-term dangers of dependence on imported oil, but its complaints fell on deaf ears at a time of increasing concern about air quality.

Con Edison's cooperation with city government to control air pollution stopped short of support for limitations on the sulfur content of fossil fuels, which the company considered costly and inflexible. When the Bureau of Smoke Control in New York City held hearings about air pollution in 1950, Con Edison objected to a proposed limit of the sulfur content of fuels used in the city to 2 percent: "We know of no evidence that would point to the need for such drastic limitation," which would place "a great financial burden not only to the Edison Company but on our customers, the people of New York City." In subsequent years the company pressed its argument that "there is no conclusive proof that stack emissions from fuel-burning equipment add to respiratory and other diseases." It hedged its bets on the future of coal by substituting oil and natural gas for coal when economically and technically possible.[18]

Little more was asked of the company until the 1960s, when smog from growing emissions of sulfur dioxide ($SO_2$) and particulates focused political attention on the health hazards from these toxic emissions. In response, Con Edison reminded all who would listen of its historical commitment to help control air pollution. It noted that it had spent $118 million on air pollution control from 1936 to 1967, with about half of that sum spent to retrofit boilers originally designed to burn coal to burn oil and natural gas. These past investments were quite small in comparison to the company's investments in new fossil-fueled plants, however, and they bought little goodwill in a new era of environmental activism that demanded much stronger efforts to clean the air.

New York City government first promulgated standards on sulfur content of fuels in 1964; the original maximum for sulfur content was 3 percent. This came down quickly to 2.2 percent by 1966, when Con Edison relied heavily on oil imports from Venezuela with an average sulfur content of 2.8 percent. Seeing a future marked by lower and lower sulfur standards, the company accelerated its efforts to get ahead of the curve by taking voluntary measures to move below 2.2 percent. Regulators took this to mean that further cuts were both possible and desirable, and sulfur content standards continued to decline into the early 1970s.[19]

Soon after coming to Con Edison, Charles Luce had reminded regulators that the largest reserves of low sulfur crude oil were in Libya and Nigeria, and the company was becoming increasingly dependent on these two volatile regions for current and future supplies of fuel. He was right to worry. Libya had emerged as the leading oil-price hawk within the Organization of Petroleum Exporting Countries (OPEC), and in 1969 a military coup placed in power Muammar al-Qaddafi, an anti-Western military dictator who pushed hard for higher oil prices. Wracked by revolution and violence, Nigeria had earned a reputation for corruption in its dealings with international oil companies. In short, the movement away from coal was poorly timed, expensive, and risky.[20]

Fuel switching from coal to oil in Con Edison's plants remained a big part of New York City's efforts to reduce air pollution and a big problem for Con Edison. The late 1960s found Luce in perpetual negotiations with the city on issues raised by air pollution. Regulation went beyond sulfur content standards for fuel to demands for Con Edison to construct new power plants outside the city. Luce did what he could to satisfy these demands of city government while also trying to protect his company's increasingly fragile financial health. He signed several memorandums of understanding with the city agreeing that Con Edison would strive to reduce sulfur emissions by using fuels with lower sulfur content and by gradually moving new power plant construction outside the city.

The creation of the federal Environmental Protection Agency (EPA) in 1970 raised the stakes—and the uncertainties—for Con Edison. No longer was the push to reduce air pollution primarily a local issue. Federal standards of air and water quality became both stricter and more eagerly enforced. Although opposed by the company, sharp reductions in the use of coal remained the key weapon in the attack on $SO_2$ emissions. Under city regulations from 1965 through 1969, coal use as a percentage of total fuel used at Con Edison fell from 43 percent to 27 percent. With added pressure from the federal EPA, that figure plummeted to 1 percent by 1973 before moving lower than 1 percent in 1974. During the eight years from 1965 to 1973, oil vaulted from 36 percent to 85 percent of the total fuel used by Con Edison. In a tight market for low sulfur fuel oil, this placed Con Edison in a precarious position if disruption of oil supplies occurred.[21]

Reductions in the sulfur content of fuels were good for the environment, but from the company's perspective, the battle plan for the war on coal was poorly conceived and implemented. Con Edison competed with many other companies to obtain existing scarce supplies of low sulfur fuel oil. An expensive pattern emerged. A new and lower sulfur content would be announced; the company would scramble to find suppliers and put in place long-term contracts to assure adequate supplies of cleaner fuel oil; then the announcement would come of even stricter standards requiring new contracts for even cleaner oil. Moving toward a single lower standard over a longer period would have been more economically efficient public policy in an era of extreme fluctuations in the supply of low sulfur oil. But the protection of human health, not economics, was the central goal of regulators, who had to define and enforce public policy in an evolving system of stricter air and water quality standards and enforcement procedures. The dramatic decline of coal use in the years prior to the oil crises of the 1970s left Con Edison extremely vulnerable to changes in the price and availability of low sulfur oil. Substituting oil for coal also sharply limited the company's option to return to coal for new base-load supply if conditions changed in the future.

## Conservation: The Available Option

There was good news, however, on the demand front. Chaotic conditions in the late 1960s and much higher oil prices after the 1973 oil embargo by the Organization of Arab Petroleum Exporting Countries (OAPEC) made a joke out of earlier projections of the future demand for electricity. Estimates based on historical patterns of demand growth proved much higher than actual demand. In 1973, for example, Con Edison forecast that peak demand in 1981 would be 12,200 MW, which turned out to be more than 4,000 MW higher than the actual demand in that year. Meeting demand for the original projection would have required the company to build the equivalent of four Big Allis power plants in the eight years after 1973. It turned out that the actual peak demand of 8,220 MW for 1981 was almost identical to that of 1973.[22] Bad forecasts were bad business, since they pushed Con Edison in directions it did not need to go. As past forecasts of demand proved wildly exaggerated, however, the company found that it had more flexibility to adapt to long-term changes in demand than it had previously assumed.

But it had no such flexibility in dealing with the mounting short-term pressures to expand power generation in the late 1960s. By then, delays in plant construction and problems in maintaining power lines and generating plants had undermined Con Edison's capacity to meet the growing demands of the oncoming summer months. In response to this crisis, the company relied on its own brand of load management. Mobilizing the service representatives for major consumers, it went public with its problems and asked customers to help meet the crisis with voluntary cuts in their consumption of electricity. In combination with system-wide voltage reductions low enough to do no harm to customers and their businesses, voluntary reductions helped the company ease through a most difficult time of recurring capacity shortages from 1969 to 1973.

This systematic approach to brownouts relied on a well-publicized color code for the likelihood of shortages of electricity on a given day. Yellow indicated the need for basic reductions in power use; amber warned of more serious conditions requiring greater cutbacks; red informed consumers of the high probability that shortages would require either the maximum reduction of 8 percent in system voltage or load shedding, the worst-case scenario in which power to large customers might need to be interrupted. The company widely publicized the color code, and some New York radio stations even began to include the code as a part of daily weather forecasts. Managing the brownouts required consumer service specialists to stay in close contact with major customers while reaching out to the general public with its color code and at times with trucks equipped with bullhorns that drove through neighborhoods asking consumers to help the company and the city through the shortage of capacity.[23]

After twenty-two voltage reductions in 1969 and 1970, Con Edison's management acknowledged the obvious: the underlying problem of insufficient capacity was not temporary. The announcement that all promotional activity would cease by the end of 1970 made clear that times had changed, and new strategies would be required to adapt to new conditions. Critics long had argued that Con Edison and other utilities created their own capacity problems with promotional advertising that helped increase demand. Con Edison now agreed. The enlistment of customers in a crusade to lower electricity consumption was incompatible with the continuation of the company's long-term promotional efforts to encourage the increased consumption of its primary product. Nor could the low promotional rates long available to the largest users of electricity be justified. Retraining of sales personnel stressed the education of consumers about the services offered by Con Edison and about the efficient use of energy. The new theme of institutional advertising became "Use all the energy you need for a safe and pleasant life, but do not waste."[24]

From there it was a small step to a more formal campaign to conserve energy, and Charles Luce decided to take that step. In the process, he became the first CEO of a major public utility to embrace conservation of electricity as a part of his company's strategy. He did not take this stance lightly. In essence, conditions in New York City had convinced Luce, the one-time power pusher, to become an advocate for the more efficient use of electricity.

Company statistics bolstered Luce's resolve by revealing a fundamental change in the assumptions underlying traditional power planning. In the old order, economies of scale in the construction of larger and larger power plants had lowered the unit costs of electricity, generating higher profits and at least the possibility of lower rates. Now, however, delays, inflation, and higher fuel costs had raised the cost of a unit of electricity from the company's new plants above that of its older plants. Instead of economies of scale from large new plants, Con Edison could expect diseconomies of scale, which would raise instead of lower the costs of electricity and the rates paid by consumers. In this new situation, conservation made economic sense, since reducing the demand for electricity would delay the need to construct increasingly expensive new power plants.[25]

With economic and environmental tensions rising within the company, Luce surveyed his choices and found few options. Nuclear power was becoming too expensive and difficult to site; pumped storage, too destructive of natural beauty; coal, too dirty; oil, too expensive; natural gas, too scarce. Research and development into renewable fuels and fuel cells had not yet advanced far enough to provide substantial contributions to capacity. In contrast, conservation had few of the constraints of these traditional options. There was no long delay getting it permitted or built; it did not require large capital investments. It had few determined opponents and some supporters among environmentalists. The initial greening of Con Edison was the available option to help squeak through the era of brownouts.

Yet over time, Luce and others within the company came to recognize the long-term benefits of a broader approach to conservation amid the challenges of the 1970s. If the company could learn to manage loads through brownouts, perhaps it also could find ways to manage demand growth by encouraging the reduction of waste and the more efficient use of energy. Higher electricity rates could help reduce consumption, but Luce sought ways to go beyond price and persuade customers that his company and its customers had mutual self-interests in reducing demand.

The idea for a conservation campaign first emerged during the wave of brownouts, but the company delayed its launch until the easing of the capacity crisis. In so doing, Con Edison hoped to prevent consumers from thinking that conserving energy was a temporary response to the crisis, not a fundamental change in the company's position. The early efforts to put together the conservation campaign used the catchphrase "Kill-a-Watt" to capture the changing of the guard after a long history of industry promotion of electricity consumption. But Luce felt uncomfortable with the heavy-handedness of this clever play on words with its obvious reference to Ready Kilowatt, the industry's longtime "spokesperson" for the traditional promotional approach of American utilities. He chose instead the catchphrase "Save-a-Watt." The slogan "It is wise to save energy" then took the place of the original slogan "It is time to save energy," which suggested that the need for conservation was temporary.[26]

In May 1971 Con Edison launched its Save-a-Watt campaign at a joint press conference featuring Luce and Mayor John Lindsay at New York's City Hall. The company justified the need for conservation by reminding listeners that energy efficiency had helped ease the shortages of electricity the previous summer. It added that the wise use of energy reduced both pollution and the nation's long-term concerns about the availability of fuel. Many observers were skeptical of Con Edison's motives, but the fact remained that the company was the first of the nation's major utilities to come out forcefully for conservation.

Following the press conference, the company employed the advertising channels developed during the promotional era to encourage consumers to conserve. Newspaper, radio, and television ads, bill inserts, a widely distributed educational kit, and numerous speeches by Con Edison representatives drove home the message. The company's service department made calls on its six thousand largest customers to urge them to conserve and to demonstrate ways to make the most efficient use of energy.

Con Edison's conservation campaign flooded New York City with a wave of tips on how to choose efficient appliances and then use them wisely. It focused special attention on air-conditioning units, which accounted for an estimated 40 percent of peak demand on hot summer days in New York City. In these efforts the company cooperated with the Association of Home Appliance Manufacturers. It urged consumers to do as much as possible to dampen peak loads by shifting nonessential uses of electricity from midday to the early morning or night. For other businesses it provided a model for making office buildings more efficient by dramatically cutting energy use at its own headquarters building.[27]

The Save-a-Watt campaign was heresy to many other utility executives, and Luce's early efforts to encourage conservation found few followers among the major utilities. The industry had long urged Americans to "live better electrically" by buying all electric homes and embracing the convenience of electric appliances. For a relative newcomer to the industry to champion conservation outraged other utility executives, making Luce an outcast in his own industry. General Electric went so far as to send its manager of market development on a national tour exhorting utility executives to continue to promote sales and avoid the "national tragedy" threatened by Luce's campaign. Ever suspicious of Con Edison, even environmentalists initially hesitated to back the Save-a-Watt initiative, although both the Sierra Club and the Friends of the Earth ultimately acknowledged its benefits and proclaimed their support.[28]

The early returns from the Save-a-Watt campaign were encouraging, but hardly world changing. The company did not achieve its goal of a 10 percent cut in projected consumption in the summer of 1971; instead, it reduced total consumption by about 5 percent and peak load by about 2.5 percent. Yet even these small percentages yielded a reduction on the summer peak load day of about 200 MW, roughly equivalent to the output of one of the company's medium-sized plants. In the next two summers, this total doubled to 400 MW. These reductions in demand certainly did not fundamentally alter the company's total peak demand of more than 8,000 MW, but they made for good public relations in an era of extreme criticism of the company. Luce acknowledged that the "economics of conservation were right for Con Edison" but also noted "a stronger motivation was to respond to the arguments of environmentalists." Whatever the motivation, Con Edison had demonstrated that greater concern for conservation could be a useful part of a new approach to utility planning.[29]

### Energy Versus Environment

The war on coal entered a new phase with the outbreak of a real shooting war in the Middle East in October 1973. The fallout from this war still reverberates through oil markets in the twenty-first century. During the winter of 1973–74 an embargo of oil exports by the Arab members of OPEC reduced supplies of much needed oil imports to the United States, shaking long-held assumptions that the nation would continue to have access to abundant supplies of relatively inexpensive oil. The energy crises of the 1970s brought an urgent search by government and industry for ways to reduce oil imports, increase the production of domestic energy, and moderate oil prices.[30]

From 1973 to the early 1980s, a more than tenfold increase in oil prices had far-reaching impacts on Con Edison. From 1970 through 1981, as environmental regulations continued to force the company to use oil instead of coal, the average price the company paid for a barrel of oil rose from about $2.50 per barrel to more than $35 per barrel. Since Con Edison used up to 100,000 barrels of oil a day, these extreme increases in oil prices brought sharp rises in utility rates. Save-a-Watt might gradually help change attitudes toward energy conservation, but the much higher prices in the 1970s and early 1980s quickly changed behavior. By reducing demand, more expensive electricity altered long-term patterns of steadily rising demand that had been the driving force in the old order.

In the chaotic years after 1973, a new cadre of energy regulators sought to manage the almost unmanageable demands of the energy crises. At the same time, environmental regulators continued their quest to control pollution and improve environmental quality. Throughout the decade after 1973, energy officials pushed Con Edison to burn less oil and more coal while it remained under a mandate by environmental officials to burn less coal and more oil. One series of events illustrates the company's struggles to sort out contradictory demands from different government agencies. Early in the embargo, with the company's oil supplies running perilously low, Luce sought permission to switch from imported oil to low sulfur domestic coal at one plant. After the city finally approved this request, the company purchased coal supplies and used them until the embargo ended only two weeks later. He recalled, "We stopped burning coal the day the embargo ended. Our request to burn the coal we had stockpiled was preemptively denied." Luce later announced that the company would better prepare itself for future embargoes by installing modern precipitators to control particulates along with coal-moving equipment at two of its newest plants. A regional director from the EPA quickly responded, informing Luce that if he did this without the agency's approval, Con Edison would face criminal penalties. Luce already had the approval of the New York Public Service Commission, so he disregarded the EPA's letter and installed the new equipment. This episode made clear the costly confusion of purpose among regulators. They grappled with energy and environmental policies separately and in a confrontational manner, rather than trying to find approaches that coordinated government responses to these two closely related sets of issues.[31]

The embargo ended in the spring of 1974, but government efforts to reduce oil imports continued until the sharp drop in oil prices in the mid-1980s. Throughout the decade Con Edison hustled to find the expensive low sulfur oil now mandated as its primary fuel source, and it continued to juggle the competing demand of energy and environmental regulations. The one place the company might have found common ground with both sets of regulators was conservation, which meant less need for building new power plants for Con Edison, less pollution for the EPA, and reductions in imports for the Department of Energy (DOE). Yet conservation never took center stage in an era when energy policy stressed the need to produce more domestic fuels, not to conserve energy.

In its largely futile decade-long effort to convince regulators to grant variances to switch from oil back to coal in some of its power plants, Con Edison noted that the nation needed to conserve oil and become less dependent on imports, and its customers needed relief from skyrocketing electricity rates. This logic seldom moved environmental regulators to grant relief. A company position paper in 1981 reported minor gains in its crusade for coal conversion, but progress "seemed like inching up a mountain." The company alone could not resolve the primary barrier to the switch back from oil to coal: "While the DOE has the power to prohibit utilities from burning oil or gas, it does not have the authority to give Con Edison or any other utility permission to burn coal. That permission must come from others—in Con Edison's case from the City of New York, the New York State Department of Environmental Conservation, and the U.S. Environmental Protection Agency."[32]

The company proved much more successful in expanding its commitment to conservation education programs for its consumers. Underneath the turmoil of the 1970s, the Save-a-Watt initiative grew stronger and more ambitious, earning a permanent role in the company's management of electricity demand. In 1980, Charles Luce's "Energy Strategy for the 1980s" outlined Con Edison's long-term strategy "to meet the twin goals of cutting oil dependence and reducing the rise in future bills for electricity." The first goal listed was to "promote energy conservation programs in New York City and Westchester County."

By this time a customer service department with a strong emphasis on energy education managed a fully developed conservation education outreach program. In effect, the company had bulked up its traditional promotional efforts, except now its specially trained staff sold energy conservation instead of energy consumption. Pamphlets, presentations, advertisements, and adjustments in its rate structure helped residential customers understand how they could save energy. The company also offered energy audits to help residential customers identify opportunities to stop waste. These audits could include the involvement of "Operation ThermoScan," which used aerial photos with infrared cameras to find areas where heat was escaping from roofs of homes. If audits identified opportunities to improve energy efficiency, the company's conservation specialists recommended improvements, referred customers to proven contractors, and even offered financing for projects that seemed capable of paying for themselves in energy savings within seven years. Until prohibited by law in 1978, the company planned to take on the role of contractor to make the improvements. For large industrial and commercial customers, Con Edison supplied load management specialists to consult on ways to reduce energy use and to shift energy demand to the lower rates of off-peak periods. The crown jewel of the conservation campaign was the Energy Conservation Center in the Chrysler Building in midtown Manhattan, where customers and tourists alike could view exhibits and talk to experts about energy conservation.[33]

Con Edison originally focused on conservation out of necessity when its fuels of choice ran into roadblocks as new agencies in a fragmented regulatory system tried to find their way toward a new balance between improved environmental quality and the supply, security, and price of energy. By 1980 the company had made a strong commitment to conservation. Saving watts did not produce immediate, sharp reductions in electricity demand, but it did contribute steady reductions in energy use while yielding public relations benefits. Save-a-Watt was a successful pioneering effort of a privately owned, publicly regulated company to use advertising and exhortation to foster conservation. The campaign affected attitudes as well as economics. It was a new way—a greener way—of thinking about system planning for utilities.

Con Edison's aggressive efforts to make the case for conservation generated useful dialogue in the city, the state, and the nation, encouraging broader acceptance of the need for using energy more efficiently. The company led the way on this issue in part because of financial and political forces unique to its region. But the leadership of Charles Luce should not be discounted. With an outsider's perspective, Luce recognized early in his tenure at Con Edison that the old order in the industry was changing. Unconstrained by inherited ideas about what could and could not be done, he put forward an innovative response to new conditions. His Save-a-Watt program minimized the need to build expensive new power plants while reducing pollution, and others in his industry gradually adopted his greener agenda for the wise use of energy.

# Chapter 12

# Entrepreneurship, Policy, and the Geography of Wind Energy

*Geoffrey Jones*

This chapter looks at the geography of the global wind energy industry before 2000. The growth of wind and other renewable energy sectors has attracted a considerable literature, especially from public policy, economics, and managerial perspectives, and rather less from the standpoint of firms and at historical levels.[1] This chapter seeks to integrate the policy and other literatures with a business history perspective to investigate a puzzle. While the phenomenon of wind is widely spread around the planet, as the modern industry emerged both the deployment of wind within national energy systems and the nationality of firms making wind turbines were highly skewed by geography.

The geographical distribution of wind power capacity and businesses was idiosyncratic. Between 1980 and 2000 the global generating capacity of wind power grew from 13 megawatts to 17,400 megawatts, but two-thirds of the capacity was in Denmark, Germany, Spain, and the United States (see Table 12.1). In 2000 wind was only a major source of electricity generation in Denmark, followed at a distance by Germany and Spain (see Table 12.2). Meanwhile wind turbine manufacture was clustered in Denmark and the United States through to the late 1980s, when there was a sudden rise of new entrants from elsewhere, and especially Germany (Table 12.3).

Table 12.1  Cumulative installed wind power capacity in top ten countries, 1980–2000 (in megawatts)

| Year | U.S. | Denmark | Germany | Spain | Italy | France | U.K. | India | China | World |
|------|------|---------|---------|-------|-------|--------|------|-------|-------|-------|
| 1980 | 8 | 5 | 0 | 0 | 0 | 0 | 0 | 0 | NA | 13 |
| 1985 | 945 | 50 | 0 | 0 | 0 | 0 | 0 | 0 | NA | 1,020 |
| 1990 | 1,484 | 343 | 62 | 0 | 0 | 0 | 0 | 0 | NA | 1,930 |
| 1995 | 1,612 | 637 | 1,130 | 140 | 32 | 3 | 200 | 576 | 38 | 4,780 |
| 2000 | 2,578 | 2,417 | 6,113 | 2,235 | 427 | 66 | 406 | 1,220 | 346 | 17,400 |

Sources: Global Wind Energy Council, Global Wind Energy Statistics 2010, compiled by Earth Policy Institute; Janet L. Sawin, "The Role of Government in the Development and Diffusion of Renewable Technologies: Wind Power in the United States, California, Denmark and Germany" (Ph.D. diss., Fletcher School of Law and Diplomacy, September 2001).

A number of explanations have been put forward for this skewed geography. The first is resource endowment. Wind speeds vary in intensity and seasonality. Both northern Europe and California, two centers of wind power, have strong and steadily westerly winds. The East Asian region, in contrast, has a monsoonal seasonal wind. However there is a weak correlation between wind energy potential and installed wind capacity.[2]

Policy decisions have been more widely perceived as key drivers behind the spread of wind energy.[3] The reason is that renewable energy, including wind and solar, is not able to compete with conventional forms of power generation from fossil fuels and nuclear energy without subsidies and guaranteed access to grids. Or more precisely, such alternative energy is only competitive if the external costs of conventional energy—such as climate change, air pollution, and water depletion—are included in the calculation.[4]

The question then arises why countries adopted different policies toward wind energy. Here there is less consensus, but a number of sociological studies have stressed variations in environmental awareness, and of social movement organizations, as being influential in shaping policies and stimulating entrepreneurship.[5] This chapter explores the influence of geography and policy during the history of wind industry, with a special focus on entrepreneurship in the industry.

## The Prehistory of Wind Energy

The business history of wind energy between the nineteenth century and World War II was tiny and primarily structured around eccentric inventors

Table 12.2 Electricity generation by energy source in selected countries at benchmark dates, 1975–2000 (thousands gigawatts and percentage share)

| Country | Product | 1975 | 1980 | 1990 | 2000 |
|---------|---------|------|------|------|------|
| **U.S** | **Electricity Generated** | **1,918** | **2,286** | **3,029** | **3,816** |
| | Nuclear % | 9.0 | 11.0 | 19.0 | 19.8 |
| | Hydro % | 15.6 | 12.1 | 9.4 | 7.2 |
| | Geothermal % | 0.2 | 0.2 | 0.5 | 0.4 |
| | Solar % | 0.0 | 0.0 | 0.0 | 0.0 |
| | Wind % | 0.0 | 0.0 | 0.1 | 0.1 |
| | All combustible fuels % | 75.2 | 76.7 | 70.9 | 72.5 |
| **Denmark** | **Electricity Generated** | **17** | **25** | **24** | **34** |
| | Nuclear % | 0.0 | 0.0 | 0.0 | 0.0 |
| | Hydro % | 0.1 | 0.2 | 0.1 | 0.1 |
| | Geothermal % | 0.0 | 0.0 | 0.0 | 0.0 |
| | Solar % | 0.0 | 0.0 | 0.0 | 0.0 |
| | Wind % | 0.0 | 0.0 | 2.5 | 12.3 |
| | All combustible fuels % | 99.9 | 99.8 | 97.4% | 87.6 |
| **Germany** | **Electricity Generated** | **360** | **437** | **509** | **538** |
| | Nuclear % | 6.5 | 12.0 | 28.4 | 29.8 |
| | Hydro % | 5.0 | 4.6 | 3.8 | 4.8 |
| | Geothermal % | 0.0 | 0.0 | 0.0 | 0.0 |
| | Solar % | 0.0 | 0.0 | 0.0 | 0.0 |
| | Wind % | 0.0 | 0.0 | 0.0 | 1.7 |
| | All combustible fuels % | 88.5 | 83.4 | 67.8 | 63.7 |
| **Spain** | **Electricity Generated** | **79** | **105** | **145** | **214** |
| | Nuclear % | 9.2 | 4.7 | 35.9 | 27.9 |
| | Hydro % | 33.7 | 28.9 | 17.8 | 14.7 |
| | Geothermal % | 0.0 | 0.0 | 0.0 | 0.0 |
| | Solar % | 0.0 | 0.0 | 0.0 | 0.0 |
| | Wind % | 0.0 | 0.0 | 0.0 | 2.2 |
| | All combustible fuels % | 57.1 | 66.4 | 46.2 | 55.2 |
| **France** | **Electricity Generated** | **179** | **247** | **401** | **517** |
| | Nuclear % | 9.8 | 23.5 | 74.3 | 76.6 |
| | Hydro % | 33.4 | 28.2 | 14.1 | 13.7 |
| | Geothermal % | 0.0 | 0.0 | 0.0 | 0.0 |
| | Solar % | 0.0 | 0.0 | 0.0 | 0.0 |
| | Wind % | 0.0 | 0.0 | 0.0 | 0.0 |
| | All combustible fuels % | 56.8 | 48.3 | 11.5 | 9.7 |

| Country | Product | 1975 | 1980 | 1990 | 2000 |
|---------|---------|------|------|------|------|
| **Italy** | **Electricity Generated** | **141** | **178** | **205** | **263** |
| | Nuclear % | 2.6 | 1.2 | 0.0 | 0.0 |
| | Hydro % | 30.1 | 26.6 | 16.9 | 19.1 |
| | Geothermal % | 1.7 | 1.4 | 1.5 | 1.7 |
| | Solar % | 0.0 | 0.0 | 0.0 | 0.0 |
| | Wind % | 0.0 | 0.0 | 0.0 | 0.2 |
| | All combustible fuels % | 65.6 | 70.8 | 81.6 | 79.0 |
| **United Kingdom** | **Electricity Generated** | **254** | **266** | **300** | **361** |
| | Nuclear % | 10.4 | 12.1 | 19.5 | 21.7 |
| | Hydro % | 1.9 | 1.9 | 2.4 | 2.1 |
| | Geothermal % | 0.0 | 0.0 | 0.0 | 0.0 |
| | Solar % | 0.0 | 0.0 | 0.0 | 0.0 |
| | Wind % | 0.0 | 0.0 | 0.0 | 0.3 |
| | All combustible fuels % | 87.7 | 86.0 | 78.1 | 75.9 |
| **Japan** | **Electricity Generated** | **456** | **552** | **810** | **1019** |
| | Nuclear % | 5.2 | 14.3 | 16.3 | 30.3 |
| | Hydro % | 18.7 | 16.5 | 19.4 | 9.5 |
| | Geothermal % | 0.0 | 0.0 | 0.1 | 0.3 |
| | Solar % | 0.0 | 0.0 | 0.0 | 0.0 |
| | Wind % | 0.0 | 0.0 | 0.0 | 0.0 |
| | All combustible fuels % | 76.1 | 69.2 | 64.2 | 59.9 |
| **India** | **Electricity Generated** | **NA** | **NA** | **275** | **NA** |
| | Nuclear % | NA | NA | 2.0 | NA |
| | Hydro % | NA | NA | 25.8 | NA |
| | Geothermal % | NA | NA | 0 | NA |
| | Solar % | NA | NA | 0 | NA |
| | Wind % | NA | NA | 0 | NA |
| | All combustible fuels % | NA | NA | 72.2 | NA |

*Sources:* International Energy Agency (IEA), *World Energy Outlook*, annual reports for 1999–2004 and 2010 (Paris: OECD, 2000–2011); China and India data, International Energy Agency, International Energy Statistics, Electricity Generation by Source, 2008.

## Table 12.3 Largest firms in wind energy manufacturing by benchmark dates

### 1945

Jacobs Wind (United States)
Lykkegaard Ltd. (Denmark)
F. L. Smidth & Co. (Denmark)

### Largest Companies by Cumulative Installed Capacity (% World Total), 1988

U.S. Windpower (United States) 26.1
Vestas (Denmark) 13.2
Fayette (United States) 11.0
Micon (Denmark) 11.0
FloWind (United States) 7.1
Bonus (Denmark) 6.3
Nordtank (Denmark) 5.2
Danwin (Denmark) 4.0
HMZ (Belgium) 3.0
Howden (United Kingdom) 2.3
ESI (United States) 1.8
Mitsubishi (Japan) 1

### Largest Companies by Cumulative Installed Capacity (% World Total), 1996

Vestas (Denmark) 20.6
U.S. Windpower (United States) 11.1
Micon (Denmark) 8.4
Enercon (Germany) 8.0
Bonus (Denmark) 7.3
Nordtank (Denmark) 6.8
Tacke (Germany) 4.5
NEPC (India) 4.2
Mitsubishi (Japan) 3.2
Windworld (Denmark) 2.9
Nedwind (Netherlands) 2.4
Windmaster (Belgium) 2.2

*Sources:* Peter Karnoe, *Dansk Vindmølleinindustri—en overaskende international success* (Copenhagen: Samfundslitterature, 1991); Peter Karnoe, "When Low-Tech Becomes High-Tech: The Social Construction of Technological Learning Processes in the Danish and the American Wind Turbine Industry," in *Mobilizing Resources and Generating Competencies*, ed. Peter Karnoe, Peer Hull Kristensen, and Poul Houman Andersen (Copenhagen: Copenhagen Business School Press, 1999), 184.

and small-scale entrepreneurs. Nonetheless this period was important as a source of path dependences, as well as providing some foundational technologies.

The historical use of wind as a source of energy for pumping water and grinding grain went back at least two thousand years, but it was rendered almost irrelevant when the use of steam took hold in the Industrial Revolution. However, during the nineteenth century the distinctive geographical conditions of the United States prompted the first attempts to develop commercial businesses using wind technologies for mechanical water pumping, using relatively small systems with rotor diameters of one to several meters. These systems appeared first with the Halladay windmill in the 1850s, developed by a Connecticut mechanic, and designed for the Great Plains. The market was the builders of the transcontinental railroads, which needed to draw water for their steam locomotives.[6] Low-cost American water-pumping windmills were made in large numbers over the subsequent decades, installed throughout the American heartland, and exported.

The first use of a large windmill to generate electricity was a system built in Cleveland, Ohio, by Charles F. Brush. Brush was a serial inventor, who had made a considerable fortune from inventing an arc-light system. In 1888 he built a sixty-foot tower in his backyard and became the first person in the world to use wind to generate electricity. To store power, he installed batteries in his basement. It worked for twenty years but could only produce twelve kilowatts from its seventeen-meter rotor blades. He dismantled his machine, and when he died in 1929, it still stood dismantled in his backyard.[7]

In Europe there was much experimentation by tinkering inventors, but it was only in Denmark that wind energy became a business.[8] The country had a long tradition of using windmills to mill grain for flour. In 1891 Poul la Cour, a teacher at the Folk High School in Askov in the south of the country, began experimenting with how wind turbines could generate electricity. He became the first person in the world to carry out systematic experiments with artificial air currents in a wind tunnel. He was motivated by a societal vision. He disliked the poor living conditions in towns as they industrialized and wanted to improve rural life so people would not leave for the towns. He perceived that electricity provided the solution, and as power plants were only built to serve the cities, he sought to find a way to generate electricity locally. La Cour's experimental windmills powered a dynamo to generate electricity. This electricity was led into a tank of water, which it would then separate into hydrogen and oxygen. The power was used first to provide the lighting for the high school and the houses of the nearby village.[9]

La Cour's work was embedded in a larger context. He drew on the research of two contemporary Danish engineers and scientists, H. C. Vogt and J. Irminger, who together with the American P. S. Langley, participated in formulating modern theory on aerodynamic lift and drag. La Cour also sought to institutionalize his work. To educate the rural population, he established a Society of Wind Electricians.[10] By 1918 250 electricity-producing wind turbines had been built in Denmark, half of which were connected to power stations.[11]

The interwar construction of national electricity grids supplied from coal-burning power stations posed an enormous challenge for wind energy. The number of power stations in Denmark using wine turbines dropped from seventy-five to twenty-five between 1920 and 1940. Nevertheless the company which La Cour and one of his students founded, known as Lykkegaard, continued to manufacture turbines. It was joined by the cement group F. L. Smidth & Co., which cooperated with the aircraft company Kramme & Zeuthen to develop a new type of wind turbine with aerodynamic wings and a tower of concrete with an output of forty to seventy kilowatts. Danish wind turbines flourished again in World War II, only to wither yet again as fossil fuels became available after the end of the war.[12]

Denmark was the only European country to have a wind turbine industry in the interwar years, albeit a small one. Meanwhile the geographical conditions of the United States continued to provide a market for wind turbines also. There was further technological development inspired by the design of airplane propellers and, later, monoplane wings. The first small electrical-output wind turbines simply used modified propellers to drive direct current generators. By the mid-1920s, one- to three-kilowatt wind generators developed by companies like Parris-Dunn and Jacobs found widespread use in the rural areas of the Great Plains. These systems were installed at first to provide lighting for farms and to charge batteries used to power crystal radio sets, but their use was extended to an entire array of direct-current motor-driven appliances, including refrigerators, freezers, washing machines, and power tools.

The Jacobs Wind Energy Company was the most important new start-up. It was the creation of Marcellus and Joe Jacobs, whose parents had relocated them in rural eastern Montana. The family wanted electricity, yet relied on gasoline from the nearest small town, which was forty miles away. Both brothers worked full-time on the farm. Joe never received formal training, while Marcellus only attended the first year of high school, where he picked up the basics of electricity, which was fundamental for people living on farms. Marcellus came back from school to the ranch and, with his brother Joe, built their first turbine in 1922. After three years they concluded that the multi-bladed wheel they used turned too slowly to produce enough electricity. As Marcellus had learned to fly, he had the intuition that an airplane propeller might solve the problem. World War I left a tremendous amount of surplus, including plane propellers and engines, which were available for purchase at a low price and were used to develop wind turbines technology.[13]

Marcellus Jacobs invented the three-bladed turbine, which later became his trademark product in 1927, and officially started a business in 1929, supported by funds from neighboring farmers. The fact that the Jacobs farm was the only one lit up at night provided a powerful demonstration effect. People would see lights from several miles and would drive to the Jacobs's ranch to find out how they could get connected as well. In 1931 the small business moved to Minneapolis.[14]

Jacobs's wind turbines were used to provide electricity to rural areas where power lines where not installed and were mostly used to charge storage batteries, operate radio receivers, and power light bulbs. The firm survived both the collapse of rural incomes with the Great Depression, and the federal government's strategies, through the Rural Electrification Association (REA), to stimulate the severely depressed agricultural economies by extending the electrical grid throughout those areas. The REA became a competitor to Jacobs, because it had excess capacity and saw the wind energy as a danger. The Jacobs company's key advantage rested in product quality, as the machines proved extremely durable. Some rural areas also continued to lack reliable electricity supplies before the 1950s. Jacobs also sold internationally. A network of dealerships across the world sold machines to primarily rich farmers with large pieces of land that needed power, who opted to use wind energy rather than use fuel that took a long time to arrive and was expensive to deliver.[15] By the 1950s the company may have built 50,000 wind plants. In contrast, experiments with larger systems, such as Palmer Putnam's giant turbine on a mountaintop in Vermont, which operated between 1941 and 1945, failed.[16]

The desire and opportunity to bring power to rural communities, then, lay behind the Danish and American entrepreneurial endeavors in wind energy before 1945. While the Danes had more of a social agenda and the Americans a primarily commercial one, both created for-profit firms that built successful machines. The only policy influence on these firms was governmental failure to extend grids to rural locations.

### Fossil Fuels Triumphant, 1945–1973

Between 1945 and the 1970s the emergent wind turbine industry was virtually swept away by the spread of grids and the availability of cheap oil. By the 1970s coal supplied 47 percent of American electricity, natural gas 21 percent, and oil 12 percent. Meanwhile the Atomic Energy Commission, created in 1946, continued to promise that a very cheap and safe primary source of power was about to come on stream.[17]

Against this unfavorable environment, there was some further technical experimentation, building on the technical results of the Putnam wind turbine, but it failed to attract support in the U.S. Congress.[18] The existing entrepreneurial wind energy companies also faced an uphill struggle. Jacobs Wind reached its peak in terms of sales from 1946 to 1950, but subsequently growth tapered off, and it filed for bankruptcy in the late 1950s. Marcellus, who had been joined by his sons, started a new business in Florida, where they built what was then called "environmental subdivisions" involving construction and wastewater management. After a few years, they went back up north to relaunch Jacobs Wind Electrics.[19] By the early 1970s many of the wind chargers built by Jacobs were rusting in junk piles on farms.[20]

The Danish firms also encountered the same problems of competing with national electric power grids providing cheap energy from fossil fuels. There was a continued interest in experimentation in Denmark, most importantly by Johannes Juul, the chief engineer at a power utility in Falster, in the south of the country, who was nearing retirement and took up his old interest in wind energy acquired when he had taken one of la Cour's courses in 1903. In 1959 his Gedser turbine began operation. The design was fairly similar to Poul la Cour's wind turbine, and the key innovation—emergency aerodynamic tip breaks—remains in use in turbines today.[21] The Gedser was efficient and reliable and ran for ten years as the largest turbine in the world until it was shut down in 1967 because of cost. In 1962 the price per kilowatt produced by the wind turbine was double that of the power produced by a power station using oil, which drove almost all of Denmark's electricity generation.[22] The Danish government opted to allocate research funding to a nuclear test plant of Risø, which was inaugurated in 1958.[23]

Although path dependency could be seen as an important component in the growth of the U.S. and Danish wind turbine sectors, it was evidently a tangential path. By the 1970s little remained of the earlier wind firms. As even remote rural areas in Western countries were connected to national grids, the need to take electricity to the countryside ceased to be a significant driver of entrepreneurial activity.

## Divergent Paths, 1973–1988

During the 1970s two exogenous factors significantly impacted the opportunities for wind energy. The first was the oil price rises of 1973–74 and 1978–79, which ended the era of cheap oil, while raising major concerns in the United States and Europe about the security of oil supplies sourced from the Middle East. Governments began to reconsider the issue of energy supplies and consumption, though with no consensus on what to do. Denmark and France were among the countries that launched new nuclear energy programs. Brazil began investing in the production of ethanol from sugarcane.[24] In the United States, some funding was even allocated to renewable energy.

A second shift in the 1970s was a rise in environmental awareness. Environmental concerns were stimulated by both a number of visible cases of pollution, especially the eutrophication of lakes caused by phosphates in detergents, and by lone voices, especially Rachel Carson with her book *Silent Spring*, published in 1962. Equally, if not more important, was the impact of the space programs of the era. There was a new awareness of humanity existing on a single planet in infinite space. In 1968 the crew of Apollo 8 took the first photograph of Earth from space. Named *Earthrise*, the photograph was widely adopted by the environmental movement.[25] On April 22, 1970, the first Earth Day was held in the United States as twenty million Americans took to the streets to demonstrate the need for a healthier environment.[26]

Coincidently, the 1970s saw the revival of scientific concerns that human activity could cause climate change, an issue that first surfaced in the 1890s, but which had remained marginal. The evidence remained inconclusive and contested for decades, but it would in time entirely transform the debate about policy support for renewable energy.[27]

Environmental concerns became important influences on a new generation of wind entrepreneurs, both in Denmark (and later Germany) and in the United States.[28] They were often provoked by the nuclear programs of governments. This was evident in Denmark where the most influential figures were involved in antinuclear protests. These included Mogens Amdi Petersen, a Maoist teacher who in the early 1970s formed a collective on farmland called Tvind in Western Jutland, and also began establishing alternative Tvind schools. His group spent three years building a turbine that opened in 1978 and attracted considerable attention. In the following year Petersen disappeared from Denmark but became a mysterious force behind the creation of a complex set of institutions, including an international relief organization and the Humana People-to-People NGO, which, by the 2000s, was the subject of allegations and court cases of massive financial fraud.[29]

A less controversial figure was Erik Grove-Nielsen, an engineer who combined an interest in flying with concerns about sustainable lifestyles, acquired while in college in the early 1970s.[30] He became involved in campaigning against the government's plans for nuclear energy, and joined a new grassroots activist organization for renewable energy, the Organisationen for Vedvarende Energi (OVE) formed in 1975, which promoted alternatives to nuclear, including wind and solar. At first experimenting with solar energy, Grove-Nielsen shifted attention to wind and began work on blade reliability and founded a bootstrap company, Økær Vind Energi, in 1977. He built a business selling blades to self-builders that struggled financially, surviving for some years only with donations from OVE, but it achieved significant improvements in blade design.[31]

Among other innovators was Christian Riisager, a small carpenter in Jutland, who installed a waterwheel in the stream in his backyard to produce electricity for his garden. As the stream was weak in the summer, in 1975 he began building a wind turbine using Juul's design with materials such as wood and truck gears that he had at hand. After a series of accidents, he created a prototype seven-kilowatt turbine, which he connected to the grid, for which he retrospectively secured permission from the local electricity distribution company. The turbine attracted journalists, and he was soon making turbines for other people, which he eventually sold to a company in 1979.[32]

The Danish industry saw significant institutionalization. The Danish Wind Turbine Owners' Association, which represented the large numbers of farmers and cooperatives that owned most of the turbines, was formed in 1978 to oppose nuclear power and to promote renewable alternatives. It lobbied electricity boards, diffused information about wind, and facilitated design features to enhance the safety of turbines. In the same year the Danish

Wind Turbine Test Station was founded by four engineers. When the government soon after required wind turbines to be certified before owner-users could gain access to subsidies, they began establishing testing criteria for gaining such subsidies.[33]

In the wake of a second round of oil price rises, three small agricultural equipment manufacturers, called Vestas, Nordtank and Bonus, diversified into wind turbines in search for new opportunities because of stagnating agricultural markets. They knew how to build heavy machinery for a rural market and augmented their competences in turbines working with activist entrepreneurs. They bought blades from Økær Vind Energi, and when Henrik Stiesdal, another young activist who had built an improved turbine, wanted to go to study at university, he licensed it to Vestas. The basis of a Denmark's successful turbine business was then in place.[34]

The development path of the emergent Danish industry was characterized by clusters of small, geographically concentrated firms engaged in incremental innovation. They relied on skilled workers, technicians, and a few practical engineers, and they accumulated practical knowledge over time. This reflected the Danish business system, which featured many small and medium-sized firms and a tradition of collaborative learning networks.[35] Geography was important too. The small size of the country enabled manufacturers to directly service their turbines. This provided huge learning opportunities and also a strong demonstration effect for potential buyers who could see turbines working.[36] Meanwhile the Wind Turbine Owners' Association published data on reliability and performance, and comparisons with manufacturer's claims, and had an annual opinion poll on the quality of service of each manufacturer.[37]

It was only with the second oil crisis that the public policy became a significant stimulus for Danish wind energy. In 1979 the government instituted a 30 percent investment subsidy for buyers of certified wind turbines. When this had little effect, subsidies were raised to 50 percent. More important, though, were voluntary agreements made in 1979 between the utilities and associations of wind turbine manufacturers. They agreed to pay owner-users for wind power at a guaranteed minimum price and to share between the utilities and the turbine owners the cost of connecting the turbines to the grid. Initially they only applied to individually owned turbines of less than 150 kW and to cooperatively owned turbines located near the cooperative.[38] These measures grew the Danish market, which reached fifty megawatts by 1985, although policies were not continuous. In 1986 the special wind farm subsidy ended.[39] The government's nuclear power program was abandoned, although the country received electricity from Swedish nuclear plant at Barsebäck, located a mere twelve miles from Copenhagen.

In the United States, in contrast to Denmark, the oil crisis of 1973–74 resulted in a sudden government intervention to support renewable energy. The federal government began to direct funds toward innovation in alternative energy, and a lead role was taken by the space agency NASA, searching for a new role after the end of moon landings.[40] Although the emphasis was on solar energy, it was predicted that wind would supply 5 percent of U.S. energy by 1979. Initially nuclear and coal were still seen as the main sources of electricity, but in the wake of the second oil crisis, President Carter announced a target that solar would supply 20 percent of electricity by the end of the century. The Wind Energy Systems Act of 1980 also promoted an aggressive research and development program to develop wind energy. Most of the funding was allocated to the development of multimegawatt turbines, in the belief that U.S. utilities would not consider wind power to be a serious power source unless large megawatt, "utility-scale," systems were available.[41]

Between 1973 and 1988 $380 million of U.S. federal money was spent on wind turbine development; the comparative spending by the German and Danish governments was $78 million and $15 million respectively.[42] The government fully funded the design and building of large turbines by leading aerospace and technology firms, including Boeing and General Electric, on the assumption that wind turbines could benefit from helicopter technology. Small companies received some money, but even research on small turbines was largely spent on big companies.[43] High spending peaked around 1981, after which the Reagan administration shifted gears and greatly reduced funding.[44] The money spent was almost entirely wasted on a technological dead end. Wind turbines operate in relatively slow moving and fluctuating air currents, which make it necessary to model aerodynamics in three dimensions rather than the two used in aircraft design.[45] The large turbines that were built experienced multiple technical failures and had to be discontinued.[46]

In contrast, a second set of public policies aimed at stimulating demand for alternative energy proved very important for the wind energy business in the United States. The Public Utility Regulatory Policies Act (PURPA) of 1978 opened the door to competition in the electricity supply by requiring utility companies to buy electricity from "qualifying facilities" also known as "nonutility facilities that produce electric power," including renewable power plants. The 1978 Energy Tax Act also offered a 30 percent investment tax credit for residential consumers for solar and wind energy equipment and a 10 percent investment tax credit for business consumers for the installation of solar, wind, and geothermal technologies.[47]

The utility commissioners of individual states were left to implement PURPA, and only those of California did. The results were spectacular. Between 1980 and 1988 the California market accounted for 97 percent of the total installations of wind power in the world.[48] By 1990 most U.S., and over three-quarters of world, wind capacity was installed in California, where wind energy produced 1.1 percent of Californian electricity at that date.[49]

California had emerged as a hot bed of environmental activism and political action during the 1970s. The state banned oil as a fuel for electricity generation, and stopped the construction of coal-fired power plants due to concerns about air pollution.[50] It also attracted activists who helped shape state policies. Among them was Tyrone Cashman, originally a Jesuit, who became interested in ecological issues and wrote a Columbia University doctoral thesis on "man's place in nature" in 1974. In 1977 he moved to a Zen Buddhist farm near San Francisco, where he encountered Sim Van der Ryn, a pioneering environmental architect, who had been appointed by Governor Jerry Brown (1975–83) as California's state architect and head of the Office of Appropriate Technology. Cashman joined the office and became instrumental in designing the policies that created the Californian wind industry.[51]

During the 1980s the state government of California aggressively implemented PURPA. It pioneered the use of feed-in tariffs, and state investment credits were used to augment federal tax credits. In California, investors in large systems exceeding $12,000 received an effective tax credit of 50 percent in the early 1980s, thereby sharply reducing up-front costs of investment. Another state policy, the Interim Standard Offer 4 (ISO4) launched in 1983, was even more important in driving the growth of the wind energy industry. Almost all new capacity between 1983 and the mid-1990s came under these contracts, which persisted after other public policies shifted. While California tax credits for wind energy declined from 25 percent in 1985 to 15 percent in 1986, and then disappeared, and oil and gas prices fell sharply in the mid-1980s, the ISO4 contracts continued for the following decade.[52]

These policies transformed wind energy into a potentially lucrative opportunity. The time length of the California contracts, fifteen to thirty years, and the fixed energy prices for the first five to ten years of the contract attracted entrepreneurial entry because they guaranteed that there would be a market for the electricity they generated and provided security for bank financing. Banks had previously not been willing to finance wind developers.[53] Also important were state-sponsored "resource studies." California was ranked only the seventeenth state for wind energy in the United States, but other states—like North Dakota, ranked number one—conducted no surveys. The surveys again facilitated entrepreneurs' obtaining financing as they could demonstrate availability of the resource.[54]

A new generation of entrepreneurial entrants was attracted to opportunities in California but there was little continuity with the past. Marcellus Jacobs himself had reentered the turbine business during the 1970s, designing a new 7.5 kW turbine, but sold the business to the computer company Control Data Corporation at the end of the decade. Both politically conservative and independent-minded, he opposed government investment in the industry and even the formation of a trade association.[55] However the machines Jacobs and others had built were inspirations to the new generation interested in wind energy. These included Paul Gipe, who began searching for old wind chargers in Montana during the 1970s, having concluded that finding renewable energy sources was vital and seeking to "make a difference." In 1983 he wrote a book on rebuilding wind turbines and moved to California.[56]

Four start-ups dominated the emergent industry, accounting for more than half of California's installed capacity by the mid-1980s.[57] The founders of each firm were quite diverse, but each had come to have concerns to promote sustainability and each moved to California as the new supportive public policies emerged. Fayette, which had started in Pennsylvania, was purchased in 1977 by CIA veteran John Eckland, who had specialized in petroleum supply issues, and who had become interested in alternative energy through concerns about future energy security. After getting a patent for a solar energy device, he refocused on wind energy and moved to Altamont, California, in 1981, initially importing machines made in Pennsylvania.[58] Eckland owned 1,600 wind turbines in the Altamont Pass, making Fayette the second largest wind farm developer in the state, but poor siting of machines and other issues resulted in the firm's demise by the end of the decade.[59] FloWind, established at San Rafael, in 1981, was the sole U.S. firm to adopt Darrieus vertical-axis turbines. It failed in the early 1990s after not getting paid for a contract in India.[60]

The two remaining firms lasted longer. In 1980 James Dehlsen, a serial entrepreneur who had already developed a fluid lubricant, founded Zond

Systems at Tehachapi, California. After becoming interested in sustainability, he sold his lubricant firm and used the proceeds to form Zond, having become convinced of the need for renewable energy and that tax incentives would attract a lot of investors.[61] In 1981 he launched the Victory Garden wind farm, buying 450 of the Storm Master machines produced by a local designer. Dehlsen undertook direct negotiations with the local utility and secured a purchase contract, but the untested Storm Masters proved unable to withstand the region's strong winds. Dehlen sought out Vestas to supply reliable turbines, and became their major customer.[62]

U.S. Windpower, the firm that grew to dominate the American industry for two decades, was founded in Cambridge, Massachusetts. The founders, Russell Wolfe and Stanley Charren, were Yale and Harvard graduates, influenced by the legendary William Heronemus, a former navy captain and one-time proponent of nuclear energy, who in the late 1960s began to predict a coming energy crisis, advocating the use of "grand scale renewables" to gradually replace fossil fuel and nuclear energy.[63] In 1978 Wolfe and Charren erected twenty windmills on New Hampshire's Crotched Mountain, which became the world's first wind farm. An early attempt to make an IPO failed, but Wolfe and Charren responded by raising money from angel investors, primarily wealthy New Englanders, and forming U.S. Windpower. To take advantage of fiscal incentives, the head office shifted to Livermore, California, near Altamont, in 1981.[64]

Wolfe and Charren excelled at fund-raising. In 1982 Merrill Lynch, to which industry insiders had recommended U.S. Windpower as the best wind farm firm, began bringing institutional investors to support the company's expansion. Its second-generation system, the Model 56-100, which it began marketing in 1983, was a major improvement over previous helicopter-blade-type systems. By the end of the decade it accounted for one-quarter of all the wind energy capacity in California.[65] The firm's revenues reached $90 million in 1985, on which it earned a profit of $6 million.[66] In 1993 it became the first wind company to make an IPO when it raised almost $100 million.[67]

The problem for many California wind companies was the quality of much of their equipment. There was limited cooperation within the American industry on standards and testing.[68] The use of untested designs caused many wind farms to experience major reliability problems. In 1986 sixty U.S. firms produced turbines, but within three years this had fallen sharply as poorly managed firms struggled under the costs of repairs, warranty issues, and complaints. The policy regime added to the quality problems of the local industry. In a later interview Cashman justified its market creation function: "We were stuck and I threw a stick of dynamite to break open a vicious cycle that was killing us. . . . What we did was make it so seductive that they would invest—even if the wind turbines didn't work. Without our program in California, the cultural knowledge would have been that wind power doesn't work."[69] Yet tax credits encouraged speculative capital flows into the industry, which were more focused on tax advantages than generating electricity. The perception that unreliable wind farms were built for tax benefits damaged the reputation of the industry and was ultimately instrumental in a policy backlash against it.

The situation laid the basis for the entry of foreign firms into the industry. While U.S. Windpower manufactured thousands of its 50–100 kW turbines, they were only installed on its own wind farms. Zond bought three thousand Vestas machines for its Tehachapi farms during the first half of the 1980s.[70] The Danish firms offered three-bladed upwind machines derived from the Gedser mill design, a primitive and inefficient, but well-understood configuration, now modernized with the addition of fiberglass blades. They had certification from the Danish test center at Risø and with statistics that showed their designs were more reliable than their U.S. counterparts. In 1987, 90 percent of new installations in California wind farms were Danish built.[71] The strong exposure to the U.S. market turned from a blessing into a curse for Danish firms as the California tax credit legislation expired. Both Nordtank and Vestas went bankrupt. In the latter case, a major restructuring finally led to the establishment of a new company called Vestas Wind Systems A/S in 1987. After large parts of the original Vestas Group had been sold off, the new company focused on wind energy.

The great California wind boom was primarily an American and Danish affair. Table 12.4 shows how American and Danish machines dominated the industry in 1992. Yet it also provided a breakthrough for others such as the Japanese heavy engineering company Mitsubishi Heavy Industries. This firm had invested in wind energy through the desire of one engineering executive at its Nagasaki plant, Kentaro Aikawa, to develop a clean energy business following his experience in manufacturing boilers for thermal power plants, which burned oil and coal. His group built wind turbines in a skunk works, hidden from the main business of the firm, and struggled in the face of a lack of a domestic market. The country's ten electric companies monopolized the energy market and had no interest in wind energy.[72] The sale of 660 units at the Tehachapi wind farm in California, then, was a breakthrough

Table 12.4  Origin of wind turbines in California, 1992

| Country of Origin | Number of Turbines | Percentage of Turbines |
| --- | --- | --- |
| United States | 7,786 | 50 |
| Denmark | 6,778 | 43 |
| Japan | 660 | 4 |
| Belgium | 174 | 1 |
| Great Britain | 112 | 1 |
| Germany | 283 | 2 |
| Netherlands | 63 | 0 |
| Total | 15,856 | |

Source: Paul Gipe, *Wind Energy Comes of Age* (New York: Wiley, 1995), 36.

and required extensive support. The project leader lived in California between 1987 and 1992, negotiating with residents.[73]

The 1980s, then, was the breakthrough decade for wind energy. Public policies in California opened up a market for wind energy. The challenge of making this market a reality was taken up by a cohort of new, mainly Danish and American, entrepreneurial firms. Their founders often had environmentalist views to which were added other components to facilitate scaling. The capabilities of the agricultural machinery industry were essential for the growth of the Danish firms, while U.S. Windpower's growth was enabled by its access to outside finance. However the combination of unproven technology and dependence on the vagaries of public polices also produced a risky environment, as the bankruptcies of many Danish and American firms indicated.

## Shifting Geographies

As Tables 12.1, 12.2, and 12.3 show, there was a large increase in installed wind capacity between 1990 and 2000, matched by a shift in the geographical location of capacity and the ownership of leading firms. In 2000 the United States contributed only 14 percent of capacity, about the same as Denmark and Spain, a country that had no wind energy in 1990. Another newcomer, Germany, had risen from almost nothing to account for the largest share of world capacity in 2000. Equally striking was the ranking of largest wind turbine firms shown in Table 12.3. By 1996 U.S. Windpower was the only U.S.-owned firm in the top ten for cumulative installed capacity, which was

dominated by Danish, German, and other firms that had emerged from almost nowhere. In most years of the 1990s, the ten leading firms accounted
for 90 percent of turbine sales worldwide.[74]

During this decade policy shifts were clear drivers of these changes. The
German government had begun a wind power development program in 1975,
but little was achieved. As in the United States, federal funding peaked in
the early 1980s, and wind energy remained marginal in the country.[75] New
policies launched in the 1990s, often adopted through pressure from environmentalist social groups and the Green Party, which was now a junior
partner in many state governments, transformed the situation. In 1989 the
German Ministry for Research and Technology (BMFT) began offering subsidies for wind turbines accepted into its research program.[76] In 1990 the
Electricity Feed Act of 1990, the first feed-in tariff legislation in Germany,
provided guaranteed and highly lucrative payments together with the obligation of utilities to buy wind-generated energy over lengthy periods, with
incentives to invest in efficiency.[77] There were also extensive tax breaks for
renewable energy technology installation.[78] Several state governments, especially in the north of the country, launched ambitious wind programs.[79] High
utility power purchase rates drove the installation of 50 kW, then 100 kW,
then 200 kW, then 500 kW, and now 1.5 MW wind turbines by cooperatives
and private landowners. In 1998, 95 percent of wind turbines in Germany
were operated by private individuals or cooperatives.[80]

In Denmark, when the voluntary agreements between the utilities and
turbine owners broke down in 1992, the government introduced a feed-in
tariff that maintained previous payments for wind power, though making
wind turbine owners pay for connecting their turbines to the low-voltage grid.
In 1991 subsidies for wind power producers were introduced. The powerful
OVE lobbied the government for these policies.[81] In 1994, the government
required municipalities to plan for future wind turbine construction and
began offering subsidies for the removal of older, inefficient, or loud turbines
with new machines.[82]

The role of policy was evident also in the sudden growth of the Spanish
wind turbine industry. In 1979 the government launched a research and development program for the use of wind energy as a source of electricity. An
experimental plant was built in Punta de Tarifa in 1983, and three years later
the government facilitated the installation of the first small-scale wind farms
through agreements with autonomous communities, utilities, and private
companies.[83] Yet the role of wind energy remained minimal until the EU's

ad valorem fund, used to promote regional development, emerged as a subsidy for wind energy projects. By 1992 there were about fourteen wind farms across Spain, but the major policy development was the Electric Power Act in 1997, which initiated an aggressive feed-in tariff policy.[84] By 2000 Spain's wind energy capacity was approaching Denmark's. In contrast, neither the British nor the French governments were interested in renewable energy, and their industries remained muted.[85]

Meanwhile, public policy shifts led both to the overall decline in importance of the U.S. market and a major geographical shift. In the 1990s, the California wind farm market began to slow sharply because of the expiration or forced renegotiation of attractive power purchase contracts with the major California utilities. Growth now started elsewhere as renewable energy initiatives were launched in other states. By 2000 twelve states had specific standards for the quantity of electricity sales from renewable energy. By the new century California's centrality had eroded, and Texas, Oregon, Washington, Oklahoma, and the Midwest became the growth centers of wind energy in the United States.[86]

These policy shifts had a direct impact on new firm creation. While the Danish firms remained heavily dependent on international markets, the sudden rise of German and Spanish firms was directly related to the growth of their national markets. Government policies favored local firms in both new markets. Between 1992 and 2000, 60 percent of new wind capacity in Germany was locally made. The government's subsidy was initially targeted at German firms, with two-thirds of the support given to local companies, enabling the German firms to build scale in the market.[87]

Aloys Wobben emerged as the leading entrepreneur in the emergent German industry. He was initially trained as an electrical engineer and built his first wind power plant in his back garden in 1975. A decade later his company, Enercon, produced fifty-five kilowatt turbines with a gearbox and capable of variable speed. The turbines were manufactured in the coastal region of East Friesland in Lower Saxony, and this was the main market initially. From the beginning, the firm provided service maintenance. As in Denmark, this simplified service and provided feedback to Enercon, enabling it to continuously improve design.[88]

Enercon became a rapid success. The firm captured about one-third of the German market for turbines and accounted for most of the German machines sold abroad, but a second tier of manufacturers emerged, including Tacke, AN Wind, and DeWind.[89] While public policies were evidently critical for the German industry, Wobben joined the ranks of entrepreneurs motivated as much by concerns for the environment as money. In an interview in 2004, he observed: "Our planet is already damaged. We have lost animal species, the state of the atmosphere is weak and we have to protect what is left. It should be immediately forbidden for everybody to increase emissions."[90]

Public policy was also important in the emergence of locally owned firms in Spain. Gamesa, which became the largest Spanish firm, was founded in 1976, and its initial activity was the construction and sale of industrial machinery. During the 1980s, after being taken over by Iberdrola, Spain's second largest Spanish electrical utility, based in Bilbao, and a local bank, Banco Bilbao Vizcaya Argentaria, the firm invested in new technologies for emerging businesses including robotics, the environment, and composite materials. Gamesa entered the wind energy business as big utilities started placing large orders to benefit from grants and as the Spanish central government and regional governments imposed aggressive local assembly and manufacture requirements before granting development concessions. In 1994 Vestas, in order to access the Spanish market, formed a joint venture with Gamesa, called Eólica, which began to build wind farms. Gamesa used the joint venture to develop its own technological capabilities, and in 2001 the Spanish bought out the Vestas share in the joint venture, with Gamesa maintaining the intellectual property rights to continue to use Vestas technology in Spain and elsewhere.[91]

Danish firms were equally important in the creation of a wind energy sector in India, but as in Spain it proved hard to sustain their position. Both Vestas and Micon formed joint ventures with local partners in the early 1990s. NEPC Micon was the largest Indian manufacturer, but the joint venture ended when Vestas acquired Micon. Vestas's own joint venture ended in 2004.[92] By 1995 India was already approaching the capacity of Denmark, but government policies were fluctuating and erratic.[93]

A local firm called Suzlon became the market leader in India. This venture developed out of a small family textile firm in Gujarat. Soaring electricity prices and erratic supplies led Tulsi Tanti, who was trained as a mechanical engineer and was working in the family business, to invest in two European-made wind turbines. When the manufacturer failed to fit them, Tanti installed them himself. After successfully reducing his power costs, Tanti founded his own company, Suzlon Energy, in 1995. Like Gamesa, Suzlon built its technological capabilities through alliances with foreign firms. The first of these was a second-tier German company, Sudwind, which in 1995 agreed to share technical knowledge in exchange for royalty payments. When the German company went bankrupt in 1997, Suzlon hired its engineers and began manufacturing its own turbines. Shortly afterward it acquired AE-Rotor Technick, a bankrupt Dutch company that made rotor blades. Tanti was an astute entrepreneur with strong views about sustainability. He later observed that he "had a very clear vision, if Indians start consuming power like Americans, the world will run out of resources. Either you stop India from developing or you find some alternate solutions."[94]

While German, Spanish, and Indian firms grew rapidly, U.S.-based companies passed through turbulent times. U.S. Windpower renamed itself Kenetech Corporation in 1988, which became a holding company for diversified activities beyond wind energy. In response to the challenge that the fixed-price purchase contracts it had signed in the mid-1980s would expire after 1991, it invested in a new generation of wind turbines. Despite falling oil and gas prices, it continued to seek growth outside California and raised $92 million for new expansion in 1993.[95] However, technical problems with the new machines compounded other serious issues, including an accumulating stock of machines for the Pacific Northwest where wind farm proposals had been delayed because of concern for birds, and the company went bankrupt in May 1996.

Zond was the remaining large U.S. company. It achieved a major coup by securing funding from the utility Florida Power and Light to complete a technically challenging Sky River wind farm in Tehachapi in 1990 and sought to build its own turbine as a means to drive innovation and reduce the cost of electricity. In 1993 Zond was awarded grant support for turbine development by the U.S. Department of Energy and started to develop a very large 550 kW Z40 turbine using variable-speed technology. The firm hired a former managing director of Vestas and acquired patent rights from the bankrupt Kenetech. The new technology was challenging and expensive, and in 1997 Dehlsen persuaded Enron, then primarily a natural gas producer and trader that was attracted to renewable energy by the opportunities to secure federal tax credits,[96] to become majority owners. The business flourished under Enron. Soon afterward Enron acquired the German-based wind turbine company Tacke.[97] Enron Wind's sales went from $50 million in 1997 to $800 million in 2001.[98]

The subsequent bankruptcy of Enron in the context of a major corporate scandal resulted in the entry into wind power of GE, the huge U.S. electrical and financial group, which had long produced turbines for power generation and which outbid Caterpillar and other firms to purchase the wind-turbine manufacturing assets of Enron in 2002. GE acquired 1,600 employees world-wide with operations in Tehachapi, California, and manufacturing opera-tions there and in Germany, Spain, and the Netherlands and became at a stroke one of the world's largest wind energy businesses for the quite modest price of $358 million.[99] After 2000 the entry of GE, and other large conven-tional firms such as Siemens, into wind energy provided a more secure finan-cial basis for the further growth of the industry, as their deep pockets made them less likely to shift strategies in an industry plagued by shifting public policies, as well as still-emergent technologies.[100]

This period, then, was one of major change in the corporate structure of the wind energy industry. The collapse of the California wind boom led to a period of upheaval in the American industry, with leading firms bankrupted or taken over and the entry into the industry of the Enron conglomerate. Many of the leading Danish firms were also bankrupted by the Californian implosion but emerged under new leadership. In Europe, huge public subsi-dies and support, and favoritism for local firms, resulted in the entry of Ger-man and Spanish firms.

## Conclusion

This chapter has explored the skewed geography in the global wind energy industry before 2000 in terms of the countries in which it was adopted and the country of origin of the leading firms. In the case of the latter, while it might have been predicted that U.S.-owned firms would be strongly repre-sented, it was less obvious that Danish-owned firms would be so important. The rapid rise of new entrants based in Germany, Spain, and India during the 1990s was also striking.

It has been shown that natural resource endowment in wind energy serves as a poor explanatory variable. Denmark was well positioned in wind capacity, but Germany was the only neighboring country that developed a strong wind industry. California was not the windiest of U.S. states. How-ever there were geographical components in the growth of firms. In both the United States and Denmark, the existence of rural areas not supplied by electricity provided a major initial stimulus to entrepreneurs and innova-tors. Subsequently, proximity between manufacture and customers helped generate corporate capabilities. The Danish companies, and Enercon in Ger-many, grew by providing service and maintenance as well as turbines to purchasers, and this was helped by smaller distances than in the United States. Geographical proximity between manufacturers and end users established a feedback loop that was important in building firm-level capabilities.

The role of public policy was important for understanding the geographical distribution of wind capacity around the globe, but it had a more nuanced impact on the rise of wind energy firms. Governments were the problem rather than an opportunity for wind entrepreneurs before the 1980s. They played virtually no part in supporting wind energy—or, rather, wind energy found its market in rural areas that lacked electricity supplies, and it was rendered uncompetitive when governments built national grids that took fossil-fuel-generated electricity to rural areas. During the 1970s, when the oil crises stimulated major shifts in energy policies, the U.S. and other governments spent huge sums of money on unproductive giant machines that further damaged the reputation of wind energy, while achieving remarkably few technological advances.

During the 1980s public policy became more important to and supportive of wind entrepreneurs. The most important policy development was in California with the establishment of feed-in tariffs, subsidies, and tax credits. While providing the opportunity for a new generation of U.S. firms, the main beneficiaries were the Danish and other foreign manufacturers who were able to supply more reliable machines and service them effectively. Although the collapse of the California wind boom proved highly disruptive to the worldwide industry, it had enabled capacities and capabilities to be built on an impressive scale. Subsequently, the combination of public policies to grow wind energy and local manufacture requirements provided an enormous stimulus for the emergence of local firms in Germany and Spain. The Janus face of public policy became evident in these years also. Subsidies and feed-in tariffs facilitated the growth of new technologies, but they generated speculative and rent-seeking behavior. Even without such behavior, distorted outcomes were frequent because of the lack of consistency in policies, especially in the United States. The boom and bust cycles in wind energy were an extreme form of creative destruction. Public policies remained chronically lopsided, with no attempt made to price environmental externalities into fossil fuels or nuclear energy.

Most important, the building of firm-level capabilities was essential. Visionary entrepreneurs were important in the industry, although the vision changed over time. For decades the vision was about bringing electricity to consumers in rural areas and elsewhere plagued by supply problems and high costs, and this tradition continued with Tulsi Tanti. From the 1970s many also entered the business through environmental concerns. It was striking, however, that some of the industry's most successful firms entered wind energy from other industries entirely, bringing in their own distinctive capabilities and connections.

The firms that succeeded were those that followed distinctive paths of learning. This either involved building capabilities incrementally, as in the case especially of Denmark, or else as in the cases of Gamesa and Suzlon, identifying partners from which to acquire technologies and in time absorbing the technologies and developing their own capabilities. The problem of many U.S. firms between the 1970s and the 1990s was their inability to develop internationally competitive products. There was no single explanation for this, but rather it was a combination of factors, including a failure to develop institutional structures for the industry as a whole; the rush to capture lucrative contracts dependent on public policies that were both generous and transient; and the pressures of banks and financiers attracted to the industry through government incentives, but who had short-time horizons. The shifting policies followed by the federal and state governments in the United States do not alone explain the torrid history of the U.S. firms in the industry—after all, the Danish firms were almost as dependent on the American market.

# Chapter 13

# Driving Change: The Winding Road to Greener Automobiles

*Brian C. Black*

"Passing Up the Hybrids" read the May 2015 headline in the *New York Times* as it discussed the impact of lower gas prices on the popularity of hybrid electric vehicles (HEVs) on American roads. After a spike in 2012 for both gas prices and HEV sales, each measure has trended downward.[1] Will the radical drop in prices caused by new technologies for fabricating oil provide the latest response to that age-old question "Who killed the electric car?"[2]

That is the type of hyberbolic conclusion that members of the media might draw from such recent developments; historical analysis of American culture, instead, provides a nuanced context that suggests a counterfactual narrative: basic fluctuations in consumer taste that most likely substantiate the inclusion of HEVs as a permanent portion of the American fleet. No longer statement icons of the environmental left, HEVs have matured into a tool to help consumers manage the fickle landscape of oil prices—a tool that manufacturers are compelled to provide by regulative requirements and consumer preferences.

The road to get manufacturers to diversify their products, however, has been similar to a windy, unpredictable country thoroughfare—on which one is never quite sure what lies around the next turn or below the dale on the horizon. For just this reason, the vehicle marketplace of the twenty-first century provides cultural observers with insight into the role that HEVs now play for an informed, contemporary consumer with buying alternatives. Additionally, the HEV marketplace speaks volumes about changes in our relationship with the automobile and its lifeblood, cheap petroleum. As consumers become more savvy about issues of price and environmental impact, the vehicles that they drive are no longer an inanimate portion of their purchasing equation; this fact alone marks a significant change from any other time in the history of American's relationship with their "rides."

For the primary origins of this shift, historians need to factor in the varied political and social impacts of the 1970s oil crisis. As historical artifacts, the vehicles driven by Americans and the policies to govern them made by national leaders in the last decades of the twentieth century evidence a seminal shift in American ideas of energy consumption. Overall, they initially offer a reflection of the U.S. reliance on cheap petroleum and of the passion for vehicular size and power; therefore, these vehicles and laws reveal the attempt by American manufacturers and consumers in ensuing decades to ignore or deny the lessons of the 1970s shift in petroleum culture. However, this reluctance to change is part of a complex cultural story that is essential to unraveling the significance of the oil shocks of the 1970s.[3]

On the ground level of this historic event, American motorists throughout 1973 to 1974 needed to wait in line for one to two hours or more—ironically, of course, with their engines running the entire time. In other regions, the worst harbinger became signs that read: "Sorry, no gas today." Expressway speeds were cut from sixty to seventy miles per hour to fifty. Many communities—as well as the White House—forwent lighting public Christmas trees. Some tolls were suspended for drivers who carpooled in urban areas. Rationing plans were leaked to the public, even if they were not implemented. For instance, in the New York City region the Federal Energy Office estimated that residents eighteen years of age and older could expect to receive books of vouchers for thirty-seven gallons per month.[4]

By the end of 1973, in fact, gas lines were plentiful throughout the nation. Supplies of petroleum were least disturbed on the West Coast, but by February even California had adopted odd/even-day rationing. Gas station operators were subjected to mistreatment, violence, and even death. Drivers also reacted with venom to other drivers attempting to cut into gas lines. At the root of such anger, of course, was the cruel reality that the events of our everyday lives—kids going to school, adults going to work or shopping, goods moving in every direction, and even cutting our grass—might be constrained, our choices limited by our reliance on finite supplies of petroleum. Nothing could seem more un-American—and nothing more completely contrasted the culture that had defined the vehicles on American roads for the decades since World War II.[5]

However, America's first true experience with petroleum scarcity did not occur in a vacuum. Discussed by historian Adam Rome, the attention generated from the 1970 Earth Day joined with public interest to spur political initiatives in the early 1970s that became known as "modern environmentalism." In a much more nuanced way, these initiatives also shaped an era in environmental thought that some scholars refer to as "green culture"—an era when a collective consciousness on behalf of environmental concerns began to shape a new paradigm organizing—to varying degrees—American life and culture. With Earth Day events emphasizing the gas-guzzling automobile, environmentalists very early identified the auto as sustainable society's primary nemesis; the actual embargo and crisis only provided additional proof and logic to such an argument.[6]

As an initial reaction to the 1970s crisis, the application of new ideas about petroleum and, in particular, its use in automobiles primarily arrived at consumers through federal policies. Although these policies included issues of safety and emissions, this chapter will primarily consider those relating to supply conservation or efficiency in order to contextualize the emergence of the HEV.[7] Although this policy story recaps periods of failure, the emergence of green consumerism and particularly the formalizing of the HEV sector of the fleet acts as an ultimate demonstration of how the American marketplace has absorbed a true energy transition within the American auto industry.

## A Century of Vehicular Complacency

Throughout the twentieth century, American auto manufacturers wowed consumers with new details, ranging from rumble seats to automatic lights and wipers. Viewed in context over time, however, the essential characteristic of the American automobile industry was a remarkable, innovative complacency and technological entrenchment. When humans redefined ideas of personal transportation at the dawn of the twentieth century, they did so through one of the most dynamic and innovative technological moments in the history of our species. With a basic devotion to redefining personal transportation away from the vagaries of animal and human power, innovators in Germany, France, and the United States took the cutting-edge technology of the bicycle and mechanized it through a series of experiments. Through trial and error, powered vehicular devices raced against one another in order to demonstrate the best alternative, ranging from steam to electric batteries and the internal combustion of explosive chemicals such as gasoline.[8]

In short, cheap petroleum and corporate dominance squashed any competitors and by midcentury, the Big Three auto manufacturers (Chrysler, General Motors, and Ford) competed against one another not through power sources and engine efficiency but, instead, through the styling of their products. In this new American marketplace, the automobile almost organically became a primary outlet for the Cold War application of conspicuous consumption.[9] By making available new accessories and decorative elements, auto manufacturers created a hierarchy of styles, models, and car lines. In trying to outdo each other, the Big Three also began cycles of review and improvement that led each one to establish annual schedules for modifying their lines. The American automobile was rapidly becoming more of a cultural icon than a transportation device.

The transformational expansion of personal transportation is truly undeniable: between 1945 and 1955 passenger car registrations doubled from 25.8 to 52.1 million. This trend was certainly a product of the new era of consumption; however, automobiles also powered other sociological trends. The effort of manufacturers of all different types of goods to generate artificial needs within the consumer public influenced all facets of American life, but auto manufacturers were among the first to master this new universe of consumption: the historian of auto styling David Gartman calls the automobile "the central icon in this spectacle of consumption."[10] New cars became the rage and the measure of success when Americans in 1955 bought a record 7.9 million cars—19 percent more than the previous best sales year in 1950! American manufacturers sold 99.2 percent of all passenger vehicles and, of these, 95 percent were made by the Big Three.

Across the fleet of vehicles, writes historian Christopher Finch, "the industry indulged in an orgy of nonfunctional styling that subordinated engineering to questionable aesthetic values."[11] Decorative features to the auto's body became standard. These also became a primary method for attempting to outdo others—at times, making the vehicle look almost cartoonish. Regardless, even the most minimal of these features served little or no purpose in assisting the vehicle to perform its duties better. The best examples included swooping fins that were added to the rear of many designs and chrome outlining that was used to accentuate the style lines. In addition to design elements such as fins and excessive size, gadgetry became a primary compulsion for consumers. Although there were no onboard computers to control such devices, the list of add-ons possible during the 1950s sounds remarkably advanced, including power seats, windows, and locks, automatic headlight dimmers, speed control, air suspension, signal-seeking radios, antennae, and polarized sun visors. With efficiency cast as largely irrelevant, auto manufacturers' research and development emphasized such minutiae while engine efficiency remained stagnant or even declined.

With only scarce exceptions, innovations to autos were organized around the abundance of affordable crude with almost no consideration of the efficiency of the transportation devices that they brought to the American public. And, this is just what the marketplace had grown to expect by the 1960s. From *American Graffiti* to muscle cars, the iconic American rides of the post–World War II era were a primary component of the culture of the Cold War. "Oppulent," "chrome-laden," "heavy," and "overpowered" were all adjectives used to describe the fleet of vehicles that imaged American consumption.

## The 1970s Gas Crisis and an Industry Under Siege

Although not innocent, the American auto industry, it can be argued, lurched into the 1970s gas crisis as a bystander. The industry's first reaction to a gap in the supply of crude was to protect its successful corporate model. Gartman writes, "In America's automotive culture, size had always connoted the importance and luxurious excess in consumption that countered the degradation and frugalities imposed in production."[12] Was it possible that some consumers' basic priorities could be changed by the urgency of petroleum scarcity? Brock Adams, secretary of transportation, spoke to manufacturers in 1978 and left no doubt about his hope: "I bring you a challenge because I think it is time to create a car that is new from the inside out—a car that represents a commitment, not a concession, to a world short on energy and concerned about the future."[13]

With a reconsideration of the basic need for vehicles to perform transportation more efficiently—to use less petroleum for their task—Americans immediately altered their view of the few small vehicles already being sold in the American market, such as the Volkswagen Beetle. Thanks to the desire for Beetles, used models from the late 1960s sold for more than new models had just prior to November 1973. The industry reported that standard-size cars outsold subcompacts by two to one just prior to the autumn of 1973. By December, smaller cars were being sold at the same rate as larger ones, and throughout 1974 their sales jumped while the guzzlers remained in the showrooms. American manufacturers simply could not immediately switch modes to fill this new demand.[14]

Stepping into this breach in the market, Japanese manufacturers made a niche for themselves with inexpensive, small vehicles. The initial forays by these companies had actually sought to appeal to existing American tastes. When Toyota began marketing in the United States in 1965, it sold a standard sedan called the Corona. Datsun/Nissan similarly began selling its 310 series in the late 1960s.[15] By 1970, Datsun had 640 U.S. distributors, and by 1972 the Japanese manufacturers had overtaken German manufacturers to sell nearly 700,000 new vehicles to become the largest overseas seller in the United States. Word spread of the reliability of these models, and when many Americans sought small vehicles, Toyota and Datsun were ready with the Corolla and 1200, respectively. The Corolla, for instance, sold for $1,953, which undercut the prices of the American competitors (Ford Pinto, Chevy Vega, and AMC Gremlin) as well as the Beetle. By the mid-1970s, the Japanese market would be joined by Mazda and Subaru.

Each of these companies focused on smaller vehicles while continuing to produce a full line of autos. However, Honda specifically organized itself to take control of the emerging subcompact market. Beginning with motorcycles, Soichuro Honda entered the auto market in 1962. Honda created the Civic, modeled after the British Mini, and released it in the United States in 1973–74. With fuel economy near 40 miles per gallon (mpg), the Civic took the American market by storm. It was followed by a Honda sedan, the Accord, in 1976—the same year that Japanese imports to the United States passed one million. By the end of the 1970s, each of the three "Big Three" U.S. auto manufacturers had entered into agreements of some type with foreign auto manufacturers to sell small models.

Overall, though, the idea of efficiency was not a smooth fit for Detroit. In addition to these new dually manufactured models, Chevrolet proclaimed in 1975, "It's about time for a new kind of American car," when it released its new Chevette, a subcompact capable of 35 mpg on the highway. AMC sought to get around the cheap, unsafe image of the subcompact by introducing the Pacer, which was billed as "the first wide small car." In its design, however, it also circumvented the efficiency of smaller vehicles and ran the heavy Pacer with a V-6 engine. Other companies created slightly downsized models, including Ford's Granada and Cadillac's Seville. Overall, though, the sales of American cars dropped precipitously in the mid-1970s. In 1974, Chrysler's sales dropped by 34 percent. To combat this free fall, Chrysler introduced the Cordoba in 1975, which, although it presented itself as a luxury vehicle, was the shortest Chrysler since World War II.

Although small was much more acceptable, the greatest impact on the overall fleet was the gaining status of small sedans that resembled Honda's Accord. Previously, as Finch explains, the U.S. manufacturers had resisted homogeneity and ideas such as efficiency and safety. The American car was, despite the pleading of consumer advocate Ralph Nader and others, about style. Finch writes, "Until 1973, the one thing that insulated the American car industry from this tendency was cheap gasoline, which permitted every man a grandiosity of expression that was forbidden to all but the rich elsewhere in the world. After 1973 many Americans began to play by the same rules as Asians and Europeans, and with this came the sameness of product that afflicts the automobile marketplace today. As fins and grinning chrome radiator grilles slipped into the past, they quickly became objects of nostalgia and veneration."[16]

"Detroit was far from dead in 1981," writes Finch, "but to a large extent it dominated the least interesting areas of the marketplace; its constituency had become the conservatives of the motoring world."[17] By the end of the 1970s, the future of the American industry, ironically, was in exploiting the consumer tastes that had been manufactured over the previous eras of petroleum decadence; not, however, in radically altering the industry's existing paradigm. The industry would need new regulations to enable such an effort.

## CAFE: Greening of Vehicle Design and Policy

Cultural preferences die hard, especially those that are particularly ingrained in our national priorities and image. In fact, they often ebb and flow without actually passing away entirely. American consumers had shopped for, purchased, and driven automobiles for more than half a century without giving primary consideration to the machine's efficiency. The first oil shock changed all of this for a time.[18] But American consumers' appetite for size and weight in their machines would flow again. In terms of auto preference, a significant portion of American consumers would (with minor adjustments) always expect certain basic qualities in their vehicles. Although some consumers had permanently reprioritized their view of the automobile, others fell under the enticing spell of an entirely new breed of mass-consumed vehicle: the light truck.

In the decade after 1978, the average weight of domestic and imported cars dropped nearly 1,000 pounds, from 3,831 to 2,921. Although there are many variables to factor in (such as shifts in design and materials), we can at least say that, overall, the weight of the cars on American roadways has decreased since the 1970s.[19] A primary component of this grew from 1977 elections that brought in new Democrats to shake up Congress. Many of these politicians were not willing to allow the manufacturers to resist meeting the new requirements discussed earlier in the decade. In spite of calls from Detroit that new mileage requirements would "shut down" American plants, Congress passed a bill requiring American vehicles to meet Corporate Average Fuel Economy (CAFE) and emissions standards. On August 7, 1977, when he signed the bill, President Jimmy Carter announced that the bill provided automakers with a "firm timetable for meeting strict, but achievable emissions standards."[20]

CAFE standards were far from perfect.[21] They did, however, represent a historic effort to stimulate the manufacture of more efficient autos in hopes of reducing American dependence on foreign oil. Each auto manufacturer was required to attain government-set mileage targets for all of its car and light trucks sold in the United States. In a compromise with manufacturers, the complex standards were calculated as a total for the entire fleet of autos and trucks made by each company. Thus, the manufacture of a few fuel-efficient models could offset an entire line of light trucks that fell below the standards. In fact, the standard is set separately for two classes of vehicles, cars and light trucks.[22] As a supplement to the original act, the 1978 CAFE standards required 18 mpg for cars (in 1974, American cars averaged 13.2 mpg; those built elsewhere, 22.2 mpg).[23] To spur innovation, the law authored by Congress increased the standard each year until 1985. With the car standard at 27.5 mpg in 1985, lawmakers expected that manufacturers would willingly surpass this goal. This standard had to be achieved for domestically produced and imported cars separately. If manufacturers failed to meet these standards, they were to be fined $5 per car per 0.1 gallon that the corporate average fuel economy fell below the standard.[24]

Interest in efficiency was compounded by regulations that derived from interests of the environmental movement, particularly as the auto related to new scientific understandings about the dangers of pollution. After federal laws and regulations from the 1960s followed the wishes of consumer activists to require safety measures such as seat belts and airbags, lawmakers also implemented the first measures to mitigate the pollution caused by the internal combustion engine.[25] The seminal event in the emergence of modern environmentalism, Earth Day 1970 contained many activities that related to air pollution. In one of the day's most dramatic and public displays, though, New York City's Fifth Avenue was transformed into an auto-free zone. Only pedestrian traffic was allowed to traverse the city's symbolic primary artery. Accomplishing its intention, this public display was meant to strip away the noise, congestion, and exhaust that the vehicles brought to the space.

The organizer of Earth Day, Gaylord Nelson, in fact, went on record in 1970, saying that "the automobile pollution problem must be met head on with the requirement that the internal combustion engine be replaced by January, 1, 1975."[26] The 1973 oil embargo added supply concerns to the calls for the construction of more efficient engines. One of the major proponents of clean air legislation was Senator Edmund Muskie, a Democrat from Maine. He acted as a bridge between the new environmental NGOs springing from middle-class America's Earth Day exuberance and the 1960s conception of using the federal government to regulate and ultimately solve the nation's various ills. Together, a conglomeration of concerns focused public opinion against the internal combustion engine as an inefficient, polluting threat to U.S. health and security. Although Nelson and others argued for banning the engine altogether, the most likely outcome appeared to be placing federal regulations (similar to those used in California) on American cars.

The battle over how far CAFE standards and emissions controls would extend required the auto industry to flex its political muscle like never before. Very quickly, the health and safety concerns morphed into threats of inflated prices on American cars and the economic threat of foreign autos encroaching on the American market. After meeting with Nixon during 1972–73, industry leaders altered their approach. When they met with President Gerald Ford in 1975 the auto industries offered to accept a 40 percent improvement in mileage standards if Congress would ease standards on emissions. Ford agreed and presented this policy to American consumers in his State of the Union address. Although Congress protested, this division (accepting CAFE while relaxing emissions) became the rallying point for the auto industry during the 1970s.

The complex terrain of the policies relating to automobiles demonstrates the technology's primacy in America's social and economic life.

Auto emissions were one of the first emphases of environmental policy with initial legislation passed in 1970 (national emission standards were contained in the Clean Air Act). As the details were worked out in Congress, Muskie won a major victory when specific pollutants contained in vehicle exhaust, such as carbon monoxide (CO) and hydrogen chloride (HCl), were required to drop 90 percent from 1970 levels by 1975. The intention, of course, was to force manufacturers to create the technologies that could meet the new standards. Individual states led the way. And, of course, one state in particular: In 1975, a California act required that vehicle exhaust systems be modified prior to the muffler to include a device, the catalytic converter. Costing approximately $300, early converters ran the exhaust through a canister of pellets or honeycomb made of either stainless steel or ceramic. The converters offered a profound, cost-effective way of refashioning the existing fleet of vehicles to accommodate new expectations on auto emissions.

In addition, the scientific scrutiny of auto emissions proceeded on one additional, much more specific front. Air testing on emissions and the smog that they created also revealed a now undeniable reality of auto use: lead poisoning. The willingness to tolerate lead additives in gasoline had persisted from the 1920s. Under the new expectations of the 1970s, though, lead emissions presented auto manufacturers with a dramatic change in the public's expectations. Even under the cultural influence of muscle cars and Hemi engines, Americans accepted that lead was an evil. Associated with poisoned children through its inclusion in paint in many schools and public buildings, lead was emerging in the 1970s as a symbol of the failure of industrial standards to protect American lives.

By this point, the amount of lead added to a gallon of gasoline hovered in the vicinity of 2.4 grams. The Department of Health, Education, and Welfare, home to the Surgeon General, had authority over lead emissions under the Clean Air Act of 1963. The criteria mandated by this statute were still in the draft stage when the act was reauthorized in 1970 and a new agency called the Environmental Protection Agency (EPA) came into existence. The days of lead's use in American gas tanks was clearly on the wane.

In January 1971, EPA's first administrator, William D. Ruckelshaus, declared that "an extensive body of information exists which indicates that the addition of alkyl lead to gasoline . . . results in lead particles that pose a threat to public health." The resulting EPA study released on November 28, 1973, confirmed that lead from automobile exhaust posed a direct threat to public health. As a result, the EPA issued regulations calling for a gradual reduction in the lead content of the nation's total gasoline supply, which includes all grades of gasoline. Following California's lead with catalytic converters, U.S. automakers responded to EPA's lead phase-down timetable by equipping new cars (starting in 1975) with pollution-reducing catalytic converters designed to run only on unleaded fuel. With the fleet largely converted, 1989 brought Congress to finally ban the use of leaded gasoline.[27] It is estimated that from the 1920s, when manufacturers had convinced Americans that lead (called "ethyl") was a safe additive to gasoline, until 1989, 15.4 billion pounds of lead dust were spewed into the air by automobiles.[28]

After the initial emergence of new expectations on automobile performance, the issue came to a political head after elections of 1977 had brought new Democrats into shake up Congress. Many of these politicians were not willing to allow the manufacturers to further forestall meeting the requirements established earlier in the decade. Congress stood up to Detroit's threat that implementing these regulations would "shut down" American plants and passed a bill requiring them to meet mandates on CAFE standards and emissions.

Given the degree of regulation and the radically new expectations placed on vehicles, American auto manufacturers came out of the 1970s feeling under siege. Each leader in the industry forecasted expensive shifts that would raise vehicle prices and put American laborers out of work. In fact, some openly speculated about whether there was hope that automobiles could still be manufactured in the United States in the twenty-first century. They would apply their considerable creativity to extending the American tradition of car making into the next century; however, American manufacturers obviously directed this creative design toward circumventing new regulations. The reform of the 1970s was viewed by manufacturers in the short term as a pitched battle to be weathered instead of as an indication of consumer and cultural change.

Following the implementation of CAFE standards, the data clearly demonstrate that the percentage of cars on American roads decreased, while the share of light trucks exploded. The standards, in short, penalized large car purchases and manufacturing, subsidized those of small cars, and left light trucks largely unregulated. Therefore, according to economist Paul Godek, one could reasonably expect that over the ensuing decades *both* small cars and light trucks would grow in popularity.[29] However, Godek's data demonstrate that, in fact, the small-car share dropped from its 1980 level. The only growth, defying logic on a number of fronts, was in the light-truck category. That is where we wade into the murky terrain of the cultural taste of the American consumer.

## The SUV: Rebuffing the Green Ride

Unintended consequences bedevil any attempt at making law; however, the experience of CAFE standards will be studied by policy makers for generations. The data demonstrates that by creating the category of "light truck," American manufacturers had found their safety valve within the very legislation that sought to restrict their designs. Following the release of the Jeep Cherokee in the mid-1980s, the form of the sport-utility vehicle (SUV) emerged to appeal to the desires of many consumers. Also in the light-truck category, minivans offered families an alternative to the station wagons that were now being phased out and pickup trucks matured from their status as a commercial, work vehicle.

Only in hindsight did auto manufacturers realize that such vehicles would sell. One of the best indicators of this changing taste in vehicle was the evolution of AMC's Jeep as it blazed the way forward in the new SUV category. From the army jeep to the Commando, CJ5, and even the early Wagoneers, Jeeps were rough, work vehicles with a tendency to rollover. AMC designers set out in 1983–84 to create a more aerodynamic, four-door Jeep. The revolutionary design became the Cherokee. When gas supplies grew and prices decreased mid-decade, the Cherokee became one of the nation's most popular vehicles. Most surprising, the sales were not in rural, specialized markets; instead, it was family-oriented, urban and suburban consumers who opted for the nation's first bona fide SUV. To take advantage of these consumers, AMC created a Limited model that sold even more briskly. The cycle was completed in 1987 when Chrysler bought American Motors for $1.5 billion. The main appeal was not the Pacer; it was the Jeep brand.

With the success of Jeep and its acquisition by Chrysler, Ford got through a generation of hesitation over developing a four-door SUV and released the Explorer in 1990. Combining the consumer interest in having such a vehicle with Ford's massive marketing capabilities, the Explorer proved the tipping point for the auto revolution begun by Jeep. Stating the Ford point of view, engineer Stephen Ross explained to journalist Keith Bradsher: "An SUV buyer is almost anti-minivan—this is a buyer who has a family but doesn't want to broadcast a docile family message."[30] Ford's surveys left no doubt that consumers wanted the vehicle to have four-wheel drive, even though the drivers were likely to never need it or, at least, to use it rarely.

Initially, the primary issue for manufacturers was vehicle weight. This is measured as "gross vehicle weight," which is the truck's weight when fully loaded with the maximum weight recommended by manufacturers. Instead of the 10,000 pounds used for trucks, light trucks were initially set at 6,000 pounds. Automakers realized that they could escape the light-truck category all together by increasing the weight of their vehicles, so, as journalist Keith Bradsher writes, they "shifted to beefier, less energy-efficient pickups even in a time of rising gasoline prices rather than try to meet regulations that they deemed too stringent."[31] During the 1980s, SUV sales rose from 1.79 percent to 6.49. Gartman finds a striking contrast between the overall style of design behind these vehicles and models of the past. He writes: "Most of these erstwhile hauling and off-road vehicles could be seen whining along freeways and suburban surface roads, their engines struggling to maintain speed with absurdly low gearing and to overcome the resistance of high, square bodies and knobby, super-traction tires."[32] Merging the attributes of the SUV with the luxury and comfort of large cars would be one of the challenges for automotive designers of the 1990s. There remained, though, one significant addition to the American roadway that must be discussed.

The other vehicle responsible for the leap in the light-truck category was the minivan, which Chrysler brought to American families in 1983. With the large station wagons of the earlier era becoming obsolete with new regulations, the minivan fit squarely into the unregulated light-truck category— with one careful bit of manipulation. Chrysler needed to prove to regulators that the vans could be used for hauling cargo as well; therefore, the first minivans were also offered with a cargo package option. The business-friendly Reagan administration was happy to oblige. Certified as light trucks, millions of minivans and SUVs have driven through this loophole and on to American roads since the mid-1980s.

Together, this segment of the American fleet is one of the remarkable developments of American technology at the close of the twentieth century. Data for the weight of light trucks is not available until 1984. From this start around 3,500 pounds, average weights of light trucks rose over the next decade and topped 4,000 pounds in 1995. With the addition of the category of large SUV, vehicle weights topped 5,000 pounds by 2006. The SUV allowed American consumers to manage the people and materiel of their busy lives, which were lived in a world connected by roads, driveways, and parking lots. A vehicle served as a device of family management and maintenance; however, the SUV always allowed its driver the potential outlet of a rugged drive through deep snow or mud. But this was only one portion of the "light truck" phenomenon.

Through careful design of both vehicle and policy by representatives of the auto industry, this new class of vehicles revolutionized the American fleet of vehicles in exactly the opposite way that CAFE standards intended. Of course, this new category of vehicles contained very few vehicles when the standards were set (decades at approximately 10 percent of entire fleet).[33] The light-truck share of the passenger vehicle fleet rose to 20.9 percent in 1975 and to 30 percent in 1987. In 1995, this had risen to 41.5 percent. And, remarkably, by the year 2001, there were almost an equal number of cars and light trucks (approximately 8.5 million of each). By 1999, the Ford F-Series and Chevrolet Silverado pickups were the best-selling vehicles in the United States.[34] Other trucks were the fifth and seventh best selling, Dodge Ram and Ford Ranger, respectively, meaning that pickups had taken four of the top ten slots in America's most popular vehicles.

In a bitter irony, the CAFE standards and ensuing legislation had created the opportunity to build large, heavy, inefficient vehicles. And, to the shock of manufacturers such as Jeep's AMC and others, Americans wanted such vehicles. What began as a gimmicky, small-selling vehicle for a specific purpose morphed into ubiquity through the odd convergence of consumer taste and auto manufacturers' interest in exploiting a specific niche in new vehicle regulations. There is no doubt that this is what a culture's failure to react to the 1970s oil shock looks like; however, this was not the end of Americans' reaction to supply scarcity. Our revision of this story grows—at least partly—from the success of green capitalism.

### "Driving Change Without Changing Driving"

As a dramatic illustration of denial after the 1970s gas crisis, American vehicle consumers completed their twentieth-century petroleum binge by staring into the face of scarcity and pressing the pedal to the metal—driving more miles in heavier cars than at any other time in history. The petroleum moment had not changed; in fact, scarcity became even more pronounced in the first decade of the twenty-first century and gasoline prices cost Americans record amounts. For this reason, writer Paul Roberts in *The End of Oil* may be stating the obvious when he writes: "The SUV represents the height of conspicuous energy consumption. The extra size, weight, and power of the vehicles are rarely justified by the way their owners drive them. Even though owners and carmakers counter that the SUV's greater size, weight, and capabilities provide an extra margin of safety, studies indicate that SUVs not only are more likely to kill people in cars they hit but, because they roll over more easily, can actually be more dangerous to their occupants as well."[35]

However, just as we assume that the conservation efforts initiated by policy initiatives of the 1970s have been lost—roadkill against the bumper of a supersized SUV—we find that simultaneous with Americans' fetish with larger, heavier trucks and SUVs a clear cultural initiative forced alternatives into the mainstream. As mass Americans veered to excess in the 1990s, the State of California worked with manufacturers and scientists to create the first serious alternative vehicles on American roadways. The electric vehicle (EV) fate—immortalized in the film *Who Killed the Electric Car?*—proved a warm-up to prepare Americans for the first release of hybrid electric vehicles (HEVs) to mass consumers at the turn of the twenty-first century.[36]

On the mass scale, the hybrid rebirth began when the Toyota Prius went on sale in Japan in 1997, making it the world's first volume-production hybrid car. Today, the five-passenger Prius is the world's most popular hybrid, but it soon was joined by the Honda Insight, first sold in the United States as a 2000 model, and the Honda Civic Hybrid, which came to market in the United States as a 2003 model. Now the HEV sector includes nearly twenty models. Additionally, other fuels, such as ethanol and other biofuels, emerged as additives and supplements in every state. Thus, we are forced to admit that the environmental ethic that emerged in the 1970s has not faded. Instead, it has persisted and even expanded from roots in the fringe to include mainstream initiatives available to all consumers. This also must be claimed as a legacy of the 1970s.

In each case, however, change to the overall fleet was minor and fleeting. That is, until the American auto industry experienced total collapse. The extravagance of the SUV and mega-SUV years carried American manufacturers into the twenty-first century while also positioning them for cataclysmic failure. Mixed in with the complex economic collapse of 2008 was a complete failure of the atrophied American auto-manufacturing empire. A historic bailout of two of the three major American manufacturers (other than Ford) formed a primary plank of the Obama administration's stimulus/recovery plan. In each case, the financial injection of federal dollars brought with it enforcement of new technologies into each company's fleet. Even at the consumer level, the stimulus/recovery effort sought to alter the composition of the American fleet.

In a remarkable reach of federal authority in 2009, Congress approved the Car Allowance Rebate System (CARS), commonly called "Cash for Clunkers," in which the public could turn over older vehicles for $4,500 that would be applied to a the purchase of a new vehicle. The $3 billion scrappage program removed 700,000 older vehicles and replaced them with new models.[37] Although the program was not renewed, many scholars have noted its transformative effect on the industry and on the marketplace.[38]

The collapse of the American car industry in 2008–9, the emergence of global markets for the reconstituted manufacturers, industry innovation, and, finally, consumer's greening taste have changed the automotive marketplace by fundamentally altering the priorities of American manufacturers.[39] Today, the vehicle marketplace has changed, with the steepest shifts occurring in large cars, while small SUVs known as crossovers grow most swiftly. The Hummer died entirely and vehicle weight, overall, is down and many varieties of smaller vehicles now are prevalent in the marketplace.

From this start, a new ethical paradigm has entered today's consumer vehicle market. Most important, though—and most distinct from the 1970s—the HEV (hybrid electric vehicle) category has proliferated, selling approximately three million units in the last decade. Although most models require consumers to check their typical desires for size and power at the door, the HEV sector marks a critical expression of green consumerism.[40] Between 1995 and 2012, alternative fuel vehicle use grew from 246,000 to nearly 1.2 million.[41]

Possibly, a vehicle such as the 1970s Gremlin represented a breadcrumb in the forest, showing the consumers the way forward that has emerged through the application of new technology. From its start with the EV1, the consumer marketplace for automobiles has truly been altered so that now it is forced to make room for the Tesla. Sold primarily through high-end shopping centers in boutique storefronts, the Tesla is marketed more like a diamond than an automobile. Since its introduction in 2012, nearly forty thousand Tesla vehicles have been sold. With sales appearing to double between 2013 and 2014, Tesla seems to indicate that a vibrant market has emerged—a niche market that will not appeal to every American able to afford an $85,000 vehicle. However, Tesla has made clear that the high costs of superhigh tech can be green; in fact, it possibly represents a high point of green capitalism: a trophy purchase for the megawealthy that is good for the environment. And, of course, Tesla's ethic will be available even more broadly with the addition of its more affordable Model 3 in 2017.

In the persistence of the HEV sector, we find the supporting historical narrative of green consumption. If the story had stopped with the mega-SUV of the 1990s, of course, the American reaction to the oil shock was a complete failure in adapting the fleet of vehicles available to consumers. However, the story that continues in the twenty-first century suggests that the ethic and priority of environmental thought has indeed resulted in a steady and intensifying transition.

## Conservation by Another Name: Green Capitalism

Environmental concern and the increasing awareness of humans' impact on earth have combined with shifts in technology and pricing to create a dynamic moment of consumption in the United States, and clearly a portion of this paradigm shift is an energy transition in the twenty-first century. In particular, at a foundational level, American ideas of energy have leapt to integrate the concept of "conservation." This profound shift has occurred as a larger conversation in the background of the automobile shifts of the late twentieth century.

In a memorable historic moment early in the presidency of George W. Bush, Vice President Dick Cheney responded stiffly when members of the press demanded access to the list of corporate representatives with whom he had consulted over the administration's new energy policy. He defiantly refused such demands beginning in May 2001 and never relented. As he faced off with the press, he defiantly stated "Conservation may be a sign of personal virtue, but it is not a sufficient basis for a sound, comprehensive energy policy."[42] Of course, such a perspective stood in stark contrast to Carter's famous effort to educate Americans in the midst of the oil crisis. He stood in the White House in 1977 and shared a very different perspective on the same subject:

> We simply must balance our demand for energy with our rapidly shrinking resources. By acting now, we can control our future instead of letting the future control us. . . .
>
>    Our decision about energy will test the character of the American people and the ability of the President and the Congress to govern.

This difficult effort will be the "moral equivalent of war"—except that we will be uniting our efforts to build and not destroy.[43]

Similar to bookends, Cheney and Carter frame the ebb and flow of a changing ethic of energy conservation in modern American politics.

When embarking on an energy transition, societies might alter the conceptions of very basic terms. Since the 1970s, for instance, terms such as "energy" and "conservation" have come to mean starkly different things. The persistence of alternatively powered vehicles is a strong symbol of the empowerment of the conservation ethic in American energy use to move from a restraining impulse to a guide for a new paradigm of consumption. In short, since the energy crisis of the 1970s, American consumers have come to consider energy in such a wholly different way that we now find green consumption as a primary force in our transition from fossil fuels. It is particularly in the area of cultural shifting that we find conservation emerging to play a primary role.[44]

The growing importance of conservation has impressed even some commentators who seem most likely to be skeptical. Daniel Yergin is the best example. A historian of petroleum who also serves as the world's leading energy consultant (and energy correspondent for CNBC, the business television network), Yergin believes "peak oil" is a myth and doubts that climate change is tied to fossil fuel use. Yet in *The Quest*, he argues that "the fifth fuel" will be central to our energy future. "It goes by different names," he explains, "*conservation, energy efficiency, energy productivity*. It could even be called *energy ingenuity*—applying greater intelligence to consumption, being more clever in how energy is used—using less for the same or greater effect."[45] Far from merely a personal virtue, conservation, he argues, is a primary component of any secure nation's future. In the current culture of energy, conservation has become technology directed by an environmental ethic and guided by consumer choices.

Since the 1970s, green culture has expanded to become a viable consideration in the marketplace of American capitalism. In its active state, this shifting moment may go by a variety of names, including: "green culture," "post-ownership," and "the sharing economy." For many consumers, such as those involved with an organization such as Transition US, green capitalism is an all-encompassing community that defines itself in this fashion: "a vibrant, grassroots movement that seeks to build community resilience in the face of such challenges as peak oil, climate change and the economic crisis.

It represents one of the most promising ways of engaging people in strength-ening their communities against the effects of these challenges, resulting in a life that is more abundant, fulfilling, equitable and socially connected."[46]

For energy—and particularly for our life with petroleum—the emergence of the viability of green capitalism carries irony: this counterbalancing cul-ture emerges while "tough oil" makes North America the world's leading producer of oil and the United States openly considers becoming an oil ex-porter for the first time since the 1950s. Particularly for this reason, however, the persistence of green capitalism suggests a shift that may last. There can be little doubt that the current trends of lower petroleum prices and over-supply (particularly thanks to manufactured oil) will not continue. There-fore, green consumerism may represent the more likely trend that is here to stay. Although it took decades to become viable, green consumerism seems to be making a long-term impact on energy markets, particularly in personal transportation.

Linking many of these initiatives and stemming from intellectual shifts of the 1970s, we find a paradigm shift in which educated, informed, and con-cerned consumption is more than a fad. Indeed, "green capitalism," com-poses a growth sector in many arenas as "sustainability" begins an uphill movement toward relevance. In the energy sector, a post-carbon movement has literally altered the way that people think about energy but also about the exact meaning of conservation. Instead of restraint, a new paradigm of green consumption has emerged that goes by a variety of names, however, the best known might be the "sharing economy."

Undercutting the very idea of ownership, businesses provide services ranging from gutter cleaning to shared office space. Where Airbnb com-modified rooms within private homes, Lyft has stimulated carpooling (one of the first energy-saving icons of the 1970s). Although "sharing" has chis-eled out an entire portion of the economy, the revolution is on the side of the empowered consumers who find themselves liberated from the perpetual cycle of purchasing new products or services. In terms of personal transpor-tation, the sharing economy joins with the HEV sector to suggest the first major shift in American automobility in a century, which leads some con-sumers away from the American rite of vehicle ownership.

Uber, begun in 2009, may provide the single most relevant illustration of the new paradigm's impact on personal transportation. Entirely made possible by an application used on an individual's smartphone, Uber flipped the very process of hailing a cab by transferring the power entirely from the cab speeding past the frustrated prospective customer to the phone's location. Using GPS locating, Uber and other applications have significantly impacted urban transportation patterns to allow consumers access, essentially, to a personal driver. And taxi hailing is not the only paradigm that Uber turns on its head, of course.[47] A recent *Forbes* article commented that by 2021 these new urban transportation services (particularly Uber and Zipcar) will be partly responsible for more than 1.2 million vehicles *not* sold to American consumers.[48]

Although the entire energy transition remains dynamic, there can be no doubt that the unifying agency of green capitalism undergirds the possibility for a different future. Unlike any time in the past, new technologies connect environmental convictions of consumers—whether founded in climate change, peak oil, or disappearing rain forest—through the new autonomy of the marketplace. While there will inevitably be fluctuations in the marketplace, the HEV sector represents a permanent change that grows from a clear energy imperative. Consumers have vibrant outlets through which to express their commitments, and the "green sector" has become one of the fastest growing segments of the American economy. The post-carbon movement has a clear footing in the new "sharing" economy, and NGOs have empowered green consumption to fan the flames of a true energy transition that traces its roots back to the 1970s.

# Notes

## Chapter 1. The Ecology of Commerce

1. Paul Hawken, *The Ecology of Commerce: A Declaration of Sustainability* (New York: Harper Business, 1993), 3, 57. I address the issues in this essay in a similar piece, "Can Capitalism Ever Be Green?" in *A Field on Fire: Essays on the Future of Environmental History Inspired by Donald Worster*, ed. Mark Hersey and Ted Steinberg (Tuscaloosa: University of Alabama Press, forthcoming).

2. Hawken, *Ecology of Commerce*, xiii, 17, 162. In addition, see Paul Hawken, *Growing a Business* (New York: Simon and Schuster, 1987). Hawken was not a typical entrepreneur, either. He was part of Stewart Brand's hip circle in the 1960s and 1970s, and he contributed to the *Whole Earth Catalog* and *Coevolution Quarterly*. See Andrew G. Kirk, *Counterculture Green: The "Whole Earth Catalog" and American Environmentalism* (Lawrence: University Press of Kansas, 2007), 102, 165, 206.

3. Rick Fedrizzi, "Ray Anderson: Great Leader of Our Time Passes," U.S. Green Building Council blog, August 9, 2011. The most publicly indebted fan of Hawken's work was Ray Anderson, CEO of the carpet manufacturer Interface, which I discuss later in this piece.

4. Ted Steinberg briefly critiques Hawken's work in "Can Capitalism Save the Planet? On the Origins of Green Liberalism," *Radical History Review* 107 (Spring 2010): 7–24.

5. The quotations are from Judith A. Layzer, *Open for Business: Conservatives' Opposition to Environmental Regulation* (Cambridge, Mass.: MIT Press, 2012), 140, 194.

6. Daniel C. Esty and Andrew S. Winston, *Green to Gold: How Smart Companies Use Environmental Strategy to Innovate, Create Value, and Build Competitive Advantage* (New Haven, Conn.: Yale University Press, 2006); Adam Werbach, *Strategy for Sustainability: A Business Manifesto* (Cambridge, Mass.: Harvard Business Press, 2009).

7. Ray C. Anderson, *Business Lessons from a Radical Industrialist* (New York: St. Martin's Griffin, 2011), 236–37; Stuart L. Hart, *Capitalism at the Crossroads: Next Generation Business Strategies for a Post-Crisis World*, 3rd ed. (Upper Saddle River, N.J.: Prentice-Hall, 2010), xv–xvi.

8. Andrew J. Hoffman, *From Heresy to Dogma: An Institutional History of Corporate Environmentalism* (Stanford, Calif.: Stanford University Press, 2001); Esty and Winston, *Green to Gold*.

9. Esty and Winston, *Green to Gold*, 106–8; Hoffman, *From Heresy to Dogma*, 217; Hart, *Capitalism at the Crossroads*, 89.

10. Peter Senge et al., *The Necessary Revolution: Working Together to Create a Sustainable World* (New York: Broadway Books, 2010), 45, 180–82, 191; Andrew J. Hoffman, *Carbon Strategies:*

*How Leading Companies Are Reducing Their Climate Change Footprint* (Ann Arbor: University of Michigan Press, 2007), 103–12.

11. Esty and Winston, *Green to Gold*, 47–48, 110, 134–35; Interface Entropy brochure, accessed August 23, 2016, http://www.interface.com/US/en-US/detail/entropy-variations -1178001999G15S001. In addition, see Ray C. Anderson, *Mid-Course Correction: Toward a Sustainable Enterprise; The Interface Model* (White River Junction, Vt.: Chelsea Green, 1998); Anderson, *Business Lessons from a Radical Industrialist*.

12. Edward Humes, *Force of Nature: The Unlikely Story of Wal-Mart's Green Revolution* (New York: Harper Business, 2011); Marc Gunther, "Game On: Why Walmart Is Ranking Suppliers on Sustainability," *GreenBiz* [online], April 15, 2013.

13. For a succinct discussion of the problematic commitment to growth by a green-capitalism booster, see Andrew S. Winston, *The Big Pivot: Radically Practical Strategies for a Hotter, Scarcer, and More Open World* (Boston: Harvard Business Review Press, 2014), 68–70.

14. Christine Meisner Rosen, "Environmental Sustainability in the Twenty-First Century," *Environmental History* 12 (April 2007): 362–63, 364. Rosen long has called for more attention to the environmental history of business. See Christine Meisner Rosen, "Industrial Ecology and the Greening of Business History," *Business and Economic History* 26 (Fall 1997): 123–37; Christine Meisner Rosen and Christopher C. Sellers, "The Nature of the Firm: Towards an Ecocultural History of Business," *Business History Review* 73, no. 4 (Winter 1999): 577–600; Christine Meisner Rosen, "The Business-Environment Connection," *Environmental History* 10 (January 2005): 77–79; Christine Meisner Rosen, "Doing Business in the Age of Global Climate Change," *Enterprise & Society* 8, no. 2 (June 2007): 221–26.

15. Donald Worster, *Dust Bowl: The Southern Plains in the 1930s* (New York: Oxford University Press, 1979), 6–7.

16. Theodore Steinberg, *Nature Incorporated: Industrialization and the Waters of New England* (Amherst: University of Massachusetts Press, 1994), 12. Many of Steinberg's other books also speak to the environmental destructiveness of capitalism, from *Down to Earth: Nature's Role in American History* (New York: Oxford University Press, 2002) to *Gotham Unbound: The Ecological History of Greater New York* (New York: Simon and Schuster, 2014).

17. William Cronon, *Changes in the Land: Indians, Colonists, and the Ecology of New England* (New York: Hill and Wang, 1983); William Cronon, *Nature's Metropolis: Chicago and the Great West* (New York: W. W. Norton, 1991); Andrew C. Isenberg, *Mining California: An Ecological History* (New York: Hill and Wang, 2005); Timothy J. LeCain, *Mass Destruction: The Men and Giant Mines That Wired America and Scarred the Planet* (New Brunswick, N.J.: Rutgers University Press, 2009); Duncan Maysilles, *Ducktown Smoke: The Fight Over One of the South's Greatest Environmental Disasters* (Chapel Hill: University of North Carolina Press, 2011); Kent A. Curtis, *Gambling with Ore: The Nature of Metal Mining in the United States, 1860–1910* (Boulder: University of Colorado Press, 2013); Brian Black, *Petrolia: The Landscape of America's First Oil Boom* (Baltimore: Johns Hopkins University Press, 2000); Christopher F. Jones, *Routes of Power: Energy and Modern America* (Cambridge, Mass.: Harvard University Press, 2014); W. Jeffrey Bolster, *The Mortal Sea: Fishing the Atlantic in the Age of Sail* (Cambridge, Mass.: Harvard University Press, 2012); Richard P. Tucker, *Insatiable Appetite: The United States and the Ecological Degradation of the Tropical World* (Berkeley: University of California Press, 2000); Adam Rome, *The Bulldozer in the Countryside: Suburban Sprawl and the Rise of American Environmentalism* (New York: Cambridge University Press, 2001).

18. Samuel P. Hays, *Beauty, Health, and Permanence: Environmental Politics in the United States, 1955–1985* (New York: Cambridge University Press, 1987), 307.

19. Richard H. K. Vietor, *Environmental Politics and the Coal Coalition* (College Station: Texas A&M University Press, 1980); Andrew Hurley, *Environmental Inequalities: Class, Race, and Industrial Pollution in Gary, Indiana, 1945–1980* (Chapel Hill: University of North Carolina Press, 1995); Thomas Dunlap, *DDT: Scientists, Citizens, and Public Policy* (Princeton, N.J.: Princeton University Press, 1981); Naomi Oreskes and Erik M. Conway, *Merchants of Doubt: How a Handful of Scientists Obscured the Truth on Issues from Tobacco Smoke to Global Warming* (New York: Bloomsbury Press, 2010); Rome, *Bulldozer in the Countryside*; James Morton Turner, *The Promise of Wilderness: American Environmental Politics Since 1964* (Seattle: University of Washington Press, 2012).

20. Timothy Silver, *Mount Mitchell and the Black Mountains: An Environmental History of the Highest Peaks in Eastern America* (Chapel Hill: University of North Carolina Press, 2003), 150–53; Christine Meisner Rosen, "Businessmen Against Pollution in Late Nineteenth Century Chicago," *Business History Review* 69, no. 3 (Autumn 1995): 351–97; Frank Uekoetter, "Divergent Responses to Identical Problems: Businessmen and the Smoke Nuisance in Germany and the United States, 1880–1917," *Business History Review* 73, no. 4 (Winter 1999): 657–60; Tom McCarthy, *Auto Mania: Cars, Consumers, and the Environment* (New Haven, Conn.: Yale University Press, 2007), 92–96.

21. Hugh S. Gorman, *Redefining Efficiency: Pollution Concerns, Regulatory Mechanisms, and Technological Change in the U.S. Petroleum Industry* (Akron, Ohio: University of Akron Press, 2001).

22. For an exception, see Bartow J. Elmore, *Citizen Coke: The Making of Coca-Cola Capitalism* (New York: W. W. Norton, 2015).

23. Hoffman, *From Heresy to Dogma*, 202–12.

24. Esty and Winston, *Green to Gold*, 20.

25. The quoted phrases are from Senge et al., *The Necessary Revolution*, 310; Chris Laszlo and Nadya Zhexembayeva, *Embedded Sustainability: The Next Big Competitive Advantage* (Stanford, Calif.: Stanford Business Books, 2011), 105–6; John R. Ehrenfeld and Andrew J. Hoffman, *Flourishing: A Frank Conversation About Sustainability* (Stanford, Calif.: Stanford Business Books, 2013), 54.

26. For a sample of radical eco-critiques of capitalism, see Jason W. Moore, *Capitalism in the Web of Life: Ecology and the Accumulation of Capital* (New York: Verso, 2015); Naomi Klein, *This Changes Everything: Capitalism vs. the Climate* (New York: Simon and Schuster, 2014); Fred Magdoff and John Bellamy Foster, *What Every Environmentalist Needs to Know About Capitalism: A Citizen's Guide to Capitalism and the Environment* (New York: Monthly Review Press, 2011); Joel Kovel, *The Enemy of Nature: The End of Capitalism or the End of the World?* (London: Zed Books, 2002).

## Chapter 2. Shades of Green

1. The Obama-Biden Plan (2009), accessed May 19, 2015, http://change.gov/agenda/energy_and_environment_agenda.

2. Peter Sasso, "Former General Electric CEO Jack Welch: Global Warming Skeptic," *MRC NewsBusters*, July 3, 2008, accessed May 7, 2015, http://newsbusters.org/blogs/peter-sasso/2008/07/03/former-general-electric-ceo-jack-welsh-global-warming-skeptic.

3. Alison van Diggelen, "Jack Welch: Why Companies Must Go Green," *Fresh Dialogues*, May 12, 2009, accessed December 20, 2014, http://www.freshdialogues.com/2009/05/12/jack-welch -why-companies-must-go-green/.

4. "Green Bonds: Green Grows the Market," *Economist*, July 5, 2014; Climate Bonds Initiative, Year 2014, "Final Green Bonds Report," accessed May 21, 2015, http://www.climatebonds.net/year -2014-green-bonds-final-report-0.

5. Heather Rogers, "The Greening of Capitalism?" *International Socialist Review* 70, no. 1 (2010), available online at http://isreview.org/issue/70/greening-capitalism.

6. Naomi Klein, *This Changes Everything: Capitalism vs. the Climate* (New York: Simon and Schuster, 2014), book jacket, 25.

7. Thomas L. Friedman, *Hot, Flat, and Crowded: Why We Need a Green Revolution—and How It Can Renew America* (New York: Farrar, Straus and Giroux, 2008), 398, 404.

8. Paul Hawken, Amory B. Lovins, and L. Hunter Lovins, *Natural Capitalism: Creating the Next Industrial Revolution* (Boston: Little, Brown, 1999), 6, 10.

9. This section draws on Hartmut Berghoff and Mathias Mutz, "Missing Links? Business History and Environmental Change," *Jahrbuch für Wirtschaftsgeschichte/Economic History Yearbook* 50, no. 2 (2009): 9–21.

10. For example, Ulrike Gilhaus, *"Schmerzenskinder der Industrie": Umweltverschmutzung, Umweltpolitik und sozialer Protest im Industriezeitalter Westfalen, 1845–1914* (Paderborn: Schöningh, 1995); Frank Uekötter, *Von der Rauchplage zur ökologischen Revolution: Eine Geschichte der Luftverschmutzung in Deutschland und den USA, 1880–1970* (Essen: Klartext, 2003). See also Frank Uekötter, *Umweltgeschichte im 19. und 20. Jahrhundert* (Munich: Oldenbourg, 2007); and "Affluence and Sustainability: Environmental History and the History of Consumption," in *Decoding Modern Consumer Societies*, ed. Hartmut Berghoff and Uwe Spiekermann, 111–24 (Houndsmill: Palgrave, 2012).

11. For example, Paul R. Josephson, *Resources Under Regimes: Technology, Environment, and the State* (Cambridge, Mass.: Harvard University Press, 2005). On the broadening of the horizons of environmental history, see Verena Winiwarter et al., "Environmental History in Europe from 1994 to 2004: Enthusiasm and Consolidation," *Environment and History* 10, no. 4 (2004): 501–30; Mathias Mutz, "Nature's Product? An Environmental History of the German Pulp and Paper Industry," in *Elements—Continents: Approaches to Determinants of Environmental History and Their Reifications*, ed. Bernd Herrmann and Christine Dahlke (Stuttgart: Wissenschaftliche Verlagsgemeinschaft, 2009), 259–64.

12. The history of Standard Oil is one of the case studies in Alfred D. Chandler, *Strategy and Structure: Chapters in the History of the American Industrial Enterprise*, 163–224 (Cambridge, Mass.: MIT Press, 1969).

13. Geoffrey Jones and Jonathan Zeitlin, eds., *The Oxford Handbook of Business History* (Oxford: Oxford University Press, 2008).

14. The term "eco-cultural business history" was coined in Christine Meisner Rosen and Christopher C. Sellers, "The Nature of the Firm: Towards an Eco-Cultural History of Business," *Business History Review* 73, no. 4 (Winter 1999): 577–600.

15. Mathias Mutz, "Managing Resources: Water and Wood in the German Pulp and Paper Industry, 1870s–1930s," *Jahrbuch für Wirtschaftsgeschichte/Economic History Yearbook* 50, no. 2 (2009): 45–68.

16. Friedrich Engels, *The Condition of the Working-Class in England in 1844* (London: Swan Sonnenschein, 1892), 45, 48–53.

17. Wolfgang von Hippel, "Wirtschafts- und Sozialgeschichte, 1800–1918," in *Handbuch der baden-württembergischen Geschichte*, vol. 3, *Vom Ende des Alten Reiches bis zum Ende der Monarchien*, ed. Hansmartin Schwarzmaier (Stuttgart: Klett, 1992), 665; Gary Herrigel, *Industrial Constructions: The Sources of German Industrial Power* (Cambridge: Cambridge University Press, 1996).

18. Hartmut Berghoff, "Marketing Diversity: The Making of a Global Consumer Product; Hohner's Harmonicas, 1857–1930," *Enterprise & Society* 2, no. 2 (2001): 338–72.

19. K. Freerk Wiersum, "200 Years of Sustainability in Forestry: Lessons from History," *Environmental Management* 19, no. 3 (1995): 321–29; Joachim Radkau, *Wood: A History* (Cambridge: Polity Press, 2012).

20. "The Story of Cadbury," accessed May 14, 2015, https://www.cadbury.com.au/About-Cadbury/The-Story-of-Cadbury.aspx.

21. Robert Fitzgerald, "Products Consumption and Firms: Cadbury and the Development of Marketing, 1900–1939," *Business History* 47, no. 4 (2005): 511–31; and *New World Encyclopedia*, s.v. "George Cadbury," accessed May 24, 2015, http://www.newworldencyclopedia.org/entry/George_Cadbury.

22. Robert Fitzgerald, *Rowntree and the Marketing Revolution, 1862–1969* (Cambridge: Cambridge University Press, 1995); Albert Pfiffner, *Henri Nestle (1814–1890): Vom Apothekergehilfen zum Marktorientierten Pionierunternehmer* (Zürich: Chronos 1993); Nancy F. Koehn, "Henry Heinz and Brand Creation in the Late Nineteenth Century: Making Markets for Processed Food," *Business History Review* 73, no. 3 (1999): 349–93; Brian C. Wilson, *Dr. John Harvey Kellogg and the Religion of Biologic Living* (Bloomington: Indiana University Press, 2014).

23. "H. J. Heinz Biography," accessed May 24, 2015, http://www.biography.com/people/hj-heinz-39251.

24. See, in general, Eva Barlösius, *Naturgemässe Lebensführung: Zur Geschichte der Lebensreform um die Jahrhundertwende* (Frankfurt: Campus, 1997); and John A. Williams, *Turning to Nature in Germany: Hiking, Nudism, and Conservation, 1900–1940* (Stanford, Calif.: Stanford University Press, 2007). More specifically, Florentine Fritzen, *Gesünder Leben: Die Lebensreformbewegung im 20. Jahrhundert* (Stuttgart: Steiner, 2006); and Fritzen, "Changing the World with Müsli," *German Research* 31, no. 3 (2009): 10–14.

25. Chris Smith, John Child, and Michael Rowlinson, *Reshaping Work: The Cadbury Experience* (Cambridge: Cambridge University Press, 1990).

26. Joachim Radkau, *Nature and Power: A Global History of the Environment* (Cambridge: Cambridge University Press, 2008), 249.

27. Steffen Hentrich, Walter Komar, and Martin Weisheimer, "Umweltschutz in den neuen Bundesländern: Bilanz im zehnten Jahr Deutscher Einheit," *IWH* [Halle Institute for Economic Research] *Discussion Papers* 128 (2000): 1–51, here 15.

28. Holger Derlien, Tobias Faupel, and Christian Nieters, "Industriestandort mit Vorbildfunktion? Das ostdeutsche Chemiedreieck," *WZB* (Berlin Social Science Center), Discussion Paper FS IV 99-16 (1999): 1–48, here 11–14.

29. Ibid., 11.

30. Robert Emmet Hernan, *This Borrowed Earth: Lessons from the Fifteen Worst Environmental Disasters Around the World* (New York: Palgrave Macmillan, 2010).

31. Ibid., 45–57.

32. Laurence Cockcroft, *Global Corruption: Money, Power and Ethics in the Modern World* (London: Tauris, 2012), 25, 44.

33. Christian Pfister, "The '1950s Syndrome' and the Transition from a Slow-Going to a Rapid Loss of Global Sustainability," in *Turning Points of Environmental History*, ed. Frank Uekötter, 90–118 (Pittsburgh: University of Pittsburgh Press, 2010).

34. Radkau, *Nature*, 252–55.

35. Robert White-Stevens, a spokesman for the chemical industry, quoted in Dorothy McLaughlin, "Fooling with Nature: *Silent Spring* Revisited," *Frontline*, PBS, accessed May 26, 2015, http://www.pbs.org/wgbh/pages/frontline/shows/nature/disrupt/sspring.html.

36. Philip Shabecoff, *A Fierce Green Fire: The American Environmental Movement*, rev. ed. (Washington, D.C.: Island Press, 2003), 199–264; Adam Rome, *The Genius of Earth Day: How a 1970 Teach-In Unexpectedly Made the First Green Generation* (New York: Hill and Wang, 2013); Frank Uekötter, *The Greenest Nation? A New History of German Environmentalism: History for a Sustainable Future* (Cambridge, Mass.: MIT Press, 2014), 74–131.

37. U.S. Energy Information Administration, "Motor Vehicle Mileage, Fuel Consumption, and Fuel Economy," *Annual Energy Review*, accessed May 26, 2015, http://www.eia.gov /totalenergy/data/annual/index.cfm.

38. *Themenpapier Energiewirtschaft* (Düsseldorf: Stahl-Zentrum, 2013), 1.

39. Hartmut Berghoff, "From the Watergate Scandal to the Compliance Revolution: The Fight Against Corporate Corruption in the United States and Germany, 1972–2012," *Bulletin of the German Historical Institute* 49, no. 2 (2013): 7–30. On the connection between corruption and environmental crime, see Cockcroft, *Corruption*, 75–78.

40. John Vidal, "Nigeria's Agony Dwarfs the Gulf Oil Spill," *Guardian* (London), May 29, 2010; BBC News, "Shell Agrees $84m Deal over Niger Delta Oil Spill," January 7, 2015; Margaret Coker and Benoît Faucon, "Shell to Pay $80 Million Compensation for Oil Spills in Nigeria," *Wall Street Journal*, January 7, 2015.

41. Kate Allen, "Shell in Nigeria: The Landmark Oil Case Is a Warning Shot to Multinationals," *Guardian*, January 9, 2015.

42. Siemens, quoted in "Lobbyismus: Joschka Fischer berät Siemens,"*Spiegel Online*, October 23, 2009.

43. United States Environmental Protection Agency, "EPA Issues Unilateral Administrative Order to General Electric Company in Rome, Georgia," press release, June 12, 2003, accessed May 27, 2015, http://yosemite.epa.gov/opa/admpress.nsf/e51aa292bac25b0b85257359003d925f/55 92f5848c70b2858525731b00674e9c!OpenDocument.

44. Political Economy Research Institute (PERI), "Toxic 100 Report: General Electric Co.," Internet Archive, accessed May 27, 2015, https://web.archive.org/web/20070927204419 /http://www.rtknet.org/new/tox100/toxic100.php?database=t1&detail=1&datype=T&reptype=a &company1=&company2=8337&chemfac=fac&advbasic=bas#.

45. Quoted in Satinder Dhiman, "Social Responsibility: Caring for People, Products, Peace, Preservation, and Planet," in *Business Administration Education: Changes in Management and Leadership Strategies*, ed. Joan Marques, Satinder Dhiman, and Svetlana Holt (New York: Palgrave Macmillan, 2012), 19–41, here 28.

46. Deb Frodl, "Ecomagination Overview," GE Global Impact 2013, accessed May 27, 2015, http://www.ge.com/globalimpact2013/#/ecomagination.

47. Peter Löscher in an interview with *Frankfurter Allgemeine Sonntagszeitung*, December 6, 2009. In general, see *Siemens Geschäftsbericht* (annual report), 2008/2009, part 1, 10–11.

48. The next two paragraphs draw on Geoffrey Jones and Loubna Bouamane, "'Power from Sunshine': A Business History of Solar Energy," Harvard Business School Working Paper, no. 12-105, May 2012.

49. *Siemens Geschäftsbericht*, 2010/2011, part 2, 191–92.

50. "Vergebliche Käufersuche: Siemens schließt seine Solarsparte," *Handelsblatt*, June 17, 2013.

51. *Siemens Sustainability Report 2012*, 6 and 7, accessed May 27, 2015, http://www.siemens.com/about/sustainability/pool/en/current-reporting/siemens-sr2012.pdf.

52. Letter from Deb Frodl, in *Powering the Future: GE Ecomagination*, accessed July 21, 2016, https://www.ge.com/sites/default/files/GE_BR15_Ecomagination_Final.pdf; and Jeff Immelt, in *GE's Approach to Sustainability*, May 2016, accessed July 21, 2016, http://dsg.files.app.content.prod.s3.amazonaws.com/gesustainability/wp-content/uploads/2014/05/12195908/GE_Sustainability_Highlights_2015.pdf.

53. *GE Ecomagination Progress*, accessed May 27, 2015, http://www.gesustainability.com/2014-performance/ecomagination/.

54. *Wikipedia*, s.v. "Desertec," accessed May 30, 2015, http://en.wikipedia.org/wiki/Desertec.

55. Alexander Gall, *Das Atlantropa-Projekt: Die Geschichte einer gescheiterten Vision; Herman Sörgel und die Absenkung des Mittelmeers* (Frankfurt: Campus, 1998).

56. Radkau, *Nature*, 256–57.

57. "The Future of Biofuels: The Post-Alcohol World," *Economist*, October 28, 2010.

58. C. Ford Runge and Benjamin Senauer, "How Biofuels Could Starve the Poor," *Foreign Affairs* 86, no. 3 (2007): 41–53.

59. Michael Fröhlingsdorf, Nils Klawitter, and Michaela Schießl, "Bio gegen Bio," *Spiegel*, November 3, 2014.

60. Heather Rogers, *Green Gone Wrong: How Our Economy Is Undermining the Environmental Revolution* (New York: Scribner, 2010).

61. William Stanley Jevons, *The Coal Question: An Inquiry Concerning the Progress of the Nation, and the Probable Exhaustion of Our Coal-Mines* (London: Macmillan, 1865), 103, 105.

62. J. Daniel Khazzoom, "Energy Saving Resulting from the Adoption of More Efficient Appliances," *Energy Journal* 8, no. 4 (1987): 85–98; Leonard G. Brookes, "The Greenhouse Effect: The Fallacies of the Energy Efficiency Solution," *Energy Policy* 18, no. 2 (1990): 199–201; Harry D. Saunders, "The Khazzoom-Brookes Postulate and Neoclassical Growth," *Energy Journal* 13, no. 4 (1992): 131–48.

63. Stan Cox, *Losing Our Cool: Uncomfortable Truths About Our Air-Conditioned World (and Finding New Ways to Get Through the Summer)* (New York: New Press, 2010), 36; David Owen, "The Efficiency Dilemma," *New Yorker*, December 20, 2010, 78–85.

64. "Aircraft Emissions: The Sky's the Limit," *Economist*, June 8, 2006; International Labor Organization, "Civil Aviation and Its Changing World of Work" (Geneva: ILO, 2013), 8 and 9, accessed May 31, 2015, http://www.ilo.org/wcmsp5/groups/public/---ed_dialogue/---sector/documents/presentation/wcms_208108.pdf.

65. U.S. Department of Justice, press statement, October 7, 1999, accessed June 2, 2015, http://www.justice.gov/archive/opa/pr/1999/October/471enr.htm.

66. Quoted in Hartmut Berghoff, "'Dem Ziele der Menschheit entgegen': Die Verheißungen der Technik an der Wende zum 20. Jahrhundert," in *Das Neue Jahrhundert: Europäische Zeitdiagnosen und Zukunftsentwürfe um 1900*, ed. Ute Frevert (Göttingen: Vandenhoeck & Ruprecht,

2000), 47–78, here 67–68. For more green utopias linked to the greening of capitalism through the application of electricity, see ibid., 66–76.

67. August Bebel, *Woman Under Socialism* (New York: New York Labor News Co., 1917), 287, 285, 288.

## Chapter 3. The Role of Businesses in Constructing Systems of Environmental Governance

1. For a work that articulates this process in U.S. environmental history, see Richard N. L. Andrews, *Managing the Environment, Managing Ourselves: A History of American Environmental Policy* (New Haven, Conn.: Yale University Press, 1999).

2. Paul S. Sutter, *Driven Wild: How the Fight Against Automobiles Launched the Modern Wilderness Movement* (Seattle: University of Washington Press, 2002).

3. Lawrence Lessig, *Code and Other Laws of Cyberspace* (New York: Basic Books, 1999).

4. Marc Cioc, *The Rhine: An Eco-Biography, 1815–2000* (Seattle: University of Washington Press, 2002).

5. Brian Black, *Petrolia: The Landscape of America's First Oil Boom* (Baltimore: Johns Hopkins University Press, 2000).

6. Theodore Steinberg, *Nature Incorporated: Industrialization and the Waters of New England* (New York: Cambridge University Press, 1991).

7. Raymond J. Burby, "Baton Rouge: The Making (and Breaking) of a Petrochemical Paradise," in *Transforming New Orleans and Its Environs*, ed. Craig E. Colten (Pittsburgh: University of Pittsburgh Press, 2000), 160–77.

8. Jonathan Joseph Wlasiuk, "The Farce of the Commons: Standard Oil and the Great Lakes," paper presented at the American Society for Environmental History Conference, San Francisco, March 12–16, 2014.

9. Carol A. MacLennan, *Sovereign Sugar: Industry and Environment in Hawai'i* (Honolulu: University of Hawai'i Press, 2014); Gregory T. Cushman, *Guano and the Opening of the Pacific World: A Global Ecological History* (New York: Cambridge University Press, 2013).

10. Samuel P. Hays, *Conservation and the Gospel of Efficiency: The Progressive Conservation Movement, 1890–1920* (Cambridge, Mass.: Harvard University Press, 1959).

11. Roderick Nash, *Wilderness and the American Mind* (New Haven, Conn.: Yale University Press, 1967).

12. Hugh S. Gorman, "Efficiency, Environmental Quality, and Oil Field Brines: The Success and Failure of Pollution Control by Self-Regulation," *Business History Review* 73, no. 4 (1999): 601–40.

13. Martin V. Melosi, *The Sanitary City: Urban Infrastructure in America from Colonial Times to the Present* (Baltimore: Johns Hopkins University Press, 1999).

14. William H. Wilson, *The City Beautiful Movement* (Baltimore: Johns Hopkins University, 1994).

15. Susan Strasser, *Waste and Want: A Social History of Trash* (New York: Henry Holt, 1999).

16. Steven W. Usselman, *Regulating Railroad Innovation: Business, Technology, and Politics in America, 1840–1920* (New York: Cambridge University Press, 2002).

17. Edwin T. Layton, *The Revolt of the Engineers: Social Responsibility and the American Engineering Profession* (Cleveland: Press of Case Western Reserve University, 1971); Bruce Sinclair with the assistance of James P. Hull, *A Centennial History of the American Society of Mechanical Engineers, 1880–1980* (Toronto: University of Toronto Press, 1980); Amy E. Slayton, *Reinforced*

*Concrete and the Modernization of American Building* (Baltimore: Johns Hopkins University Press, 2001).

18. Craig N. Murphy and JoAnne Yates, *The International Organization for Standardization (ISO): Global Governance Through Voluntary Consensus* (New York: Routledge, 2009).

19. Hugh S. Gorman, *Redefining Efficiency: Pollution Concerns, Regulatory Mechanisms, and Technological Change in the U.S. Petroleum Industry* (Akron, Ohio: University of Akron Press, 2001).

20. Samuel P. Hays and Barbara D. Hays, *Beauty, Health, and Permanence: Environmental Politics in the United States, 1955–1985* (New York: Cambridge University Press, 1987).

21. Hugh S. Gorman, "Laying the Foundation for the Control of Industrial Pollution, 1930–1970: Two Canals, a Refinery, and Clarence W. Klassen," *Journal of Illinois History* 8, no. 3 (2005): 182–208.

22. Cesare Dosi and Michele Moretto, "Is Ecolabelling a Reliable Environmental Policy Measure?" *Environmental and Resource Economics* 18 (2001): 113–27.

23. Samir A. Qadir and Hugh S. Gorman, "The Use of ISO 14001 in India: More than a Certificate on the Wall?" *Environmental Practice* 10, no. 2 (2008): 53–65.

24. Paul T. Anastas and Julie B. Zimmerman, "Design Through the Twelve Principles of Green Engineering," *Environmental Science and Technology* 37, no. 5 (2003): 94A–101A.

25. Paul T. Anastas and John C. Warner, *Green Chemistry: Theory and Practice* (New York: Oxford University Press, 1998).

26. For example, a major proponent of "Green Chemistry," Paul Anastas, downplays the role of regulations in efforts to change industrial practices; see Paul T. Anastas and Mary M. Kirchoff, "Origins, Current Status, and Future Challenges of Green Chemistry," *Accounts of Chemical Research* 35 (2002): 686–94.

27. Richard V. Ericson, Aaron Doyle, and Dean Barry, *Insurance as Governance* (Toronto: University of Toronto Press, 2003).

28. John Galiette, "The Price-Anderson Act: A Constitutional Dilemma," *Environmental Affairs* 6 (1977): 565–96.

29. Gard Paulsen et al., *Building Trust: The History of DNV, 1864–2014* (Lyskaker: Dinamo Forlag, 2014).

30. David Stradling, *Smokestacks and Progressives: Environmentalists, Engineers, and Air Quality in America, 1881–1951* (Baltimore: Johns Hopkins University Press, 1999); James E. Krier and Edmund Ursin, *Pollution and Policy: A Case Essay on California and Federal Experience with Motor Vehicle Air Pollution, 1940–1975* (Berkeley: University of California Press, 1977).

31. Gorman, "Laying the Foundation."

32. John Kvinge, "Morally Hazardous Chemical Regulations: Why Effective Reform of the TSCA Requires Reduction of the Toxic Data Gap," *Minnesota Journal of Law, Science, and Technology* 12 (2011): 313–34.

33. Hugh S. Gorman, "The Houston Ship Channel and the Changing Landscape of Industrial Pollution," in *An Environmental History of Houston and the Gulf Coast*, ed. Martin V. Melosi and Joseph Pratt (Pittsburgh: University of Pittsburgh Press, 2007), 52–68.

34. Gorman, *Redefining Efficiency.*

35. Stuart Banner, *American Property: A History of How, Why, and What We Own* (Cambridge, Mass.: Harvard University Press, 2011).

36. Walter Rosenbaum, *Environmental Politics and Policy*, 8th ed. (Washington, D.C.: CQ Press, 2014).

37. Naomi Oreskes and Erik Conway, *Merchants of Doubt: How a Handful of Scientists Obscured the Truth on Issues from Tobacco Smoke to Global Warming* (New York: Bloomsbury Press, 2010).

38. Frank Cameron, *Cottrell: Samaritan of Science* (Garden City, N.Y.: Doubleday, 1952); Timothy LeCain, "The Limits of 'Eco-Efficiency': Arsenic Pollution and the Cottrell Electrical Precipitator in the U.S. Copper Smelting Industry," *Environmental History* 5, no. 3 (2000): 336–51.

39. Mark Tebeau, *Eating Smoke: Fire in Urban America, 1800–1950* (Baltimore: Johns Hopkins University Press, 2003).

40. Lara Johannsdottir, "The Geneva Association Framework for Climate Change Actions of Insurers: A Case Study of Nordic Insurers," *Journal of Cleaner Production* 75 (2014): 20–30.

41. Christopher Hayes, "The New Abolitionism," *Nation*, April 22, 2014.

42. Gorman, *Redefining Efficiency*.

43. Kristina Söderholm, "Governing Socio-Technical Transitions: Historical Lessons from the Implementation of Centralized Water and Sewage Systems in Northern Sweden, 1900–1950," *Environmental Innovations and Societal Transitions* 7 (2013): 37–53; Kristina Söderholm and Ann-Kristin Bergquist, "Growing Green and Competitive—A Case Study of a Swedish Pulp Mill," *Sustainability* 5, no. 5 (2013): 1789–805; Ann-Kristin Bergquist et al., "Command-and-Control Revisited: Environmental Compliance and Technological Change in Swedish Industry, 1970–1990," *Ecological Economics* 85 (2013): 6–19.

44. Hugh S. Gorman and Barry D. Solomon, "The Origins and Practice of Emissions Trading," *Journal of Policy History* 14 (2002): 293–320.

45. Hugh S. Gorman, *The Story of N: A Social History of the Nitrogen Cycle and the Challenge of Sustainability* (New Brunswick, N.J.: Rutgers University Press, 2013).

46. Thomas A. Birkland, *After Disaster: Agenda Setting, Public Policy, and Focusing Events* (Washington, D.C.: Georgetown University Press, 2007).

47. Velma L. Grover and Gail Krantzberg, eds., *Great Lakes: Lessons in Participatory Governance* (Boca Raton, Fla.: CRC Press, 2012).

48. Jeroen C. J. M. van den Bergh and Frank R. Bruinsma, eds. *Managing the Transition to Renewable Energy: Theory and Practice from Local, Regional, and Macro Perspectives* (Cheltenham: Edward Elgar, 2008).

49. Ronald D. Brunner and Amanda H. Lynch, *Adaptive Governance and Climate Change* (Boston: American Meteorological Society, 2010).

## Chapter 4. Business Leadership in the Movement to Regulate Industrial Air Pollution in Late Nineteenth- and Early Twentieth-Century America

1. This chapter is a revised version of Christine Rosen, "Business Leadership in the Movement to Regulate Industrial Air Pollution in Late Nineteenth and Early Twentieth Century America," *Jahrbuch für Wirtschaftsgeschichte/Economic History Yearbook* 50, no. 2 (2009): 23–44. It is reprinted with permission.

2. John Duffy, *A History of Public Health in New York City, 1625–1866* (New York: Russell Sage Foundation, 1968); John Duffy, *A History of Public Health in New York City, 1866–1966* (New York: Russell Sage Foundation, 1974), 1–49, 128–32; John Duffy, *The Sanitarians: A History of American Public Health* (Urbana: University of Illinois Press, 1992), 66–125; Howard D. Kramer, "Early Municipal and State Boards of Health," *Bulletin of the History of Medicine* 24, no. 6 (November–December 1950): 503–29. For a legal history perspective, see Ronald M. Labbe and

Jonathan Lurie, *The Slaughterhouse Cases: Regulation, Reconstruction, and the Fourteenth Amendment* (Lawrence: University Press of Kansas, 2003). In making heroes of the public health reformers responsible for the regulations that led to the epic legal battles that are their main concern, Labbe and Lurie are rescuing them from an earlier generation of legal scholars who demonized the reformers as the corrupt allies of the evil New Orleans abattoir monopoly. For a very different perspective, see Christine Meisner Rosen, "The Role of Pollution Regulation and Litigation in the Modernization of the U.S. Meat Packing Industry, 1865–1880," *Enterprise & Society* 8, no. 2 (June 2007): 297–347, which discusses the impact stench regulation had on innovation relating to waste reduction and recycling in the meat and related industries. For a piece that seeks to elevate the positive role that business leaders played in public health reform in general, see John H. Ellis, "Businessmen and Public Health in the Urban South During the Nineteenth Century: New Orleans, Memphis, and Atlanta," *Bulletin of the History of Medicine* 44, no. 3 (May–June 1970): 197–212 (part 1); and no. 4 (July–August): 346–71 (part 2). Some historians are now focusing on the broad cultural and social meanings and land use impacts of slaughterhouse regulation. See Paula Young Lee, ed., *Meat, Modernity, and the Rise of the Slaughterhouse* (Durham: University of New Hampshire Press, 2008), 198–215.

  3. Harold L. Platt, *Shock Cities: The Environmental Transformation and Reform of Manchester and Chicago* (Chicago: University of Chicago Press, 2005), 468–91; Robert D. Grinder, "The Battle for Clean Air: The Smoke Problem in America, 1880–1917," in *Pollution and Reform in American Cities, 1870–1930*, ed. Martin V. Melosi (Austin: University of Texas Press, 1980), 83–103; Harold L. Platt, "Invisible Gases: Smoke, Gender, and the Redefinition of Environmental Policy in Chicago, 1900–1920," *Planning Perspectives* 10 (1995): 67–97; Angela Gugliotta, "Class, Gender, and Coal Smoke: Gender Ideology and Environmental Justice in Pittsburgh, 1868–1914," *Environmental History* 5 (April 2000): 165–93; David Stradling, *Smokestacks and Progressives: Environmentalists, Engineers, and Air Quality in America, 1881–1951* (Baltimore: Johns Hopkins University Press, 1999).

  In contrast, Frank Uekoetter, "Divergent Responses to Identical Problems: Businessmen and the Smoke Nuisance in Germany and the United States, 1880–1917," *Business History Review* 73 (Winter 1999): 641–76, presents an analysis of business's role in the American antismoke movement that is similar to the one I develop here. See also Joel A. Tarr and Carl Zimring, "The Struggle for Smoke Control in St. Louis," in *Common Fields: An Environmental History of St. Louis*, ed. Andrew Hurley (St. Louis: Missouri Historical Society Press, 1997), 199–220; Christine Meisner Rosen, "Businessmen Against Pollution in Late Nineteenth Century Chicago," *Business History Review* 69, no. 3 (Autumn 1995): 351–97; David Stradling and Joel A. Tarr, "Environmental Activism, Locomotive Smoke, and the Corporate Response: The Case of the Pennsylvania Railroad and Chicago Smoke Control," *Business History Review* 73, no. 4 (Winter 1999): 677–704. Angela Gugliotta, "'Hell with the Lid Taken Off': A Cultural History of Air Pollution—Pittsburgh" (Ph.D. diss., University of Notre Dame, 2004), examines the interactions between male and female smoke reformers in Pittsburgh. For a comparative analysis of the distinctive and often conflicting ways by which women approached environmental reform compared to men see Adam W. Rome, "'Political Hermaphrodites': Gender and Environmental Reform in Progressive America," *Environmental History* 11, no. 3 (July 2006): 440–62.

  4. Duffy, *The Sanitarians*, quote is from p. 120; Duffy, *A History of Public Health in New York City, 1625–1866*, 545–54, 565, 569; Gert H. Brieger, "Sanitary Reform in New York City: Stephen Smith and the Passage of the Metropolitan Health Bill," *Bulletin of the History of Medicine* 40 (September–October 1966): 413–19, 428–29; Kramer, "Early Municipal and State Boards of

Health," 508–9; Citizens' Association of New York, Council of Hygiene and Public Health, *Sanitary Condition of the City: Report of the Council of Hygiene and Public Health of the Citizens' Association of New York* (1866; reprint, New York: Arno Press, 1970), xv–xvi; Stephen Smith, *The City That Was* (New York: F. Allaben, 1911), reprinted in *The City That Was; The Report of the General Committee of Health, New York City, 1806* (Metuchen, N.J.: Scarecrow Reprint Corp., 1973), 39–41.

5. Duffy, *A History of Public Health in New York City, 1625–1866*, 545–70; Brieger, "Sanitary Reform," 413–25; Kramer, "Early Municipal and State Boards of Health," 510–13; Smith, *The City That Was*, 40–46, 163–77; Stephen Smith, "The History of Public Health, 1871–1921," in *A Half Century of Public Health*, ed. Mazyck P. Ravenel (New York: American Public Health Association, 1921), 8–9. The Citizen's Association published a very detailed, seventeen-volume report of its findings, in addition to *Sanitary Condition of the City*, which was its general overview of these findings and a call for reform.

6. John Duffy, "Nineteenth Century Public Health in New York and New Orleans: A Comparison," *Louisiana History* 15 (Fall 1974): 1–29. For a biographical sketch of Jackson Schultz, see Gordon Atkins, "Health, Housing, and Poverty in New York City, 1865–1895" (Ph.D. diss., Columbia University, 1947), 35–36. See also Rosen, "Role of Pollution Regulation," 309–11.

7. Rosen, "Role of Pollution Regulation," 306–12.

8. On the establishment of sanitary abattoirs, see "Metropolitan Board of Health," *New York Times*, March 23, 1866, 8; "Abattoirs at Communipaw," *New York Times*, May 5, 1866, 2; "The Communipaw Abattoirs," *New York Times*, September 20, 1866, 2; "The Communipaw Abattoirs," Local Intelligence, *New York Times*, June 29, 1866, 2, and August 23, 1867, 8; "An Abattoir for New York," *Scientific American* 15, no. 8 (August 18, 1866): 120; "The Great Abattoirs at Communipaw, New Jersey," *Scientific American* 19, no. 25 (December 16, 1868): 392. On the upgrading of the New York City's disgusting offal dock by the New York Rendering Company, see Moreau Morris and E. H. Janes, "'G': Report upon the Operations of the New York Rendering Company," in *Second Annual Report of the Metropolitan Board of Health of the State of New York, 1867* (New York: Union Printing House, 1868), 308–10; the owners of the New York Rendering Company described their innovative technologies in "Communications—The Refuse of the City," *New York Times*, September 3, 1870, 2. See also E. H. Janes, "Sanitary View of Abattoirs and the Slaughtering Business in New York," *Public Health Reports and Papers* 3 (1877): 24–31.

9. This organization has yet to find its historian. Richard Schneirov, *Labor and Urban Politics: Class Conflict and the Origins of Modern Liberalism in Chicago, 1864–97* (Urbana: University of Illinois Press, 1998), 53–63, views the organization from a critical, left perspective, focusing on its role in political, antimachine government reform (in other words, reform associated with opposition to the interests of the laboring classes), not environmental improvement. For a more appreciative, but only slightly less sketchy view, see Donald David Marks, "Polishing the Gem of the Prairie: The Evolution of Civic Reform Consciousness in Chicago, 1874–1900" (Ph.D. diss., University of Wisconsin, 1974), 58–88. The Citizen's Association's interest in and advocacy for a broad range of improvements in Chicago's built and sanitary environment is evident in its annual reports.

10. Rosen, "Role of Pollution Regulation," 321–29; Louise Carroll Wade, *Chicago's Pride: The Stockyards, Packingtown, and Environs in the Nineteenth Century* (Urbana: University of Illinois Press, 1987), 130–38.

11. Rosen, "Role of Pollution Regulation," 329; Citizens' Association of Chicago, *Annual Report* (1882), 7–8; (1883), 8–10; (1884), 8–11; (1885), 9–14. See also Citizens' Association of Chicago,

*Report of the Committee of the Citizens' Association on the Main Drainage and Water Supply of Chicago* (Chicago, 1885).

12. Harmon v. City of Chicago, 110 Ill. 400, 51 Am. Rep. 698 (1884). Chicago Department of Health, *Annual Report for 1881 and 1882* (Chicago, 1882), 31–32, 34–44; Citizens' Association of Chicago, *Annual Report* (1880), 8; (1882), 6–7; (1883), 6–8; (1884), 5–6, 15; (1887), 13; (1888), 25–26; (1889), 8–9.

13. Rosen, "Businessmen Against Pollution."

14. Tarr and Zimring, "Struggle for Smoke Control," 202–4.

15. Stradling, *Smokestacks and Progressives*, 52–55 and 211 n. 40. See the list of "Subscribers and Donors" in the Smoke Abatement League's annual reports for names of individual and corporate members. For an interesting first-person description of how league members helped the city inspector enforce the law, see Matthew Nelson, "Smoke Abatement in Cincinnati," *American City* 2 (January 1910): 8–10. See also David Stradling, "To Breathe Pure Air: Cincinnati's Smoke Abatement Crusade, 1904–1916," *Queen City Heritage* 55 (Spring 1997): 2–18.

16. Other problems resulted from technical flaws and limitations of the era's smoke abatement technologies, the administrative difficulty and cost of regulatory enforcement, the vicissitudes of municipal politics, and the exclusion of residential coal furnaces and boilers from the regulations.

17. Gugliotta, " 'Hell with the Lid Taken Off,' " 183–313. See also John O'Connor Jr., "The History of the Smoke Nuisance and of Smoke Abatement in Pittsburgh," *Industrial World*, March 24, 1913, 353–54.

18. Gugliotta, " 'Hell with the Lid Taken Off,' " 313–27; O'Connor, "History of the Smoke Nuisance," 354–55.

19. Rosen, "Businessmen Against Pollution," 358.

20. Gugliotta, " 'Hell with the Lid Taken Off,' " 192.

21. Ibid., 240–44; O'Connor, "History of the Smoke Nuisance," 354.

22. Lance E. Davis and Douglass C. North, *Institutional Change and American Economic Growth* (Cambridge: Cambridge University Press, 1971), 47; see also 16–19, 182–83.

23. Rosen, "Businessmen Against Pollution," 352–54. Uekoetter, "Divergent Responses," 657–58. One reason economists give for them to refrain from supporting regulation, despite the benefits of smoke abatement, has to do with the free rider problem. A boiler owner could enjoy cleaner air at no cost simply by letting all the other owners of smoking boilers do the cleaning up. In other words, the owner could "free ride" on the abatement activities of the others (Rosen, "Businessmen Against Pollution," 361–62). Uekoetter provides additional insight, pointing out how relatively small a part of a businessman's operating expenses coal costs usually were, how disinterested most businessmen were in what happened in their boiler rooms and ignorant about the benefits of more efficient coal combustion ("Divergent Responses," 645–46).

24. Davis and North, *Institutional Change*, 15–17; Rosen, "Businessmen Against Pollution," 361–62.

25. Uekoetter, "Divergent Responses." For an example of the research that supported this claim see John O'Connor Jr., "The Economic Cost of the Smoke Nuisance to Pittsburgh," Smoke Investigation Bulletin No. 4 of the Mellon Institute of Industrial Research and School of Specific Industries (Pittsburgh, 1913).

26. These problems are some of the reasons engineers were so insistent that government regulators provide technical assistance to polluters to help them come into compliance with smoke abatement ordinances. Rosen, "Businessmen Against Pollution," 359–60, 365–66, 371–73,

379; Stradling, *Smokestacks and Progressives*, 91–107; see also Uekoetter, "Divergent Responses," 645–46, 663–70.

27. Rosen, "Role of Pollution Regulation," 321–28; Wade, *Chicago's Pride*, 130–38.

28. Duffy, *History of Public Health in New York City*, 552–53; Citizens' Association of New York, *Sanitary Condition of the City*, xv–xvi.

29. Labbe and Lurie, *Slaughterhouse Cases*, 54–65, 84–88.

30. Rosen, "Businessmen Against Pollution," 363–64, 367–71.

31. Gugliotta, " 'Hell with the Lid Taken Off,' " 240–44, 247.

32. Ibid., 241–43; Rosen, "Businessmen Against Pollution," 365–66.

33. Platt, *Shock Cities*, 468–73, 481–91; Stradling, *Smokestacks and Progressives*, 119–31.

34. Platt, *Shock Cities*, 468–69.

35. Stradling, *Smokestacks and Progressives*, 120, 470, 485–86; Platt, *Shock Cities*, 469–70, 485–86. See also Stradling and Tarr, "Environmental Activism," 690–91; Uekotter, "Divergent Responses," 669.

36. Stradling, *Smokestacks and Progressives*, 125–26; Platt, *Shock Cities*, 486–91. See also Uekoetter, "Divergent Responses," 659.

37. Stradling, *Smokestacks and Progressives*, 125–26; Platt, *Shock Cities*, 486–91; Chicago Association of Commerce and Industry, Committee of Investigation on Smoke Abatement and Electrification of Railway Terminals, *Smoke Abatement and Electrification of Railway Terminals in Chicago* (Chicago, 1915). Stradling and Tarr, "Environmental Activism," 689–702, is an in-depth analysis of this episode from the perspective of the management of the Pennsylvania Railroad.

38. Platt, *Shock Cities*, 474, 479–80; Stradling, *Smokestacks and Progressives*, 38, 102, 206 n. 5.

39. Christopher Sellers, "Factory as Environment: Industrial Hygiene, Professional Collaboration, and the Modern Sciences of Pollution," *Environmental History Review* 18 (Spring 1994): 55–84; Christopher Sellers, *Hazards of the Job: From Industrial Disease to Environmental Health Science* (Chapel Hill: University of North Carolina Press, 1997), 107–19, 145; Christian Warren, *Brush with Death: A Social History of Lead Poisoning* (Baltimore: Johns Hopkins University Press, 2000), 84–133. See also Gerald Markowitz and David Rosner, *Deceit and Denial: The Deadly Politics of Industrial Pollution* (Berkeley: University of California Press; New York: Milbank Memorial Fund, 2002), 12–57.

40. John D. Wirth, *Smelter Smoke in North America: The Politics of Transborder Pollution* (Lawrence: University Press of Kansas, 2000), 45–70.

41. Gugliotta, " 'Hell with the Lid Taken Off,' " 368–450.

42. Tarr and Zimring, "Struggle for Smoke Control," 205–20; Stradling, *Smokestacks and Progressives*, 163–67.

43. Stradling, *Smokestacks and Progressives*, 108; Robert Dale Grinder, "From Insurgency to Efficiency: The Smoke Abatement Campaign in Pittsburgh Before World War I," *Western Pennsylvania Historical Magazine* 61 (July 1978): 187–202; Gugliotta, "Class, Gender, and Coal Smoke," 178–81.

## Chapter 5. "Constructive and Not Destructive Development"

1. T. Asbury Wright, "The Exposition," *Knoxville Sentinel*, August 27, 1913, 4. See also "Conservation Show Ready," *San Francisco Call*, August 31, 1913, 32; Robert Douglas Lukens, "Portraits of Progress in New South Appalachia: Three Expositions in Knoxville, Tennessee, 1910–1913" (M.A. thesis, University of Tennessee, 1996), 46–65.

2. "Bas-Relief Maps Southern States," *Tulsa Daily World*, June 16, 1912, 11; W. M. Goodman, ed., *The First Exposition of Conservation and Its Builders: An Official History of the National Conservation Exposition* (Knoxville, Tenn.: Knoxville Lithographing Co., 1914), 108–40; "Educational Exhibit Is Quite Creditable," *Knoxville Sentinel*, September 6, 1913, 11; "Deforestation Dangers Emphasized in Exhibit," *Knoxville Sentinel*, September 4, 1913, 7; "Conservation Exposition Attracts Great Interest," *Atlanta Constitution*, October 27, 1912, A8.

3. As quoted in Goodman, *First Exposition of Conservation*, 411.

4. *The National Conservation Exposition: Knoxville, Tennessee, Sept. 1st to Nov. 1st, 1913* (Knoxville, Tenn.: The Exposition, 1913); advertisement, *Atlanta Constitution*, June 4, 1913, 94.

5. "Booster for Knoxville Favors Conservation," *Atlanta Constitution*, May 27, 1911, 3.

6. Robert J. Lowry, "The Cry of Conservation," *Atlanta Constitution*, July 27, 1913, 5B.

7. Ulrich Grober, *Sustainability: A Cultural History* (Devon: Green Books, 2012); Jeremy L. Caradonna, *Sustainability: A History* (New York: Oxford University Press, 2014).

8. World Commission on Environment and Development, *Our Common Future* (New York: Oxford University Press, 1987), 43. See also Donald Worster, "The Shaky Ground of Sustainable Development," in *The Wealth of Nature: Environmental History and the Ecological Imagination* (New York: Oxford University Press, 1993), 142–55.

9. Chris Turner, *The Geography of Hope: A Tour of the World We Need* (Toronto: Vintage Canada, 2007), as quoted in Caradonna, *Sustainability*, 1.

10. Edmund Ruffin, *Nature's Management: Writings on Landscape and Reform, 1822–1859*, ed. Jack Temple Kirby (Athens: University of Georgia Press, 2000), 323.

11. *Manufacturers' Record*, January 1888, as quoted in Paul M. Gaston, *The New South Creed: A Study in Southern Myth-Making* (New York: Alfred A. Knopf, 1970), 1.

12. Gaston, *The New South Creed*, 7.

13. James C. Cobb, *Industrialization and Southern Society* (Lexington: University Press of Kentucky, 1984), 16–18.

14. *Greenville [Ala.]Advocate*, March 16, 1898, as quoted in Edward L. Ayers, *The Promise of the New South: Life After Reconstruction* (New York: Oxford University Press, 1992), 62.

15. Caradonna, *Sustainability*, 21–88.

16. *Proceedings of a Conference of Governors* (Washington, D.C.: Government Printing Office, 1909), 12; quoted in Ian Tyrell, *Crisis of the Wasteful Nation: Empire and Conservation in Theodore Roosevelt's America* (Chicago: University of Chicago Press, 2015), 82.

17. Theodore E. Burton to Theodore Roosevelt, October 3, 1907, in *Proceedings of a Conference of Governors*, viii.

18. Gifford Pinchot, *Breaking New Ground* (New York: Harcourt, Brace, and Co., 1947), 13; quoted in Char Miller, *Gifford Pinchot and the Making of American Environmentalism* (Washington, D.C.: Shearwater Books, 2001), 85.

19. Pinchot, *Breaking New Ground*, 505.

20. *Idaho Daily Statesman*, June 21, 1907, quoted in Miller, *Gifford Pinchot*, 168.

21. "Addresses at the Southern Conservation Congress," *American Lumberman*, October 15, 1910, 53.

22. National Conservation Commission, *Report of the National Conservation Commission, February 1909* (Washington, D.C.: Government Printing Office, 1909), 161–62, 169–70.

23. *Addresses and Proceedings of the Second National Conservation Congress* (Washington, D.C.: National Conservation Congress, 1911), 135.

24. Ibid., 135–38.

25. Miller, *Gifford Pinchot*, 278; Samuel P. Hays, *Conservation and the Gospel of Efficiency* (1959; New York: Atheneum, 1974), 29–35.

26. Lowry, "The Cry of Conservation."

27. Richard H. Edmonds, "The Utilization of Southern Wastes," *Publications of the American Economic Association*, 3rd ser., vol. 5, no. 1 (February 1904): 166–67.

28. "Useful Products from Sawmill Waste," *Southern Field* 18 (1928): 16.

29. U.S. Bureau of the Census, *Cotton Production and Distribution, Year Ending July 31, 1964*, Bulletin 201 (Washington, D.C.: Government Printing Office, 1965), 52.

30. National Conservation Commission, *Report of the National Conservation Commission, February 1909*, 162.

31. B. F. Williamson Statement on Florida Conference, Box 62, Charles Holmes Herty Papers, Emory University Libraries; George B. Tindall, *The Emergence of the New South* (Baton Rouge: Louisiana State University Press, 1967), 465–67.

32. Thomas D. Clark, *The Greening of the South* (Lexington: University Press of Kentucky, 1984), 52–53, 102–4.

33. William Boyd, "The Forest Is the Future? Industrial Forestry and the Southern Pulp and Paper Complex," in *The Second Wave: Southern Industrialization from the 1940s to the 1970s*, ed. Philip Scranton (Athens: University of Georgia Press, 2001), 168–73.

34. "It's a Poor Tree That Doesn't Go to Modern Market," *Natural Resources* 1, no. 7 (July 28, 1923): 2.

35. Boyd, "The Forest Is the Future?" 173–83.

36. *Pineland Bag Corporation v. Riley, Auditor*, 142 Miss. 574, 582 (Miss. 1926).

37. Boyd, "The Forest Is the Future?" 168–69. For more on twentieth-century industrial recruitment, see James C. Cobb, *The Selling of the South: The Southern Crusade for Industrial Development, 1936–1990*, 2nd ed. (Urbana: University of Illinois Press, 1993).

38. Michael Williams, *Americans and Their Forests: A Historical Geography* (New York: Cambridge University Press, 1989), 265.

39. A. C. Goodyear, "Forestry," in *Reforestation in the South*, Pamphlets on Silviculture, vol. 17 (Bogalusa: Great Southern Lumber Company, 1923), 12.

40. "Bogalusa Mill Part of Utilization Plan," *Southern Lumberman*, December 20, 1924, 148.

41. C. W. Goodyear, *Bogalusa Story* (Buffalo, N.Y.: Wm. J. Keller, 1950), 138–39.

42. Ibid., 137–40, 160–71; Michael Curtis, "Early Development and Operations of the Great Southern Lumber Company," *Louisiana History* 14, no. 4 (Autumn 1973): 355–67; "Great Southern Outlines Reforestation Program," *Bogalusa Enterprise and American*, December 2, 1920, 8.

43. A. C. Goodyear, "Forestry," 11.

44. As quoted in Meigs O. Frost, "Wonderful Story of a Wonderful City—Bogalusa," *Bogalusa Enterprise and American*, March 31, 1921, 6; originally published in the *New Orleans Item*.

45. "World's Greatest Paper Manufacturer Praises Bogalusa," *Bogalusa Enterprise and American*, April 28, 1921, 1.

46. Courtenay De Kalb, *Bogalusa: Perpetual Timber Supply Through Reforestation as Basis for Industrial Permanency of Bogalusa* (Baltimore: Manufacturers' Record, 1922).

47. Robert W. Griffith, "Industrial Development of Western North Carolina," *Southern Tourist* (March 1926): 100–106.

48. Ibid.

49. Miller, *Gifford Pinchot*, 376.

50. Donald Worster, *Dust Bowl: The Southern Plains in the 1930s* (New York: Oxford University Press, 1979), 197.

51. C. Vann Woodward, "The Irony of Southern History," *Journal of Southern History* 19, no. 1 (February 1953): 3–19.

## Chapter 6. Utilities as Conservationists?

1. "The Age of Reckless Waste," *Electrical World* 39, no. 16 (1902): 674.

2. Samuel P. Hays, *Conservation and the Gospel of Efficiency: The Progressive Conservation Movement, 1890–1920* (Pittsburgh: University of Pittsburgh Press, 1959). Hays delineates the utilitarian approach to conservation during the Progressive Era and details the policy and politics of the movement at the federal level. For recent updates on the historiography of conservation and environmental movements, see Robert Lifset, *Power on the Hudson: Storm King Mountain and the Emergence of Modern American Environmentalism* (Pittsburgh: University of Pittsburgh Press, 2014); Thomas Raymond Wellock, *Preserving the Nation: The Conservation and Environmental Movements, 1870–2000*, American History Series (Wheeling, Ill.: Harlan Davidson, 2007).

3. One example of this type of dispute took place between 1910 and 1912. Small towns in Massachusetts contested the right of utilities to use eminent domain to erect new transmission lines. Town leaders cited concerns about health, safety, aesthetics, and local control. The state determined not to give the utilities the right of eminent domain at that time. "Public Control of Electricity: Interesting Hearing by State Board; W. R. Peabody Urges Bill for Eminent Domain Right; Predicts Doom of All the Small Companies," *Boston Globe*, September 16, 1910, 2; *Twenty-Seventh Annual Report of the Board of Gas and Electric Light Commissioners of the Commonwealth of Massachusetts for the Calendar Year 1911, Including Tables from the Annual Returns for the Year Ending June 30, 2011* (Boston: Wright & Potter, State Printers, 1912), 314a–42a.

4. For detailed studies of electrification in the United States, see Richard F. Hirsh, *Technology and Transformation in the American Electric Utility Industry* (New York: Cambridge University Press, 1989); Paul W. Hirt, *The Wired Northwest: The History of Electric Power, 1870s–1970s* (Lawrence: University Press of Kansas, 2012); Thomas Parke Hughes, *Networks of Power: Electrification in Western Society, 1880–1930* (Baltimore: Johns Hopkins University Press, 1983); David E. Nye, *Electrifying America: Social Meanings of a New Technology, 1880–1940* (Cambridge, Mass.: MIT Press, 1990).

5. *Central Electric Light and Power Stations, 1902* (Washington, D.C.: Government Printing Office, 1905), 6.

6. "Station Efficiencies," *Electrical World* 52, no. 22 (1908): 1158.

7. National Association of Regulatory Utility Commissioners (NARUC), "Regulatory Commissions," accessed July 27, 2016, http://www.naruc.org/about-naruc/regulatory-commissions/.

8. Public Utilities Commission of Rhode Island v. Attleboro Steam and Electric Company, 273 U.S. 83 (1927).

9. The federal government exercised multiple roles in power development: through construction projects of the Army Corps of Engineers and the Bureau of Reclamation; through regulatory responsibilities established by the Public Utility Holding Company Act (1935) and the Federal Power Act of 1935; following creation of the Tennessee Valley Authority (1933), the Public Works Administration (1933), the Rural Electrification Administration (1935), and the Bonneville Power Administration (1937); and through numerous additional financing and loan mechanisms.

10. For a discussion of how Samuel Insull and Commonwealth Edison effected this in Chicago at the turn of the century, see Harold L. Platt, *The Electric City: Energy and the Growth of the Chicago Area, 1880–1930* (Chicago: University of Chicago Press, 1991).

11. *Merriam-Webster Online*, s.v. "conservation" and "conserve," accessed February 17, 2013, http://www.merriam-webster.com.

12. *Encyclopedia Britannica Online*, s.v. "conservation of energy," accessed February 17, 2013, http://www.britannica.com.

13. Theodore Roosevelt, *Presidential Addresses and State Papers*, vol. 1 (New York: Review of Reviews, 1910), 249–57 (speech given at a meeting of the Society of American Foresters, March 26, 1903).

14. Ibid., 6:1183 (letter to create the Inland Waterways Commission, March 14, 1907).

15. *Proceedings of a Conference of Governors in the White House, Washington, D.C., May 13–15, 1908*, ed. Newton C. Blanchard et al. (Washington, D.C.: Government Printing Office, 1908), x.

16. H. St. Clair Putnam, "Conservation of Power Resources," *Transactions of the American Institute of Electrical Engineers* 27, no. 1 (1908): 378.

17. Ibid., 396.

18. Louis Bell, "Electrical Power Transmission," *Electrical World* 37, no. 1 (1901): 32.

19. In 1907, the Technologic Bureau of the Geological Survey produced a report stating that "nearly one-half of the total coal supply is being left underground." "National Waste," *Electrical World* 50, no. 15 (1907): 771; see also Chas. F. Scott, "Conservation of Power Resources," *Electric Journal* 5, no. 9 (1908): 486–88.

20. "The Conservation of Natural Resources," *Electrical World* 51, no. 11 (1908): 550.

21. Bell, "Electrical Power Transmission."

22. "Anthracite Coal Situation," *Electrical World* 60, no. 22 (1912): 1128; Charles P. Steinmetz, "America's Energy Supply," *Transactions of the American Institute of Electrical Engineers* 37 (1918): 164.

23. "Smoke Production," *Electrical World* 49, no. 13 (1907): 645; "Smoke Prevention," *Electrical World* 49, no. 18 (1907): 909; "Smoke Nuisance," *Electrical World* 50, no. 23 (1907): 1124; "Relation of Government Fuel Investigation to the Solution of the Smoke Problem," *Electrical World* 52, no. 1 (1908): 5; W. F. Murphy, "Smokeless Combustion of Slack and Natural Gas," *Electrical World* 52, no. 23 (1908): 1234; "Smokeless Combustion," *Electrical World* 53, no. 16 (1909): 908; "Some Advances in Producer Gas," *Electrical World* 54, no. 6 (1909): 287.

24. "Electricity Directly from the Coal Mine in Pennsylvania," *Electrical World* 59, no. 19 (1912): 1002–3; "Unmarketable Coal Used for Generating Electricity—I," *Electrical World* 63, no. 19 (1914): 1035–40; "A Real Case of Conservation," *Electrical World* 63, no. 20 (1914): 1079.

25. Scott, "Conservation of Power Resources."

26. "Coal Consumption of New York's Generating Stations," *Electrical World* 64, no. 14 (1914): 660.

27. "A Wasteful Century," *Electrical World* 36, no. 8 (1900): 272.

28. "The Value of Water Storage," *Electrical World* 44, no. 20 (1904): 811.

29. *Electric Power Development in the United States: Letter from the Secretary of Agriculture Transmitting a Report . . . as to the Ownership and Control of the Water-Power Sites in the United States*, 3 vols. (Washington, D.C.: U.S. Department of Agriculture, 1916), 15.

30. "The National Water-Power Situation," *Electrical World* 58, no. 23 (1911): 1333.

31. "Low Priced Fuels for Energy Transmission," *Electrical World* 60, no. 5 (1912): 229.

32. "The Conservation Movement," *Electrical World* 61, no. 4 (1913): 184.

33. William B. Jackson, "The Water-Power Situation," *Electrical World* 63, no. 1 (1914): 13.

34. A.C. Dunham, "The Comparative Values of Water-Power and Steam Power," *Electrical World* 59, no. 1 (1912): 41.

35. "The Alleged Water-Power Trust," *Electrical World* 54, no. 8 (1909): 409–10.

36. "Beautifying Niagara," *Electrical World* 48, no. 25 (1906): 1189.

37. "Niagara Falls Power," *Electrical World* 60, no. 19 (1912): 1006.

38. "Hydroelectric Developments," *Electrical World* 59, no. 22 (1912): 1144.

39. "The Growth of a Transmission Network," *Electrical World* 51, no. 16 (1908): 799.

40. "Getting After the 'Electric Trust,'" *Electrical World* 54, no. 23 (1909): 1327.

41. "The Great Southern Transmission Network," *Electrical World* 63, no. 22 (1914): 1201.

42. Carl Hering, "San Gabriel–Los Angeles Transmission," *Electrical World* 33, no. 1 (1899): 24; "Power Transmission in Utah," *Electrical World* 37, no. 15 (1901): 587, 593–94.

43. "The Year in Power Transmission," *Electrical World* 45, no. 1 (1905): 5.

44. "The Tendency of Central Station Development—III," *Electrical World* 30, no. 26 (1897): 75.

45. Howard S. Knowlton, "The Storage Battery in Transmission Plants," *Electrical World* 41, no. 20 (1903): 831.

46. Hering, "San Gabriel–Los Angeles Transmission"; "San Gabriel Electric Company," *Engineering* (1899): 781–83.

47. Hering, "San Gabriel–Los Angeles Transmission."

48. "Pacific Coast Notes: An 81-Mile Transmission Line in Successful Operation," *Electrical World* 33, no. 6 (1899): 188; "83 Miles Power Transmission," *Electrical World* 34, no. 20 (1899): 750.

49. R. F. Hayward, "Some Practical Experiences in the Operation of Many Power Plants in Parallel," in *Transactions of the International Electrical Congress, St. Louis, 1904*, vol. 2 (St. Louis, Mo.: J. B. Lyon, 1905), 443–63.

50. For an examination of utility efforts to manage the unpredictability of the Susquehanna River through interconnections, see Christopher F. Jones, *Routes of Power: Energy and Modern America* (Cambridge, Mass.: Harvard University Press, 2014), 167–68.

51. A search for "conservation" in Compendex for the years 1884 (when the records begin) to 1908 produced sixty-two results, the first occurring in 1895. Of the sixty-two, thirty-nine were published in English and did not refer to chemical processes. Engineering Village, Compendex database, accessed May 15, 2012, http://www.engineeringvillage.com/home.url.

52. "Progress in Power Transmission," *Electrical World* 47, no. 1 (1906): 4.

53. "The Preservation of Niagara," *Electrical World* 48, no. 1 (1906): 5.

54. "Economic Limitations to Aggregation of Electrical Systems," *Electrical World* 57, no. 8 (1911): 468.

55. "Modern Transmission Problems," *Electrical World* 57, no. 12 (1911): 710.

56. "World's Largest Transmission System," *Electrical World* 59, no. 22 (1912): 1203.

57. "Electrical Interconnections to Conserve Fuel," *Electrical World* 71, no. 1 (1918): 12–14.

58. Cornelius G. Weber, "Interconnecting Industrial and Central-Station Plants," *Power* 51, no. 26 (1920): 1049.

59. "Interconnection in Southern Vermont," *Electrical World* 76, no. 1 (1920): 9.

60. Ross B. Mateer, "Another Opportunity for Interconnection," *Electrical World* 76, no. 24 (1920): 1162; "An Interconnection of Increasing Value," *Electrical World* 78 (1921): 204, 216–17.

61. W. S. Murray, "The Superpower System as an Answer to a National Power Policy," *General Electric Review* 25, no. 2 (1922): 72–76; "Power from Coal Mines by Wire Seen as the Next

Big Economy," *New York Times*, September 30, 1923; Gus Norwood, *Columbia River Power for the People: A History of Policies of the Bonneville Power Administration* (Portland, Ore.: U.S. Department of Energy, Bonneville Power Administration, 1981), 51–52.

62. Federal Power Act of 1935, 16 U.S.C.§ 791a, section 202 (a).

63. *National Power Survey: A Report* (Washington, D.C.: Government Printing Office, 1964).

## Chapter 7. Plastic Six-Pack Rings

1. Ougljesa Jules Poupitch, Container Carrier and Package, U.S. Patent 2,874,835, filed December 1, 1958, and issued February 24, 1959.

2. In a 1971 article on recent inventions, author Peter Blake described the problem of the paperboard six-pack holder. He wrote, "The six-pack designer put all those finger-holes into the six-pack carrying case, and these holes are just dandy—but then he printed instructions on the carrying case that tell you how to zip off this cardboard string and that one, and you do just that, and then you pick up the six-pack carrying case by its finger-holes and all the bottles crash to the floor and you have foam in your living room." Peter Blake, "It May Be Art, But It Won't Cut Cheese," *New York Magazine*, December 6, 1971, 65.

3. Gregory E. Lang, "Plastics, the Marine Menace: Causes and Curbs," *Journal of Land Use & Environmental Law* 5, no. 2 (Spring 1990): 730.

4. See Ocean Conservancy's International Coastal Cleanup, *Tracking Trash: 25 Years of Action for the Ocean*, Trash Free Seas Marine Debris 2011 Report, http://issuu.com/oceanconservancy/docs/marine_debris_2011_report_oc.

5. The exhibit, which can be accessed at http://www.hidden-heroes.net, is underwritten by Hi-Cone to showcase the array of everyday products developed by the company.

6. Finn Arne Jørgensen explores the intersections of technology, waste, and disposability in his fascinating study of automated beverage recycling machines. See Finn Arne Jørgensen, *Making a Green Machine: The Infrastructure of Beverage Container Recycling* (New Brunswick, N.J.: Rutgers University Press, 2011). Also see Bartow J. Elmore, *Citizen Coke: The Making of Coca-Cola Capitalism* (New York: W. W. Norton, 2015). Other works on plastic waste tend to focus on the myriad of plastic products produced, sold, shipped, and thrown out. See, for example, recent works such as Susan Freinkel, *Plastic: A Toxic Love Story* (Boston: Houghton Mifflin Harcourt, 2011); Stephen Fenichell, *Plastic: The Making of a Synthetic Century* (New York: HarperBusiness, 1997); and Donovan Hohn, *Moby-Duck: The True Story of 28,800 Bath Toys Lost at Sea and of the Beachcombers, Oceanographers, Environmentalists, and Fools, Including the Author, Who Went in Search of Them* (New York: Viking, 2012). Scholars such as Martin Melosi, Susan Strasser, and Carl Zimring have examined the history of sanitation, waste, and recycling, and the creation of a "throw-away society." See Martin Melosi, *Garbage in the Cities: Refuse Reform and the Environment* (Pittsburgh: University of Pittsburgh Press, 2004); Susan Strasser, *Waste and Want: A Social History of Trash* (New York: Henry Holt, 1999); and Carl Zimring, *Cash for Your Trash: Scrap Recycling in America* (New Brunswick, N.J.: Rutgers University Press, 2004).

7. Jørgensen, *Making a Green Machine*.

8. Christine Kreiser, "Canned Beer," *American History* 45, no. 3 (August 2010): 15; Jane Busch, "An Introduction to the Tin Can," *Historical Archaeology* 15, no. 1 (1981): 95–101; Greg Hatala, "Made in Jersey: Canned Beer—Krueger Brewing Co. Proved 'Yes, We Can Can!'" NJ .com, October 28, 2013; "America's Experience with Refillable Beverage Containers," in Brenda Platt and Doug Rowe, *Reduce, Reuse, Refill!* (Washington, D.C.: Institute for Local Self-Reliance, 2002; produced under a joint project with the GrassRoots Recycling Network, Grrn.org).

9. William L. Dempsey Jr., "Multiple Packaging: A Merchandising Tool," *Journal of Marketing* 23, no. 3 (January 1959): 287–92; *American Brewer* (1949). Also see Jess Kibben, "Beer Talk: First Six Pack Holder," *Beer Advocate*, June 14, 2013, http://www.beeradvocate.com/community/threads/first-six-pack-holder.96664/.

10. Jørgensen, *Making a Green Machine*, 13.

11. Regional bottling facilities were one way beer and soda manufactures developed to reduce transportation costs. Elmore, *Citizen Coke*.

12. "Time Out to Take Stock," *Modern Plastics*, January 1948, 5.

13. Jeffrey L. Meikle, "Into the Fourth Kingdom: Representations of Plastic Materials, 1920–1950," *Journal of Design History* 5, no. 3 (1992): 177; and Jeffrey L. Meikle, *American Plastic: A Cultural History* (New Brunswick, N.J.: Rutgers University Press, 1995), esp. 63–90.

14. "Plastic 1962: A Critical Analysis," *Modern Plastics*, January 1963, 54–103.

15. E. S. Stevens, *Green Plastics: An Introduction to the New Science of Biodegradable Plastics* (Princeton, N.J.: Princeton University Press, 2002), 6

16. "New Day for Thin-Wall Containers," *Modern Plastics*, May 1964, 84–88, 160–62.

17. "Die Cut PE Outperforms Paperboard," *Modern Plastics*, September 1960, 110–11.

18. Ibid., 111.

19. Kris Frieswick, *ITW: Forging the Tools for Excellence* (Bainbridge Island, Wash.: Fenwick Publishing Group, 2012), 29.

20. ITW Annual Report 1977, 10; and ITW Annual Report 1979, 10.

21. Bartow J. Elmore, "The American Beverage Industry and the Development of Curbside Recycling Programs, 1950–2000," *Business History Review* 86 (Autumn 2012): 478. Also see Elmore, *Citizen Coke*, esp. 224–61.

22. John A. Kouwenhoven, *The Beer Can by the Highway: Essays on What's American About America* (1961; Baltimore: Johns Hopkins University Press, 1988), 218; John McHale, "The Plastic Parthenon," *Dot Zero 3* (Spring 1967), reprinted in *The Futurists*, ed. Alvin Toffler (New York: Random House, 1972); Alvin Toffler, *Future Shock* (New York: Random House, 1970), 221; and Victor Papanek, *Design for the Real World: Human Ecology and Social Change* (New York: Pantheon Books, 1971), 212–13, and 77. Also see Jennifer Price, *Flight Maps: Adventures with Nature in Modern America* (New York: Basic Books, 1999), esp. 111–66; and Vance Packard, *The Waste Makers* (New York: David McKay, 1960).

23. Barry Commoner, *The Closing Circle: Nature, Man, and Technology* (New York: Knopf, 1971), 164.

24. Nelson Bryant, "Wood, Field and Stream: A Rare Owl Lures Bird Watchers," *New York Times*, March 2, 1973, 29; *Field and Stream*, March 1974, 24.

25. Edward J. Carpenter and K. L. Smith Jr., "Plastics on the Sargasso Sea Surface," *Science* 175, no. 4027 (March 17, 1972): 1240–41; Gwenda Matthews, "Pollution of the Oceans: An International Problem?" *Ocean Management* 1 (March 1973): 161–70; A. M. Cundell, "Plastic Materials Accumulating in Narragansett Bay," *Marine Pollution Bulletin* 4, no. 12 (December 1973): 187–88; "Plastic Cups Found in Fish," *Marine Pollution Bulletin* 6, no. 10 (October 1975): 148.

26. Convention on the Prevention of Marine Pollution by Dumping of Wastes and Other Matter of 1972, art. 2. Also see Gregory E. Lang, "Plastics, the Marine Menace: Causes and Cures," *Journal of Land Use & Environmental Law* 5, no. 2 (Spring 1990): 729–52.

27. MARPOL, Annex V. Also see Rebecca Becker, "MARPOL 73/78: An Overview in International Environmental Enforcement," *Georgetown International Environmental Law Review* 10

(1998): 625–42; and Gerard Peet, "The MARPOL Convention: Implementation and Effectiveness," *International Journal of Estuarine and Coastal Law* 7, no. 4 (1992): 277–95.

28. Richard S. Shomura and Howard O. Yoshida, eds., *Proceedings of the Workshop on the Fate and Impact of Marine Debris, 27–29 November 1984, Honolulu, Hawaii*, NOAA Technical Memorandum NMFS-SWFC 54 (Honolulu: U.S. Department of Commerce, National Oceanic and Atmospheric Administration, National Marine Fisheries Service, Southwest Fisheries Center, 1985); quotations at pp. 3 and 11.

29. Judie Neilson, *Get the Drift and Bag It: Final Report*, NWAFC Processed Report 86–11 (Seattle, Wash.: U.S. Department of Commerce, National Oceanic and Atmospheric Administration, National Marine Fisheries Service, Northwest and Alaska Fisheries Center, 1986); quotation at p. 21.

30. Hi-Cone was not the first to develop ethylene carbon monoxide. The compound was first developed by the Eastman Corporation in the 1940s and commercialize by DuPont Chemical Corporation. See U.S. Environmental Protection Agency, Proposed Rule, 40 CFR Parts 238, "Degradable Ring Rule," *Federal Register* 58, no. 65 (April 7, 1993): 18064. Also see Stevens, *Green Plastics*; and George Harlan and Chester Kmiec, "Ethylene-Carbon Monoxide Copolymers," in *Degradable Polymers: Principles and Applications*, ed. Gerald Scott and Dan Gilead (London: Chapman & Hall, 1995), 153–68.

31. ITW Annual Report 1977, 6; 1979, 10; 1980, 8; and 1987, 10.

32. Michael Hudson, ITW vice president of public affairs, testimony, in U.S. Congress, House Committee on Merchant Marine and Fisheries, Subcommittee on Fisheries and Wildlife Conservation and the Environment, *Degradable Six-Pack Rings: Joint Hearing Before the Subcommittee on Fisheries and Wildlife Conservation and the Environment of the Committee on Merchant Marine and Fisheries and the Subcommittee on Transportation, Tourism, and Hazardous Materials of the Committee on Energy and Commerce, House of Representatives, One Hundredth Congress, Second Session, on S. 1986 . . . July 26, 1988* (Washington, D.C.: Government Printing Office, 1988), 43 (hereafter *Degradable Six-Pack Rings Hearing*).

33. Hans Y. Tammemagi, *The Waste Crisis: Landfills, Incinerators, and the Search for a Sustainable Future* (New York: Oxford University Press, 1999); K. S. Shrader-Frechette, *Burying Uncertainty: Risk and the Case Against Geological Disposal of Nuclear Waste* (Berkeley: University of California Press, 1993); and Peter Little, *Toxic Town: IBM, Pollution, and Industrial Risks* (New York: New York University Press, 2014). Also see David Naguib Pellow, *Garbage Wars: The Struggle for Environmental Justice in Chicago* (Cambridge, Mass.: MIT Press, 2004); Rob Nixon, *Slow Violence and the Environmentalism of the Poor* (Cambridge, Mass.: Harvard University Press, 2013); and Robert Bullard, *Dumping in Dixie: Race, Class, and Environmental Quality*, 3rd ed. (Boulder, Colo.: Westview Press, 2000).

34. They are (with date of law in effect): Vermont (January 1, 1977); Maine (January 1, 1978); Oregon (September 1, 1978); Alaska (October 1, 1981); California (November 1, 1982); Delaware (January 15, 1983); Massachusetts (January 17, 1983); New York (September 13, 1983); Connecticut (October 1, 1984); New Jersey (April 21, 1986); and Rhode Island (July 1, 1987).

35. *Report of the Interagency Task Force on Persistent Marine Debris* ([Rockville, Md.]: The Administration, [1988]).

36. *Congressional Record*, 100th Cong., 1st sess., 1987, 133. pt. 4:4600–4603 (S. 633, a bill to prohibit disposal of plastic products in U.S. waters).

37. *Degradable Six-Pack Rings Hearing*.

38. Ibid., 1.

39. Barbara Mandula, letter to the editor, "Plastic Debris Poses a Threat to Wildlife," *New York Times*, July 8, 1987.

40. *Congressional Record*, 100th Cong., 1st sess., 1987, 133. pt. 4:4600–4603 (S. 633, a bill to prohibit disposal of plastic products in U.S. waters).

41. *Degradable Six-Pack Rings Hearing*, 10.

42. Ibid., 68.

43. Ibid., 8.

44. Ibid.

45. ITW Annual Report 1976, 4; 1977, 4; 1978, 5.

46. "Sustainability," Hi-Cone website, accessed March 20, 2014, http://www.hicone.com /index.php.

47. Quoted in John Holusha, "Business Technology: Doubts Are Voiced on 'Degradable' Plastic Waste," *New York Times*, October 25, 1989; and "New Study Challenges 'Biodegradable' Claims," *New York Times*, March 5, 1991. Also see "Technology: The Plastic Pollution Fight," *New York Times*, May 16, 1985; Stephen Budiansky, "The World of Crumbling Plastics," *U.S. News & World Report*, November 24, 1986, 76; "A Step Toward Cheap Plastic That Doesn't Pollute," *Business Week*, October 28, 1985, 111; and William J. Jewell, *Reflections on an Academic Career* (Ithaca, N.Y.: Internet-First University Press, 2015), esp. 118–38.

48. Quoted in Holusha, "Business Technology: Doubts Are Voiced."

49. My colleague at Fredonia Dr. Sam Mason has done some innovative research on microplastic pollution in the Great Lakes. Similar work on plastic waste in the ocean is being done by 5 Gyres, Woods Hole Oceanographic Institution, Scripps Institution of Oceanography, among others. See, for example, Christopher Johnson, "Personal Grooming Products May Be Harming Great Lakes Marine Life," *Scientific American*, June 25, 2013; Anthony L. Andrady, "Microplastics in the Marine Environment," *Marine Pollution Bulletin* 62, no. 8 (August 2011): 1596–605; and Lorena M. Rios et al., "Quantitation of Persistent Organic Pollutants Adsorbed on Plastic Debris from the Northern Pacific Gyre's 'Eastern Garbage Patch,'" *Journal of Environmental Monitoring* 12 (2010): 2226–36.

50. Frieswick, *ITW*, 30.

51. Hi-Cone Sustainable Packaging, 2011, http://www.ringleader.com/downloads/Hi-Cone %20Sustainable%20Packaging-2011web.pdf.

52. "The Ring Leader Recycling Program," accessed March 20, 2014, http://www.ringleader .com/program.html.

53. Conrad B. MacKerron, "Waste and Opportunity 2015: Environmental Progress and Challenges in Food, Beverage, and Consumer Goods Packaging," National Resources Defense Council and As You Sow report, January 2015, 4.

54. See note 48 above. See also Chris Wilcox, Erik Van Sebille, and Britta Denise Hardesty, "Threat of Plastic Pollution to Seabirds Is Global, Pervasive, and Increasing," *PNAS* 112, no. 38 (2015): 11899–904.

## Chapter 8. The Rise and Fall of an Ecostar

I would like to thank Duke University's Hartman Center for Sales, Marketing, and Advertising History for a grant to support this research.

1. Northeast Sustainable Energy Association, "Quick Facts, 1994 Tour de Sol," undated broadsheet, File AFV Ecostar, 1993–94, Box FM10, Inventory of the J. Walter Thompson Company, Account Files, 1885–2008 and undated, bulk 1920–95 (hereafter, JWT Account Files),

John W. Hartman Center for Sales, Advertising, and Marketing History, Duke University (hereafter, Hartman Center).

2. The major companies included GM, Ford, Chrysler, Toyota, Honda, and Nissan. Gustavo Collantes, "The California Zero-Emission Vehicle Mandate: A Study of the Policy Process, 1990–2004" (Ph.D. diss., University of California, Davis, 2006), vi.

3. Ibid., 17–29; Leslie Harrison Reed Jr., "California Low-Emission Vehicle Program: Forcing Technology and Dealing Effectively with the Uncertainties," *Boston College Environmental Affairs Law Review* 24 (1996): 695.

4. Curtis Darrel Anderson and Judy Anderson, *Electric and Hybrid Cars: A History* (Jefferson, N.C.: McFarland, 2005), 9, 47.

5. Gustavo Collantes and Daniel Sperling, "The Origin of California's Zero Emission Vehicle Mandate," *Transportation Research Part A: Policy and Practice* 42, no. 10 (December 2008): 1304.

6. David Vogel, "The 'New' Social Regulation in Historical and Comparative Perspective," in *Regulation in Perspective: Historical Essays*, ed. Thomas K. McCraw (Cambridge, Mass.: Harvard University Press, 1981), 155–85; Paul Charles Milazzo, *Unlikely Environmentalists: Congress and Clean Water, 1945–1972* (Lawrence: University Press of Kansas, 2006), 218.

7. Lettie McSpadden, "Industry's Use of the Courts," in *Business and Environmental Policy: Corporate Interests in the American Political System*, ed. Michael E. Kraft and Sheldon Kamieniecki (Cambridge, Mass.: MIT Press, 2007), 233–62; "Detroit Strikes Familiar Stance on Clean Air," *New York Times*, March 26, 1990, A1; Jim Motavalli, "The Sky Is Falling for Carmakers, Again," *New York Times*, February 8, 2009.

8. CARB officials saw the history of the agency as one of successfully setting "the pace for manufacturers to meet progressively more stringent vehicle emissions standards." Both officials quoted in Collantes and Sperling, "Origin of California's Zero Emission Vehicle Mandate," 1306–7.

9. Sherry Boschert, *Plug-In Hybrids: The Cars That Will Recharge America* (Vancouver: New Society Publishers, 2006), 10.

10. Joe Sherman, *Charging Ahead* (New York: Oxford University Press, 1998), 65.

11. Michael Shnayerson, *The Car That Could: The Inside Story of GM's Revolutionary Electric Vehicle* (New York: Random House, 1996), 48.

12. According to a CARB member, Ford initially said it would go along with a mandate so long as it was given enough time to phase in the technology. Collantes, "California Zero-Emission Vehicle Mandate," 34.

13. "Ford's Electric Vehicle History," *EM: Air & Waste Management Association's Magazine for Environmental Managers*, May 1998, 10; on the state of Ford's EV research circa 1990, see Shnayerson, *The Car That Could*, 84–85.

14. Collantes and Sperling, "Origin of California's Zero Emission Vehicle Mandate," 1308.

15. "Ford's Electric Vehicle History"; on GM, Chrysler, and the USABC, see Shnayerson, *The Car That Could*, 88–89.

16. Collantes and Sperling, "Origin of California's Zero Emission Vehicle Mandate," 1305.

17. Kateri Callahan, executive director of Electric Transportation Coalition, to members not in attendance, November 10, 1993; Electric Transportation Coalition, Full Coalition Meeting, November 8, 1993; no author, handwritten note "Electric Transportation Coalition," November 8, 1993; all in File Electric Transportation Coalition, 1993–94, Box FM10, JWT Account Files.

18. Collantes notes that Ford and Chrysler were worried about their environmental image. Collantes, "California Zero-Emission Vehicle Mandate," 34, 45–46. However, as documented

below, Ford and JWT clearly believed that Ford was soon seen as the most aggressive opponent of the ZEV mandate.

19. J. Walter Thompson (JWT), "Ecostar Electric Vehicle 1994 American Tour de Sol Race Win Advertising Proposal," May 23, 1994, File AFV Ecostar, 1993–94, Box FM10, JWT Account Files. Japanese companies stayed neutral or feigned support for the mandate even though they also did not have a commercially viable EV. Ford and analysts did not elaborate on this strategy, but it may have also been geared toward avoiding an appearance of antienvironmentalism. Or it may have been that Japanese companies, which had relatively developed electric vehicle technology, did not think they would be any worse off than American companies. See ibid.; and Daniel Sperling et al., *Future Drive: Electric Vehicles and Sustainable Transportation* (Washington, D.C.: Island Press, 1995), 37.

20. New management contributed to Ford's harder stance. Shnayerson, *The Car That Could*, 168.

21. "Don Johnston on Advertising Credibility," JWT News, in Folder JWT News, 1982–84, Box MN19, JWT Newsletters; "Since Greenwatch 2," *JWT Greenwatch* 3 (Spring/Summer 1991), in Folder JWT Greenwatch, 1991–93, Box RN2, JWT Newsletters.

22. Casey Bukro, "Shopping for an Ideal," *Chicago Tribune*, November 17, 1991; Carl F. Patka, "Of Diapers, Lawnbags, and Landfills: The Federal Trade Commission Cracks Down on False Advertising in the Environmental Marketplace," *Loyola Consumer Law Reporter* 5 (1993): 43.

23. Ford believed its NAS batteries would ultimately "blow its rivals away," in Shnayerson's words. Shnayerson, *The Car That Could*, 86.

24. For example, a Ford representative criticized the first draft of JWT's brochure for the Ecostar because it claimed that Ford had a "commitment" to the environment. "Does this pass the 'red face' test?" the representative asked. It was California's ZEV mandate, he noted, not Ford's "commitment to preserve and protect the environment," that was responsible for building the Ecostar. JWT subsequently changed the brochure to emphasize that Ford technologies had made the environment cleaner. JWT, "Ford Ecostar Brochure Overview," May 25, 1993; first draft of brochure (no date, circa late May or June 1993); Bill Canever, "Ecostar Spec Sheet Summary of OGC Comments," no date; all in Folder AFV Ecostar, 1993–94, Box FM10, JWT Account Files.

25. Ford Communications Network, "Change Is in the Air," draft, June 16, 1992, Folder Change is in the Air, Box FM13, JWT Account Files.

26. Al Chambers to Tom Benjamin, memo, July 1, 1992, Folder Change is in the Air, Box FM13, JWT Account Files.

27. Ford Communication Network, "Driving Toward a Cleaner, Greener, Environment," Folder Change Is in the Air, Box FM13, JWT Account Files.

28. Publicly, Ford was silent on its plans for selling the Ecostar to individual consumers. Shnayerson's reporting on EVs in 1996, however, revealed that Ford had no plans to sell the Ecostar, only to use it to test the technology (Shnayerson, *The Car That Could*, 85), and, evidently, to use that testing as part of its green marketing.

29. Merson to Doyle, December 27, 1993; JWT Eco Expo Task Force, "Objective of Ford's Participation in Eco Expo," circa 1994, in Folder AFV Eco Expo 1994, Box FM10, JWT Account Files, Hartman Center.

30. JWT, "Ecostar Electric Vehicle 1994."

31. Sherman, *Charging Ahead*, 5.

32. Ibid., 158.

33. Minutes of the California Air Resources Board, October 26, 1995, accessed July 15, 2015, http://www.arb.ca.gov/board/mt/mt102695.txt. For battery study, see pp. 142–60; for consumer viability, p. 124.

34. One of the first full-book assessments of EVs and California's ZEV mandate described the sulfur-sodium battery as the "greatest disappointment." Sperling et al., *Future Drive*, 50. Another review also stated that NAS batteries presented the most serious safety hazards. U.S. General Accounting Office, *Electric Vehicles: Likely Consequences of U.S. and Other Nations' Programs and Policies* (Darby, Pa.: Diane Publishing, 1995), 26.

35. Louise Wells Bedsworth and Margaret R. Taylor, "Learning from California's Zero-Emission Vehicle Program," *California Economic Policy* 3, no. 4 (2007): 13–14.

36. Ibid., 9–11.

## Chapter 9. Dilemmas of Going Green

1. For a recent overview, see Geoffrey Jones and Christina Lubinski, "Making 'Green Giants': Environment Sustainability in the German Chemical Industry, 1950s–1980s," *Business History* 56, no. 4 (2014): 623–49.

2. Ann-Kristin Bergquist and Magnus Lindmark, "Sustainability and Shared Value in the Interwar Swedish Copper Industry," *Business History Review* 90, no. 2 (2016): 197–225.

3. See Christine M. Rosen, "Industrial Ecology and the Transformation of Corporate Environmental Management: A Business Historian's Perspective," in *Inventing for the Environment*, ed. Arthur P. Molella and Joyce Bedi (Cambridge, Mass.: MIT Press, 2003); Christine Meisner Rosen and Christopher Sellers, "The Nature of the Firm: Towards an Ecocultural History of Business," *Business History Review*, 73, no. 4 (1999): 577–600. Drawing on theoretical and empirical research from different disciplines, such as business history, environmental history, and the history of technology, Rosen and Sellers concluded that few efforts generally had been made to understand businesses' internal processes in relation to environmental issues. They even argued that business historians had tended to treat the environmental dimension of business development as if natural goods and supplies (including pollution and other harms) were "externalities to the enterprise of business history itself" (586).

4. Andrew J. Hoffman, *From Heresy to Dogma: An Institutional History of Corporate Environmentalism* (San Francisco: New Lexington Press, 2007), 6.

5. Ann-Kristin Bergquist and Kristina Söderholm, "Transition to Greener Pulp: Regulation, Industry Responses and Path Depenency," *Business History* 57, no. 6 (2015): 862–84; Frank Ueköt-ter also points to several parts of this complexity in comparing the evolution of national styles of air pollution regulation in Germany and the United States between 1880 and 1970. See Frank Uekötter, *The Age of Smoke* (Pittsburgh: University of Pittsburgh Press, 2009).

6. Richard R. Nelson and Nathan Rosenberg, "Science, Technological Advance and Economic Growth," in *The Dynamic Firm: The Role of Technology, Strategy, Organization and Regions*, ed. Alfred D. Chandler, Peter Hagström, and Örjan Sölvell (Oxford: Oxford University Press, 1999); Nathan Rosenberg, *Exploring the Black Box: Technology, Economics and History* (Cambridge: Cambridge University Press, 1994).

7. Nelson and Rosenberg, "Science," 54.

8. Michael E. Porter and Claas van der Linde, "Toward a New Conception of the Environment-Competitiveness Relationship," *Journal of Economic Perspectives* 9, no. 4 (1995): 119–32.

9. Porter and van der Linde argue that the pressure from a strict and properly designed environmental regulation might, according to this line of reasoning, foster innovative solutions

that fully or partly mitigate environmental investment costs. For an overview, see Stefan Ambec et al., *The Porter Hypothesis at 20: Can Environmental Regulation Enhance Innovation and Competitiveness?* RFF Paper DP 11-01, Resources for the Future, Washington, D.C. (January 2011).

10. Clases Bernes and Lars J. Lundgren, *Use and Misuse of Nature's Resources: An Environmental History of Sweden* (Stockholm: Swedish Environmental Protection Agency, 2010), 53.

11. John R. McNeill, *Something New Under the Sun: An Environmental History of the Twentieth-Century World* (New York: W. W. Norton, 2000), 32.

12. Timothy J. McCain, *Mass Destruction: The Men and Giant Mines That Wired America and Scarred the Planet* (New Brunswick, N.J.: Rutgers University Press, 2009). Another known example of severe environmental destruction caused by copper production is found in Ducktown, Tennessee. See Duncan Maysilles. *Ducktown Smoke: The Fight over One of the South's Greatest Environmental Disasters* (Chapel Hill: University of North Carolina Press, 2011).

13. In short, the method separated the arsenic from the dust and obtained the arsenic in a "safe" form that could be stored or sold as a product on the market. Bergquist and Lindmark, "Sustainability and Shared Value."

14. Between 1931 and 1940, the emissions of sulfur dioxide ($SO_2$) increased from 4,000 tons per year to around 100,000 tons in 1940, according to emission data sent from Boliden to the author.

15. Swedish Environmental Protection Agency, "Swedish Pollutant Release and Transfer Register," 2014, http://utslappisiffror.naturvardsverket.se/Sok/Anlaggningssida/?pid=4505.

16. Boliden fact sheet, accessed August 13, 2015, http://www.boliden.com/Documents/Press/Publications/Fact%20sheets/facts-ronnskar-sv.pdf.

17. Boliden Annual Report 1980, 1981.

18. In 1989 Trelleborg acquired 50 percent of the shares in the Canada-based mining company Falconbridge. "Noranda, Trelleborg Succeed in Offer for Falconbridge," *Northern Miner* 75, no. 29 (1989).

19. The company was listed on the Toronto Stock Exchange.

20. This disaster threatened to bankrupt the company. Ann-Kristin Bergquist, "Guld och Gröna Skogar? Miljöanpassningen av Rönnskärsverken, 1960–2000" [Going Green? A Case Study of the Rönnskär Smelter, 1960–2000], Umeå Studies in Economic History, no. 36 (Ph.D. diss., Umeå University, 2007), 61.

21. Ibid., appendix 2.

22. For an overview of regulations, see Kristina Söderholm and Ann-Kristin Bergquist, "Firm Collaboration and Environmental Adaptation: The Case of the Swedish Pulp and Paper Industry, 1900–1990," *Scandinavian Economic History Review* 60, no. 2 (2012): 183–211.

23. Lars J. Lundgren, *Vattenförorening: Debatten i Sverige, 1890–1921* (Lund: Gleerup, 1974).

24. Ann-Kristin Bergquist and Kristina Söderholm, "Green Innovation Systems in Swedish Industry, 1960–1989," *Business History Review* 85, no. 4 (2011): 677–98.

25. Bertil Wedin, *Luftens föroreningar* (Stockholm: Ivar Hagströms Boktryckeri AB, 1960), 11.

26. The Swedish Nature Conservation Association arranged a "mercury conference" in 1963, the same year Rachel Carson's book *Silent Spring* was translated into Swedish.

27. Lars J. Lundgren, "Från Miljöproblem till Miljövård: Ett genombrott med fördröjning," *Daedalus* (Tekniska Museets Årsbok, 1999), 242.

28. The Swedish government appointed the so-called emission experts in 1963, a committee assigned to investigate the issue of all interference from stationary plants. This then formed the basis for the Environmental Protection Act (EPAct) passed in 1969.

29. Lennart J. Lundqvist, "Sweden," in *National Environmental Policies: A Comparative Study of Capacity-Building*, ed. Martin Jänicke and Helmut Weidner (Berlin: Springer, 1997), 45–72.

30. Boliden Archive Rönnskärsverken (BaR), vol. 137.05, notes printed March 2, 1963.

31. BaR, vol. 137.05, minutes, June 13, 1966, "Protokoll fört vid sammanträde den 13.6.66. med avloppsgruppen."

32. BaR, vol. 137.04, manuscript, "Miljö och individen—Aktuell probleminventering i dagsläget: Anförande av direktör Folke Nilsson, Boliden Aktiebolag, Skelleftehamn, Konferens i Skellefteå den 12 November 1970."

33. Ann-Kristin Bergquist and Kristina Söderholm, "Miljöforskning i Statens och Industrins tjänst: Institutet för Vatten och Luftvårdsforskning (IVL), 1960-tal till 1980-tal," Umeå Papers in Economic History, no. 40 (2010).

34. Ibid.

35. BaR, vol. 137.02, note, February 9, 1968, "Besök på Naturvårdsverket 9.2.1968." For the agency, the issue of mercury had emerged as the most serious and urgent problem needing to be handled. The Swedish parliament had tasked the agency with charting the emissions of mercury in the whole country and identifying polluted areas.

36. Ibid.

37. BaR, vol. 137.05, Interna organ; 137.06, minutes, March 19, 1968, "Ärende: Vatten och luftvårdsfrågor."

38. BaR, vol. 137.05, Interna organ; 137.06, minutes, June 19, 1968, "Protokoll vid sammanträde den 19 juni 1968 med Bolidens arbetsgrupp för vatten och luftvård."

39. Lars J. Lundgren, *Acid Rain on the Agenda: A Picture of a Chain of Events in Sweden, 1966–1968* (Lund: Lund University Press, 1998).

40. BaR, vol. 137.05, minutes, June 9, 1971, "Protokoll 9.6.71: Ärende Miljövårdsammanträde."

41. Erland Mårald, *Svenska miljöbrott och miljöskandaler, 1960–2000* (Halmstad: Gidlunds, 2007), 10.

42. BaR, vol. 137.04, manuscript, November 1970, "Miljö och individen—Aktuell probleminventering i dagsläget."

43. The LBEP was formed the same year the Environmental Protection Act was implemented, in 1969, to administer the licenses.

44. Swedish National Archive (NA), Dnr Ä 57/73, vol. EI: 313, Aktbil.1

45. BaR, notes, June 14, 1972, Bolidens arbetsgrupp för vatten och luftvård, Pärm 7, "Minnesanteckningar från besök av Naturvårdsverket och Länsstyrelsen vid Rönnskärsverken 1972-06-14," 9.

46. Ibid., 5–6.

47. BaR, vol. 137.02, 1973–75, minutes, September 10, 1974, "Protokoll: Sammanträde i Skelleftehamn 1974-09-10."

48. Ibid.

49. Ibid., 8.

50. Bergquist, "Guld och Gröna Skogar?" 102–104, 177–182.

51. Västerbotten County Administrative Board's Archive (VCABA) Dossie för miljövård 2482-M-107, vol. EIc:49 (Koncession 1971–1975), "Beslut Jordbruksdepartementet 1975-06-18."

52. Bergquist, "Guld och Gröna Skogar?" appendix 2.

53. Donella H. Meadows et al., *The Limits to Growth: A Report for the Club of Rome's Project on the Predicament of Mankind* (New York: New American Library, 1972).

54. Ann-Kristin Bergquist, "Guld och Döda Skogar: Rapport från Rönnskärsverken, Sveriges Skitigaste Industri," *Pockettidningen R* (1978).

55. Boliden Annual Report 1978.

56. Ibid., 19.

57. In 1980, the company concluded that productive investment had been delayed or shelved in favor of mandatory environmental investments.

58. NA, Koncessionsnämnden för miljöskydd, Dnr Ä 57/73, Inlaga till Koncessionsnämnden, June 1980.

59. Ibid., chap. 1: "Allmänt, H. Ramprogram för yttre miljö under 1980-talet."

60. NA, Koncessionsnämnden för miljöskydd, Dnr Ä 57/73 "Beslut Nr 192/86, Aktbil. 284," 138–45.

61. See the Swedish Environmental Protection Agency's Archive (SEPAA), vol. F2GK:88, Dnr 311-1305-83-Ti2, "Studiebesök vid smältverk i England och Tyskland 14–18 mars och 16–27 maj enligt Koncessionsnämndens förordnande 1983-03-27"; SEPAA, vol. F2GK:78, "Reserapport från studieresa till Metallverk i Japan, USA, Kanada och Belgien januari–februari 1986, 1986-03-27." See also "Guld och Gröna Skogar?" 95–96, 140–45. In 1974 trips were made to smelters in the United States and Canada. Trips were also made in 1983 to the United Kingdom (British Lead Mills, Welvur Garden City and Holman Mickel Ltd.) and the Federal Republic of Germany (Hüttenwerke Kayser AG, Lünen and Norddeutsche Affineri, Hamburg). Finally, trips were made in 1986 to Japan (Furukawa, Ashio Smelter, Furukawa Co. Ltd.; Mitsui Mining & Smelting Co. and Onahama Smelting Unit Refining Co., Ltd); Belgium (Hoboken), Canada (Noranda Horne Smelter and Noranda CCR Refinery), and the United Sates (ASARCO Hayden Copper Smelter, Arizona; ASARCO Hayden, Inspiration Consolidated Copper Co., Arizona, and St. Joe Lead Herculaneum, Missouri).

62. SEPAA, vol. F2GK:88, "Studiebesök vid smältverk i England och Tyskland 14–18 mars och 16–27 maj enligt Koncessionsnämndens förordnande 1983-03-27"; vol. F2GK:78, "Reserapport från studieresa till Metallverk i Japan, USA, Kanada och Belgien januari–februari 1986, 1986-03-27," 58–66.

63. Ibid., 39.

64. Interview with Björn Lindqvist, environmental manager at Rönnskär smelter from 1973 to 1978, Boliden Contec, Skellefteå, December 15, 2003.

65. Interview with Lars-Erik Nilsson, manager of the water purification works, September 12, 2003.

66. Erik Solby, "Reningskrav på Rönnskär utvecklade ny teknik," Bergsmannen 6 (1989): 10–11.

67. One unit focused on emissions and one unit on waste management.

68. Solby, "Reningskrav på Rönnskär."

69. The acidification made the metals bioavailable.

70. NA, Koncessionsnämnden för miljöskydd, Dnr Ä 57/73 Aktbil, 279 "Protokoll 1986-06-10–12," 18.

71. NA, Koncessionsnämnden för miljöskydd, Dnr Ä 57/73 "Beslut Nr 192/86, Aktbil. 284."

72. NA, Industri- och näringsdepartementets arkiv, vol. E1A:1630. Dnr 4-1260/87, letter signed by Rune Andersson and Kjell Nilsson, July 10, 1987.

73. NA, Industri- och näringslivsdepartements arkiv, vol. E1A:1577, regeringsbeslut 1988-01-28 nr 1, regeringsbeslut 1988-01-28 nr 2. See also appendix 2 for minutes to the goverment meeting of January 28, 1988.

74. Bergquist, "Guld och Gröna Skogar?" 186.

75. Bergquist, "Guld och Döda Skogur," 215.

76. Financial institutions, such as the World Bank, the European Investment Bank, and the European Bank for Reconstruction, were also invited. For an overview of the development of the Baltic Sea environmental cooperation, see Ronnie Hjorth, "Baltic Sea Environmental Cooperation: The Role of Epistemic Communities and the Politics of Regime Change," *Cooperation and Conflict* 29 (1994): 11–31.

77. Ibid., 18.

78. Swedish Environmental Protection Agency, "Miljöplan för Sveriges del av Östersjön och Västerhavet," Rapport 3879 (1991), 19.

79. Government Bill 1990/91:90, 14.

80. BaR, vol. Arkivkod, reg. 137.02, "Ärende: Räddningsplan för Östersjön."

81. Ibid.

82. BaR, vol. Rönnskär, Ny koncession. Rönnskär+200, MUR -96. 1995–1998, "Rönnskär+200: Marknadspåverkande miljötrender, koppar."

83. Bergquist, "Guld och Gröna Skogar?" 229–30, 240.

84. Per Henricsson, "Rönnskär—Slutstationen för din mobil," *Elektronik Tidningen*, accessed August 17, 2015, http://www.etn.se/index.php?option=com_content&view=article&id=56918.

85. Interview with Michael Borell, environmental director, Boliden Mineral, August 12, 2012.

86. This information is not based on firsthand sources, but the data come from current company employees, the media, and conversations with a lawyer for the prosecution. For information, see, for example, "In Focus: Deliveries of Smelting Residues to Chile During the 1980s," accessed August 17, 2015, http://www.boliden.com/Sustainability/Arica/.

87. The claim amounts to approximately SEK 90 million plus interest and relates to deliveries of smelter sludge made from Boliden to the Chilean company PROMEL.

88. The Swedish Green Party has proposed a global framework with a strict liability of responsibility for exported materials, even for old environmental transgressions. Proposal 2013/14 MJ304, accessed August, 17, 2015, http://data.riksdagen.se/fil/C55787F5-2A93-46AC-A1DA-14A2D2345A76.

89. Hoffman, *From Heresy to Dogma*, 14.

## Chapter 10. Private Companies and the Recycling of Household Waste in West Germany, 1965–1990

1. Finn Arne Jørgensen, *Making a Green Machine: The Infrastructure of Beverage Container Recycling* (New Brunswick, N.J.: Rutgers University Press, 2011), 14–15.

2. Agnes Bünemann, "Duales System Deutschland: Ein Rückblick über die Entwicklung in Deutschland," in *Ressource Abfall: Politische und wirtschaftliche Betrachtungen anlässlich des 50-jährigen Bestehens des BDE*, ed. Peter Kurth (Neuruppin: TK-Verlag, 2011), 18–31.

3. Exceptions are, for instance, Mathias Mutz, "Managing Resources: Water and Wood in the German Pulp and Paper Industry, 1870s–1930s," *Jahrbuch für Wirtschaftsgeschichte* 50, no. 2 (2009): 45–68; Jørgensen, *Making a Green Machine*.

4. Peter Münch, *Stadthygiene im 19. und 20. Jahrhundert: Die Wasserversorgung, Abwasser- und Abfallbeseitigung unter besonderer Berücksichtigung Münchens* (Göttingen: Vandenhoeck & Ruprecht, 1993), 243.

5. Richard Wines, *Fertilizer in America: From Waste Recycling to Resource Exploitation* (Philadelphia: Temple University Press, 1985).

6. Joel A. Tarr, *The Search for the Ultimate Sink: Urban Pollution in Historical Perspective* (Akron, Ohio: University of Akron Press, 1996).

7. Thomas Bauer, *Im Bauch der Stadt: Kanalisation und Hygiene in Frankfurt am Main 16.–19. Jahrhundert* (Frankfurt am Main: Kramer, 1998), 176.

8. Gottfried Hösel, *Unser Abfall aller Zeiten: Eine Kulturgeschichte der Städtereinigung* (Munich: Jehle, 1987), 197–202.

9. Jinhee Park, "Von der Müllkippe zur Abfallwirtschaft: Die Entwicklung der Hausmüllentsorgung in Berlin (West) von 1945 bis 1990" (Ph.D. diss., Technische Universität Berlin, 2004), 27; Münch, *Stadthygiene im 19. und 20. Jahrhundert*, 325.

10. Geoffrey Jones and Andrew Spadafora, "Waste, Recycling and Entrepreneurship in Central and Northern Europe, 1870–1940," Harvard Business School Working Paper 14-084, March 4, 2014.

11. Reinhold Reith, "'Altgewender, humpler, kannenplecker': Recycling im späten Mittelalter und in der Frühen Neuzeit," in *Recycling in Geschichte und Gegenwart*, ed. Roland Ladwig (Freiberg: Georg Agricola-Gesellschaft, 2003), 41–79.

12. Georg Stöger, *Sekundäre Märkte? Zum Wiener und Salzburger Gebrauchtwarenhandel im 17. und 18. Jahrhundert* (Vienna: Oldenbourg, 2011); Laurence Fontaine, ed., *Alternative Exchanges: Second-Hand Circulations from the Sixteenth Century to the Present* (New York: Berghahn, 2008).

13. Hermann Stern, *Die geschichtliche Entwicklung und die gegenwärtige Lage des Lumpenhandels* (Erlangen: Noske, 1914); Georg Hafner, *Der deutsche Schrotthandel und die Probleme seiner neueren Entwicklung: Ein Beitrag zur Frage der Rohstoffversorgung der deutschen Eisenindustrie* (Rostock: Hinstoff, 1935); Ulrich Wengenroth, *Unternehmensstrategien und technischer Fortschritt: Die deutsche und die britische Stahlindustrie, 1865–1895* (Göttingen: Vandenhoeck & Ruprecht, 1986), 37–43; W. Silberschmidt, "Müll (mit Hauskehricht)," in *Städtereinigung*, vol. 2 of *Handbuch der Hygiene*, ed. Theodor Weyl (Leipzig: Barth, 1912), 573–714, 622–54.

14. Friedrich Huchting, "Abfallwirtschaft im Dritten Reich," *Technikgeschichte* 48 (1981): 252–73; Susanne Köstering, "'Pioniere der Rohstoffbeschaffung': Lumpensammler im Nationalsozialismus," *Werkstatt Geschichte* 17 (1997): 45–65, esp. 55–56.

15. Paul Erhardt to Wirtschaftsminister des Landes NRW, September 25, 1947, State Archive Nordrhein-Westfalen, NW 354, Nr. 1096.

16. Raymond G. Stokes, Roman Köster, and Stephen C. Sambrook, *The Business of Waste, 1945 to the Present* (Cambridge: Cambridge University Press 2013), 188–213.

17. Axel Priebs, "Suburbane Siedlungsflächen: Wucherung oder gestaltbare Stadtregion?" in *Stadt und Kommunikation in bundesrepublikanischen Umbruchszeiten*, ed. Adelheid von Saldern (Stuttgart: Steiner 2006), 147–62, esp. 148–51; Tilman Harlander, "Wohnen und Stadtentwicklung in der Bundesrepublik," in *Geschichte des Wohnens*, vol. 5, *1945 bis heute: Aufbau, Neubau, Umbau*, ed. Ingeborg Flagge (Stuttgart: DVA 1999), 233–417.

18. Announcement Verband Kommunaler Fuhrparks- und Stadtreinigungsbetriebe 3/1972: 1912–1972, 60 Jahre VKF, Federal Archive Koblenz, B 106, Nr. 69727.

19. Deutscher Städtetag to Mitgliedsstädte and Landesverbände, May 28, 1962, State Archive Nordrhein-Westfalen, NW 354, Nr. 587.

20. Verband Privater Städtereinigungsbetriebe to Hans-Dietrich Genscher, June 15, 1973, Federal Archive Koblenz, B 106, Nr. 25177; VPS to Federal Ministry of Labor, March 20, 1973, Federal Archive Koblenz, B 106, Nr. 69731.

21. Deutscher Städtetag to Mitgliedsstädte and Landesverbände, May 28, 1962, State Archive Nordrhein-Westfalen, NW 354, Nr. 587.

22. Vorstand der Rethmann AG & Co., *"Verantwortung übernehmen und unternehmerisch handeln": Ein Buch über den Unternehmer Norbert Rethmann, sein Unternehmen und eine großartige Leistung* (Selm: Rethmann, 1999), 44–45; *Edelhoff 40 Jahre* (Bielefeld: Edelhoff, 1992), 20.

23. Jörg Mueller, "Expansion: Konsolidierung und Wachstum," in *1961–2001: 40 Jahre BDE; Von der Stadthygiene zur Kreislaufwirtschaft; Eine Zeitreise mit der Entsorgungswirtschaft*, ed. Bundesverband der deutschen Entsorgungswirtschaft (Cologne: BDE 2001), 70–95, 84.

24. Ibid.

25. Altvater & Co. to Stadtkämmerei Mannheim, February 16, 1967, Mannheim City Archive, Zugang 52/1979, 1463.

26. Court verdict, Oberverwaltungsgericht Lüneburg, Horst Marthen, Lingen/Ems, against Landkreis Grafschaft Bentheim, March 30, 1977, State Archive Nordrhein-Westfalen, NW 455, Nr. 816.

27. Hanskarl Willms and Stephan Mlodoch, *Wiederaufbau, Wirtschaftswunder, Konsumgesellschaft: Stadtentwicklung, Stadthygiene und Abfallwirtschaft in Deutschland 1945 bis 1975* (Selm: Sase 2014), 108; Informationsschrift Edelhoff et al., "1979/80: Gerechtigkeit für die 'Dritten,'" Federal Archive Koblenz, B 106, Nr. 69732.

28. Report Jahreshauptversammlung VPS in Berlin, October 10/11, 1974, Federal Archive Koblenz, B 106, Nr. 69731.

29. BDI (Department for Environmental Protection) to Federal Ministry of the Interior, September 25, 1979, Federal Archive Koblenz, B 106, Nr. 70539; Horst P. Sander, "Abfallrecht verhindert Wiederverwertung," *Umwelt* 6, no. 3 (1976): 170–72.

30. Stokes, Köster, and Sambrook, *The Business of Waste*, 209–13.

31. Jürgen Klowait, *Die Beteiligung Dritter an der Abfallentsorgung* (Baden-Baden: Nomos, 1995), 24.

32. Bernd Aschfalk, *Besteuerung und Abfallwirtschaft: Auswirkungen des Steuerrechts auf die Abfallbeseitigung* (Berlin: Schmidt, 1983), 48–49.

33. Wolfgang Borelly, "Die Mannheimer Müllabfuhr heute" (1961), Mannheim City Archive, Hauptregistratur, Zugang 40/1972, Nr. 291.

34. Dirk Wiegand, "Der NKT und die Normung des MGB 240—Eine Erfolgsgeschichte," *DIN-Mitteilungen* (January 2011): 15–22.

35. Cf. Gewerkschaft Öffentliche Dienst, Transport und Verkehr (ÖTV), ed., *Rationalisierung und ihre Auswirkung im Bereich der Stadtreinigung (Müllabfuhr)* (Stuttgart: ÖTV, 1983).

36. Wiegand, "Der NKT und die Normung des MGB 240."

37. ÖTV, *Rationalisierung und ihre Auswirkungen*, 26.

38. For a more detailed explanation, see Roman Köster, "Abschied von der verlorenen Verpackung: Das Recycling von Hausmüll in Westdeutschland," *Technikgeschichte* 1 (2014): 33–60.

39. Reith, "'Altgewender, humpler, kannenplecker,'" 41–56.

40. Köstering, "'Pioniere der Rohstoffbeschaffung.'"

41. Michael Prinz, *Der Sozialstaat hinter dem Haus: Wirtschaftliche Zukunftserwartungen, Selbstversorgung und regionale Vorbilder; Westfalen und Südwestdeutschland, 1920–1960* (Paderborn: Schöningh, 2012), 306–7.

42. Ulrike Lindner, "Rationalisierungsdiskurse und Aushandlungsprozesse: Der moderne Haushalt und die traditionelle Hausfrauenrolle in den 1960er Jahren," in *Demokratisierung und gesellschaftlicher Aufbruch: Die 1960er Jahre als Wendezeit der Bundesrepublik*, ed. Matthias Frese, Julia Paulus, and Karl Teppe (Paderborn: Schöningh, 2005), 83–106; Staffan B. Linder, *The Harried Leisure Class* (New York: Columbia University Press, 1970).

43. Bundesministerium des Inneren, ed., *Verwertung von Altpapier: Untersuchung über die Möglichkeit der Verwertung von Altpapier; Gegenwärtiger Stand und zukünftige Entwicklung; Bericht des Battelle-Instituts Frankfurt am Main* (Berlin: VDI, 1973), 11.

44. Hans Onasch, "Ist die Umstellung auf Einwegflaschen aus Kunststoff verantwortbar? Beurteilung aus Sicht einer Stadtreinigung," *Städtehygiene* 10 (1968): 228–30; Werner Best to Georg Leber, May 28, 1971, Federal Archive Koblenz, B 106, Nr. 25134.

45. Bürgermeisteramt Stuttgart to Städteverband Baden-Württemberg, May 18, 1967, Mannheim City Archive, Bauverwaltungsamt, Zugang 52/1979, Nr. 1463.

46. Annotation, "Hösel: Throwaway Packagings," July 13, 1971, Federal Archive Koblenz, B 106, Nr. 25190.

47. Köster, "Abschied von der verlorenen Verpackung."

48. Friedrich Arnst to Hans Evers, January 7, 1974, Federal Archive Koblenz, B 106, Nr. 25136; Stadtreinigungsamt to Dezernat VII, May 21, 1974, Mannheim City Archive, Bauverwaltungsamt, Zugang 52/1979, Nr. 950.

49. Loetz to Federal Ministry of the Interior, November 12, 1979, statement, Verband kommunaler Städtereinigungsbetriebe: Abfallbeseitigungsgesetz, 2. Novelle (September 17, 1979), Federal Archive Koblenz, B 106, Nr. 70539; Werner Schenkel, presentation, "Future Developments of Waste Management," May 30, 1979, Federal Archive Koblenz, B 106, Nr. 69732.

50. Regierungsbezirk Detmold to MELF, May 18, 1978, State Archive Nordrhein-Westfalen, NW 455, Nr. 826.

51. Kommission der Europäischen Gemeinschaften, draft on wastepaper in the European Community, August 16, 1977, Federal Archive Koblenz, B 106, Nr. 69771.

52. Werner Best to Georg Leber, May 28, 1971, Federal Archive Koblenz, B 106, Nr. 25134.

53. Andreas Eberhardt, "Abfallwirtschaft als Alternative," in *Müllverbrennung: Fortbildungsveranstaltung 85 am 3.5.1985,* ed. Fachhochschule Lübeck et al. (Lübeck: FHL, 1985), 53–59, 58.

54. Ralf Nünke to Umweltzeitung, August 1, 1978, Federal Archive Koblenz, B 106, Nr. 58838.

55. Wolfgang Glatzer and Wolfgang Zapf, "Die Lebensqualität der Bundesbürger," *Aus Politik und Zeitgeschichte (Beilage zur Wochenzeitschrift das Parlament)* 44 (November 3, 1984): 3–25, 17.

56. Karl Pulver, "Von der Abfuhranstalt zum Eigenbetrieb: 125 Jahre Stadthygiene in Mannheim" (Mannheim, 2005), 124; Michael Homberg, *Die Abfallwirtschaft in unterschiedlich strukturierten Räumen—an Beispielen aus Westfalen* (Bochum: Brockmeyer, 1990), 148; minutes of VPS–UBA meeting, April 5, 1979 (June 11, 1979), Federal Archive Koblenz, B 106, Nr. 69732.

57. Volker Grassmuck and Christian Unverzagt, *Das Müll-System: Eine metarealistische Bestandsaufnahme* (Frankfurt am Main: Suhrkamp, 1991), 99.

58. Gerhard Neckermann and Hans Wessels, *Die Glasindustrie—Ein Branchenbild* (Berlin: Duncker & Humblot, 1987), 171–72.

59. Bernhard Gallenkemper and Heiko Doedens, *Getrennte Sammlung von Wertstoffen des Hausmülls: Planungshilfen zur Bewertung und Anwendung von Systemen der getrennten Sammlung* (Düsseldorf: Ministry for Environmental Protection North Rhine–Westphalia, 1987), 33.

60. Neckermann and Wessels, *Die Glasindustrie,* 171–72.

61. "'Menschen, die sich um jeden Dreck kümmern': Von der wichtigen Arbeit der Stadtreinigung und Müllabfuhr/Jeder Frankfurter >produziert< jährlich 550 Kilo Abfall," *Seniorenzeitschrift* 1 (1981), Frankfurt City Archive, Sammlung Ortsgeschichte S3/V, 24.134.

62. Report on environmental protection measures of the Dortmund Cleansing Department, 1989, Dortmund City Archive.

63. Neckermann and Wessels, *Die Glasindustrie,* 11.

64. Ibid., 236.

65. Homberg, *Die Abfallwirtschaft in unterschiedlich strukturierten Räumen,* 148.

66. Verband Privater Städtereinigungsbetriebe to the Gesetzgeber in Bund und Ländern, open letter, May 20, 1974, State Archive Nordrhein-Westfalen, NW 354, Nr. 883.

67. Willms and Mlodoch, *Wiederaufbau, Wirtschaftswunder, Konsumgesellschaft*, 146.

68. Rethmann AG & Co., *Verantwortung übernehmen*, 52.

69. Jørgensen, *Making a Green Machine*.

70. Bernd Wimmer, "Von der Abfallbeseitigung zur Abfallwirtschaft," *Kommunalwirtschaft* 1 (1982): 42–47, 43–44.

71. Gewerkschaft Öffentliche Dienste, Transport und Verkehr, ed., *ÖTV-Geschäftsbericht 1987–1991* (Stuttgart: ÖTV, 1992), 740.

72. Bünemann, "Duales System Deutschland."

## Chapter 11. Kill-a-Watt

Research for this chapter is drawn from Joseph A. Pratt, *A Managerial History of Consolidated Edison, 1936–1982* (New York: Consolidated Edison, 1988). This is a corporate history written under contract with Con Edison in the early 1980s. I had access to internal records and personnel for interviews. I also had editorial control of the content of the manuscript; Con Edison had the choice to publish it or not. After some delay, the company published the book and printed copies for internal use and for me. My thanks to Charles F. Luce, the president and chairman of Con Edison from 1967 to 1982, and to Bernard P. Stengren for their assistance. When citing references, I will refer to copied documents in my possession as the Pratt Con Ed Collection.

1. The profile of Charles F. Luce is taken from his book, Charles F. Luce, *Some Lessons Learned: Recollections of 15 Years as Chairman of Consolidated Edison, 1967–1982* (New York: Con Edison, 1990). Other sources include a series of interviews I conducted with Luce in 1981 and 1982. In his introduction to *Some Lessons Learned*, Luce described his book as "a supplement" to "Professor Pratt's history with some personal recollections of my experience as chairman of Con Edison, 1967–1982, and some lessons I think I learned."

2. The most valuable overview of Con Edison modern history is a manuscript written by Dorothy Ellison, longtime editor of the Con Edison in-house magazine, *Around the System*; a copy is in the Pratt Con Ed Collection. For a general comprehensive history of Consolidated Gas, a predecessor to Con Edison, see Frederick L. Collins, *Consolidated Gas Company of New York: A History* (New York: Consolidated Gas Company, 1934).

3. For long-term trends in planning at Con Edison, see "Planning for Capacity, Fuel, and Reliability," in Pratt, *Managerial History of Con Edison*, 101–56.

4. Ibid., 262–70. See also Scott Dewey, *Don't Breathe the Air: Air Pollution and U.S. Environmental Politics, 1945–1970* (College Station: Texas A&M University Press, 2000), 113–74; and Marc J. Roberts and Jeremy S. Bluhn, *The Choice of Power: Utilities Face the Environmental Challenge* (Cambridge, Mass.: Harvard University Press, 1981).

5. George Mazuzan, "'Risky Business': A Power Reactor for New York City," *Technology & Culture* 27, no. 2 (April 1986): 261–84; for background on both Indian Point 1 and Ravenswood A, see Pratt, *Managerial History of Con Edison*, 215–44.

6. Con Edison's ill-fated Storm King project has been the subject of numerous studies. See Robert Lifset, *Power on the Hudson: Storm King Mountain and the Emergence of Modern American Environmentalism* (Pittsburgh: University of Pittsburgh Press, 2014); Allan Talbot, *Power Along the Hudson: The Storm King Case and the Birth of Environmentalism* (New York: E. P. Dutton, 1972); William Tucker, "Environmentalism and the Leisure Class," *Harper's*, December 1977.

7. Pratt, *Managerial History of Con Edison*, 189–99; for relative size of Con Edison's operating power plants, see chart 5.2, "Growth in Capacity of Con Edison Electric Generating Units," 190.

8. Richard Hirsh wrote the best historical analysis of this "old order" and its breakdown in the 1970s. See Richard F. Hirsh, *Technology and Transformation in the American Electric Industry* (Cambridge: Cambridge University Press, 1989). Hirsh argues convincingly that technological stasis in the 1960s and 1970s limited the continued expansion of the size of fossil-fuel-burning power plants. Before this time, economies of scale from the construction of larger power plants drove down the price of electricity, but this era came to an end as thermal efficiency became harder to increase in new, larger plants. He returns to this theme in a broader context in *Power Loss: The Origins of Deregulation and Restructuring in the American Electric Utility System* (Cambridge: Mass.: MIT Press, 1999), 55–70, where he argues that the combination of technological stasis, the energy crisis, and the environmental movement undermined the consensus supporting the old order in the electric utility industry.

9. Thomas O'Hanlon, "Con Edison: The Company You Love to Hate," *Fortune*, March 1966, 122–26, 170–73.

10. Luce, *Some Lessons Learned*, 7–12.

11. Charles F. Luce to James A. Lundy, chairman of the New York Public Service Commission, letter dated August 12, 1969. Quoted in Pratt, *Managerial History of Con Edison*, 107. Charles Luce called himself an old "power pusher" in an interview, August 6, 1981, Con Edison headquarters, New York City, notes in Pratt Con Ed Collection.

12. Pratt, *Managerial History of Con Edison*, 236–44; "ultimate in safety" quote is on p. 237.

13. Scenic Hudson Preservation Conference to Mr. Luce, September 12, 1968, in Pratt Con Ed Collection.

14. Note that in the citations in note 6 above, the book on Storm King by Allan Talbot in 1972 and the more recent study of the Storm King controversy by Robert Lifset in 2014 characterize the episode as the "birth" or the "emergence" of modern environmentalism.

15. Pratt, *Managerial History of Con Edison*, 287–305; Luce, *Some Lessons Learned*, 81–85.

16. Harry Knecht and R. C. Wolin, "Design Features of the 1000 Mw Ravenswood Steam Generating Unit," *Combustion*, April 1963, 34–38. For public reaction to the problems of Big Allis, see "Daddy's Late, He's Out with Finicky Allis," *New York Daily News*, June 13, 1971; "A Lemon Named Big Allis," *Time*, July 19, 1971, 41; and "Con Edison's Biggest Power Plant Fails," *Wall Street Journal*, August 5, 1969. For an overview of the problems of Big Allis, see Pratt, *Managerial History of Con Ed*, 197–202.

17. Fundamental regulatory adjustments in this era in search of a new balance between energy and environment can be seen in various histories of energy policy. See for example, John C. Whitaker, *Striking a Balance: Environment and Natural Resource Policy in the Nixon-Ford Years* (Washington, D.C.: American Enterprise Institute for Public Policy Research, 1976) and Richard H. K. Vietor, *Environmental Politics and the Coal Coalition* (College Station: Texas A&M University Press, 1980). For the economic position of coal in the production of electric power, see Richard L. Gordon, *U.S. Coal & the Electric Power Industry* (Baltimore: The John Hopkins University Press, 1980).

18. Pratt, *Managerial History of Con Edison*, 267; testimony of Henry Bauer (president of New York Steam Corporation) before New York City Bureau of Smoke Control, August 3, 1950.

19. Pratt, *Managerial History of Con Edison*, 271–81 and chart 7.3, "Sulfur Dioxide Concentrations in New York City, 1960–1990," 286.

20. Ibid., 282. See also "Statement of Charles Luce at Public Hearing for Adoption by the New York City Air Pollution Control Board of a Rule for the 'Prevention and Control of Air Contamination and Air Pollution by Regulating Fuel Composition in the New York City Metropolitan Area,'" September 13, 1967; "Electricity vs. Clean Air in New York," *Wall Street Journal*, August 8, 1981. For a broader view of the regulation of the entire electric power industry, see John C. Moorhouse, ed., *Electric Power: Deregulation and the Public Interest* (San Francisco: Pacific Research Institute for Public Policy, 1986).

21. Pratt, *Managerial History of Con Edison*, 277–88 and chart 4.4, "Growth in the Use of Oil, 1965–1981," 128. An excellent overview of the history of coal in power plants is Richard L. Gordon, *U.S. Coal and the Electric Power Industry* (Washington, D.C.: Resources for the Future, 1975).

22. For information on Con Edison's projected peak loads versus their actual peak loads in this era, see Pratt, *Managerial History of Con Edison*, chart 4.2, "Projected Peaks Versus Actual Peaks, 1970–1981," 108.

23. For the creation of the Save-a-Watt program, see Luce, *Some Lessons Learned*, 118–23; interview with Luce, August 6, 1981; and Pratt, *Managerial History of Con Edison*, 116–27.

24. For Con Edison's earlier support of these promotional efforts, see "Live Better . . . Electrically," *Around the System* 21, no. 3 (March 1956): 4–5. Luce did not think that these ads "could have been very important" but felt that they played two contradictory roles: investors saw them as a symbol of a growing company, while environmentalists saw them as a symbol that the utilities were creating their own problems. Interview with Charles Luce, February 9, 1982, Con Edison headquarters, New York City, notes in Pratt Con Ed Collection.

25. For Charles Luce's views of the broad changes in utility planning in this era, see Charles F. Luce, "Planning for Con Edison's Future," presentation before Finance Club of the Graduate School of Business Administration, Harvard University, December 9, 1975, copy in Pratt Con Ed Collection.

26. Pratt, *Managerial History of Con Edison*, 123; interview with Luce, August 6, 1981.

27. Pratt, *Managerial History of Con Edison*, 124–27.

28. "Save-a-Watt? No, Replies G.E.," *New York Times*, September 18, 1972; interview with Luce, February 9, 1982.

29. Interview with Charles Luce, August 1, 1981, Con Edison headquarters, New York City, notes in Pratt Con Ed Archives.

30. For a detailed history of the coming of the energy crises, see Daniel Yergin, *The Prize* (New York: Free Press, 2008).

31. Luce, *Some Lessons Learned*, 58.

32. "Con Edison Makes Progress Toward Coal Conversion," Con Edison background paper, 1981, 3–4, copy in Pratt Con Ed Collection.

33. Con Edison, "A Call for Action: An Energy Strategy for New York City and Westchester County for the 1980s . . . and Beyond," 1–8, copy in Pratt Con Ed Collection. For an excellent perspective on energy conservation in the United States in the 1970s, see Robert Stobaugh and Daniel Yergin, *Energy Future* (New York: Random House, 1979), 136–82.

### Chapter 12. Entrepreneurship, Policy, and the Geography of Wind Energy

This chapter draws partially on Geoffrey Jones, *Profits and Sustainability* (Oxford: Oxford University Press, 2017); and Geoffrey Jones and Loubna Bouamane, "Historical Trajectories and Corporate Competences in Wind Energy," Harvard Business School Working Paper 11-112, May 2011.

1. Ben Backwell, *Wind Power: The Struggle for Control of a New Global Industry* (New York: Routledge, 2015), does focus heavily on individual firm strategies, but the majority of the book deals with the period after 2000. Matt G. Hopkins, "The Makings of a Champion; or, Wind Innovation for Sale: The Wind Industry in the United States, 1980–2011" (University of Massachusetts, Lowell, 2012), is essential reading on the U.S. wind energy industry.

2. Janet L. Sawin, "Mainstreaming Renewable Energy in the 21st Century," *Worldwatch Paper* 169 (May 2004): 8; Ion Bogdan Vasi, *Winds of Change: The Environmental Movement and the Global Development of the Wind Energy Sector* (Oxford: Oxford University Press, 2011), 4.

3. Janet L. Sawin, "The Role of Government in the Development and Diffusion of Renewable Technologies: Wind Power in the United States, California, Denmark and Germany" (Ph.D. diss., Fletcher School of Law and Diplomacy, September 2001); Katherine L. Dykes and John D. Sterman, "Boom and Bust Cycles in Wind Energy Diffusion Due to Inconsistency and Short-term Bias in National Energy Policies," *ICSD 2010 Conference Proceedings*, July 25–30, 2010.

4. Sawin, "Mainstreaming," 12–13.

5. Vasi, *Winds of Change*; Wesley D. Sine and Brandon H. Lee, "Tilting at Windmills? The Environmental Movement and the Emergence of the U.S. Wind Energy Sector," *Administrative Science Quarterly* 54 (2009): 123–55.

6. Robert W. Righter, *Wind Energy in America: A History* (Norman: University of Oklahoma Press, 1996), 24–25.

7. Ibid., 42–54; Darrell M. Dodge, "Illustrated History of Wind Power Development," *Telos-Net*, accessed February 9, 2011, www.telosnet.com/wind/.

8. Righter, *Wind Energy in America*, 62, 86.

9. Flemming Tranaes, "Danish Wind Energy," accessed June 21, 2015, http://www.spok.dk/consult/reports/danish_wind_energy.pdf; Righter, *Wind Energy in America*, 61.

10. Per Dannemand Andersen, "Review of Historical and Modern Utilization of Wind Power," 1999, accessed February 17, 2011, http://www.risoe.dk/rispubl/VEA/dannemand.htm.

11. Jens Vestergaard, Lotte Brandstrup, and Robert D. Goddard, "A Brief History of the Wind Turbine Industries in Denmark and the United States," *Academy of International Business (Southeast USA Chapter) Conference Proceedings*, November 2004, 322–27.

12. Ibid.; Paul Gipe, *Wind Energy Comes of Age* (John Wiley: New York, 1995), 53–54. A kilowatt (kW) is a unit of power that measures the rate at which energy is generated.

13. Interview with Paul Jacobs, December 1, 2010, Minnetonka, Minnesota. Paul Jacobs was the son of Marcellus.

14. Righter, *Wind Energy in America*, 90–104.

15. Interview with Paul Jacobs, December 1, 2010.

16. Righter, *Wind Energy in America*, 126–36.

17. Adam Harris Serchuk, "Federal Giants and Wind Energy Entrepreneurs: Utility-Scale Wind Power in America, 1970–1990" (Ph.D. diss, Virginia Polytechnic Institute, 1995), 10; Righter, *Wind Energy in America*, 144.

18. Righter, *Wind Energy in America*, 136–43.

19. Interview with Paul Jacobs, December 1, 2010.

20. Righter, *Wind Energy in America*, 163.

21. Søren Krohn, "Danish Wind Turbines: An Industrial Success Story," 2002, accessed May 10, 2010, http://www.talentfactory.dk.media.

22. Righter, *Wind Energy in America*, 150; Tranaes, "Danish Wind Energy."

23. Søren Krohn, "Creating a Local Wind Industry: Experience from Four European Countries," testimony on behalf of the Regroupement national des Conseils Régionaux de l'environnement du Québec before the Régie de l'énergie du Québec, Helios Center for Sustainable Energy Strategies, May 4, 1998.

24. Thomas Friedman, *Hot, Flat and Crowded: Why We Need a Green Revolution—and How It Can Renew America*, Release 2.0, updated and expanded (New York: Picador/Farrar, Straus and Giroux, 2009), 41–42.

25. *Our Common Future: World Commission on Environment and Development* (Oxford: Oxford University Press, 1987), 3: "In the middle of the 20th century, we saw our planet from space for the first time."

26. Adam Rome, *The Genius of Earth Day: How a 1970 Teach-In Unexpectedly Made the First Green Generation* (New York: Hill and Wang, 2013).

27. Spencer R. Weart, *The Discovery of Global Warming* (Cambridge, Mass.: Harvard University Press, 2008).

28. Vasi, *Winds of Change*, chap. 5; Sine and Lee, "Tilting at Windmills."

29. Backwell, *Wind Power*, 8–10; Michael Durham, "Enigma of the Leader," *Guardian* (London), June 8, 2003.

30. Erik Grove-Nielsen, "The Blade Story: Økær, AeroStar, RISØ-Test; A Personal Story in Photos," accessed March 28, 2014, http://www.windsofchange.dk.

31. Vasi, *Winds of Change*, 144–48.

32. The company was Windmatic. "Danish Turbine Makes, 1975–1985," accessed March 22, 2011, http://www.windsofchange.dk.

33. Raghu Garud and Peter Karnoe, "Bricologe Versus Breakthrough: Distributed and Embedded Agency in Technology Entrepreneurship," *Research Policy* 32 (2003): 282.

34. Vasi, *Winds of Change*, 150–52; Gipe, *Wind Energy Comes of Age*, 56; Peter Karnoe, "When Low-Tech Becomes High-Tech: The Social Construction of Technological Learning Processes in the Danish and the American Wind Turbine Industry," in *Mobilizing Resources and Generating Competencies*, ed. Peter Karnoe, Peer Hull Kristensen, and Poul Houman Andersen (Copenhagen: Copenhagen Business School Press, 1999), 167.

35. Garud and Karnoe, "Bricolage"; Karnoe, Kristensen, and Andersen, *Mobilizing Resources*.

36. Gipe, *Wind Energy Comes of Age*, 56.

37. Krohn, "Danish Wind Turbines."

38. Vasi, *Winds of Change*, 68–69.

39. Garud and Karnoe, "Bricologe," 292–93. One megawatt (MW) is one thousand kilowatt-hours every hour.

40. Gipe, *Wind Energy Comes of Age*, 103.

41. Sawin, "Role of Government," 86–89.

42. Righter, *Wind Energy in America*, 158, 180.

43. Sawin, "Role of Government," 102.

44. Ibid., 101.

45. Krohn, "Danish Wind Turbines."

46. Righter, *Wind Energy in America*, 180–83.

47. Sawin, "Role of Government," 105–6.

48. Karnoe, "When Low-Tech Becomes High-Tech," 183.

49. Sawin, "Role of Government," 200–202.

50. Peter Asmus, "Gone with the Wind: How California Is Losing Its Clean Power to . . . Texas?!!" Hewlett Foundation Energy Series (San Francisco: Energy Foundation, 2002), 4.

51. Righter, *Wind Energy in America*, 161–66, 194–97.

52. Sawin, "Role of Government," 205–8.

53. Ibid.

54. Ibid., 216.

55. Righter, *Wind Energy in America*, 166–69.

56. Ibid., 163.

57. Sawin, "Role of Government," 198

58. Peter Asmus, *Reaping the Wind: How Mechanical Wizards, Visionaries, and Profiteers Helped Shape Our Energy Future* (Washington, D.C.: Island Press, 2001), 86–87.

59. Ibid., 98–99.

60. Ibid., 151.

61. Vasi, *Winds of Change*, 161–62; "Wind Power Pioneer Interview: Jim Dehlsen, Clipper Windpower," October 1, 2003, http://apps2.eere.energy.gov/wind/windexchange/filter_detail.asp?itemid=683.

62. Asmus, *Reaping the Wind*, 106–7.

63. Forrest Stoddard, "The Life and Work of Bill Heronemus, Wind Engineering Pioneer," http://www.umass.edu/windenergy/about.history.heronemus.php.

64. Asmus, *Reaping the Wind*, 57–62.

65. Righter, *Wind Energy in America*, 211–15; Dave Mote, "Kenetech Corporation," *International Directory of Company Histories* (1995 edition), Encyclopedia.com, accessed March 16, 2011, http://www.encyclopedia.com/doc/1G2-2841500081.html.

66. Asmus, *Reaping the Wind*, 95

67. Righter, *Wind Energy in America*, 211–15; Mote, "Kenetech Corporation"; Asmus, *Reaping the Wind*, 95; Hopkins, "Makings of a Champion."

68. Sawin, "Role of Government," 213.

69. Quoted in Asmus, *Reaping the Wind*, 124.

70. Righter, *Wind Energy in America*, 219–20.

71. Ibid., 181; Vasi, *Winds of Change*, 162.

72. Dave Englander, "Japan's Wind-Power Problem," *Greentech Media*, April 23, 2008, http://www.greentechmedia.com/articles/read/japans-wind-power-problem-828/.

73. Interview with Yuji Matsunami, Mitsubishi Heavy Industries, May 28, 2010.

74. Sawin, "Role of Government," table 8.1.

75. Ibid., 271–72.

76. Gipe, *Wind Energy Comes of Age*, 38.

77. Vasi, *Winds of Change*, 55–64.

78. Sawin, "Role of Government," 289–91.

79. Gipe, *Wind Energy Comes of Age*, 39.

80. Sawin, "Role of Government," 269.

81. Vasi, *Winds of Change*, 66–75.

82. Svend Auken, "Answers in the Wind: How Denmark Became a World Pioneer in Wind Power," *Fletcher Forum on World Affairs* 26, no. 1 (2002): 149–57.

83. Cayetano Espejo Marín, "La energía eólica en España," *Investigaciones Geográficas* 35 (September–December 2004): 45–65.

84. Vasi, *Winds of Change*, 75–76.

85. Gipe, *Wind Energy Comes of Age*, 42–44

86. Hopkins, "Makings of a Champion," 5.

87. Gipe, *Wind Energy Comes of Age*, 39–40.

88. Ibid., 56.

89. Sawin, "Role of Government," 293–94.

90. Aloys Wobben, Chairman and Managing Director, "Enercon," *Wind Directions*, May/June 2004.

91. Joanna I. Lewis, "A Comparison of Wind Power Industry Development Strategies in Spain, India and China," prepared for the Center for Resource Solutions, San Francisco, Calif., July 19, 2007.

92. Backwell, *Wind Power*, 65.

93. Vivek Patel, "Wind Energy: India's Prospects," Polymer/Composite/Chemicals/Life Sciences Market blog, September 23, 2010.

94. Richard H. K. Vietor and Juliana Seminerio, "The Suzlon Edge," Harvard Business School Case 708-051, June 2008 (rev. August 2008).

95. Mote, "Kenetech Corporation."

96. Malcolm Salter, *Innovation Corrupted: The Origins and Legacy of Enron's Collapse* (Cambridge, Mass.: Harvard University Press, 2008), 235–36; Loren Fox, *Enron: The Rise and Fall* (Hoboken, N.J.: Wiley, 2003), 131–32.

97. Asmus, *Reaping the Wind*, 202–3.

98. Christopher Mumma, "Firm Tells Bankruptcy Judge It Overpaid for Manufacturing Assets It Bought in May," *Los Angeles Times*, November 15, 2002.

99. Ibid.

100. Backwell, *Wind Power*, chap. 2.

## Chapter 13. Driving Change

1. Lawrence Ulrich, "Passing Up the Hybrids," *New York Times*, May 15, 2015.

2. Toyota Prius brochure, 2014.

3. This chapter will not examine the oil shocks of the 1970s with detail. For more detailed consideration, see, for instance, Brian C. Black, *Crude Reality: Petroleum in World History*, updated ed. (Lanham, Md.: Rowman & Littlefield, 2014).

4. *New York Times*, January 21, 1974. See Karen R. Merrill's collection, *The Oil Crisis of 1973–1974: A Brief History with Documents* (Boston: Bedford/St. Martin's, 2007).

5. For the construction of this paradigm, see Brian Black, "Oil for Living: Petroleum and American Conspicuous Consumption," *Journal of American History* 99, no. 1 (June 2012): 40–50. This chapter is part of my effort to extend this argument to demarcate the 1970s as shift to a new paradigm of oil consumption in the United States.

6. Adam Rome, *The Genius of Earth Day: How a 1970 Teach-In Unexpectedly Made the First Green Generation* (New York: Hill and Wang, 2013).

7. In constructing a timeline of environmental policy, see Richard N. L Andrews, *Managing the Environment, Managing Ourselves: A History of American Environmental Policy* (New Haven, Conn.: Yale University Press, 2006). In addition, new work has begun to explore the complex cultural connections of modern environmentalism, including Andrew G. Kirk, *Counterculture Green: The Whole Earth Catalog and American Environmentalism* (Lawrence: University Press of Kansas, 2007); Frank Zelko, *Make It a Green Peace! The Rise of Countercultural Environmentalism* (New York: Oxford University Press, 2013); and others.

8. See Black, *Crude Reality*.

9. This is an expansion of the argument forwarded by Lizabeth Cohen, *A Consumer's Republic: The Politics of Mass Consumption in Postwar America* (New York: Knopf; distributed by Random House, 2003), among others.

10. David Gartman, *Auto Opium: A Social History of American Automobile Design* (New York: Routledge, 1994), 157.

11. Christopher Finch, *Highways to Heaven: The Auto Biography of America* (New York: HarperCollins, 1992), 286.

12. Gartman, *Auto Opium*, 223.

13. Quoted in Michael D. Meyer and Marvin L. Manheim, "Energy Resource Use: Energy, the Automobile, and Public Policy," *Science, Technology, and Human Values* 5, no. 31 (1980): 24; see also p. 25: "The history of transportation policy through the late 1960s can be best described as one of accommodation to the automobile. Politicians and planners alike viewed the rise of the automobile and the concomitant highway construction as signs of progress, as clear indications of the superiority of the American political and economic system." Meyer and Manheim's article offers a superb overview of the incredible shift of priorities toward the automobile that was brought by 1970s legislation.

14. Finch, *Highways to Heaven*, 298–99.

15. Ibid., 318–19.

16. Ibid., 306.

17. Ibid.

18. These classifications are argued in Andrews, *Managing the Environment*. I discuss them in more depth elsewhere. Overall, however, given the degree of regulation and the immensely new expectations placed on vehicles, American auto manufacturers came out of the 1970s feeling under siege. Each leader in the industry forecast expensive shifts that would raise vehicle prices and put American laborers out of work. In fact, some openly speculated about whether automobiles could hope to still be manufactured in the United States in the twenty-first century.

In terms of vehicles, though, increased efficiency came slowly over the next few decades. Instead of demonstrating failure, this lag in transition is part of the story—it is what shows us that Americans' post-shock transition has been a culturally driven one. As one considers vehicle transition in the United States after 1970, the lesson appears to be the very dynamic relationship between market and consumer. In fact, the primary evidence for scholars to claim as a failure the American energy transition of the 1970s is the (at-times) complete, unabashed failure of American manufacturers to alter the consumer fleet. Closer inspection of trends in American auto purchases during the ensuing decades demonstrates a pattern much worse than failure to change; the fleet did, in fact change, becoming heavier and rife with the largest consumer vehicles in history. In one of the epic cases of unintended consequences in American political history, the primary environmental legislation produced from the 1970s oil crisis provided the template for manufacturers to completely resist any mandate to improve vehicle efficiency.

19. Jack Doyle, *Taken for a Ride: Detroit's Big Three and the Politics of Pollution* (New York: Four Walls Eight Windows, 2000), 148.

20. Ibid.

21. There is a healthy scholarly debate over whether or not CAFE standards were an appropriate response to the energy crisis. Stephen Ross's point is that such regulations created a format that could adjust over time, including to be used facing current environmental issues. See

Keith Bradsher, *High and Mighty: SUVs—The World's Most Dangerous Vehicles and How They Got That Way* (New York: PublicAffairs, 2002).

22. Doyle, *Taken for a Ride*, 240.

23. Rudi Volti, *Cars and Culture: The Life Story of a Technology* (Westport, Conn.: Greenwood Press, 2004), 124.

24. One other initiative begun in the 1970s was a federally mandated speed limit. In the 1970s, federal safety and fuel conservation measures included a national speed limit of 55 miles per hour (today, consumers have led some states to loosen such restrictions). Doyle, *Taken for a Ride*, 251–62. Journalist Paul Roberts writes that perhaps "the most discouraging example of how developed nations misspend their efficiency dividend is transportation—and nowhere more so than in the United States." Prior to the early 1970s, energy costs were "trivial," and, therefore, "carmakers made no effort to build cars that were fuel-efficient." This changed with the implementation of CAFE standards. Paul Roberts, *The End of Oil: On the Edge of a Perilous New World* (Boston: Houghton Mifflin Harcourt, 2004), 152.

25. Air pollution was documented to possess health impacts for humans since the early 1900s. In the 1940s, air pollution was more broadly construed to be a product of many facets of urban life, not just factories. In cities such as Los Angeles, the phenomenon became known as "smog" and was directly connected to exhaust from the automobile's internal combustion engine (typically "smog" is not merely used to blend the words "smoke" and "fog" but also to include chemical compounds that linger in the air when sunlight interacts with smoke put off by burning hydrocarbons). The existence of carbon monoxide, carbon dioxide, and sulfur dioxide in such air pollution was not clarified for a few more decades. The connection between smog and auto exhaust is credited to Arie Haagen-Smit, a researcher at the California Institute of Technology. During the 1950s, Haagen-Smit fought off the savage criticism of the auto manufacturers, who claimed that a well-tuned vehicle had no such adverse effects on the air. Severe smog episodes in California kept the issue in the public arena and helped to make it one of the primary issues for the nascent environmental movement.

26. Doyle, *Taken for a Ride*, 64.

27. Hugh S. Gorman, *Redefining Efficiency: Pollution Concerns, Regulatory Mechanisms, and Technological Change in the U.S. Petroleum Industry* (Akron, Ohio: Akron University Press, 2001).

28. Jim Motavalli, *High Voltage: The Fast Track to Plug In the Auto Industry* (Emmaus, Pa.: Rodale, 2011), 40.

29. Paul E. Godek, "The Regulation of Fuel Economy and the Demand for 'Light Trucks,'" *Journal of Law and Economics* 40, no. 2 (1997): 503.

30. Bradsher, Ross quote at p. 51.

31. Ibid., 13.

32. Gartman, *Auto Opium*, 223.

33. Volti, *Cars and Culture*, 143.

34. Data findings are derived from *Transportation Energy Data Book* and *Automotive News Annual Reports*.

35. Roberts, *The End of Oil*, 154.

36. See, for instance, Motavalli, *High Voltage*.

37. At the end of the program, Toyota accounted for 19.4 percent of sales, followed by General Motors with 17.6 percent, Ford with 14.4 percent, Honda with 13 percent, and Nissan with 8.7 percent (from *Transportation Energy Data Book* and *Automotive News Annual Reports*).

38. Political perspective appears to have a significant bearing on the perception of CARS success or failure. For one of the more even reports on the topic, see Michael Sivak and Brandon Schoettle, "The Effect of the 'Cash for Clunkers' Program on the Overall Fuel Economy of Purchased New Vehicles," University of Michigan, Transportation Research Institute, Report No. UM-TRI-2009-34, September 2009, http://deepblue.lib.umich.edu/bitstream/handle/2027.42/64025/102323.pdf;jsessionid=F113E78D630E41414BED7ADE816B4E0F?sequence=1. Other sources include National Highway Traffic and Safety Administration, "Cash for Clunkers Wraps Up with Nearly 700,000 Car Sales," DOT 133-09, August 26, 2009, http://www.nhtsa.gov/About+NHTSA/Press+Releases/2009/Cash+for+Clunkers+Wraps+up+with+Nearly+700,000+car+sales+and+increased+fuel+efficiency,+U.S.+Transportation+Secretary+LaHood+declares+program+%E2%80%9Cwildly+successful%E2%80%9D; and Ted Gaynor and Emily Parker, "The Car Allowance Rebate System: Evaluation and Lessons for the Future," Economic Studies at Brookings, Policy Brief, October 31, 2013, http://www.brookings.edu/~/media/research/files/papers/2013/10/cash%20for%20clunkers%20evaluation%20gayer/cash_for_clunkers_evaluation_policy_brief_gayer.pdf.

39. Discussion of the 2008–9 economic collapse can be found in journalistic accounts such as Steve Coll's *Private Empire: ExxonMobile and American Power* (New York: Penguin Press, 2012).

40. These figures come from U.S. Department of Transportation, Office of the Assistant Secretary for Research and Technology, Bureau of Transportation Statistics, "Table 4-23: Average Fuel Efficiency of U.S. Light Duty Vehicles," http://www.rita.dot.gov/bts/sites/rita.dot.gov.bts/files/publications/national_transportation_statistics/html/table_04_23.html.

41. U.S. Energy Information Administration, "Frequently Asked Questions: How Many Alternative Fuel and Hybrid Vehicles Are There in the United States?" http://www.eia.gov/tools/faqs/faq.cfm?id=93&t=4.

42. Richard Benedetto, "Cheney's Energy Plan Focuses on Production," *USA Today*, May 1, 2001.

43. Daniel Horowitz, *Jimmy Carter and the Energy Crisis of the 1970s: The "Crisis of Confidence" Speech of July 15, 1979; A Brief History with Documents* (Boston: Bedford/St. Martin's, 2005), 43–46.

44. John R. McNeil., *Something New Under the Sun: An Environmental History of the Twentieth-Century World* (New York: W. W. Norton, 2000), 298.

45. Daniel Yergin, *The Quest: Energy, Security, and the Remaking of the Modern World* (New York: Penguin Press, 2011), 629.

46. Transition US, "About Us," http://www.transitionus.org/about-us.

47. Nick Judd, "A Recent History of Uber: Lobbying, Lawsuits, and a 'Scuffle,'" July 18, 2014, http://www.vice.com/read/a-recent-history-of-uber-lobbying-lawsuits-and-a-scuffle-718.

48. Mark Rogowsky, "Zipcar, Uber and the Beginning of Trouble for the Auto Industry," *Forbes*, February 8, 2014, http://www.forbes.com/sites/markrogowsky/2014/02/08/viral-marketing-car-sharing-apps-are-beginning-to-infect-auto-sales/.

# Contributors

**Hartmut Berghoff** was director of the German Historical Institute in Washington, D.C., from 2008 until 2015. He is currently director of the Institute of Economic and Social History at the University of Göttingen in Germany.

**Ann-Kristin Bergquist** is associate professor in economic history at Umeå University, Sweden.

**Brian C. Black** is professor of history and environmental studies at Penn State Altoona, where he currently serves as head of Arts and Humanities. He is the author of several books, including the award-winning *Petrolia: The Landscape of America's First Oil Boom* (2003) and *Crude Reality: Petroleum in World History* (2014).

**William D. Bryan** teaches history at Georgia State University in Atlanta. He is completing his first book, which considers how the conservation of natural resources shaped the American South after the Civil War.

**Julie Cohn** is a research historian with the Center for Public History at the University of Houston. She is currently completing a book project titled *The Grid: Biography of an American Technology*.

**Leif Fredrickson** is Ambrose Monell Fellow in Technology and Democracy at the Miller Center of Public Affairs and a Ph.D. candidate in history at the University of Virginia. His research has been published in *Global Environment* and *Environment and History*. He is writing a dissertation titled "The Age of Lead: Environmental Health, Suburbanization, and Urban Underdevelopment in Baltimore, 1900–2000."

**Hugh S. Gorman** teaches in the graduate Environmental and Energy Policy program at Michigan Technological University as professor of environmental history and policy. He is the author of *The Story of N: A Social History of the Nitrogen Cycle and the Challenge of Sustainability* (2013).

**Geoffrey Jones** is Isidor Straus Professor of Business History at Harvard Business School. His recent books include *Beauty Imagined: A History of the Global Beauty Industry* (2010) and *Entrepreneurship and Multinationals: Global Business and the Making of the Modern World* (2013).

**David Kinkela** is an associate professor of history at the State University of New York at Fredonia. He is author of *DDT and the American Century: Global Health, Environmental Politics, and the Pesticide That Changed the World* (2011). He is also the coeditor of *Nation-States and the Global Environment: New Approaches to International Environmental History* (2013).

**Roman Köster** is an assistant professor at the Chair for Economic, Social and Technical History at the University of the Bundeswehr in Munich. His publications include *The Business of Waste* (together with Raymond G. Stokes and Stephen C. Sambrook; 2013) and *Die Wissenschaft der Außenseiter* (2011), a history of German political economics during the 1920s.

**Joseph A. Pratt** is the NEH-Cullen Professor of History and Business at the University of Houston, where he is the director of the Energy and Sustainability minor. His research focuses on energy and environmental history and the history of the Houston region.

**Adam Rome** is professor of history at the State University of New York at Buffalo. He is the author of *The Bulldozer in the Countryside: Suburban Sprawl and the Rise of American Environmentalism* (2001) and *The Genius of Earth Day: How a 1970 Teach-In Unexpectedly Made the First Green Generation* (2013).

**Christine Meisner Rosen** is an associate professor at the Haas School of Business and the associate director for Business and Economics of the Berkeley Center for Green Chemistry at the University of California at Berkeley. She is finishing up a book on business leadership in America's early struggles with industrial pollution, 1840–1920.

# Acknowledgments

Our biggest debt is to Roger Horowitz, director of the Center for the History of Business, Technology, and Society at the Hagley Museum and Library. Roger had the idea of bringing environmental and business historians together for this volume. He then was involved at every step of the way, from selecting the authors to working with the press. His wisdom and administrative ability were invaluable.

The Hagley Museum and the German Historical Institute generously supported our project and made it possible to involve scholars from Europe as well as the United States. Carol Lockman of Hagley provided tremendous staff support. Casey Sutcliffe of the German Historical Institute also helped by polishing the texts of our nonnative authors.

In conceptualizing this project, Erik Rau of Hagley and Yda Schreuder of the University of Delaware were very helpful. The contributors also shared ideas. So did a number of other scholars: Brian Balogh, Regina Lee Blaszczyk, Emily Brock, Ben Cohen, David Cohen, Bart Elmore, Ann Greene, Rachel Gross, Ai Hisano, Simone Müller-Pohl, and Frank Uekoetter. Thanks to all.

Christine Meisner Rosen's chapter is drawn from "Business Leadership in the Movement to Regulate Industrial Air Pollution in Late Nineteenth and Early Twentieth Century America," *Jahrbuch für Wirtschaftsgeschichte/ Economic History Yearbook* 50, no. 2 (2009), and we are grateful to the editors and publishers of the *Jahrbuch* for their permission to include Rosen's article in this volume.

We are delighted that this volume is part of the Hagley Perspectives on Business and Culture series published by the University of Pennsylvania Press. Senior editor Robert Lockhart saw the potential in this project, and his suggestions helped us to produce a more focused collection. We also appreciate the expert work of the press's production staff. Amanda Ruffner did a great job in guiding the book through the production process.

Lightning Source UK Ltd.
Milton Keynes UK
UKHW01n1100030518
322054UK00005B/88/P